GOD,
HISTORY,
AND HISTORIANS

God,
History,
and Historians

An Anthology
of Modern Christian Views of History

Edited by
C. T. McINTIRE

New York
OXFORD UNIVERSITY PRESS

OXFORD UNIVERSITY PRESS
Oxford   London   Glasgow
New York   Toronto   Melbourne   Wellington
Nairobi   Dar es Salaam   Cape Town
Kuala Lumpur   Singapore   Jakarta   Hong Kong   Tokyo
Delhi   Bombay   Calcutta   Madras   Karachi

Library of Congress Cataloging in Publication Data
Main entry under title:

God, history, and historians.

　　Bibliography: p.
　　Includes index.
　　1. History (Theology)—Addresses, essays, lectures.
I. McIntire, C. T.
BR115.H5G63　　　901　　　76-47428
ISBN 0-19-502203-3
ISBN 0-19-502204-1 pbk.

PRINTED IN THE UNITED STATES OF AMERICA

This reprint, 1979

PREFACE

I dreamed I saw Saint Augustine alive as you or me.
—BOB DYLAN, 1968

A people without history is not redeemed from time, for history is a pattern of timeless moments.
—T. S. ELIOT,
"Little Gidding," 1942

The renewal of Christian views of history in the twentieth century, especially since 1939, is the theme of this volume of essays. As the table of contents reveals, the authors are people of learning and insight—historians, philosophers, theologians, and writers from many Christian traditions. In their writings they take us to the interdisciplinary terrain where religion, philosophy, and history meet. The implications of what they show us reach into many fields of study and everyday living.

The renewal began in the 1930's and 1940's as a response to a series of monumental catastrophes and crises inaugurated by the first world war. A new awareness of history contributed to a rethinking of theology, ethics, and the church. More generally, a growing sense of the inadequacy of the secular and liberal beliefs about history and human nature which dominated the civilization stimulated a quest for alternative certainties. The authors of these essays, for the most part, were among those who found a satisfying alternative in Christian views of history in the lineage of the biblical prophets, Paul, and Augustine. The crises of the age induced others to follow different avenues. Some thinkers have turned outside western civilization to Buddhism, Taoism, or other Oriental religions. A few looked to the pagan or classical roots of our culture. Many more have found a revitalized Marxist view of history and human nature appealing, while others have placed their hopes in conservatism.

The renewal of Christian views has continued through the 1960's and 1970's as many writers have used their understanding of history to illuminate some basic issues of theology and hermeneutics, revolution and social change, philosophy of history, culture, and historiography.

There was a day when Christian views of history prevailed in western civilization. Saint Augustine, that fifth-century Christian bishop of the unlikely place called Hippo, now vanished in North Africa, left his legacy in a Christian vision of human destiny which was worked into the very structure of the whole civilization. Simultaneously there developed a Christian historiography which ran through Bede, Dante, Bodin, Bossuet, and Acton.

Sometime, probably during the nineteenth century, Christian views of history lost their privileged position as the civilization underwent a radical and pervasive secularization. In general culture, by the 1920's, a secular idea of history as progress, especially as measured by capitalist economic growth and liberal political achievement, became preeminent in North America and western Europe. In historiography, the secularization begun by Machiavelli, Voltaire, and Gibbon came, via rationalism, positivism, and historicism in the nineteenth century, to dominate the field in the twentieth.

The regeneration of Christian views of history in our time demonstrates the belief of these authors that a Christian perspective possesses ongoing validity in a secular age. The renewal reestablishes a bond with an ancient tradition while it develops entirely fresh insights germane to the new circumstances of contemporary history. Through all their diversity and disagreement the writers of these essays offer to us discoveries which are beneficial to theology, philosophy, and history, and perhaps even more generally to our secular culture.

ACKNOWLEDGMENTS

The theme and major theses which I put forward in this volume of essays derive from my work in the seminar in philosophy of history and historiography at the Institute for Christian Studies, Toronto. I wish especially to thank the participants in the seminar since 1973 for their involvement. To my co-workers at the Institute for Christian Studies since 1973, the Senior and Junior Members and supporting staffs, who provide a creative community in which to teach and research, I thankfully dedicate this volume.

I am very grateful for invaluable comments and leads from a number of people who kindly read my introductory essay and looked at the table of contents—Herbert Butterfield, Martin E. Marty, Hendrikus Berkhof, George Marsden, Albert F. Gedraitis, and Al Wolters. Professor Marty gave some very special support to the project for which I am particularly thankful. Robert Swierenga suggested one of the selections, and W. Stanford Reid gave helpful criticism. Various staff members of the libraries of the University of Toronto made the work go easily. Mary Carolyn Kennedy McIntire shared in every aspect of the work from beginning to end, and I am deeply thankful and indebted to her for it.

C. T. McIntire

Institute for Christian Studies, Toronto

CONTENTS

II
THE NATURE OF HISTORY AND CULTURE

III
HISTORIANS AND HISTORICAL STUDY

GOD,

HISTORY,

AND HISTORIANS

C. T. McINTIRE

Introduction

THE RENEWAL OF
CHRISTIAN VIEWS OF HISTORY
IN AN AGE OF CATASTROPHE

Christianity and History

While Hitler annexed Czechoslovakia in the spring of 1939 and
then invaded Poland in the fall, Reinhold Niebuhr delivered his
Gifford Lectures in Scotland on the nature and destiny of man.
Niebuhr recorded his sense of the monumentality of these events
in a diary partially serialized in *The Christian Century*.[1] His lectures possessed a timeliness that created a sensation among his
hearers. Making use of Augustine and the Bible he challenged the
prevailing views of human nature and history and declared them
failures before the experience of contemporary history.

He reworked the lectures as the war unfolded. In 1943 he
published the ones on history as volume two of *The Nature and
Destiny of Man,* with the subtitle, *Human Destiny.* "The belief
that informs these pages," he wrote in January 1943, "is that the
Christian faith represents deeper sources of power for the fulfillment of life than has been assumed in the main currents of modern culture." [2]

Niebuhr's lectures mark a beginning point in what has become a widespread renewal of interest in a Christian view of history.[3] During the late 1940's book after book and article after article by a diverse set of authors appeared on the theme of Christianity and history.[4]

Professor E. Harris Harbison of Princeton University commented on this phenomenon in December 1951 at the meeting of the American Historical Association in New York. In a paper on "The 'meaning of history' and the writing of history," he said he believed there was "a kind of Augustinian revival of interest in the meaning of history." Its proponents included theologians and philosophers, and it had begun to influence even the writing of history by historians.[5]

In a book review published in the first issue of *History and Theory*, in 1960, Harbison expressed his appreciation of the number and the creativity of the publications on Christianity and history which continued to appear. He wrote,

> Whether these works mark the swansong of an expiring *Weltanschauung*, or whether they herald a vigorous Renaissance of Christian thought it is perhaps too early to tell. But it is already clear that it is no mere revival of the conception of history which dominated Western thinking from Augustine to Bossuet.

His own essays on the subject were collected posthumously in 1964 under the title *Christianity and History*.[6]

The renewal of a Christian view of history about which Harbison wrote, and which continued into the 1970's, acquired the proportions of a major movement of contemporary thought. The main contributors to it are represented in this anthology. They include notable historians—Butterfield, Dawson, Link, Cochrane, Marrou, Toynbee, Florovsky, Latourette, Harbison—as well as some of the most creative Christian theologians, philosophers, and writers of our time—Niebuhr, Tillich, Barth, Bultmann, Pannenberg, Berkhof,[7] Gutiérrez, Maritain, Dooyeweerd, C. S. Lewis, T. S. Eliot. They come from Protestant, Catholic, and Orthodox traditions. The Protestants are Methodist, Anglican, Reformed, Lutheran, Baptist, Evangelical. They have lived and worked in the United States, Great Britain, France, Switzerland, Germany, The Netherlands, Canada, and Peru, and their influence has extended to many other countries. Most have had something to do with the

Ecumenical Movement among Protestants, Orthodox, and Catholics. Their work has influenced scholars in many fields as well as the general public, clergy and laity alike, in all kinds of denominations.

The range of issues concerning history to which they and others have addressed themselves covers the theology of history, the philosophy of history, and historiography. It includes questions of the meaning of history, time, the nature of history, God's work in history, laws in history, religion and culture, the character of historical study and historical knowledge. The renewal of Christian views of history is no narrow phenomenon.

In a larger context, this revival can be seen as part of a general increase of interest in philosophy of history among all schools of thought since World War II. Among what can be termed, broadly, liberal schools of thought, the new attention to philosophy of history is perhaps symbolized by the founding of *History and Theory* in 1960, the first English language publication in the field. This journal has documented the general revival by publishing a series entitled *Bibliography of Works in the Philosophy of History* with volumes covering blocks of years since 1945.[8]

Marxists, too, have demonstrated new interest in the large questions of history. What used to be the concern of a relatively few people in the 1930's, when Marxism in its Soviet form appeared attractive to many disenchanted liberals, has, since 1945, become the vocation of an increasing number of New Left historians and philosophers. In North America and Europe as well as the Third World, a new Marxist view of history, where it has not replaced the traditional liberal philosophies, is the primary rival available.[9]

Philosophy of history in general is a special concern of the post-1945 period.

The Sources: Biblical Studies and Catastrophe

The renewal of interest in a Christian view of history emerges from two main sources. The secondary one is the "problem of history" in Old and New Testament studies and theology. The primary one is a response to the catastrophes of our secular age and the search for an alternative view of human nature and human history.

In biblical studies, the "problem of history" has long been regarded as troublesome. Since the 1940's it has become central as a look at some of the leading biblical scholars will illustrate. Rudolf Bultmann tended at first to minimize the importance of history to faith by affirming a radical difference between the Jesus of history and the Christ of faith. He chose an existentialist philosophy of history as an answer to the weaknesses of the older liberal-positivist view of history which had prevailed. In *The Presence of Eternity: History and Eschatology* (1957), the most systematic presentation of his position, he claimed that the advent of Christ was "above time and history" and that in the faith of the Christian today "time and the world's history are overcome." Writes Bultmann, ". . . the meaning in history lies always in the present." Even as he minimized the importance of history to faith, however, he devoted considerable attention to the question of the nature and meaning of history.[10]

James M. Robinson's *The New Quest of the Historical Jesus* (1959) represented the concerns of the heirs of Bultmann who, while holding to an existentialist view of history, desired to see what *can* be known about the Jesus of history, and whether the Jesus of history and the Christ of faith cannot be seen as more of a unity. Van A. Harvey's *The Historian and the Believer* (1967) found such a line not far-reaching enough. He argued for a "radical historical confessionalism" which affirmed that the historicity of all human existence in which Jesus and we share is the proper basis on which to approach the Jesus Christ of history and faith.

The work of Wolfhart Pannenberg and his circle tries to put history and faith back together again. For him history is not merely crucial to the faith, but is in itself God's revelation. *Revelation As History* (1968) summarizes the thesis that the message of the Christian kerygma is meaningless if separated from history as we know it. He has probed the nature of the process of history and of universal history.[11]

More generally, in theology and church doctrine the problem of history is related to questions of the relativity of history and the constancy of truth, of the development of doctrine and the finality of biblical revelation, of the *aggiornamento* of the church and the continuity of the ancient traditions. The achievements of the second Vatican Council (1962–65), for example, are dependent upon a changed view of history in relation to truth.[12]

It happens that the debate on the "problem of history" in biblical studies and theology receives such wide attention in theological circles that one is tempted to think foremostly of it when speaking of a renewal of interest in a Christian view of history. Significant as it is, however, its import is limited largely to questions of the life of Jesus, the history of Israel, the nature of revelation, hermeneutics, the authority of the traditions and structures of the church, and similar theological issues.[13]

The primary source of the new Christian interest in the meaning and nature of history lies elsewhere: in a response to the crisis of the secular age. The conviction runs through much of the writings of the figures represented in this anthology, as well as numerous others, that western civilization in its secular form is coming to the end of an era and needs radical transformation.

The world war of 1914–18 began a two-generation-long series of crises of immense scale which shook intellectuals and political, social, and cultural leaders out of a complacency toward the condition of the civilization.[14] Such leaders, along with great numbers of their middle-class followers, came to understand what the poor and outcast had always known—that life could be catastrophic and that our most prized achievements could be swept away in an instant. The first world war demonstrated that the barbarities of war could, via exquisite technology, be multiplied so as to engulf whole populations and cultures. Once the Bolshevik Revolution of 1917 had been achieved, the reign of Stalin showed that tyranny could outdo tyranny as a Marxist-Leninist totalitarianism was established on a scale more vast than Czarism. After a decade of semi-chaos in Germany, the Nazi revolution during the 1930's furnished a case of inhumanity and neo-pagan tribalism massively organized with great technological skill. Meanwhile industrial capitalism increased its capacity to dehumanize by reducing still more of life to the economic and by transforming personalities into efficient supports of a huge productive apparatus. The Great Depression during the 1930's crippled the United States, Britain, France, Germany, and smaller countries as well. The second world war surpassed even the first as the entire globe convulsed. The hubris of the in-

dustries, the science, the politics, and the militaries of western civilization up to 1945 seemed to be summarized by the atomic bomb
which annihilated Hiroshima.

The world-wide era of crisis gave no evidence of ending into
the third and fourth generations: the Cold War, the bomb, Viet
Nam, economic glut and squander, maldistribution of wealth, oppression of the poor, technocracy, depletion of resources, pollution,
urban disintegration, revolution, dictatorships, and more revolution.

For many Christian thinkers this "time of troubles," as Toynbee called it,[15] shook loose the idea of progress and the trust in
human reason which underlay both the old liberal as well as the
Marxist views of history. The glorious day of the liberal idea of
progress during the Pax Britannia for a century prior to 1914 led
the elites and even many of the common people, whether
bourgeois or not, to enjoy the most optimistic expectations about
their present and their future. The accomplishments of industrial
capitalism and western imperialism were to them the most tangible proof of progress. Early Marxists, while not enamored with the
promises of the liberal view of history, nonetheless firmly believed
their own unabashedly optimistic view of the course of human history.

Before 1914 some of the most thoughtful advocates of the
Christian social gospel, while critical of capitalism and Marxism,
shared the secular optimism about progress in history. In 1907,
during the heyday of Teddy Roosevelt's Progressivism, Walter
Rauschenbusch spoke confidently of helping "to build the coming
Messianic era of mankind":

> Perhaps these nineteen centuries of Christian influence have been a
> long preliminary stage of growth, and now the flower and fruit are al-
> most here. If at this juncture we can rally sufficient religious faith
> and moral strength to snap the bonds of evil and turn the present un-
> paralleled economic and intellectual resources of humanity to the
> harmonious development of a true social life, the generations yet un-
> born will mark this as the great day of the Lord for which the ages
> waited, and count us blessed for sharing in the apostolate that pro-
> claimed it.

He was convinced, in 1912, that only the domain of business and
industry remained to Christianize.[16]

That was *before* the cataclysm.

During the gestation of the Great War, Oswald Spengler wrote the first draft of *The Decline of the West*. He reworked it during the war and published it in 1918. Though obtuse and clumsy it met an immediate need for an explanation of catastrophe and became a German bestseller. And so it did in the United States after the English translation appeared in 1926. Spengler certainly broke with the secular idea of progress, but he replaced it with a neo-pagan idea of inevitable decay.[17] The notion was not an ultimately satisfying alternative.

As the "time of troubles" lengthened during the 1920's and 1930's the situation was ready for another alternative view of history. Christopher Dawson saw the opportunity in 1929 when he published *Progress and Religion: An Historical Enquiry*. He argued that we need not lament the passing of "the English middle-class version of the optimistic liberal creed, which had set out to refashion the world in the preceding century." We must not "take refuge in fatalistic theories of the inevitability of cultural decline." [18] And neither will we find help in a Marxist or communist faith. Rather, Dawson concluded, only in a recovery of Christianity which supplied the original spiritual dynamic of the civilization could we hope for a renaissance:

> If our civilization is to recover its vitality, or even to survive, it must cease to neglect its spiritual roots and must realize that religion is not a matter of personal sentiment which has nothing to do with the objective realities of society, but is, on the contrary, the very heart of social life and the root of every living culture.[19]

A number of Christian thinkers did publish books in the 1930's which, in response to the catastrophe, reflected on the meaning and nature of history. Dawson, a Catholic, was central. So was the nominal Anglican Arnold Toynbee, who issued the early volumes of *A Study of History* in 1934 and 1939. Nicholas Berdyaev, Russian Orthodox, published *The Meaning of History* in English in 1936. Paul Tillich, from a German Lutheran tradition, brought out *The Interpretation of History* the same year. The papers of the 1933 meeting of the American Catholic Historical Association appeared in 1936 under the title *The Catholic Philosophy of History*. H. G. Wood, a Quaker, gave the Hulsean Lectures at Cambridge

University in 1933–34 on *Christianity and the Nature of History* (1934). One of the official books of the 1937 Oxford conference on church, community, and state was devoted to history, *The Kingdom of God and History* (1938), and included articles by Tillich, Dawson, and H. G. Wood.

When Reinhold Niebuhr presented the Gifford Lectures on history in Edinburgh in 1939 the catastrophe had deepened and the situation was prepared for a renewal of interest in a Christian view of history on a wide scale. In the movement of historical thought which developed thereafter, Niebuhr no doubt was the most influential figure. He continued to reflect on the large questions of the nature and meaning of history during the 1940's, and in 1949 published *Faith and History*. Another central figure was Herbert Butterfield, then professor of modern history at Cambridge University. In 1948 he presented a course of lectures at Cambridge which he repeated over the BBC, and then revised and published in 1949 as *Christianity and History*. Dawson and Toynbee continued to be significant after the war as their thought developed and they reached new audiences.

Many of the other thinkers included in the anthology were influenced by these four figures—Niebuhr, Butterfield, Dawson, and Toynbee. On the whole, however, it is important to notice that most of them come to their views of history and culture chiefly as the result of their own experience of and reflection upon the crisis of contemporary history in the light of the Christian tradition. These include Latourette, Brunner, Barth, Tillich, C. S. Lewis, T. S. Eliot, Dooyeweerd, Maritain, Harbison, Florovsky, Marrou, Gutiérrez. Two of the figures—Bultmann and Pannenberg—came to their thought on history in the context of their New Testament and theological studies, but they too were not untouched by the turmoil of contemporary history. Tillich expressed the feeling of many in his generation:

> We are not scholars according to the pattern of our teachers at the end of the nineteenth century. We were forced into history in a way which made the analysis of history and of its contents most difficult. Perhaps we have had the advantage of being nearer to reality than they were. Perhaps this is only a rationalization of our shortcomings.[20]

It should not be surprising that an age of catastrophe has yielded significant Christian reflection on the meaning and nature of history. It is at such times that the fundamental matters of life which calmer days take for granted especially come to attention. It is no mere coincidence that many of these thinkers, whatever their ecclesiastical tradition, in some way or another have felt the power of Augustine's thought about history. Perhaps the twentieth century with its terrible civilization-wide calamities is not unlike the fifth when Augustine experienced evidences of the fall of Roman civilization and then developed his Christian view of history.

Augustine, from his vantage point in North Africa, was scandalized in 410 when Alaric and his barbarian army invaded the eternal city of Rome and for three days ran riot, destroying, pillaging, burning as much as they could. He could not glory in the humiliation of the greatest city of the world. To him, Christian though he was, the pagan city of Rome was the center of all civilized life as contrasted with barbarism. The near-universal conviction of the time was that Rome would not die. The plunder of Rome suggested otherwise. Jerome wrote, "If Rome can perish, what can be safe." [21] Alaric's invasion passed, but the prospect of catastrophe was enough to prompt Augustine's thinking along monumental lines. Prior to 410 he had reflected often on the contrast between the life of Christians and that of the pagan culture around them. Now his thought moved on. By 413 he published the first three sections of the *City of God*. Thirteen years later he completed all of the twenty-two sections of the work. In the process, from out of the biblical sources, his knowledge of history, and his experience of the disintegration of the culture of Rome, he defined a Christian philosophy of history.[22]

Augustine's *City of God* proved more durable than the classical city of Rome. His thought still generates thought. Through his life and writings, says Marrou, he "instructs us by his example in the art of living through an age of catastrophe." [23]

Niebuhr and Butterfield

A look at two of the leading thinkers can serve to indicate the character of a major portion of the renewal of Christian views of history. The books in the 1940's by Niebuhr—*The Nature and Destiny of Man,* II (1943), and *Faith and History* (1949)—and by Butterfield—*Christianity and History* (1949)—stimulated considerable thought on the subject. Their books are in many ways very different from each other, treating different aspects of the subject in different manners and for different audiences. Yet they display a generally common outlook—a remarkable point since they were apparently written independently of each other.[24]

For both Niebuhr and Butterfield the character and scale of the crisis of the age directly stimulated their thought. Wrote Niebuhr:

> The crisis in which we live today is more than a political one. While political institutions are being shaken to their foundations by the world catastrophe which has overwhelmed us, it will become increasingly apparent that the philosophical and religious presuppositions by which men live are as seriously challenged by world events as are the political institutions by which they have ordered their lives.[25]

Butterfield observed:

> Whether we escape the deluge or not, therefore, we are confronted by the threat of it on a scale out of all comparison with what was even feared in 1914. And history has resumed its risky and cataclysmic character.[26]

Niebuhr and Butterfield both believed that the crisis was partially due to an optimistic view of history which liberalism and Marxism shared. Such optimism was characterized by two features. First, both liberalism and Marxism were certain that complete redemption would come within the course of history, and, second, both philosophies were convinced that history could be entirely understood from inside history. The followers of these philosophies believed, according to Niebuhr's compelling phrase, "that history is itself Christ."[27] They had come, said Butterfield, to "regard these human systems and organizations as being the actual end of life, the ultimate purpose of life."[28] Needless to say, these messianic and optimistic convictions possessed tremendous power, and the scale and intensity of the cataclysm demonstrated it.

Both Niebuhr and Butterfield believed that secular views of history were also dependent upon an optimism about human nature which attributed redemptive character to human reason. They detected a seemingly congenital inability to recognize or ac- knowledge human evil, unless of course the evil be the enemy's.

To find a radical alternative to these beliefs, both Niebuhr and Butterfield turned to the biblical sources of the Christian faith, Butterfield more to the Old Testament and Niebuhr more to the Gospels and Paul. The starting point in a Christian view of history for both men was a two-sided belief. On one side was the acknowl- edgment of the reality of evil in human nature, what Butterfield called "the universal element of human cupidity." On the other side was the affirmation, for Niebuhr, of the image of God in human nature, and, for Butterfield, of the primacy of human per- sonality in history.[29]

Both writers saw the Christian view of history as catastrophic and tragic, but not ultimately so. Because of evil, history is a drama of conflict, not of gradual improvement. Niebuhr regarded the cross of Christ as the secret of the story of history, and the para- digm of history. In the death of Christ evil appears to triumph, but in the resurrection of Christ we come to see that God, not evil, triumphs in the end. History, now and in the *eschaton,* moves "beyond tragedy." [30] Butterfield saw in the conflicts of history a particularly clear manifestation of God's Providence. Providence takes the compound of all the human wills which clash in any his- torical event or process and constantly brings good out of evil. Conflict in history leads not to mere dissolution, but to "that kind of history-making which goes on so to speak over our heads, now deflecting the results of our actions, now taking our purposes out of our hands, and now turning our endeavours to ends not real- ized." [31]

Butterfield believed that the Christian has "in his religion the key to his conception of the whole human drama." Niebuhr, too, stressed that the biblical view of history treated history as a whole and understood it from the perspective of the end. God, through Israel and especially Christ, revealed the end of history in the mid- dle of history, so to speak, and thereby provided from outside his- tory the terms in which the process of history made sense. History was not annihilation or annulment, but fulfillment and consum- mation. At the same time, Butterfield could affirm that each per- son and each moment is "equidistant from eternity." No human act depended upon absorption in a developmental process to be worthwhile.[32]

Niebuhr and Butterfield took very different routes to such relatively similar views of history. Butterfield's was the more straightforward one. He was raised in a devoutly Methodist family in Yorkshire, England. He never significantly altered the essentially Augustinian beliefs he learned early about the worth of human personality, the doctrine of sin, the relativity of human achievement in history, and futility of worshipping anything other than God.[33] *The Whig Interpretation of History* (1931) established his genius as a historian as he did battle with a one-sided, whig-liberal view of progress in history. Marxism never seriously tempted him, but he did study it carefully in the 1930's and learned from it: history as conflict, the place of economic and social factors in history, process and law in history.[34] He wrote *Christianity and History* (1949) by request, but hesitantly, because as he says, "It had never occurred to me to set myself up as a theologian." He simply said those things which he thought post-war, non-Christian students might do well to hear about history. The crisis of the times, it seems, did lead him after 1945 to begin publishing a fair number of books and articles on the themes of Christianity and history, diplomacy, and politics, such as *Christianity, Diplomacy, and War* (1953), *International Conflict in the Twentieth Century: A Christian View* (1960), and "Christianity and Politics" (1966–67). Without having an elaborate schema, or indeed without interacting closely with anyone on such matters, he worked for the renewal of Christianity in relation to the principles of those areas of life. His writings as a historian on topics like modern science, George III, Napoleon, and especially on the history of historical writings are, demonstrably, dependent upon the sorts of Christian presuppositions about human nature and history which he explicitly treats in *Christianity and History, History and Human Relations* (1951), "God in history" (1958), and elsewhere.[35]

Niebuhr's development was more spectacular. His intellectual biography reveals a dramatic and complicated series of "conversions of thought" surrounding a rather constant commitment to love and serve God and to offer help to the practical affairs of industrial workers, politics, and international diplomacy.[36] He began a thirteen-year pastorate in industrial Detroit as a fairly typical liberal idealist in the line of the social gospel. Toward the end of the 1920's he questioned the optimism of the old liberal view of human nature and history. When he moved to New York in 1928 to teach at Union Theological Seminary he also began to move toward Marxism. During the 1930's in his books *Moral Man and Immoral Society* (1932) and *Reflections on the End of an Era* (1934), he worked out a Christian social theory influenced by Marxism which gave him an instrument with which to criticize liberalism. The Marxist view of history as catastrophe and conflict gave him support in his critique of the liberal view of history as gradual progress. By the 1940's, when his seminal books on history were published, he moved completely away from Marxism toward Augustine and a new reading of the Bible. He called himself a Christian realist. During the 1950's he continued to shift toward a Christian pragmatism. He used his developing Christian view of history to interpret the history of America, democracy, and world politics in several books: *The Irony of American History* (1952); *The Structure of Nations and Empires* (1959); *A Nation So Conceived: Reflections on the History of America from Its Early Visions to Its Present Power* (1963); and *The Democratic Experience: Past and Prospects* (1969).

By the 1940's Niebuhr believed that the experiences of recent history refuted both the liberal and the Marxist views of history. He wrote in 1949, "This refutation has given the Christian faith, as presented in the Bible, a new relevance." [37] He wanted his work to contribute to a renewal of Christianity in our culture.

Christian Alternatives and the Ecumenical Movement

The idea of finding a Christian alternative to the prevailing philosophies of history functions decisively in the thought of most of the people in this anthology. In fact most of them went on to propose ideas for general cultural reconstruction: Niebuhr, Tillich, Maritain, Butterfield, Marrou, Eliot, Dawson, Toynbee, Dooyeweerd, Brunner, Florovsky, Gutiérrez, perhaps even Barth. In an age of crisis they hoped to find a way out somehow enlightened by the spirit and power of Christ and the Christian tradition.

It is evident that, common though this concern be, what appears is a remarkable diversity among them. One must use the plural in saying that, in fact, they found a number of Christian alternatives and offer a variety of Christian views of history. The differences often are not minor, and the essays here presented make this clear. For example, Brunner, Toynbee, and Dawson think that a linear view of history is important, while Bultmann does not. Pannenberg and Gutiérrez stress how inseparable salvation and ordinary history are, while Bultmann insists upon their divorce, and Maritain speaks of two distinct realms of the sacred and secular which are nonetheless closely linked. Dooyeweerd and Maritain look for specific laws in history, Butterfield claims there probably are such laws, but does not name any, and Barth and C. S. Lewis disparage or deny the validity of identifying any laws. Eliot stresses the leaders, while Gutiérrez emphasizes the outcast. Marrou and Florovsky prefer the large questions of interpretation in history, while Butterfield and Link start with the particulars. Link perceives the connection between his Christian faith and his historical vocation to be specialized on the point of his concern for the truth, while Florovsky, Butterfield, Marrou, and Dawson see the connection to be much more pervasive throughout their historical study. Latourette detects a gradual improvement of the position of Christianity in history, while most of the others do not.

The theological differences among the authors are great as well and often underlie their diversity of views on history. We need only think of how different are the approaches to the Bible of Latourette, Bultmann, and Tillich, or how opposite are Gutiérrez's, Toynbee's, and Dooyeweerd's views of human salvation through Christ.

Moreover, their searches for a Christian alternative varied considerably, some of them being very complex. Along their routes some of them experienced attraction to persons or viewpoints which were contradictory, or which they later rejected as inconsistent with Christian beliefs even if they learned something in the meantime.

The more spectacular searches are worth mentioning. The journey of Reinhold Niebuhr we have already seen as he moved from old liberal idealism, to a Marxist-influenced Christianity, to Christian realism, to Christian pragmatism. Maritain began as a

liberal Bergsonian, then converted to Roman Catholicism, and as a
Catholic was attracted briefly to the proto-fascist Charles Maurras,
then discovered Thomism and finally developed neo-Thomism.
Dawson was raised a nominal liberal Anglican, later converted to
Roman Catholicism and, in working out his Augustinian Catholic
Christianity, experienced attraction at various times to certain fea-
tures of Marxism, fascism, and liberalism. T. S. Eliot was raised
Unitarian, converted to Anglo-Catholicism, and in the process
briefly spoke well at different times of Maurras, Marxism, and
Social Credit.

The similarity underlying these pilgrimages as well as that of
others was their conviction of the need to mark out a Christian
way which offered an alternative to mere identification with liberalism, conservatism, fascism, and Marxism. Such people have often
been misunderstood. For example, reviewers of Dawson's books
have used conflicting labels to identify his ideas—capitalist, Marxist, fascist, liberal, conservative, reactionary.[38] In reality the label
most befitting Dawson should start with "Roman Catholic" and
then add adjectives like "Augustinian" and "social pluralist." What
one commentator said about Toynbee is true of most thinkers in
this anthology who hope for a renewal of Christianity in the culture:

> At bottom, secular ideologies, whether liberal, socialist, capitalist or
> whatever do not mean much to Toynbee. It is, of course, only religion
> that counts.[39]

The point being made here can be generalized. Whatever
their differences in their views of history, or their theology, or their
biographies, the term to use first in describing all the authors of
these essays as well as their views of history is "Christian." They
all share a common characteristic: Christ and Christian belief
are decisive for their lives and their views of history.

One significant cultural movement tended at the beginning to
direct their diversity toward a common Christian renewal. All but
one of the Protestant thinkers in this anthology have had some
connection with the Ecumenical Movement. The Catholics among
them have been ecumenically minded. The Ecumenical Movement itself began as a search for a Christian way in the modern

world. W. A. Visser 't Hooft, long-time General Secretary of the World Council of Churches, once characterized the Ecumenical Movement as "a third way" which cut across accepted dichotomies and deadlocks and rejected the current alternatives.[40]

Many of the thinkers have been leaders in the Ecumenical Movement.[41] The Oxford conference on church, community, and state in 1937 received the help of Niebuhr, Tillich, Barth, Brunner, Dawson, Latourette, and Florovsky. Barth, Brunner, Niebuhr, and Florovsky were principal speakers in Amsterdam at the founding of the World Council of Churches in 1948, and Tillich was present. Florovsky was for a time a member of the council's Central Committee and the Faith and Order Commission, as was Hendrikus Berkhof. Toynbee was once a member of the Commission of the Churches on International Affairs. T. S. Eliot, Niebuhr, Barth, Brunner, and Florovsky were members of the Advisory Commission on the theme of the second assembly of the council in 1954, and Toynbee was a member of that assembly's section on international affairs. Latourette was active in the International Missionary Council. John Baillie, who wrote two books on Christianity and history, was a president of the World Council.[42] All the Catholics— Maritain, Gutiérrez, Marrou, Dawson, and Cochrane—have supported Protestant-Catholic ecumenism.

The Ecumenical Movement from the 1930's through the 1960's was a significant influence in the revival of Christian views of history—by reflecting the renewal of thought on history, by providing a forum of common discussion, and by stimulating interest in the topic among member churches. The theme of Christianity and history was one of the most durable in ecumenical affairs on the world level.

As already noted, one of the books of the Oxford conference in 1937 was *The Kingdom of God and History*. The Amsterdam assembly of the World Council of Churches in 1948 took the theme "Man's disorder and God's design" and faced directly the reality of catastrophe in history in the context of trust in God's work in history. Two of the assembly sections studied Christian renewal amid the disorder of society and international disorder. Addresses by Niebuhr, Barth, Brunner, Florovsky, John Baillie, and C. D. Dodd, among others, spoke with varying emphases of the meaning and nature of history.[43]

The theme of the second assembly in Evanston in 1954 was "Christ, the hope of the world." The issue now became philosophies of history and eschatology. The report of the Advisory Commission on the theme presented a Christian view of history in contrast with rival secular hopes:

> The centre of world history is the earthly life, the cross and the resurrection of Jesus Christ. In Him God entered history decisively to judge and forgive. . . . Because God is the Lord of history, Christians must reject all doctrines of automatic progress or of fated decline. Man's hope is not in any process or achievement of history.

The false hopes identified were democratic humanism, scientific humanism, and Marxism. The document directly reflected Niebuhr's, and possibly Butterfield's, thought. Barth drafted the concluding section.[44]

In New Delhi at the third assembly in 1961, the World Council of Churches voted to study during the 1960's the theme of God's work in history. The proposal originated in the Division of Studies and was supported by the Department of Church and Society. The urgent question was how to discern what God is doing in history in an age of revolution and immense changes in every sphere of human life. One section at New Delhi reported this conviction:

> The Christian must always recognize that *Jesus Christ is the Lord of history and he is at work today in every nation of the world* in spite of, and through, the ambiguous political, economic, or social structures and actions in any given country.[45]

In the fall of 1962 the Division of Studies published *The Finality of Jesus Christ in the Age of Universal History,* which included a discussion of the themes of God and history, and the nature of universal history. The aim was "to help clarify the witness which the churches are called to make in the modern age." [46] Certain members of the committee for the Division of Studies felt that more specific work was needed on the historical questions in the study. This concern led to a further study, "God in Nature and History," written by Hendrikus Berkhof and published in 1965. After extensive study by groups in many parts of the world and by a consultation in Geneva the document was revised. It went next to the conference of the Faith and Order Commission in Bristol in

1967. The Commission published it, with some further revisions, as its own.[47] Berkhof reported on the study and addressed the fourth assembly of the World Council of Churches at Uppsala in 1968.[48] A request by Faith and Order for a parallel study on "Man in Nature and History" resulted, after Uppsala, in the establishment of Humanum, a centralized study program on human nature in the context of social change.[49]

For more than thirty years, at the world level of the Ecumenical Movement, sustained attention was given to the question of history. The consequences continued to be felt in all the major areas of concern of the World Council of Churches—social change, revolution, and the Third World, missions, faith and order.

The major way in which the renewal of Christian views of history proceeded from the 1930's to the 1960's was by means of thinkers reflecting on the problems and issues involved, and through the ordinary course of people reading their relevant books and articles. But the Ecumenical Movement provided a timely and organized support for the renewal, while the spirit of ecumenism in some manner animated most of the authors of these essays. In such ways, the new interest in history contributed its share to making Christianity, with all its internal diversity, a live option in world culture.[50]

The Anthology

The selections which follow include representative writings by the most important thinkers on Christianity and history. The books that are represented have all exercised considerable influence, like Niebuhr's *Faith and History,* Butterfield's *Christianity and History,* Maritain's *On the Philosophy of History,* Bultmann's *History and Eschatology,* Pannenberg's *Revelation As History,* Eliot's *Notes toward a Definition of Culture,* Tillich's *Systematic Theology,* and Gutiérrez's *A Theology of Liberation: History, Politics, and Salvation.* In the case of Dawson and Toynbee relatively unknown articles are included which summarize some of the thought found in their more famous books. Some of the articles have been particularly influential, like Latourette's presidential address before the American Historical Association in 1948, and the World Council of Churches' Faith and Order document, "God in Nature and History" (1967). In as many cases as possible entire chapters and articles have been given. The entries cover a period of about thirty years.[51]

The selections reveal the range of issues included in a Christian view of history, as well as some of the diversity and disagreement which exists. They are grouped in three parts.

Part I is devoted to the questions of the meaning of history, topics which often come under the heading theology of history. Here the writers treat how the revelation of Jesus Christ provides a transcendent approach to interpreting the course of history as a whole from the origins to the *eschaton*. The main themes are the Incarnation of Jesus Christ, the cross and resurrection, Christianity in history, the goal of history and Christian hope, the transcendent meaning of time, the interplay of redemption and sin in history, God's work in history, the relation between salvation history and history as we ordinarily know it, the uniqueness of a Christian view of history. The writers on these themes include three historians (Dawson, Latourette, Toynbee), one philosopher (Niebuhr), and five theologians (Tillich, Bultmann, Brunner, Pannenberg, Gutiérrez).

Part II on the nature of history and culture concerns what is often called the philosophy of history. The main issues have to do with discerning patterns, regularities, or laws in history, the relationship of a philosophy of culture to philosophy of history, and religion and culture. Important to some of the writers is to see how the understanding which Christians have of the meaning of history illuminates the structure of the historical process. Represented are two philosophers (Maritain, Dooyeweerd), one historian (Butterfield), one theologian (Barth), two "cultural thinkers" (Eliot, Lewis), and one document of the World Council of Churches, drafted by a theologian (Berkhof).

Part III on historians and historical study shifts attention to historiography, the study and writing of history. Topics include what it means to be a Christian historian, the character of historical scholarship and historical inquiry, and the relationship between the historian and historical reality. The issue is how being a Christian and having a Christian understanding of the meaning and nature of history affects the task of interpreting history. All six writers are historians (Harbison, Florovsky, Link, Butterfield, Marrou, and Cochrane).

The bibliography of further reading at the end of the volume lists some other people who have written on Christian views of history from the 1930's to the 1970's. Historians, theologians, and philosophers continue to devote themselves to the questions discussed in the essays presented in this anthology.[52]

Harbison was right in regarding the renewal since the 1930's as no mere return to an earlier form of Christianity. It reflects an urgently felt need to restore contact with an ancient tradition reaching back to Augustine, Paul, the Gospels, the prophets, and the Torah. At the same time it involves a development of new insights aroused by the experience of history in our times in interaction with the Christian tradition. As this anthology demonstrates, Christian approaches to understanding history are concerned with the same kinds of problems treated by other approaches—liberal or Marxist, idealist or positivist, analytic or phenomenological. Moreover, Christian approaches often discuss problems rarely considered by some other viewpoints. Accordingly, Christian views of history may be regarded as offering additional and, in many cases, alternative suggestions for philosophy of history and historiography, as well as contributing to the theology of history, which most non-Christian viewpoints neglect.

The work of the thinkers represented in this anthology and listed in the bibliography can be picked up with benefit by people studying history, theology, and philosophy, as well as by anyone who has been led by the crises and catastrophes of our times to question the assumptions which underlie our secular civilization.

NOTES

1. Reinhold Niebuhr, "Leaves from the notebooks of a war-bound American," *Christian Century*, 56 (1939), 1298–99, 1405–6, 1502–3, 1607–8.

2. Niebuhr, *The Nature and Destiny of Man*, II (New York: Scribner's, 1943), vii.

3. This anthology always has primarily in view the renewal in English-speaking North America and Great Britain. Writings which originated elsewhere are considered relative to their influence in English language areas.

4. Some statistical indication of the trend in the number of publications involved
can be gathered from Robert North's "Bibliography of Works in Theology and History," *History and Theory*, XII (1973), 55–140. From the perspective of the thesis
of this introduction, North's bibliography is very incomplete. It stresses theology
and biblical studies, and does not include all of the relevant works on a Christian
view of history by, for example, Dawson, Niebuhr, Butterfield, Toynbee, Tillich,
Harbison, and many others. But it can serve as a suggestion nonetheless. The figures give combined totals by year for all categories in North's bibliography, which
includes articles, books, reviews, and translations.

	Totals, English	Totals, all languages
1907–29	1	18
1930–34	3	37
1935–39	16	37
1940–44	3	16
1945–49	10	41
1950–54	21	76
1955–59	36	103
1960–64	83	225
1965–69	150	291

1949 starts the English upturn, with 7. 1948 starts the upturn for all languages
with 13, while 1949 has 18.

5. First published in *Church History*, XXI (1952), 97–106.

6. Review of M. C. D'Arcy, *The Meaning and Matter of History: A Christian View*,
in *History and Theory*, I (1960–61), 86. See p. 330.

7. Hendrikus Berkhof, professor of theology at the University of Leiden, was the
original author of the World Council of Churches' document, "God in Nature and
History." See. p. 291.

8. John C. Rule, *1945–1957* (Beiheft 1, 1961, with Supplement, Beiheft 3, 1964);
M. Nowicki, *1958–1961* (Beiheft 3, 1964); Lewis D. Wurgaft, *1962–1965* (Beiheft
7, 1967, with addenda, Beiheft 10, 1970); Lewis D. Wurgaft and others, *1966–1968*
(Beiheft 10, 1970, with addenda, Beiheft 13, 1974); Sylvia Pruitt and Astrid
Witschi-Bernz, 1969–1972 (Beiheft 13, 1974).

9. *History and Theory* intends to publish a separate bibliography of Marxist works
on history. See Lionel M. Munby and Ernst Wangermann, eds., *Marxism and History: A Bibliography of English Works* (London: Lawrence and Wishart, 1967).

10. The book is Bultmann's Gifford Lectures in Scotland in 1955 which he gave in
English. See p. 97. This is perhaps the place to notice that the thinkers in this anthology who were probably the most influential were Gifford lecturers: Barth, Niebuhr, Dawson, Toynbee, Bultmann, and Butterfield.

11. See p. 112. Also, Pannenberg, *Basic Questions in Theology*, I (Philadelphia:
Fortress, 1970).

12. For example, see the collection of papers which originated in German Catholic
circles after Vatican II, Walter Kasper, *et al. The Crisis of Change: Are Church and
Theology Subject to Historical Laws?* (Chicago: Argus, 1969).

13. Two summaries of the debate on the "problem of history" are James M. Connolly, *Human History and the Word of God: The Christian Meaning of History in*

Contemporary Thought (New York: Macmillan, 1965); and Carl E. Braaten, *History and Hermeneutics, New Directions in Theology*, II (Philadelphia: Westminster, 1966).

14. The experiences and developments mentioned in this and the next paragraph are the ones the authors themselves refer to most often.

15. Toynbee, in *A Study of History*, IV (New York: Oxford University Press, 1939), believes all civilizations experience a "time of troubles" as part of their breakdown. It may last centuries, and can be overcome by a revitalization of religion. See p. 176.

16. Rauschenbusch, *Christianity and the Social Crisis* (New York: Macmillan, 1907), 352, 422; *Christianizing the Social Order* (New York: Macmillan, 1912), chapters 2 and 3.

17. See Spengler's and the translator's prefaces in *The Decline of the West: Form and Actuality*, translated by Charles Francis Atkinson (New York: Knopf, 1926).

18. Dawson, *Progress and Religion: An Historical Enquiry* (London and New York: Sheed & Ward, 1929), preface.

19. Dawson, *Enquiries into Religion and Culture* (London and New York: Sheed & Ward, 1933), introduction. Also see p. 28.

20. Tillich, "Autobiographical Reflections," in *The Theology of Paul Tillich*, edited by Charles W. Kegley and Robert W. Bretall (New York: Macmillan, 1952), 21. See p. 57.

21. Peter Brown, *Augustine of Hippo: A Biography* (London: Faber and Faber, 1967), 287–98.

22. Brown, 299–312.

23. Henri-Irénée Marrou, *St. Augustine and His Influence through the Ages*, translated by Patrick Hepburne-Scott (New York: Harper Torchbooks, 1957), 7. Also see p. 390.

24. Butterfield claims he did not read Niebuhr until after he had published these Cambridge lectures (Personal interview, Peterhouse, Cambridge, 17 June 1975). Butterfield could not, however, have been unaware of the general discussion of Niebuhr's lectures, or of the emphases of neoorthodoxy.

25. Niebuhr, *Nature and Destiny*, II, vii.

26. Butterfield, *Christianity and History* (London: Bell, 1949), 70.

27. Niebuhr, *Faith and History: A Comparison of Christian and Modern Views of History* (New York: Scribner's, 1949), viii.

28. Butterfield, *Christianity and History*, 64.

29. Butterfield, *Christianity and History*, introduction and chapter 2; Niebuhr, *The Nature and Destiny of Man*, I (New York: Scribner's, 1941), chapter 6.

30. Niebuhr, *Faith and History*, chapter IX. See p. 68. Niebuhr, *Beyond Tragedy: Essays on the Christian Interpretation of History* (New York: Scribner's, 1937).

31. Butterfield, *Christianity and History*, 94. Compare this with Butterfield, "God in History," R. J. W. Bevan, ed., *Steps to Christian Understanding* (New York: Oxford University Press, 1958), 111–13. See p. 192. Also, Butterfield, *The Whig Interpretation of History* (London: Bell, 1931), chapter 3.

32. Niebuhr, *Nature and Destiny*, II, chapter 10. Butterfield, *Christianity and History*, 22–25, 65–67. See p. 357.

33. Most personal biographical details derive from a personal interview, Peterhouse, Cambridge, 17 June 1975. Butterfield's friend Professor David Knowles writes: "These pages on St. Augustine may not be out of place in a book dedicated to Herbert Butterfield, for he is in more than one way himself Augustinian." Knowles, "St. Augustine," in J. H. Elliot and H. G. Koenigsberger, eds., *The Diversity of History: Essays in Honour of Sir Herbert Butterfield* (London: Routledge and Kegan Paul, 1970), 19.

34. Butterfield, "History and the Marxian Method," *Scrutiny*, I (1933), 339–55; and Butterfield, "Marxist history," in *History and Human Relations* (London: Collins, 1951), 66–100.

35. See the Butterfield bibliography, complete to 1968, in *The Diversity of History*, 317–25.

36. Of the many studies on Niebuhr, the most helpful on this point are the political biography by Ronald N. Stone, *Reinhold Niebuhr: Prophet to Politicians* (Nashville and New York: Abingdon, 1972), and Paul Merkley, *Reinhold Niebuhr: A Political Account* (Montreal and London: McGill-Queen's University Press, 1975).

37. Niebuhr, *Faith and History*, viii.

38. Anne Woolever, *Christopher Dawson: A Study in Anti-Democratic International Thought, 1920–1960* (Ph.D. thesis, University of Toronto, 1969), *passim*.

39. Roland N. Stromberg, *Arnold J. Toynbee: Historian for an Age in Crisis* (Carbondale and Edwardsville, Ill.: Southern Illinois University Press, 1972), 86.

40. Edward Duff, *The Social Thought of the World Council of Churches* (New York: Association, 1956), 288–90. He wrote this in 1953 when the world seemed dominated by a struggle between liberal democracy and communism.

41. Most of what follows is gathered from David P. Gaines, *The World Council of Churches: A Study of Its Background and History* (Peterborough, N.H.: Richard R. Smith, 1966).

42. John Baillie, a professor at the University of Edinburgh, wrote *What Is Christian Civilization* (New York: Scribner's, 1945); and *The Belief in Progress* (New York: Scribner's, 1950).

43. Gaines, part III, *passim*. The texts of the sectional reports are on the disorder of society, 292–97; and on international disorder, 301–6.

44. The text of the report is in Gaines, 1140–67. Visser 't Hooft says Barth wrote the conclusion (*Memoirs* [London: SCM, 1973], 247). On the Evanston theme, Visser 't Hooft wrote: "The eschatological problem—that is the problem of the relation of the Kingdom of God to human history and of the ultimate hope to the proximate hope—is the key-problem of modern theology and had dominated ecumenical discussion ever since the Stockholm conference of 1925" (*Memoirs*, 246).

45. *The New Delhi Report, the Third Assembly of the World Council of Churches, 1961*, ed. Visser 't Hooft (New York: Association, 1962), 102, italics in the original report. See also *Workbook: New Delhi, 1961* (Geneva: World Council of Churches, n.d.), 68–73, 87.

46. Published in *Bulletin of the Division of Studies,* WCC, VIII, no. 2 (Autumn 1962), 1–42. A shorter version, without the appendices, is in *Ecumenical Review*, XV (1962–63), 320–31.

47. Berkhof's original article in *Study Encounter,* I (1965), 142–60. The final version in *New Directions in Faith and Order: Bristol 1967* (Geneva: World Council of Churches, 1968), 7–31. See p. 291.

48. Berkhof's report of the history of the study is in *Ecumenical Review,* XX (1968), 464–65. His address is in *The Uppsala Report 1968: Official Report of the Fourth Assembly of the World Council of Churches* (Geneva: WCC, 1968), 304–12. The title was "The Finality of Jesus Christ: Our Common Confession and Its Implications for Today."

49. See *Workbook: Uppsala 1968* (Geneva: WCC, 1968), 12–13. Dietrich Ritschl presented a paper with that title before the working committee of the Faith and Order Commission in Sweden, 1968. (*Minutes* of the working committee, Faith and Order Commission, Uppsala and Sigtuna, 1968, 16–21.)

50. It should be kept in mind that a revival of Christian presence in the world has taken many diverse and contradictory forms, such as, in the United States, that represented by the resurgence of conservative churches and the Evangelicalism symbolized by Billy Graham, by movements such as the new social consciousness among Evangelicals, the Jesus Movement, the "underground churches," the charismatic movement in Catholic and Protestant churches, and so on. The World Council of Churches is one kind of presence and not necessarily the most important.

51. Entries in the anthology grouped by decade: post-war 1940's, 5; 1950's, 7; 1960's, 8; 1970's, 2. Works first published in another language are listed according to the date of their English publication, both in this essay and in the brief introductions to each section.

52. See C. T. McIntire, *The Ongoing Task of Christian Historiography* (Toronto: Institute for Christian Studies, 1974). Historians working on the questions treated in this anthology may be found in professional societies like the American Catholic Historical Association, the American Society of Church History, the Conference on Faith and History, the Society of Ecclesiastical History in Great Britain, and the Canadian Catholic Historical Association.

THE MEANING
OF HISTORY

CHRISTOPHER DAWSON

Christopher Dawson (1889–1970) offers a good place to begin. In this essay he summarizes the salient features of a Christian view of history, and urges its rescue from the disfavor of both secular and certain Christian critics. Very quickly he identifies the heart of the matter: the Incarnation of Christ in the "fullness of time." He writes, "The history of the human race hinges on the unique divine event which gives spiritual unity to the whole historic process." The Incarnation is the central event of a continuum of world-transforming events which the Bible reveals, but which, he writes, "have occurred as it were under the surface of history unnoticed by the historians and the philosophers."

Dawson's approach, typically, is sweeping. He surveys the development of a Christian view of history from Israel to Christ and Paul, to Augustine, Bede, and Dante. Then he shows us the secular children of Christianity, the offspring of a classical marriage— Machiavelli, Hobbes, Marx. For Dawson, as a Catholic, the church holds the secret of history and human redemption.

Dawson knew best the history of Christendom from Augustine to the Renaissance, partly covered by his most influential book, *The Making of Europe* (1932). But he ranged widely from ancient to modern history, from western to eastern history, wherever he needed to look to understand the question of religion and culture. His many books include his Gifford Lectures, *Religion and the Rise of Western Culture* (1950), and *The Dividing of Christendom* (1965), lectures given while a professor at Harvard University.

The Christian View of History

The problem of the relations of Christianity to History has been very much complicated and, I think, obscured by the influence of nineteenth-century philosophy. Almost all the great idealist philosophers of that century, like Fichte and Schelling and Hegel, constructed elaborate philosophies of history which had a very considerable influence on the historians, especially in Germany, and on the theologians also. All these systems were inspired or coloured by Christian ideas and they were consequently eagerly accepted by Christian theologians for apologetic purposes. And thus there arose an alliance between idealist philosophy and German theology which became characteristic of the Liberal Protestant movement and dominated religious thought both on the Continent and in this country during the later nineteenth century.

Today the situation is entirely changed. Both philosophic idealism and liberal Protestantism have been widely discredited and have been replaced by logical positivism and by the dialectic theology of the Barthians. The result is that the idea of a Christian philosophy of history has also suffered from the reaction against philosophic idealism. It is difficult to distinguish the authentic and original element in the Christian view of history from the philosophic accretions and interpretations of the last century and a half, so that you will find modern representatives of orthodox Christianity like Mr. C. S. Lewis questioning the possibility of a Christian interpretation of history, and declaring that the supposed connection between Christianity and Historicism is largely an illusion.[1]

Reprinted by permission of *New Blackfriars* from *Blackfriars,* XXXII (1951), 312–27.

If we approach the subject from a purely philosophical point of view there is a good deal to justify Mr. Lewis's scepticism. For the classical tradition of Christian philosophy as represented by Thomism has devoted comparatively little attention to the problem of history, while the philosophers who set the highest value on history and insist most strongly on the close relation between Christianity and history, such as Collingwood and Croce and Hegel, are not themselves Christian and may perhaps have tended to interpret Christianity in terms of their own philosophy.

Let us therefore postpone any philosophical discussion and consider the matter on the basis of the original theological data of historic Christianity without any attempt to justify or criticize them on philosophical grounds. There is no great difficulty in doing this, since the classical tradition of Christian philosophy as represented by Thomism has never devoted much attention to the problem of history. Its tradition has been Hellenic and Aristotelian, whereas the Christian interpretation of history is derived from a different source. It is Jewish rather than Greek, and finds its fullest expression in the primary documents of the Christian faith— the writings of the Hebrew prophets and in the New Testament itself.

Thus the Christian view of history is not a secondary element derived by philosophical reflection from the study of history. It lies at the very heart of Christianity and forms an integral part of the Christian faith. Hence there is no Christian "philosophy of history" in the strict sense of the word. There is, instead, a Christian history and a Christian theology of history, and it is not too much to say that without them there would be no such thing as Christianity. For Christianity, together with the religion of Israel out of which it was born, is an historical religion in a sense to which none of the other world religions can lay claim—not even Islam, though this comes nearest to it in this respect.

Hence it is very difficult, perhaps even impossible, to explain the Christian view of history to a non-Christian, since it is necessary to accept the Christian faith in order to understand the Christian view of history, and those who reject the idea of a divine revelation are necessarily obliged to reject the Christian view of history as well. And even those who are prepared to accept in theory the principle of divine revelation—of the manifestation of a religious truth which surpasses human reason—may still find it hard to face the enormous paradoxes of Christianity.

That God should have chosen an obscure Palestinian tribe—not a particularly civilized or attractive tribe either—to be the vehicle of his universal purpose for humanity, is difficult to believe. But that this purpose should have been finally realized in the person of a Galilean peasant executed under Tiberius, and that this event was the turning point in the life of mankind and the key to the meaning of history—all this is so hard for the human mind to accept that even the Jews themselves were scandalized, while to the Greek philosophers and the secular historians it seemed sheer folly.

Nevertheless, these are the foundations of the Christian view of history, and if we cannot accept them it is useless to elaborate idealistic theories and call them a Christian philosophy of history, as has often been done in the past.

For the Christian view of history is not merely a belief in the direction of history by divine providence, it is a belief in the intervention by God in the life of mankind by direct action at certain definite points in time and place. The doctrine of the Incarnation which is the central doctrine of the Christian faith is also the centre of history, and thus it is natural and appropriate that our traditional Christian history is framed in a chronological system which takes the year of the Incarnation as its point of reference and reckons its annals backwards and forwards from this fixed centre.

No doubt it may be said that the idea of divine incarnation is not peculiar to Christianity. But if we look at the typical examples of these non-Christian theories of divine incarnation, such as the orthodox Hindu expression of it in the Bhagavad-gita, we shall see that it has no such significance for history as the Christian doctrine possesses. It is not only that the divine figure of Khrishna is mythical and unhistorical, it is that no divine incarnation is regarded as unique but as an example of a recurrent process which repeats itself again and again *ad infinitum* in the eternal recurrence of the cosmic cycle.

It was against such ideas as represented by the Gnostic theosophy that St. Irenaeus asserted the uniqueness of the Christian revelation and the necessary relation between the divine unity and the unity of history—"that there is one Father the creator of Man and one Son who fulfils the Father's will and one human race in which the mysteries of God are worked out so that the creature conformed and incorporated with his son is brought to perfection."

For the Christian doctrine of the Incarnation is not simply a theophany—a revelation of God to Man; it is a new creation—the introduction of a new spiritual principle which gradually leavens and transforms human nature into something new. The history of the human race hinges on this unique divine event which gives spiritual unity to the whole historic process. First there is the history of the Old Dispensation which is the story of the providential preparation of mankind for the Incarnation when "the fulness of time," to use St. Paul's expression, had come. Secondly there is the New Dispensation which is the working out of the Incarnation in the life of the Christian Church. And finally there is the realization of the divine purpose in the future: in the final establishment of the Kingdom of God when the harvest of this world is reaped. Thus the Christian conception of history is essentially unitary. It has a beginning, a centre, and an end. This beginning, this centre, and this end transcend history; they are not historical events in the ordinary sense of the word, but acts of divine creation to which the whole process of history is subordinate. For the Christian view of history is a vision of history *sub specie æternitatis,* an interpretation of time in terms of eternity and of human events in the light of divine revelation. And thus Christian history is inevitably apocalyptic, and the apocalypse is the Christian substitute for the secular philosophies of history.

But this involves a revolutionary reversal and transposition of historical values and judgments. For the real meaning of history is not the apparent meaning that historians have studied and philosophers have attempted to explain. The world-transforming events which changed the whole course of human history have occurred as it were under the surface of history unnoticed by the historians and the philosophers. This is the great paradox of the gospel, as St. Paul asserts with such tremendous force. The great mystery of the divine purpose which has been hidden throughout the ages has now been manifested in the sight of heaven and earth by the apostolic ministry. Yet the world has not been able to accept it, because it has been announced by unknown insignificant men in a form which was inacceptable and incomprehensible to the higher culture of the age, alike Jewish and Hellenistic. The Greeks demand philosophical theories, the Jews demand historical proof. But the answer of Christianity is Christ crucified—*verbum crucis*—the story of the Cross: a scandal to the Jews and an absurdity to the Greeks. It is only when this tremendous paradox with its reversal of all hitherto accepted standards of judgment has been accepted that the meaning of human life and human history can be understood. For St. Paul does not of course mean to deny the value of understanding or to affirm that history is without a meaning. What he asserts is the mysterious and transcendent character of the true knowledge—"the hidden wisdom which God ordained before the world to our glory which none of the rulers of this world know." [2] And in the same way he fully accepted the Jewish doctrine of a sacred history which would justify the ways of God to man. What he denied was an external justification by the manifest triumph of the Jewish national hope. The ways of God were deeper and more mysterious than that, so that the fulfilment of prophecy towards which the whole history of Israel had tended had been concealed from Israel by the scandal of the Cross. Nevertheless the Christian interpretation of history as we see it in the New Testament and the writings of the Fathers follows the pattern which had already been laid down in the Old Testament and in Jewish tradition.

There is, in the first place, a sacred history in the strict sense, that is to say, the story of God's dealings with his people and the fulfilment of his eternal purpose in and through them. And, in the second place, there is the interpretation of external history in the light of this central purpose. This took the form of a theory of successive world ages and successive world empires, each of which had a part to play in the divine drama. The theory of the world ages, which became incorporated in the Jewish apocalyptic tradition and was ultimately taken over by Christian apocalyptic, was not however Jewish in origin. It was widely diffused throughout the ancient world in Hellenistic times and probably goes back in origin to the tradition of Babylonian cosmology and astral theology. The theory of the world empires, on the other hand, is distinctively biblical in spirit and belongs to the central message of Hebrew prophecy. For the Divine Judgment which it was the mission of the prophets to declare was not confined to the chosen people. The rulers of the Gentiles were also the instruments of divine judgment, even though they did not understand the purposes that they served. Each of the world empires in turn had its divinely appointed task to perform, and when the task was finished their power came to an end and they gave place to their successors.

Thus the meaning of history was not to be found in the history of the world empires themselves. They were not ends but means, and the inner significance of history was to be found in the apparently insignificant development of the people of God. Now this prophetic view of history was taken over by the Christian Church and applied on a wider and universal scale. The divine event which had changed the course of history had also broken down the barrier between Jews and the Gentiles, and the two separated parts of humanity had been made one in Christ, the corner-stone of the new world edifice. The Christian attitude to secular history was indeed the same as that of the prophets; and the Roman Empire was regarded as the successor of the old world empires, like Babylon and Persia. But now it was seen that the Gentile world as well as the chosen people were being providentially guided towards a common spiritual end. And this end was no longer conceived as the restoration of Isreal and the gathering of all the exiles from among the Gentiles. It was the gathering together of all the spiritually living elements throughout mankind into a new spiritual society. The Roman prophet Hermas in the second century describes the process in the vision of the white tower that was being built among the waters, by tens of thousands of men who were bringing stones dragged from the deep sea or collected from the twelve mountains which symbolize the different nations of the world. Some of these stones were rejected and some were chosen to be used for the building. And when he asks "concerning the times and whether the end is yet," he is answered: "Do you not see that the tower is still in process of building? When the building has been finished, the end comes."

This vision shows how Christianity transfers the meaning of history from the outer world of historic events to the inner world of spiritual change, and how the latter was conceived as the dynamic element in history and as a real world-transforming power. But it also shows how the primitive Christian sense of an imminent end led to a foreshortening of the time scale and distracted men's attention from the problem of the future destinies of human civilization. It was not until the time of the conversion of the Empire and the peace of the Church that Christians were able to make a distinction between the end of the age and the end of the world, and to envisage the prospect of a Christian age and civilization which was no millennial kingdom but a field of continual effort and conflict.

This view of history found its classical expression in St. Augustine's work on *The City of God* which interprets the course of universal history as an unceasing conflict between two dynamic principles embodied in two societies and social orders—the City of Man and the City of God, Babylon and Jerusalem, which run their course side by side, intermingling with one another and sharing the same temporal goods and the same temporal evils, but separated from one another by an infinite spiritual gulf. Thus St. Augustine sees history as the meeting point of time and eternity. History is a unity because the same divine power which shows itself in the order of nature from the stars down to the feathers of the bird and the leaves of the tree also governs the rise and fall of kingdoms and empires. But this divine order is continually being deflected by the downward gravitation of human nature to its own selfish ends—a force which attempts to build its own world in those political structures that are the organized expression of human ambition and lust for power. This does not, however, mean that St. Augustine identifies the state as such with the *civitas terrena* and condemns it as essentially evil. On the contrary, he shows that its true end—the maintaining of temporal peace—is a good which is in agreement with the higher good of the City of God, so that the state in its true nature is not so much the expression of self-will and the lust for power as a necessary barrier which defends human society from being destroyed by these forces of destruction. It is only when war and not peace is made the end of the state that it becomes identified with the *civitas terrena* in the bad sense of the word. But we see only too well that the predatory state that lives by war and conquest is an historical reality, and St. Augustine's judgment on secular history is a predominantly pessimistic one which sees the kingdoms of this world as founded in injustice and extending themselves by war and oppression. The ideal of temporal peace which is inherent in the idea of the state is never strong enough to overcome the dynamic force of human self-will, and therefore the whole course of history *apart from divine grace* is the record of successive attempts to build towers of Babel which are frustrated by the inherent selfishness and greed of human nature.

The exception, however, is all-important. For the blind forces of instinct and human passion are not the only powers that rule the world. God has not abandoned his creation. He communicates to man, by the grace of Christ and the action of the Spirit, the spiritual power of divine love which alone is capable of transforming human nature. As the natural force of self-love draws down the world to multiplicity and disorder and death, the supernatural power of the love of God draws it back to unity and order and life. And it is here that the true unity and significance of history is to be found. For love, in St. Augustine's theory, is the principle of society, and as the centrifugal and destructive power of self-love creates the divided society of the *civitas terrena,* so the unitive and creative power of divine love creates the City of God, the society that unites all men of good will in an eternal fellowship which is progressively realized in the course of the ages.

Thus St. Augustine, more perhaps than any other Christian thinker, emphasizes the social character of the Christian doctrine of salvation. For "whence," he writes, "should the City of God originally begin or progressively develop or ultimately attain its end unless the life of the saints were a social one?" [3] But at the same time he makes the individual soul and not the state or the civilization the real centre of the historic process. Wherever the power of divine love moves the human will there the City of God is being built. Even the Church which is the visible sacramental organ of the City of God is not identical with it, since, as he writes, in God's foreknowledge there are many who seem to be outside who are within and many who seem to be within who are outside.[4] So there are those outside the communion of the Church "whom the Father, who sees in secret, crowns in secret." [5] For the two Cities interpenetrate one another in such a way and to such a degree that "the earthly kingdom exacts service from the kingdom of heaven and the kingdom of heaven exacts service from the earthly city." [6]

It is impossible to exaggerate the influence of St. Augustine's thought on the development of the Christian view of history and on the whole tradition of Western historiography, which follows quite a different course from that of Eastern and Byzantine historiography. It is true that the modern reader who expects to find in St. Augustine a philosophy of history in the modern sense, and who naturally turns to the historical portions of his great work, especially Books XV to XVIII, is apt to be grievously disappointed, like the late Professor Hearnshaw who wrote that the *De Civitate Dei* contains neither philosophy nor history but merely theology and fiction. But though St. Augustine was never a Christian historian such as Eusebius, his work had a far more revolutionary effect on Western thought. In the first place, he impressed upon Christian historians his conception of history as a dynamic process in which the divine purpose is realized. Secondly, he made men realize the way in which the individual personality is the source and centre of this dynamic process. And finally, he made the Western Church conscious of its historical mission and its social and political responsibilities so that it became during the following centuries the active principle of Western culture.

The results of St. Augustine's work find full expression three centuries later in the Anglo-Saxon Church. Unlike St. Augustine, St. Bede was a true historian, but his history is built on the foundations that St. Augustine had laid, and thus we get the first history of a Christian people in the full sense of the word—a history which is not primarily concerned with the rise and fall of kingdoms—though these are not omitted; but with the rise of Christ's kingdom in England, the *gesta Dei per Anglos*. Of course Bede's great work can hardly be regarded as typical of mediaeval historiography. It was an exceptional, almost an unique, achievement. But at any rate his historical approach is typical, and, together with his other chronological works, it provided the pattern which was followed by the later historians of the Christian Middle Ages. It consists in the first place of a world chronicle of the Eusebian type which provided the chronological background on which the historian worked. Secondly there were the histories of particular peoples and Churches of which St. Bede's *Ecclesiastical History* is the classical example, and which is represented in later times by works like Adam of Bremen's *History of the Church of Hamburg* or Ordericus Vitalis's *Ecclesiastical History*. And thirdly there are the biographies of saints and bishops and abbots, like Bede's life of St. Cuthbert and the lives of the abbots of Wearmouth.

In this way the recording of contemporary events in the typical mediaeval chronicle is linked up on the one hand with the tradition of world history and on the other with the lives of the great men who were the leaders and heroes of Christian society. But the saint is not merely an historical figure; he has become a citizen of the eternal city, a celestial patron and protector of man's earthly life. So that in the lives of the saints we see history transcending itself and becoming part of the eternal world of faith.

Thus in mediaeval thought, time and eternity are far more closely bound up with one another than they were in classical antiquity or to the modern mind. The world of history was only a fraction of the real world and it was surrounded on every side by the eternal world like an island in the ocean. This mediaeval vision of a hierarchical universe in which the world of man occupies a small but central place finds classical expression in Dante's *Divina Commedia*. For this shows better than any purely historical or theological work how the world of history was conceived as passing into eternity and bearing eternal fruit.

And if on the one hand this seems to reduce the importance of history and of the present life, on the other hand it enhances their value by giving them an eternal significance. In fact there are few great poets who have been more concerned with history and even with politics than Dante was. What is happening in Florence and in Italy is a matter of profound concern, not only to the souls in Purgatory, but even to the damned in Hell and to the saints in Paradise, and the divine pageant in the Earthly Paradise which is the centre of the whole process is an apocalyptic vision of the judgment and the reformation of the Church and the Empire in the fourteenth century.

Dante's great poem seems to sum up the whole achievement of the Catholic Middle Ages and to represent a perfect literary counterpart to the philosophical synthesis of St. Thomas. But if we turn to his prose works—the *Convivio* and the *De Monarchia*—we see that his views on culture, and consequently on history, differ widely from those of St. Thomas and even more from those of St. Augustine. Here for the first time in Christian thought we find the earthly and temporal city regarded as an autonomous order with its own supreme end, which is not the service of the Church but the realization of all the natural potentialities of human culture. The goal of civilization—*finis universalis civitatis humani generis*— can only be reached by a universal society and this requires the political unification of humanity in a single world state. Now it is clear that Dante's ideal of the universal state is derived from the mediaeval conception of Christendom as a universal society and from the tradition of the Holy Roman Empire as formulated by Ghibelline lawyers and theorists. As Professor Gilson writes, "if the *genus humanum* of Dante is really the first known expression of the modern idea of Humanity, we may say that the conception of Humanity first presented itself to the European consciousness merely as a secularized imitation of the religious notion of a Church." [7]

But Dante's sources were not exclusively Christian. He was influenced most powerfully by the political and ethical ideals of Greek humanism, represented above all by Aristotle's *Ethics* and no less by the romantic idealization of the classical past and his devotion to ancient Rome. For Dante's view of the Empire is entirely opposed to that of St. Augustine. He regards it not as the work of human pride and ambition but as a holy city specially created and ordained by God as the instrument of his divine purpose for the human race. He even goes so far as to maintain in the *Convivio* that the citizens and statesmen of Rome were themselves holy, since they could not have achieved their purpose without a special infusion of divine grace.

In all this Dante looks forward to the Renaissance rather than back to the Middle Ages. But he carries with him so much of the Christian tradition that even his secularism and his humanism have a distinctively Christian character which make them utterly different from those of classical antiquity. And this may also be said of most of the writers and thinkers of the following century, for, as Karl Burdach has shown with so much learning, the whole atmosphere of later mediaeval and early Renaissance culture was infused by a Christian idealism which had its roots in the thirteenth century and especially in the Franciscan movement. Thus the fourteenth century which saw the beginnings of the Italian Renaissance and the development of Western humanism was also the great century of Western mysticism; and this intensification of the interior life with its emphasis on spiritual experience was not altogether unrelated to the growing self-consciousness of Western culture which found expression in the humanist movement. Even in the fifteenth and sixteenth centuries the humanist culture was not entirely divorced from this mystical tradition; both elements co-exist in the philosophy of Nicholas of Cusa, in the culture of the Platonic Academy at Florence and in the art of Botticelli and finally in that of Michelangelo. But in his case we feel that this synthesis was only maintained by an heroic effort, and lesser men were forced to acquiesce in a division of life between two spiritual ideals that became increasingly divergent.

This idealization of classical antiquity which is already present in the thought of Dante developed still further with Petrarch and his contemporaries until it became the characteristic feature of Renaissance culture. It affected every aspect of Western thought, literary, scientific and philosophic. Above all, it changed the Western view of history and inaugurated a new type of historiography. The religious approach to history as the story of God's dealings with mankind and the fulfilment of the divine plan in the life of the Church was abandoned or left to the ecclesiastical historians, and there arose a new secular history modelled on Livy and Tacitus and a new type of historical biography influenced by Plutarch.

Thus the unity of the mediaeval conception of history was lost and in its place there gradually developed a new pattern of history which eventually took the form of a threefold division between the ancient, mediaeval and modern periods, a pattern which in spite of its arbitrary and unscientific character has dominated the teaching of history down to modern times and still affects our attitude to the past.

This new approach to history was one of the main factors in the secularization of European culture, since the idealization of the ancient state and especially of republican Rome influenced men's attitude to the contemporary state. The Italian city state and the kingdoms of the West of Europe were no longer regarded as organic members of the Christian community, but as ends in themselves which acknowledged no higher sanction than the will to power. During the Middle Ages the state as an autonomous self-sufficient power structure did not exist—even its name was unknown. But from the fifteenth century onwards the history of Europe has been increasingly the history of the development of a limited number of sovereign states as independent power centres and of the ceaseless rivalry and conflict between them. The true nature of this development was disguised by the religious prestige which still surrounded the person of the ruler and which was actually increased during the age of the Reformation by the union of the Church with the state and its subordination to the royal supremacy.

Thus there is an inherent contradiction in the social development of modern culture. Inasmuch as the state was the creation and embodiment of the will to power, it was a Leviathan—a sub-moral monster which lived by the law of the jungle. But at the same time it was the bearer of the cultural values which had been created by the Christian past, so that to its subjects it still seemed a Christian state and the vice-gerent of God on earth.

And the same contradiction appears in the European view of history. The realists like Machiavelli and Hobbes attempted to interpret history in non-moral terms as a straightforward expression of the will to power which could be studied in a scientific (quasi-biological) spirit. But by so doing they emptied the historical process of the moral values that still retained their subjective validity so that they outraged both the conscience and the conventions of their contemporaries. The idealists, on the other hand, ignored or minimized the sub-moral character of the state and idealized it as the instrument of divine providence or of that impersonal force which was gradually leading mankind onwards towards perfection.

It is easy to see how this belief in progress found acceptance during the period of triumphant national and cultural expansion when Western Europe was acquiring a kind of world hegemony. But it is no less clear that it was not a purely rational construction, but that it was essentially nothing else but a secularized version of the traditional Christian view. It inherited from Christianity its belief in the unity of history and its faith in a spiritual or moral purpose which gives meaning to the whole historical process. At the same time its transposition of these conceptions to a purely rational and secular theory of culture involved their drastic simplification. To the Christian the meaning of history was a mystery which was only revealed in the light of faith. But the apostles of the religion of progress denied the need for divine revelation and believed that man had only to follow the light of reason to discover the meaning of history in the law of progress which governs the life of civilization. But it was difficult even in the eighteenth century to make this facile optimism square with the facts of history. It was necessary to explain that hitherto the light of reason had been concealed by the dark forces of superstition and ignorance as embodied in organized religion. But in that case the enlightenment was nothing less than a new revelation, and in order that it might triumph it was necessary that the new believers should organize themselves in a new church whether it called itself a school of philosophers or a secret society of *illuminati* or freemasons or a political party. This was, in fact, what actually happened, and the new rationalist churches have proved no less intolerant and dogmatic than the religious sects of the past. The revelation of Rousseau was followed by a series of successive revelations—idealist, positivist and socialistic, with their prophets and their churches. Of these today only the Marxist revelation survives, thanks mainly to the superior efficiency of its ecclesiastical organization and apostolate. None of these secular religions has been more insistent on its purely scientific and non-religious character than Marxism. Yet none of them owes more to the Messianic elements in the Christian and Jewish historical traditions. Its doctrine is in fact essentially apocalyptic—a denunciation of judgment against the existing social order and a message of salvation to the poor and the oppressed who will at last receive their reward after the social revolution in the classless society, which is the Marxist equivalent of the millennial kingdom of righteousness.

No doubt the Communist will regard this as a caricature of the Marxist theory, since the social revolution and the coming of the classless society is the result of an inevitable economic and sociological process and its goal is not a spiritual but a material one. Nevertheless the cruder forms of Jewish and Christian millenniarism were not without a materialistic element since they envisaged an earthly kingdom in which the saints would enjoy temporal prosperity, while it is impossible to ignore the existence of a strong apocalyptic and Utopian element in the Communist attitude towards the social revolution and the establishment of a perfect society which will abolish class conflict and social injustice.

There is in fact a dualism between the Marxist myth, which is ethical and apocalyptic, and the Marxist interpretation of history, which is materialist, determinist and ethically relativistic. But it is from the first of these two elements that Communism has derived and still derives its popular appeal and its quasi-religious character which render it such a serious rival to Christianity. Yet it is difficult to reconcile the absolutism of the Marxist myth with the relativism of the Marxist interpretation of history. The Marxist believer stakes everything on the immediate realization of the social revolution and the proximate advent of the classless society. But when these have been realized, the class war which is the dialectical principle of historical change will have been suppressed and history itself comes to an end. In the same way there will no longer be any room for the moral indignation and the revolutionary idealism which have inspired Communism with a kind of religious enthusiasm. Nothing is left but an absolute and abject attitude of social conformism when the revolutionary protest of the minority becomes transformed into the irresistible tyranny of mass opinion which will not tolerate the smallest deviation from ideological orthodoxy. By the dialectic of history the movement of social revolution passes over into its totalitarian opposite, and the law of the negation finds its consummation.

Thus, in comparison with the Christian view of history, the Marxist view is essentially a short-term one, the significance of which is concentrated on the economic changes which are affecting modern Western society. This accounts for its immediate effectiveness in the field of political propaganda, but at the same time it detracts from its value on the philosophical level as a theory of universal history. The Marxist doctrine first appeared about a century ago, and could not have arisen at any earlier time. Its field of prediction is limited to the immediate future, for Marx himself seems to have expected the downfall of capitalism to take place in his own lifetime, and the leaders of the Russian revolution took a similar view. In any case the fulfilment of the whole Marxist programme is a matter of years, not of centuries, and Marxism seems to throw no light on the historical developments which will follow the establishment of the classless society.

The Christian view, on the other hand, is co-extensive with time. It covers the whole life of humanity on this planet and it ends only with the end of this world and of man's temporal existence. It is essentially a theory of the interpenetration of time and eternity: so that the essential meaning of history is to be found in the growth of the seed of eternity in the womb of time. For man is not merely a creature of the economic process—a producer and a consumer. He is an animal that is conscious of his mortality and consequently aware of eternity. In the same way the end of history is not the development of a new form of economic society, but is the creation of a new humanity, or rather a higher humanity, which goes as far beyond man as man himself goes beyond the animals. Now Christians not only believe in the existence of a divine plan in history, they believe in the existence of a human society which is in some measure aware of this plan and capable of co-operating with it. Thousands of years ago the Hebrew prophet warned his people not to learn the ways of the nations who were dismayed at the signs of the times. For the nations were the servants of their own creatures—the false gods who were the work of delusion and who must perish in the time of visitation. "But the portion of Jacob is not like these, for he that formed all things has made Israel to be the people of his inheritance." The same thing is true today of the political myths and ideologies which modern man creates in order to explain the signs of the time. These are our modern idols which are no less bloodthirsty than the gods of the heathen and which demand an even greater tribute of human sacrifice. But the Church remains the guardian of the secret of history and the organ of the work of human redemption which goes on ceaselessly through the rise and fall of kingdoms and the revolutions of social systems. It is true that the Church has no immediate solution to offer in competition with those of the secular ideologies. On the other hand, the Christian solution is the only one which gives full weight to the unknown and unpredictable element in history; whereas the secular ideologies which attempt to eliminate this element, and which almost invariably take an optimistic view of the immediate future are inevitably disconcerted and disillusioned by the emergence of this unknown factor at the point at which they thought that it had been finally banished.

NOTES

1. In his article on "Historicism" in *The Month*, October, 1950 [see p. 224].

2. Col. ii; cf. Eph. iii.

3. *De Civ. Dei*, xix, V.

4. *De bapt.*, V, 38.

5. *De Vera Religione*, vi, II.

6. *In Psalmos*, li, 4.

7. E. Gilson, *Dante the Philosopher*, p. 179.

KENNETH SCOTT LATOURETTE

Latourette's (1884–1968) aim is plainly, but politely, evangelistic. He was for most of his career a professor of missions and Oriental history at Yale University, but he remained a Baptist missionary at heart. In this his presidential address before the American Historical Association in 1948 he invited the historians assembled to consider the Christian interpretation of history as a solution to the problem of framework in the writing of history.

He surveys some of the central elements of a Christian view of history—the sovereignty of God, the Incarnation of Christ, the universality of outlook, the motive of love, and the fellowship of the People of God. Even though these crucial convictions "cannot be subject to the tests which the historian is able to apply," he believes that the history of Christianity and the legacy of Christ in the world supports "the truth of the Christian understanding." He published two large works to demonstrate his point: *The History of the Expansion of Christianity* (7 volumes, 1937–45), and *Christianity in a Revolutionary Age* (5 volumes, 1958–69).

True to his universality of viewpoint Latourette was a pioneer in the study of Chinese history and wrote *The Chinese: Their History and Culture* (2 volumes, 1934, rev. 1964) which became a standard in the field.

The Christian Understanding of History

Do patterns exist in history? All historians make selections from the multitude of happenings which constitute the quarry in which they work. Do they do so arbitrarily or in accord with what is inherent in the events? If there are patterns, can they be discerned? Is history governed by laws? If so, what are they? Does history have meaning, or is it simply sound and fury, signifying nothing? Does it have an end toward which it is moving, or is it movement without direction? These are questions which continue to trouble members of our craft. In various lands, cultures, and ages they have been repeatedly raised and many answers have been given. Whether in the ancient civilizations of the Nile and the Tigris-Euphrates Valley, in Hebrew Palestine, in China, in India, in Greece, in Rome, in the Middle Ages of Europe, or in the modern Occident, explicitly or by implication they have been posed and pondered.

We need no full catalogue to recall how various have been the purposes which have governed selection from the fragmentary records of the past, how numerous have been the patterns which observers of man's course on this planet have seen as giving coherence to the many incidents which are the crude stuff with which historians deal, how diverse have been the laws which have been said to mold the course of events, and the meaning—or the absence of meaning—which has been thought to characterize the stream of human life. Many scribes, both ancient and modern, have centered their stories upon men and women who have loomed large in the collective life of the group—rulers, statesmen,

Reprinted by permission of the American Historical Association from the *American Historical Review*, LIV (1949), 259–76.

artists, authors, scholars, religious leaders. Some of this, as in early
China, has been from a mixture of reverence for ancestors and the
desire of insuring prestige to a particular family. Some has been at
the instance of those in the public eye who have wished to perpetuate the memory of their greatness—from some of the most ancient inscriptions and chronicles to the archives amassed and preserved by recent Presidents of the United States and the spate of
autobiographies which has been mounting since the invention of
the printing press. Many arrangements of events have had as their
principle of selection admiration and affection for a friend, a
teacher, or a saint, or concern for the perpetuation and spread of a
religious or political faith—as in the case of Confucius, the Buddha, Jesus, and Lenin. Some historians have centered their narratives upon a war, or series of wars—the Peloponnesian struggle,
the Gallic Wars, the American Civil War, and World Wars I and II.
Many have concentrated on the state and politics. Some, especially
in recent times, have viewed economic factors as determinative.
Others have attempted to discern a science of society. Influenced
by the temper which has characterized much of the Occidental
mind for the past few generations, historians have debated
whether history is a science. Whatever their answer, in general
they have attempted to apply scientific methods to their work.
Modern historians usually believe in causation—that events and
movements are in large part or entirely determined by preceding
events and movements. Yet there are those who declare a time
sequence to be all that can be demonstrated. For at least twenty-
five hundred years there have been those who have insisted that
no meanings or patterns are to be observed in history. Often, as in
the case of Yang Chu, this has been in protest against those who
believed such to exist. Those who have viewed this world, including human life, as illusion, as has been so widely the case in India,
naturally have had little or no regard for history. Many observers
across the centuries have believed that history is cyclical, repeating itself. This has been true of the Greeks, of many Buddhists,
and of some of the most widely read of modern Occidental authors.
Others have held that progress is discernible, whether by steady
movement, by pulsations, or by the dialectical process. Some are
passionately convinced that progress culminates in an ideal society
in which all man's ills will have been resolved. Others, while be-

lieving in progress, do not envision mankind as ever escaping from struggle. These are merely a few of the many attitudes which men have taken as they have sought to record or to understand the past. Some contradict one another. Others can be embraced in a larger synthesis.

Faced with this multiplicity of convictions, it is not surprising that the experienced historian tends to be wary of committing himself to any of them. Yet history cannot be written without some basis of selection, whether artificial and purely subjective or inherent in man's story. A survey of the presidential address made before this Association reveals the fact that no one single topic has so attracted those who have been chosen to head this honorable body as have the possible patterns and meanings of history. A few of the addresses have been critical of particular interpretations or even of all interpretations of history. More have presented interpretations—although usually with such modesty and cautious tentativeness as befits those who submit themselves to the judgment of their peers. Frequently the patterns have been assumed or implied.

The historian, then, is faced with a dilemma. On the one hand he is painfully aware of the many interpretations and philosophies of history which have been put forward and is therefore hesitant to accept wholeheartedly any one of them. On the other hand he is confronted with the necessity of acting on some principle of selection, even though it be arbitrary, and is haunted by the persistent hope that a framework and meaning can be found which possess objective reality.

This hope is peculiarly insistent in our day. We appear to be living in a time of major revolution. As historians we are familiar with many earlier periods of rapid change. Indeed, if there is one feature which we are agreed upon as characterizing history it is flux. It seems probable that no culture—if we can assent to the existence of such an entity—and no institution remains permanently unaltered. Yet so far as we are aware, never before has all mankind been so drastically on the march. Never at any one time have so many cultures been in what appears to be disintegration. In no other era have all men been faced with such colossal possibilities of what they deem good and ill. Never before has the race as a whole been so assailed by those who urge upon it dogmatically one or another interpretation of the historical process to explain and to guide in humanity's painful transition.

May I make bold under these circumstances to invite your consideration to one of the oldest interpretations of history, the one which bears the name Christian? I do so realizing that many now regard it as quite outmoded, as associated with a stage of thinking which mankind is discarding, and as being held only by those who are victims of what is indulgently denominated social lag. I do so as one who accepts the Christian understanding of history and is more and more attracted by what he believes to be the accuracy of its insight. But it is not as an advocate, as one in the long succession of those who would seek to justify the ways of God to men, that I would once more draw your attention to it. I would, rather, raise with you the question of whether the Christian understanding of history may not offer the clue to the mystery which fascinates so many of our best minds.

May I first outline what the Christian understanding of history is? Then may I go on to suggest the degree to which it eludes testing by the methods employed by historians of our day? May I next note the ways in which it can be approached by these methods and indicate possible conclusions from these tests? The subject is rendered pertinent partly by reason of the claims which continue to be made for the Christian understanding of history, partly because, through the geographic expansion of Christianity, the Christian view is held by individuals and groups in more and more peoples and is, indeed, more widely spread than any other, in part from the challenges, some old and some new, to which the view is submitted, and because recent experience may shed fresh light on a familiar question.

What is the Christian understanding of history? At first sight there may seem to be no single view held by all Christians and given the Christian name, but rather a number of views, related but reciprocally contradictory and having little in common. Some differences are to be found near the very beginning of Christianity and are imbedded in the earliest documents of the faith, those assembled in the New Testament. Most of the others arise from varying interpretations of these documents.

The chief differences are quickly summarized. Jesus had much to say of what he called the Kingdom of Heaven or the Kingdom of God. Presumably he meant by this the doing of God's will, for one of the central petitions of the prayer which all Christians agree to have been taught by him, "Thy Kingdom come, thy will be done on earth as it is in Heaven," in the fashion of Hebrew poetry makes the second part repeat in different words the idea in the first part. But Christians disagree as to how and when that petition is to be answered. Is the Kingdom of God to come by slow stages and by the cooperation of men until God's will is perfectly accomplished—within history? This view was widely cherished in Protestant circles late in the nineteenth century and in some quarters survives today. It is believed to have support in the words of Jesus. This, obviously, is akin to evolution and has been congenial to many who have accepted the evolutionary hypothesis. The opposite view has been held that the world is becoming no better, and, indeed, may even be deteriorating, and that God by His own unaided act will bring history to a sudden dramatic end and will then accomplish His perfect will. Eminent scholars have contended that Jesus himself expected this consummation and very soon. From time to time through the centuries there have been those who have believed the end of history to be imminent. Indeed, we have them with us today. Some Christians identify the Kingdom of God with the Church. Others would not so identify it. Some have held that the human will is so hopelessly corrupted by sin that every effort by man to better his condition is foredoomed and that we must quietly wait for God to accomplish His purposes. Others, with more confidence in human ability, make God dependent on man's efforts in bringing in the Kingdom.

Striking and important though these differences are, they occur within a framework to which most informed Christians give general assent. They state their faith in a wide variety of ways, but back of the many formulations lies a large measure of agreement. Christians believe that God is the creator of the universe and rules throughout all its vast reaches, whether, to man, the unimaginable distances and uncounted suns or the inconceivably minute world of the atom, whether in what men call matter or in what they call spirit. This means that man lives and history takes places in a universe, that all of reality is one and under the control of God, and that the human drama is part and parcel of the far larger unity of God's creation. Ultimately and in His own way, so the Christian view maintains, God is sovereign in the affairs of men. Physically frail though he is, man, the Christian declares, was created in the likeness of God and with the possibility of fellowship with God. For this reason, as the Christian sees it, mankind is one; history embraces all mankind and is universal. In creating man in His image, God gave to man a certain measure of His own free will. Man's freedom is limited by various factors, among them heredity and physical and social environment, but his freedom is still real. Human history is in large part tragedy, and the tragedy consists in man's abuse of his freedom. Man is prone to ignore the fact that he is a creature. In one fashion or another he arrogates to himself full autonomy and seeks to do not God's will but his own will. He places other loyalties above his loyalty to God and gives to them the allegiance due to God. Thus one's own fancied security and pleasure, the family, a set of ideas, the state or some other organization, even a church, may be given priority. God, who is always working in the universe and in history, meets this perversion of man's will, so the Christian goes on to say, in two ways, by judgment and by mercy. Through what are sometimes described as His inexorable laws written into the structure of the universe and so in man's own constitution and environment, God judges man and whatever man sets up in place of God. Hence comes most of man's misery and frustration. But God wishes man to repent, and as often as men truly repent, whether individually or in groups, He forgives them and gives them fresh opportunity to grow toward the purpose which He has for them. Ultimately God will triumph. History moves toward a culmination. Whether within or beyond time God's will is to be accomplished and His full sovereignty will be seen to have prevailed.

Thus far the Christian understanding of the universe and of history resembles several non-Christian views. What is here outlined is largely true of Judaism, to a certain extent of Islam, and has partial parallels in theistic or near-theistic systems in China, ancient Persia, and elsewhere.

The distinctively Christian understanding of history centers upon historical occurrences. It has at its heart not a set of ideas but a person. By a widespread convention historians reckon history as B.C. and A.D. They are aware of many other methods of recording dates and know that this particular chronology has acquired extensive currency because of the growing dominance during the past few centuries of a civilization in which Christian influences have been potent. To the Christian, however, this reckoning of time is much more than a convention. It is inherent in history. In Jesus of Nazareth, so the Christian holds, God once for all disclosed Himself and acted decisively. The vast majority of Christians believe that Jesus was God incarnate. Historians are well aware of the long debates and the ecclesiastical struggles, some of them in stark contradiction to the love which is the supreme Christian virtue, over the relation of the divine and human in Jesus. That so many of the debates should have been an occasion for this temper is part of a larger problem to which we must later recur and which had its most dramatic and, so Christians believe, its decisive expression in the crucifixion of Jesus. In spite of and, perhaps, in part because of their acrimony, the controversies over the relation of the human and divine in Jesus are evidence of the struggle of the human mind and spirit to comprehend what Christians hold to have been a quite unique event. The large majority of Christians agree with the conviction expressed in one of the early Christian documents, that in Jesus the eternal Word which was and is God became flesh. In Jesus, so Christians maintain, God's Kingdom began in a fresh way. This was partly because Jesus, being both God and man, disclosed by his life and his teachings what God intended man to be and what man might become. It was also because in and through Jesus God revealed His inmost nature and accomplished a work of central and supreme importance.

God, so the Christians declare, is love. The English word "love" is clumsy and ambiguous. It is used to cover a wide range of meanings. The Greek which the early Christians employed was more discriminating. But even that was inadequate. In "love," as that term is applied to God, the Christian discerns a self-giving which can never be perfectly described in words but which was disclosed in Jesus. This love was especially seen in the death of Jesus. Here, as one of the earliest Christians declared, although it appeared to be weakness and folly, were displayed both the power of God and the wisdom of God.[1] The crucifixion was followed by the resurrection. Through the resurrection, so Christians believe, God demonstrated that physical death not only does not end all but that it may be a stage in an endless life beyond history which is not

merely continued existence—this might be and presumably will
for some men be extraordinarily unhappy—but which is one of
growing fellowship with God, God who is love. In the earliest documents the name for what God did in Jesus is not Christianity: it is
Gospel, "Good News." The Gospel judges man by making clear as
in no other way man's perversity and sin. It also releases life to
overcome that perversity and sin. The purpose of God in history is
that men shall be "conformed to the image of His son."[2]

The Christian understanding of history goes on to say that following the crucifixion and the resurrection God continued to
operate through what Christians call the Holy Spirit. Through the
Holy Spirit men can be remade and can enter upon the radiant,
eternal life which from the beginning was God's plan for men.
Those who have that life are characterized by faith, hope, and
especially love, the kind of love which is of the very nature of God.
They form a fellowship, the Church, which takes on a visible form
or forms within history but which is never completely identical
with any historic expression and continues beyond history. The
course of history is God's search for man. God is judge, but He
judges man that He may save him and transform him. God's
grace, the love which man does not deserve and cannot earn, respects man's free will and endeavors to reach man through the incarnation, the cross, and the Holy Spirit. Here, to the Christian, is
the meaning of history and its unifying core.

From the outset, the Christian view of history has embraced
all men. From the Christian standpoint man is not necessarily central in the universe. There may be many other beings and on other
planets or in other stellar systems whom God creates in His likeness, to whom He gives free will, and who abuse that free will. If
so, His love also seeks them. If God is love, His love must be at
work in all the universe. Yet on this planet God's love certainly
includes all men. The early disciples were commanded to be "witnesses" "unto the uttermost parts of the earth," [3] to "make disciples of all nations," baptizing them, and teaching them to observe all that Jesus had commanded his original followers.[4] This,
presumably, also becomes the obligation of all subsequent Christians. It implies that the Christian goal can be nothing short of the
full obedience of all men to God as He disclosed Himself in Jesus.
This would entail the complete transformation of human society to

bring society into entire conformity with God's will for man. Yet it seems clear that neither Jesus nor the early Christians expected within history the full conformation of mankind to the "measure of the stature of the fullness of Christ." [5] Both the wheat and the tares, the good and the evil, were expected to "grow" until the consummation of history.[6] Beyond history, presumably outside of time, God is "to gather together all things in one in Christ, which are in heaven and which are on earth." [7] God has always been sovereign, and in the cross and the resurrection He signally triumphed,[8] but beyond history His sovereignty is to be seen as complete.

The Christian understanding of history differs radically from other views. It is in contrast with the ancient Persian dualism, for the latter implies separate origins of good and evil. This dualism means that the good God is not sovereign in history, because He has not created the universe as a whole, whereas Christianity regards God as creator and lord of all. Only a sovereign God can forgive sins as the Christian believes Him to do. Nor is Christianity pantheistic, as is so much of Indian philosophy, for it does not make God the author of what men call evil. Man's misery, so Christianity declares, arises from the abuse of the free will which God has given him. The Christian understanding of history is not exclusively cyclical. It recognizes eras and ages, but it holds that novelty enters, that new things happen. The great event, as the Christian sees it, was Jesus and Jesus was without precedent. So, too, the consummation will be new. Some interpretations of history seem to expect perfection within history, the coming of the ideal human society. This is the communist message. It appears to have been true of Comte and of Hegel. The Christian understanding of history does not necessarily deny progress. Obviously, the criteria for measuring advance must be established before we can say whether progress has occurred, and the Christian criteria are peculiarly Christian—growth in the likeness of God as God reveals Himself in Jesus. Christians are not agreed as to whether progress occurs in history. Some affirm it and others deny it. Yet few if any Christians have maintained that man will attain his full destiny within history.

All this is, or should be, a commonplace to historians. It is simply an attempt at a restatement of what the majority of Christians have always believed. Many Christians would add to this or would amplify it. Many would regard it as inadequate and incomplete. Yet the overwhelming proportion would say that so far as it goes it is a summary of what Christians have held and hold today to be the Christian view of history. I would apologize for repeating it were it not necessary for any assessment of the Christian understanding of history.

Several features of the Christian outlook must be especially noted if the historian would seek an appraisal by the standards which the members of his craft are currently inclined to apply.

First of all, he must be clear that here are frankly a perspective and a set of values which are the complete reverse of those which mankind generally esteems. We are told that unless a man is born again not only can he not enter, but he cannot even see (or presumably recognize) the Kingdom of God.[9] On one memorable occasion the "prince of the apostles" was rebuked by Jesus for thinking like man and not like God.[10] This was because he was shocked by the prospect of the crucifixion and sought to dissuade his master from it. Centuries before Jesus a famous story of the one of the prophets who was counted as among his greatest predecessors declared that God was not in the thunder nor in a mighty wind, where He was expected, but in a still small voice.[11] Another of the prophets in whose succession Jesus stood was emphatic that God's thoughts are not man's thoughts nor man's ways God's ways.[12] Of the crucifixion Paul declared that the "wise man" and the "scribe," namely the scholar, completely miss its significance and that God makes foolish the wisdom of this world.[13] In other words, if he is to understand history as God sees it, the historian must focus his attention upon events which he would normally ignore. From the Christian standpoint, the usual historian has an entirely distorted view of history and misses the most important features. This, may we add parenthetically, may be true of those who deal with ecclesiastical as well as with political, economic, or intellectual history.

Even when the historian gives attention to the events which the Christian understanding deems most significant he may miss their real import. There is deep meaning in the plea, "Father forgive them for they know not what they do." [14] Had those who crucified Jesus dreamed that they were executing the Son of God they would, presumably, have drawn back in terror or in horror.

In the second place, the historian must recognize that from the viewpoint of Jesus the individual is of outstanding importance. In this he declared that he was expressing the mind of God. The Christian faith exalts the individual. Each human being, as we have said before, is regarded as intended for fellowship with the eternal God Who is love. It was to individuals that Jesus gave his attention. He healed men one by one. Some of his best remembered stayings and parables were to single persons. He spoke again and again of the value which God places on individuals. The concern of God for the erring, so he said, is like that of the shepherd who leaves the ninety and nine who are safe in the fold and seeks for the one sheep who is lost until he finds it,[15] or like the father who longs for the return of a wayward son and rejoices when he appears, repentant.[16]

Jesus was deeply concerned for the fate of his people. In his day Palestine was seething with unrest which a few years later broke out in open revolt and was followed by the destruction of Jerusalem. He clearly foresaw what was coming, as must any intelligent, well-poised observer who took account of the mounting nationalistic and religious fanaticism and who knew the power of Rome. He believed that the destruction had not been unavoidable, that had its inhabitants been willing to heed him Jerusalem might have escaped, but that they were so blind that the doom of the city was sealed. So deeply pained was he by the prospect that he wept.[17]

Yet so far as we know Jesus never engaged in politics. Indeed, at the outset of his public career he had put aside as a palpable temptation the suggestion that he enter the political arena.[18] To be sure, he was accused of treasonable aspirations and was crucified derisively as "the King of the Jews," [19] but it is quite clear that he believed his kingdom to be "not of this world" [20] and that as applied to what he had in mind and what he believed to be God's purpose, the term had for him far other significance than that given it by men. From the standpoint of political wisdom and when viewed prudently the program which Jesus followed seemed the sheerest madness. On the visit to Jerusalem which issued in his death he pursued a course which could not but bring down on his head the wrath of the established authorities of religion and the state and yet he declined either to flee or to permit his followers to organize or to use armed force to defend him and his cause.

However, in the third place, Jesus did not ignore the social structures of mankind. He said much of the relation of individuals to other individuals and declared that the corollary of love for God is love for one's neighbor.[21] The Kingdom of God, of which he so often spoke, is a society. Men are to enter that Kingdom one by one. When they enter it, as they can here and now, they are to act as its members and as though the Kingdom were already here. The standards of that Kingdom are so far above the actual attainments of any other society that Christians as members of the Kingdom are always a revolutionary force. It is not the purpose of the Gospel to save any culture. The rise and fall of cultures and empires are important in so far as they affect individuals, but the rise and fall may harm the individual no more than do the cultures and empires themselves. There is that in the Gospel, so Christians maintain, which enables individuals to pass through such experiences triumphantly, centers of healing and strength. Indeed, the collapse of an empire or a culture may make it possible to build what, from the Christian standpoint, is better. Christians must always challenge any civilization in which they are set. Yet they are not to be primarily destructive but constructive. They are to be "the salt of the earth" and "the light of the world." [22]

Here at last appears to be something tangible on which the historian would like to believe that he can lay his hand and begin to measure. Surely he can determine where Christians, because of their faith, have been a molding force in history. Yet he is warned that, since the Christian set of values is different from that of the rank and file of men, the record of the accomplishments of Christians may not be preserved in the documents on which he relies. "The last shall be first and the first last." [23] The Kingdom of God, he is told, comes not by observation. Neither can men say about it "lo here and lo there." [24]

In the fourth place, the Christian understanding of history regards history and time as surrounded by eternity. Christianity centers upon historical events and views God as acting in history. Yet it holds that the human drama is not completed in time, and that one must go beyond the events with which the historian deals and even beyond what is still to occur in time in order completely to see God's dealings with man. Of necessity and by its very nature history deals with time. Christianity centers upon events in time and also transcends them.

When he is confronted with the Christian understanding of history the historian may well feel baffled and even impatient. He may say with a wry smile that the Christian is like the Taoist who declared that those who know do not speak and that those who speak do not know.[25] Some of the key Christian convictions about history are not and cannot be subject to the tests which the historian is able to apply. For instance, the historian can neither absolutely prove nor disprove that God created man in His own image. Obviously he cannot reach beyond time and verify the Christian conviction concerning the goal of history. God cannot be fully known within history. If He could, He would be limited and would cease to be what the Christian faith believes Him to be.

The difficulty is inherent in the methods to which the historian is confined. He must deal with records. Through whatever channels are open to him he must attempt to determine what actually happened. The records which are accessible to the historian are usually very faulty. In appraising them and in arranging and interpreting events the historian relies on his reason. He knows that in most of the records and in his arrangement and interpretation of them there is subjectivity, a subjectivity from which he can never be entirely emancipated. He seeks through reason to reduce the subjective element to a minimum, but if he is honest and well equipped he knows something of the limitations of reason and also suspects that the subjective element can never be completely eliminated. The historian is himself part of history. He is caught in it and cannot fully stand apart from it or view it with undiluted objectivity.

These limitations on his work handicap the historian in all his endeavors, including his attempt to appraise any interpretation of history. It is not merely when he applies his tools to the Christian understanding of history that he is hampered. The historian is dealing with visible events, but there are also invisible forces which he cannot measure. If he is not to do violence to history the historian can never abstract fact from value. Yet his training, at least as usually given in our day, does not equip him to deal with the latter. Unless he is a thoroughgoing skeptic, the historian tries to discover a standard of values. Christianity professes to provide him with an absolute standard of values. Christianity professes to provide him with an absolute criterion. Yet by the processes which he normally employs the historian is clumsy and baffled when he comes to appraise the Christian or any other set of values.

However, limited though they are, the historian must employ such tools as he possesses. When he does so, much comes to light which tends to support the Christian understanding of history. The historian as historian can neither refute nor demonstrate the Christian thesis, but he can detect evidence which suggests a strong probability for the truth of the Christian understanding.

Increasingly it is apparent that history must be seen in its entire setting and that that setting is the universe. This is what the Christian has all along contended. More and more man by the scientific method is recognizing that the universe is orderly. This supports theism. An orderly universe which can be explored by human reason implies a reason and a will controlling that universe to which the human mind is akin.

In the development of life on the earth there seems to be purpose. Man appears to be the culmination, at least at this stage, of the life process on the planet. So far as we know, man is the only creature who is interested in his own past and in seeking to understand the universe. It is quite unlikely that this is the outcome of blind chance. Moreover, in support of the Christian conviction, as life reaches what we believe to be higher stages, the biological process appears to be increasingly interested in the individual rather than the mass. Certainly individuals are more and more differentiated from one another.

The Christian belief about what happens beyond history gives relevance to the development of life on the earth. As we have said, it appears to be true that this development issues in ever higher forms of life of which man is, at least in the present stage, the highest. But man is obviously incomplete within history. He has longings which cannot be satisfied in the brief span of the existence of individuals in this flesh. The Christian view of history regards what occurs beyond physical death as essential to the realization of man's capacities and holds out confident hope of that fulfillment. This is what is embraced in what the theologian terms apocalypticism and eschatology.

The Christian conception of man provides an intelligible and responsible explanation of the tragic dilemma in which man increasingly finds himself. On the one hand man aspires to understand the universe and adds more and more to his fund of knowledge. This is what we would expect if man, as the Christian faith declares, is created in the image of God. Man is thinking God's thoughts after Him. It is clear, too, that were man to follow the law of love which the Christian declares is written by God in man's nature, he would be freed from the ills which he now brings on himself. He would live in reverence and love of God and love of his neighbor. War would be banished. Men would co-operate the globe over in utilizing the resources of their environment for the physical and spiritual well-being of all. Just as clearly through his departure from this law man brings on himself misery. The more his knowledge and mastery of his physical environment increase, the more man employs them on the one hand for his benefit and on the other for his woe. Indeed, through his misuse of that knowledge he threatens the existence of the civilization which he has created and even the race itself. In this the Christian sees the judgment by which God seeks to constrain man to do His will.

But what of the redeeming love which the Christian believes God to have displayed in Jesus? What evidence, if any is there that this is present and is proving effective? It is, of course, clear that Jesus lived, that he taught and was crucified, that his disciples were profoundly convinced that he was raised from the dead and in the strength of that conviction set out to win the world to allegiance to him. As the centuries pass the evidence is accumulating that, measured by his effect on history, Jesus is the most influential life ever lived on this planet. The influence appears to be mounting. It does not increase evenly but by pulsations of advance, retreat, and advance. It has had an unprecedented growth in the past four and a half centuries and especially in the last century and a half. Christianity is now more widely spread geographically than it or any other religion has ever been. Only a very few peoples and tribes exist where it is not represented by organized groups.

This advance has been associated with the expansion of the

Occident. As we all know, that expansion is a recent historical phenomenon. As we also know, Western Europe, from which that expansion stemmed, appears to be waning and at times it seems that in Western Europe itself Christianity is declining. Yet nations, notably the United States, which trace their source to Western Europe, are still continuing the expansion of the Occident, and the culture which had its origin in the West spreads ever more widely and rapidly. It has become global. That Occidental civilization is in part the product of Christianity is obvious. In art, literature, thought, education (for universities and many other new types of schools have owed to it an incalculable debt), in morals, and in social, economic, and political institutions Christianity has been a major factor. Democracy as the West understands that term is largely its child. A case can be made for the claim that science sprang from Christianity. Precisely to what degree Jesus is responsible for Western culture is by no means clear. On that question large volumes could be written and the answers would not be definitive. Now the expansion of the Occident and its culture has by no means been an unmixed blessing to mankind. If Jesus has had a major share in the development of that culture and in its dynamic spread, we may well ask whether the redemption which the Christian declares that God wrought through him has been sufficiently potent to offset the ills that have accompanied the growth of what is often described as Christendom.

As the influence of Jesus has spread geographically, various results have followed which are evidence that the transforming power which Christians claim for it is at work. Because of it more languages have been reduced to writing than through all other agencies in the history of mankind. Literacy is not an unmixed blessing, but it can be and has been used to further the enrichment of man's life. Through the expansion of Western peoples and their culture, mankind has for the first time been brought together. To the degree that this is the result of the influence of Jesus it is a partial implementation of the dream of the unity of mankind which is a feature of the Christian understanding of history. The struggle to regulate and eventually to eliminate the wars which make our shrinking globe so perilous a neighborhood owes much to Jesus. That he was potent in such pioneers of international law as Francisco de Vitoria and Hugo Grotius is well attested. He can also be shown to have had a part in the initiation of the Hague conferences of the last generation. Such attempts at world-wide co-operation as the League of Nations and the United Nations are demonstrably to some extent from him. However, just how large his share has been in these achievements cannot accurately be measured.

Much clearer is the decisive part which Jesus has had in the efforts to combat slavery and other forms of the exploitation of men by their fellows. It is significant that the first Christian priest ordained in the New World, Bartolomé de Las Casas, was the chief pioneer in the struggle to protect the Indians against the cruelties of the Spaniards, to write humane statutes in the Laws of the Indies, and to seek their enforcement. The list is long of the Spanish and Portuguese laymen and clergy who, inspired and sustained by their Christian faith, labored to guard the non-Europeans in the colonies in both hemispheres from the callous selfishness of their fellow countrymen. The place of his Christian faith in impelling Wilberforce in his campaign against the Negro slave trade is well known. So, too, is the role of the Quakers, Samuel Hopkins, and those touched by the Finney revival, consciences made sensitive by commitment to the Christian faith, in the movement for the emancipation of Negro slaves in the United States. We are all aware of the efforts of the Christian missionary, David Livingstone, to curb the slave trade in Africa itself. Less familiar is the share of such Christian missionary leaders as John Philip and Cardinal Lavigerie in the campaign against African slavery. Christianity has been one of the most potent forces making for the liberation and advance of the depressed classes of India. Jesus was a major inspiration of Gandhi. In land after land he has contributed to the emancipation of women. In the impact of Occidental upon non-Occidental peoples Christian missions and other agencies inspired by him have made for improved medical care, for public health, for better methods of agriculture, and for schools and universities better adapted to the new day than were their predecessors. Increasingly these features of the influence of Jesus have been spreading and now in varying measure embrace mankind.

More and more the ecclesiastical organizations which we call churches are becoming world-wide. They seek, not unsuccessfully, to perpetuate the influence of Jesus and to incarnate the self-giving and the fellowship which are of the essence of the Christian Gospel. Their divisions and quarrels are familiar to the historian, but in spite of them the churches have become global. The largest, the Roman Catholic Church, is to be found in almost every land and people. The non-Roman Catholic churches are fully as widely distributed and have been drawing together through new types of organizations, several of which include some Roman Catholics.

The transforming love of God through Jesus is seen, so the Christian believes, not only in collective movements but also and primarily in individuals. Some of these individuals loom large in the records which are at hand for the historian. Among these are Paul of Tarsus, Augustine of Hippo, Francis of Assisi, Martin Luther, Ignatius Loyola, George Fox, and John Wesley. Indeed, the list could be extended to many pages. What from the Christian standpoint would be a full and therefore an accurate list can never be compiled, for it would need to include untold millions for whom no record survives. Moreover, for those whose records we have, we cannot determine with complete accuracy just which qualities and changes of character are due to the Christian faith and which to other factors. For the qualities of character, too, which the Christian view prizes no accurate measurements are possible. They are real, but are not capable of being plumbed by the methods which are at the historian's disposal. Nor can we judge their full effects on other lives and upon human society as a whole. Yet we have enough information to permit some generalizations which possess rough accuracy. We know that under Christian influence changes in character take place. Sometimes these appear to be sudden. More often they come by gradual, almost imperceptible stages. In some lives they are outstanding. In many they are slight. Yet when we see them we recognize them. They are the qualities commended in the Sermon on the Mount and in other parts of the Gospels and in the Epistles of the New Testament. Often we find them nourished in small groups of those who have sought to commit themselves fully as Christians. Indeed, those in whom the Christian faith predominates as a transforming force have always been small minorities. Yet often they have had effects which far outstrip their own borders.

These many results of Christianity, in society at large, in individuals, and in groups, are what we would expect from what the Christian calls the Holy Spirit. They are, so the Christian maintains, in consequence of stimuli issuing from the divine initiative, stimuli marked by the characteristics displayed in Jesus and tied up historically with him. Yet they are more than the lengthened influence of a great life. The Christian understanding of history is that it is through the Holy Spirit which is God Himself that God continues to work in history. Thus God respects man's will but continuously brings His love to bear on man. It is through the Holy Spirit, the Christian believes, that as the centuries pass the influence of Jesus grows rather than wanes.

Somewhere in this region lies a possible explanation of one of the most perplexing questions provoked by the Christian understanding of history. Why is it that what the Christian deems evil and good continue side by side in individuals and in groups? Why do even ecclesiastical bodies display both, bodies presumably the result of God's love, the embodiment of the Christian community of love? Why do some of the chronic ills of mankind, notably war, attain their most colossal dimensions in lands and through peoples that have long been under Christian influence? Why are some of what seem to be the gifts of God and the effects of Christianity twisted to man's hurt? Here we recall the fashion in which science and its fruits are so often turned to man's destruction. Has God failed? Is His sovereignty compromised? Is His salvation through Jesus frustrated? Is the influence of Jesus, though growing, always to be a minority force, outstripped by the forces opposed to it and perhaps even provoking them to greater activity? Is, therefore, the Christian view of history an illusion?

As we meditate on these persistent questions we need to remind ourselves again that the Christian understanding of history presupposes a degree of freedom of man's will, sufficient for man to accept or reject God's love. We must also recall that the issues are not new. They are posed in their most vivid form in the crucifixion of Jesus. Here, as the Christian sees it, man's blindness to God's purpose and man's self-assertiveness were in stark contrast with the seeming weakness and futility of God's chosen way of showing His love. Indeed, this is what we should expect if the Christian teaching of man and God is in accord with the facts.

Man's rebellion becomes most marked when God's love is most clearly displayed. In the cross and in the other perversions of God's gifts is seen the judgment as well as the love of God.

Yet, if God is love and is sovereign, His judgments must be a way to the triumph of His love. It is, therefore, not surprising that following the crucifixion there came a fresh release of power in the lives of those who began to see something of the significance of the death of Jesus and freely accepted the forgiveness and love of God. It is understandable that the cross became the symbol of the Christian faith and has been the confidence and inspiration of millions to face triumphantly the evil in them and about them. Similarly the abuses of God's love which have followed the crucifixion and have been painfully apparent in those cultures where the influence of Jesus has been most marked have been the occasion for millions to seek to eliminate the evils of which they are the symptoms and thus have given rise to something better than had been there before, both in individual lives and in the collective life of mankind.

The struggle continues. Civilization becomes more complex. All mankind is bound together ever more closely in the bundle of life and the disorders of one segment affect the whole. Yet the efforts to combat these disorders mount and more and more make themselves felt throughout the earth. Increasingly they have a major source in Jesus, and what Christians have believed about his birth, his life, his death, and his resurrection. Here is one of the strongest reasons for confidence in the accuracy of the Christian view of history. The historian, be he Christian or non-Christian, may not know whether God will fully triumph within history. He cannot conclusively demonstrate the validity of the Christian understanding of history. Yet he can establish a strong probability for the dependability of its insights. That is the most which can be expected of human reason in any of the realms of knowledge.

NOTES

1. I Cor. 1:18–25.
2. Rom. 8:29.
3. Acts 1:8.
4. Matt. 28:19, 20.
5. Eph. 4:13.
6. Matt. 13:24–30.
7. Eph. 1:10.
8. Col. 2:15.
9. John 3:3, 5.

10. Matt. 16:23.
11. I Kings 19:11–13.
12. Isaiah 55:8.
13. I Cor. 1:20.
14. Luke 23:34.
15. Luke 15:3–6.
16. Luke 15:11–24.
17. Luke 19:41–44.

18. Luke 4:5–8.
19. Mark 15:18, 26; Luke 23:1, 2.
20. John 18:36.
21. Matt. 22:34–40.
22. Matt. 5:13, 14.
23. Matt. 19:30.
24. Luke 17:20, 21.
25. *Tao Tê Ching*, 56.

REINHOLD NIEBUHR

Niebuhr (1892–1971), in this selection from *Faith and History* (1949), takes us to the Gospels' revelation of Christ in order to appreciate "the seeming absurdity and the ultimate wisdom of faith in Christ as the end of history and the fulfillment of life's meaning." The cross, a recurrent theme in Niebuhr's writings, signifies the power of sin in human nature which is broken by the greater power of God in Christ. It, together with the resurrection, marks a new beginning in history which becomes "the pattern of all subsequent confrontations between God and man."

Niebuhr's thinking on history was nourished by a fresh reading of the Bible, Augustine, Luther, and Calvin. Volume II of *The Nature and Destiny of Man* (1943) represents his first systematic probing of the meaning of history. Then in *Faith and History* he clarifies the features of a Christian view of history by comparing it with classical Greek and modern secular views. At the same time, and typical of all his thought, he engaged intensely in reflection upon the chaotic course of contemporary history. He regarded himself as a social philosopher and directed his thought toward the practical world of politics. He had no doubt that the biblical truth of the cross and the resurrection could not be contained by the theologizing of specialists, including himself, but would work through to the benefit of ordinary human affairs.

The Foolishness
of the Cross and
the Sense of History

I

The New Testament makes the startling claim that in Christ history has achieved both its end and a new beginning. The affirmation that Christ is the end of history signifies that in His life, death, and resurrection the meaning of man's historic existence is fulfilled. The divine sovereignty, which gives it meaning, is revealed to have an ultimate resource of mercy and forgiveness, beyond judgement, which completes history despite the continued fragmentary and contradictory character of all historic reality. The affirmation that in Christ there is a new beginning, that a "new age" has been initiated in the history of mankind, means that the wisdom of faith which apprehends the true meaning of life also contains within it the repentance which is the presupposition of the renewal of life.

The New Testament claim seems equally incredible from the standpoint of either Hebraic messianism or a modern man's conception of history, because both preserve their sense of meaning for human life by the hope that its obscurities and ambiguities will be overcome in history itself. Hebraic messianism hoped for a messianic end in which the moral obscurity of history, which permitted the righteous to suffer and the wicked to triumph, would be overcome; or in which the righteous would be given a new heart so that they would deserve the victory which was assured them. In modern culture the process of historical growth is expected gradually to overcome both the inexactness of rewards and punishments in history and the inclination of the human heart to violate the laws of life. The New Testament, on the contrary, regards the defiance by man of the very structure of his existence as a permanent factor in history which is never completely overcome except by divine grace. Yet it promises a new beginning in the life of any man, nation, or culture which recognizes the depth and persistence of man's defiance of God. Where such self-knowledge is achieved both the release from sin through forgiveness and the hope of a new life are possible.

Such a faith came into the world by a highly improbable revelation and it maintains itself whenever the power of that revelation penetrates through human pretentions and discovers men in their true situation on any level of their historical development. As St. Paul insisted its acceptance could not be achieved in the first instance by "worldly wisdom." The revelation of a divine mercy in a suffering saviour was not a conclusion about the nature of God at which men might arrive if they analyzed the causes, sequences, and coherences of the world and deduced the structure of existence from these observable phenomena. Any such procedure is bound, however, to be "foolish" despite its seeming wisdom. In the case of Greek wisdom the mind which rose to the knowledge of God was separated from history. History was reduced to the level of nature. In this process man himself was lost, since man is something more than nature and something less than spirit. The problem of the meaning of history is always the problem of the meaning of life itself, since man is an historic creature involved, and yet not involved, in the flux of nature and time, but always involved in a false solution of his predicament. Thus man is always in the position either of negating the meaning of history or of completing it falsely, if he seeks to complete it from the standpoint of his own wisdom. Yet it can be completed by a revelation, the acceptance of which is possible only through a contrite recognition of the human situation of sinfulness. Such repentance is possible, in turn, only if the judgment overhanging man is known to be prompted by love and to be crowned by forgiveness.

Whether in the period when the Gospel of Christ was first proclaimed and accepted, or in our own day, the acceptance of such a gospel is always experienced as a miracle of revelation in the sense that the relation between God and man which it establishes is not the achievement of a rational analysis of life. Yet it is felt to be a new wisdom and power. From its standpoint it is possible to "make sense" out of life; whereas alternative approaches either destroy the sense of life entirely or make false sense of it.

II

In order to appreciate the seeming absurdity and the ultimate wisdom of faith in Christ as the end of history and the fulfillment of life's meaning, it will be helpful to distinguish between the form and the content of the drama, recorded in the New Testament, as the focal point of this revelation. The form is that of a story, an event in history which becomes, by the apprehension of faith, something more than a mere event. It is an event through which the meaning of the whole of history is apprehended and the specific nature of the divine sovereignty of history is revealed. It is presented as the last in a series of God's "mighty acts," and one which has a particularly definitive character. Whatever may happen in subsequent ages, nothing can occur which will shake the faith of a true believer in God's sovereignty over all history. He is "persuaded, that neither death, nor life, nor angels, nor principalities, nor powers, . . . nor height, nor depth, nor any other creature shall be able to separate us from the love of God, which is in Christ Jesus our Lord" (Romans 8:38–39). The specific content of this revelation involves the crucifixion of the Messiah. In that drama all forms of human righteousness are made problematic, except a type of perfect love which seems untenable in history. The revelatory power of this whole story, drama, event, and person requires that it be viewed not as a spectator might view an ordinary drama. Both the form and the content of the drama require that it be apprehended by man in the total unity of his personality and not merely by his reason. For it will not touch him essentially if he does not recognize that its form as revelation challenges him as a rational though finite creature who is incapable of giving meaning to the total dimension of his individual and collective history, whatever partial and tentative meanings he may be able to discern by tracing its sequences and tendencies. The specific content of the revelation, on the other hand, challenges man as a sinful creature, whose various alternative methods of bringing his history to a meaningful conclusion always involve some pretension which is revealed in the light of the Cross to be a false conclusion. Thus the claims of Christ can only be heard by man in the unity of his personality and in the recognition of the self-contradiction in which that unity is involved in actual life.

The specific content of the Christian revelation is concerned with the story of a Jewish teacher, rabbi, and prophet who made messianic claims for himself and yet sought to keep his messianic mission a provisional secret since his own view of the messianic end differed radically from all current hopes. He rejected every version of the messianic hope which involved God's miraculous intervention in history for the purpose of eliminating its moral obscurity. He was extremely critical of the claims of virtue of the professionally holy class or oligarchy of his day and preferred to consort with "publicans and sinners." The conclusion reached by St. Paul in the light of the revelatory power of Christ's life, that "there is no difference for all have sinned and come short of the glory of God" (Romans 3:22–23) is anticipated in every searching criticism made by Jesus of all human pretensions of virtue. The Messiah would not bring victory to the virtuous but would die and "give his life a ransom for many" (Mark 10:45). The guiltless one would expiate the guilt of the guilty; and that would be the only way of ending the chain of evil in history. Thus the suffering of the guiltless, which is the primary problem of life for those who look at history from the standpoint of their own virtues, is made into the ultimate answer of history for those who look at it from the standpoint of the problematic character of all human virtue. This suffering of the guiltless one was to become in Christian faith a revelation of God's own suffering. It alone was seen to have the power to overcome the recalcitrance of man at the very center of man's personality, however successful the divine power might be to set outer limits beyond which human defiance could not go. But it alone was also the final dimension of the divine sovereignty over human history. To make suffering love rather than power the final expression of sovereignty was to embody the perplexity of history into the solution.

The actual incidents in the drama serve to add vividness to

this final meaning. The Christ was not crucified by criminals or by men who fell below the ordinary standards of human virtue. Such criminals were crucified with Christ. One of the instruments of crucifixion was the Roman system of jurisprudence which rightly boasted the highest achievements of justice in the ancient world. But even a boasted system of impartial justice is sufficiently human to fear that its majesty may be challenged by one who proclaimed himself a king. The kingdom of truth is a threat to every historical majesty. Every historical majesty is more anxious and insecure than it pretends. A priestly oligarchy was also implicated in the crucifixion. This oligarchy was certain that it was merely defending a very sublime system of religious legalism against an impious rebel; but it was also defending the moral prestige of all "good" men and more particularly its own prestige and its security. That is the fate of all historic oligarchies and institutions. There is always an anxious life, individual or collective, behind the most imposing façade of ideals and principles, of values and eternal verities, to the defense of which men rise in history.

Christian piety has sometimes foolishly sought to limit the guilt of involvement in the crucifixion to the particular instumentalities depicted in the actual story. But that is to miss the real point. In its profounder moments the church has known that Pilate and the priests are symbolic of the fact that every majesty or virtue, which is tenable in history, is involved in the crucifixion of a "prince of glory" who incarnates a love which is normative for, but not tenable in, history. That love which could not maintain itself in history becomes the symbol both of the new beginning which a man could make if he subjected his life to the judgement of Christ, and of the mercy of God which alone could overcome the fateful impotence of man ever to achieve so perfect a love.

In this double facet of the *Agape* of Christ is the point where a story in history becomes something more. It is recognized by the eyes of faith as the point where the heavens are opened and the divine mystery is disclosed and the love of God toward man shines down upon him; and man is no longer afraid, even though he knows himself to be involved in the crucifixion.

Obviously such a life and such a tragic drama could not be regarded as a revelation of divine majesty, and as concluding the meaning of man's existence, except by a faith which presupposed repentance. There is no justification in the revelation for any good man. The natural anxiety of good men about the threat which they face from evil men or from nature is forced into a subordinate position. No individual or nation is promised either moral justification or ultimate triumph. The meaning of history is not completed within itself. It is completed only from beyond itself as faith apprehends the divine forgiveness which overcomes man's recalcitrance. Thus Biblical faith, which begins with a sense of mystery, embodying meaning, and moves to a sense of meaning in history which contains perplexity and ambiguity, ends by seeing human history perpetually, and on every level of its achievements, in contradiction to the divine. It sees the possibilities of new beginnings in history only upon the basis of the contrite recognition of this contradiction. Significantly the same suffering love, the same *Agape* of Christ which reveals the divine mercy is also the norm of a new life. Men may have this new life if they discern what they are and what God is in this focal point of God's self-disclosure. Such a point in human history can be regarded both as the beginning of a new age for all mankind and as a new beginning for every individual man who is "called" by it, because both the individual and the collective realities of human existence are fully disclosed in it. If apprehended at all they are so apprehended that the old self, which makes itself its own end, is destroyed and a new self is born. That is why a true revelation of the divine is never merely wisdom but also power.

III

The form and dimension of this story of Christ, namely its revelatory significance as the point in history where the meaning of history is completed, is not presented as an afterthought to the story. On the contrary the whole story is pieced together within a Christian community, already united upon the basis of faith that this Jesus is the Christ. The Pauline theological formulations of the meaning of God's revelation in Christ actually precede the Gospel accounts chronologically. But though the story is written from the standpoint of its special significance in the eyes of faith, it still embodies the perplexities of the disciples in accepting its true significance and the tortuous path by which Jesus moved against the obtuseness of his own disciples. It is not presented as a theophany, revealing the meaning of the eternal world to finite man; nor yet merely as the story of a "God-man" who overcame the breach between the eternal and the temporal or the divine and the temporal. On the contrary it is a part of history though the claim is made that in it history has found its true fulfillment.

St. Paul recognizes the seeming absurdity of such a claim. It is as difficult for a rational man to accept the possibility and necessity of such a disclosure as for a virtuous man to accept its specific content. Its specific content challenged the virtue of the virtuous; and its form and dimension challenged the self-sufficiency of human reason. Greek rationalism had difficulty with the claim that history could be the locus of the final revelation of God and of man's true relation to God, because history belonged to nature and made such a revelation impossible; and human reason belonged to eternity and made it unnecessary. Modern rationalism has a different problem. Since it regards history as intelligible from within itself and expects that it will gradually overcome its own frustrations and moral ambiguities it combines, as it were, the objections to the Gospel of both Jews and Greeks. With the Greeks modern culture does not require the Gospel to make life intelligible; and with the Jews it does not require the Gospel to make history meaningful. Modern culture is particularly offended by the claim of finality of any disclosure of the ultimate at an antecedent point of history, partly because it believes that history itself changes the human situation radically and partly because it hopes that historical culture will be able to refine and perfect any valid solution of whatever may be perennial in the human situation. This modern objection to the Gospel seems so plausible that it has been a great embarrassment to the Gospel's theological protagonists in the past two centuries. They have done everything possible to prove that the Gospel message was practically identical with modern man's conception of a redemptive history.

Modern theology did not recognize that the new objection to the Gospel was merely an old objection in a new form. Men are inclined in every age to resist a truth which discloses the contingent character of their existence and discredits the false answer to this problem of their contingent life in which they are always involved. To make faith the requirement of the ultimate meaning of existence is to recognize the divine mystery as impenetrable by human reason. To find that revelation in an historical drama and person is to understand history as potentially meaningful rather than meaningless. To experience a divine forgiveness reaching out to man in his predicament is to recognize that the human situation, both individually and collectively, is such that man is not only unable to complete his fragmentary life but that, viewed ultimately, there is always false and sinful completion in it. Thus faith is the final expression of man's freedom; but it is an expression which involves the consciousness of an element of corruption in any specific expression of that freedom. It is the expression of his final freedom in the sense that faith achieves a point of transcendence over all the contingent aspects of man's historic existence, individually and collectively. But it must contain a recognition of the contingent and the false element in all his actual knowing. It is thus recognized as a knowledge beyond the capacity of human wisdom, as a gift of "grace." The New Testament insists that the recognition of Jesus as the Christ is possible only by the Holy Spirit.[1] And Jesus himself assures Peter that his understanding of the messianic calling could have been inspired only by God.[2]

While all Gospel narratives are written in the consciousness of the revelatory significance of the story they tell, the sense of the dimension of the story influences the telling of the narrative particularly in the accounts of the resurrection of Christ. It seems fairly certain that the earlier narratives reported an experience of communion by the disciples with the resurrected Lord in Galilee (I Corinthians 15:1–8), while later narratives not only fixed this event at Jerusalem but sought to validate it by factual details of which the empty tomb was the most significant. The story of this triumph over death is thus shrouded in a mystery which places it in a different order of history than the story of the crucifixion. Yet the church as a fellowship of believers was obviously founded upon the conviction of the fact of the resurrection. This "fact" contained an alteration in the story through faith's apprehension of the significance of the story. To recognize that the Cross was something more than a noble tragedy and its victim something else than a good man who died for his ideals; to behold rather that this suffering was indicative of God's triumph over evil through a love which did not stop at involvement in the evil over which it triumphed; to see, in other words, the whole mystery of God's mercy disclosed is to know that the crucified Lord had triumphed over death and "when he had by himself purged our sins, sat down on the right hand of the Majesty on high" (Hebrews 1:3). It is the revelatory depth of the fact which is the primary concern of faith.

The effort to certify this triumph through specific historical details may well be regarded as an expression of a scepticism which runs through the whole history of Christianity. The account of Christ's virgin birth serves the same purpose. Christ can not be known as the revelation of God except by faith and repentance; but a faith not quite sure of itself always hopes to suppress its scepticism by establishing the revelatory depth of a fact through its miraculous character. This type of miracle is in opposition to true faith.

On the other hand the belief in the resurrection is itself a miracle of a different order, and a miracle without which the church could not have come into existence or could not continue in existence. It is the miracle of recognizing the triumph of God's sovereignty in what seem to be very ambiguous facts of history. There is significantly no hint in the Gospel record of any gradual understanding even in the inner circle of disciples of the true meaning of Christ's death. Peter's confession of his Master's messianic ministry was immediately followed by a rejection of the tragic culmination of it which Christ predicted. In the Lukan account of Christ's appearance to his disciples at Emmaus they remain oblivious of the real meaning of his life, ruefully confessing, "We trusted that it had been he who would have redeemed Israel" (Luke 24:21).

The church is thus not grounded upon a slowly dawning consciousness of the true significance of Christ. It is founded in the miracle of the recognition of the true Christ in the resurrection. From the first covenant of God to the resurrection, God's revelations to a people are imbedded in history. God speaks "at sundry times and in divers manners" (Hebrews 1:1). And the revelations move toward a climax through a course of history, the climax being that He "hath in these last days spoken unto us by his Son" (Hebrews 1:2). The acceptance of that revelation in faith involves a radical break in the community in which the revelations occur. It ceases to be a particular people or nation. The revelation creates an "Israel of God" (Galatians 6:16) which is gathered together upon the basis of its acceptance of the revelation by faith.

Insofar as these various confrontations between God and His people have a history, there is also a history of revelation. But this is not the history of a broadening religious consciousness or of a more and more successful yearning or searching after God. For every step in the story requires that divine judgement be accepted in repentance against the human inclination to complete human virtue and wisdom within the historical structure; and that the divine mercy which prompts and qualifies the judgement be apprehended by faith.

The climax of the crucifixion and resurrection thus becomes not merely the culmination of the whole series of revelations but the pattern of all subsequent confrontations betwween God and man. They must contain the crucifixion of self-abandonment and the resurrection of self-recovery. Men must die to sin with Christ and arise with him to newness of Life.[3]

In Christian thought the resurrection of Christ is, however, not only indicative of the triumph of Christ over sin in the very Cross which seemed to make him its victim, but also is proof of God's power to overcome death. St. Paul, in fact, deduces both the resurrection from the dead and the triumph over sin from Christ's resurrection.[4]

The logic of such a faith might be expressed in the following propositions: 1) Life is fragmentary, ending in death. 2) Man seeking to live and to avoid death destroys himself in the very process of seeking to establish his life. 3) If man would truly live he must die to self; but this dying to self is no guarantee of the preservation of his physical life. 4) Men will make nonsense of life if they seek to make sense of it only upon the basis of their physical survival. But the alternative requires that they believe in the sublimation of its fragmentary character. This-worldly religions try to make sense out of life in the dimension of nature-history which man transcends. Other-worldly religions try to make sense out of life by abstracting some eternal essence of man from the fragments of history. Christianity insists upon the potential meaningfulness of man's fragmentary life in history and its final completion by a power and love not his own.

The "final enemy," declares St. Paul, is death. And the final pinnacle of the Christian faith is this confidence in the completion of life's meaning by the power of God.

This pinnacle of faith in New Testament religion is the final expression of certainty about the power of God to complete our fragmentary life as well as the power of His love to purge it of the false completions in which all history is involved. This pinnacle has no support from miraculous facts in history; neither can it be deduced from a careful observation of the general facts of human nature and history. With Plato men have always sought some rational certainty about the immortality of the soul by seeking to prove that the dimension of human existence which transcended the mortality of the body would survive the death of the body. But that which survives, according to the thought of Plato, bears no resemblance to the human self, being no more than the eternal validity of the logical faculties of the human mind. Modern Christian theories of immorality are frequently invalid mixtures of Christian conceptions of personality with this Platonic assurance.

The Biblical sense of the unity of man in his body, mind, and soul makes the Platonic escape from the contingent character of human existence impossible. If, therefore, the New Testament faith ends in the pinnacle of the hope of the resurrection this is also the final expression of a faith which sees no hope that man may overcome or escape the contingent character of his existence; yet is not without hope, for it is persuaded that a divine power and love have been disclosed in Christ, which will complete what man can not complete; and which will overcome the evil introduced into human life and history by man's abortive effort to complete his life by his own wisdom and power.

NOTES

1. *Cf.* I Corinthians 12:3: "Wherefore I give you to understand that no one . . . can say that Jesus is the Lord, but by the Holy Spirit."

2. Matthew 16:17 ff: "Blessed art thou, Simon Bar-Jonah: for flesh and blood hath not revealed it unto thee, but my Father which is in heaven." Significantly Peter

misunderstands the messianic mission in the same moment in which he understands it, seeking to dissuade Jesus not to follow the logic of his messianism, which demanded the Cross rather than triumph. For Jesus "from that time forth began to shew unto his disciples, how that he must go unto Jerusalem, and suffer many things of the elders and chief priests and scribes, and be killed, and be raised again the third day." Peter's rejoinder, "Be it far from thee, Lord: This shall not be unto thee." is rebuked by Jesus in the words: "Get thee behind me, Satan, thou art an offence unto me; for thou savourest not the things that be of God, but those that be of men."

This encounter is an accurate symbolic description of the mixture of ultimate and human viewpoints which remain in the Christian church throughout the ages. Insofar as it is the community in which Jesus is acknowledged as the Lord it is a new community, different from all other human communities. Insofar as it joins in Peter's abhorrence of the Cross it is a sinful community, engulfed in the securities and insecurities of human history.

3. Galatians 2:20. Colossians 2:12. Romans 6:3. II Timothy 2:11.

4. I Corinthians 15:12: "Now if Christ be preached that he rose from the dead, how say some among you that there is no resurrection of the dead?" 5:17. "And if Christ be not raised, your faith is vain; ye are yet in your sins."

EMIL BRUNNER

The Christian view of history, says Brunner (1889–1966), portrays time as moving from a beginning toward a goal, a fulfillment. In this it differs radically from Oriental and Greek ideas of time as cyclical recurrence. Using a striking metaphor, Brunner writes that with Christ's Incarnation, "God himself has entered this circular time at a certain point, and with His whole weight of eternity has stretched out this time-circle and given the time-line a beginning and an end, and so a direction." Eternity entered time and revealed that time is meaningful, although not the last word. Consequently Christian hope is not bound to time, but transcends it. The modern secular idea of history distorts the Christian view on which it is dependent by treating history as self-contained and continually progressive.

The way Brunner sees it the biblical revelation about Christ and time actually led to a transformation of how people understood time in western civilization. The faith, in other words, had decisive cultural consequences. Brunner would like Christianity to have further impact upon culture. In his Gifford Lectures, *Christianity and Civilization* (2 volumes, 1947–48), from which this chapter comes, he worked out a comprehensive Christian philosophy of culture which he hoped would contribute to that end.

Brunner was professor of theology at the University of Zurich and one of the most creative minds in dialectic theology. As even this selection suggests, his theology regarded the Christian task in history and culture much more highly than Barth. His *Man in Revolt* (1939) influenced Niebuhr's thinking on sin. He presented his theology systematically in *Dogmatics* (3 volumes, 1946–62).

The Problem of Time

The relation of man to time is an essential factor determining the character of existence for the individual, as well as for whole epochs and different civilisations. Everyone knows that the haste and rush which characterise our life are something typically modern, and probably a symptom of a deep-seated disease. But there are few who take account of the basic elements which determine man's relation to time. It is not because modern man has watches and time-saving machinery that his life shows an ever-increasing speed; modern man has watches and time-saving machinery because he has a certain relation to time, which expresses itself most crudely in that often heard phrase: I don't have time! Now that even children in the nursery use this phrase, we can no longer postpone investigating the roots of the apparent time-disease of the present world.

All who have travelled in the East with open eyes and an impressionable mind are at one in finding an immense contrast between the quiet of the Orient and the unrest of the West. Although we cannot deny that certain external elements of technical civilisation contribute towards this striking difference, its real cause does not lie on this superficial level, but in a different relation to time. The Orient has a conception of time entirely different from that of the West, and this difference belongs to the religious and metaphysical sphere. In all Oriental philosophy and religion, time is something irrelevant and illusory compared with eternity, although the individual interpretations of this basic conception may differ. Reality is beyond and above the time-process. Change means imperfection. Just as a man looking for change does so because he is not satisfied with what he has, so nothing that is subject to change can be looked upon as true being. That which exists must have duration, persistence; it must be changeless, being satisfied with itself. It is not possessed by an urge to get what it does not have, to become what it is not yet. True being is eternal. This idea is common to the whole Eastern world, however differently this eternal being may be interpreted. The radical expression of this idea is again found in India. The world of change is unreal. Reality is . . . the One and All which cannot change, and therefore has no relation to time. It is timeless, motionless, self-satisfied eternity; therefore it is the deepest desire of the Indian thinker to enter into or to share in that motionless eternal being, in Nirvana.

This conception, however, was not foreign to ancient Greece. We find it in its most daring expression in the system of Parmenides, and in a less extreme form in Plato's idealism. The ὄντως ὄν, the true being of the world of ideas, is distinguished from mere appearance or the half-reality of the world of sensations by this very fact, that it is timeless eternity beyond all change. This world of sensible experience, however, is taken up with an incessant stream of change and becoming. There is a clear-cut opposition between eternity and the temporal world. Eternity is the negation of time: time is the negation of eternity. How this time-world came into being, and what kind of being it has, is a question which can hardly be answered satisfactorily from Plato's presuppositions. On the one hand, Plato wants to get away from the blunt negation of the temporal world as represented by Parmenides; on the other hand, he does not seem to succeed in giving the world of time and becoming its proper place. Neoplatonism which . . . is so important for the formation of the mediæval world, tried to solve the problem by the concept of emanation, emanation meaning at the same time a kind of degeneration. By a process of flowing out or going down, a whole hierarchy of half-realities is established between the eternal, true being and absolute nothingness. In this hierarchy the distance of each step from the eternal is also its distance from true being or the measure of its approach to nothingness. Thus a continuum reaching from eternal true being to zero is conceived, which forms a parallel to the modern concept of evolution but runs in the opposite direction.

Modern man's understanding of time is quite different from this conception. To him the temporal is the real. Whether there is anything eternal is uncertain; but that the things in time are, is beyond question. But what is his concept of time? As it is quantity which determines his concept of reality, time also is a quantum— measurable time, time which consists of time-units, time-atoms. The second hand of the watch is the symbol of modern man's understanding of time. He looks for reality in the present moment, but the present moment is the smallest indivisible element or fraction of time. Life, then, cannot be but the sum or addition of such fractional time-entities, of time-atoms. This quantified physical time has completely lost its distinctiveness from space; it has become a fourth dimension of space.[1] Quantified time is spatialised time. Time dwindles away into space. It has no quality of its own. It is interchangeable with the dimensions of space, and is therefore always about to pass into zero.

It is this conception—not the watch or the telephone or the aeroplane—which is the cause of man's not having time. Time was lost to him metaphysically long before he had overcome it technically. The exact time-signal on the radio, which every decent citizen notes in order to set his watch correct to the second, the wrist watch, which at any moment shows him the exact time—all these devices have been invented because man wants them, because time vanishes under his fingers, because he does not have time any longer. We have reached here the opposite pole from the Oriental view. Reality is pulverised temporarily. It is in vain that Faust wishes to see that moment to which he can say: "Verweile doch, Du bist so schön!" It is in vain that Nietzsche exclaims in a superb poem: "Denn alle Lust will Ewigkeit, will tiefe, tiefe, Ewigkeit." If once you have declared your option for the moment, the fate of your reality as radical temporality is determined, and radical temporality is vanishing time. Time dwindles away, constantly approaching zero.

It is for this reason that modern man wants to snatch as much of this time as possible, to get as much "into his time" as he can. He begins, so to say, a race with time, and in this race man is inevitably the loser, because it is the last moment which decides, and the last moment is death. Man races death, but death wins. Over the whole of life there looms this certainty of a lost race with death. But no one likes to face it. The thought of it is avoided, because man's chances are so absolutely hopeless. Modern man puts out of sight as well as he can all reminders of death; he does not want to hear of it, because the thought reminds him of his being the loser. All the same, the remembrance of death stands behind him with its whip like a slave-driver and urges him on. This—and this—and this I must have, cries man, before it is too late, before the door closes for ever. It is the panic of the closed door. This panic explains many of the features which are typical of modern life: man's hasty enjoyment, his all-dominating craving for security, to which finally he sacrifices freedom and his soul.

The Christian understanding of time and its relation to eternity stands midway between, but also above and beyond, the opposing views of East and West. At first sight it seems much more similar to the Eastern than to the Western concept, its main thesis being that God is eternal, and that therefore true reality is eternity. Is not the Gospel the promise of eternal life? Is it not said that God is unchangeable? "With Him there can be no variation, neither shadow that is cast by turning." [2] He is the same yesterday, to-day and in eternity. "For a thousand years in Thy sight are but as yesterday, when it is past." The time-process in its totality, from beginning to end, is present in Him. For Him there is no surprise. Everything that happens does so according to His eternal decree. God is eternal.

But the relation of this eternal God to temporal being and becoming is totally different from what it is in Indian thought or in the systems of Parmenides, Plato or the Neoplatonists. God creates the time, He *gives* time. As He, the Almighty, gives man room for his freedom, so He creates time for him, for his becoming and for his free action. Temporality is not an approach to nothingness any more than the created world is unreal. God has created time together with the world, He has set a beginning to time and will set an end of time. He gives every man his time, with a beginning and an end to his temporal existence, but the end of time and the beginning are not the same. The time-process does not come back to its beginning. Between these two points, the start and the finish, something happens, which even for God is real and significant. There is history, an individual and a universal human history, in which God is infinitely interested. He is so intensely concerned with this history that He not only looks down on the scene of human life like an interested spectator, but He Himself intervenes in it. Even more, at a certain point in this time-process, He Himself enters the scenery of temporal life; He, the eternal, appears in the shape of a historical person and, as such, performs, once and for all, the decisive act of all history. The incarnation of the word of God is at once the insertion into time of the eternal God: "When the fulness of time came, God sent forth His son." [3] And in Him He revealed unto us the eternal secret of His will. [4]

This event charges the time of man's history with an extreme tension. [5] It is the time of expectation of the end, that end which is not the closed door, but the open door. It is the expectation of fulfilment. Time conceived in that fashion is the time of decision and probation. It is that time in which the eternal fate of the individual is decided. Therefore this sense of time is as remote from Oriental indifference to the temporal as from that time-panic of the modern Westerner. It is of the utmost significance, because it is within time that everything is decided for us, and every moment is a moment of decision. In every moment we have to keep faith; the servants must be awake all the time, for they do not know the day and the hour when the Lord comes; they do know, however, that if the Lord finds them sleeping they are lost, and that it will be said to them, as to those foolish virgins battering in vain on the closed door of the wedding-feast, "I know you not." [6]

All the same, in spite of the tremendous tension and the weight of decision involved, this temporality is not the ultimate reality; it is an intermezzo between divine election in the beginning and eternal perfection beyond time, beyond the limit of death, beyond this historical movement.

These two aspects of time enable us to understand the Christian concept of history. As has often been observed, neither in Oriental nor in classical Greek thought does the problem of history play any rôle. For the Oriental as well as for the Greek—and, we may say, for all humanity outside of Biblical revelation—the image of temporal happening is that of the circle. Temporality, as far as it has any reality and any significance, is a circular movement, always returning on itself. It is the same movement which we observe in nature: day and night, summer and winter, birth and death in perpetual rotation. This movement, then, has no climax; it leads nowhere. It is therefore not worth while making it a problem of thought. This is why Greek philosophy, to which everything else has become a problem, never made history an object of philosophic reflection.

The theme of history as a topic of thought is Judeo-Christian, brought into our consciousness by the Old Testament prophets and by the New Testament Gospel. Here history is no circular movement. History is full of new things, because God works in it and reveals Himself in it. The historical time-process leads somewhere. The line of time is no longer a circle, but a straight line, with a beginning, a middle and an end. This is so because—if I may use a simile—God Himself has entered this circular time at a certain point, and with His whole weight of eternity has stretched out this time-circle and given the time-line a beginning and an end, and so a direction. By this incarnation or "intemporation" of the word of God, time has been charged with an immense intensity. It has become, as we have said, the time of waiting, of decision and probation. Thus history has become interesting as a theme even for the thinker. It is now worth while for a thinker of the highest calibre, like St. Augustine, to write his *De Civitate Dei* as a kind of Christian philosophy of history, in fact the first philosophy of history ever written.[7]

We have been speaking of the tension of temporality. Comparing, however, the Christian existence with that of the panic-stricken modern man, we could also speak of a removal of tension. "For I am persuaded, that neither death nor life . . . nor things present, nor things to come . . . shall be able to separate us from the love of God, which is in Christ Jesus our Lord."[8] "For I reckon that the sufferings of this present time are not worthy to be compared with the glory which shall be revealed in us."[9] Christian man, through his faith in Christ Jesus, is time-superior, time-exempt; he lives already in the coming eternity. Important as earthly events may be in his life and that of other men, the all-important, the true decision has already been made in Christ, and the believer's life consists only in living on the basis of this earlier decision. This is what is meant by "Living by faith."

The Christian conception of time, then, permits and even obliges us to partake in temporal happenings with the utmost intensity—the picture presented by the New Testament being usually that of an athlete on the race-course, spending his last energy to reach the goal—and at the same time to be free from the haste and over-excitement created by the panic of the closed door. Those who live in faith are seriously intent on something going forward on this earth, something being bettered, so that the will of the Creator may be more fully expressed in His creation than it is now, under the domination of evil. But at the same time the life-feeling of the Christian is not dependent on whether or not this earthly goal is reached. He knows that whatever he can do for the realisation of God's will is at best something relative. He knows that whatever goes on within this temporality is encircled by the limits of death and fragility. And yet this insight into the insurmountable barrier does not make him resigned. His true, ultimate hope is not based on what can be achieved within temporal history, but upon that realisation of the divine purpose, which is neither dependent on man's action, nor happens within time, but sets an end to the temporal world, and which is not *a* goal, but *the* goal, the ultimate τέλος, the perfection of all things, which God gives and effects in bringing about life eternal.

The Christian understanding of history and its goal is sharply distinct from the idea of progress and evolution, which is characteristic of our era. Such a concept of universal evolution is unknown not only in the Eastern world but also in the West, so far as regards antiquity, the Middle Ages, and the period from the Reformation right up to the 18th century. Where the totality of temporal reality is interpreted by the symbol of a circle, there is no room for the idea of universal progress. Neither Heraclitus' πάντα ρεῖ, nor Aristotle's entelechy means anything like a directed time-process. The stream of happenings of which Heraclitus speaks is a movement without direction and goal, an eternal fluctuation comparable to the moving sea. But neither does Aristotle's entelechial movement have any reference to history. It is an eternal movement without beginning or end. No Greek thinker ever conceived the Cosmos in such a way that it represents a movement in time directed towards a goal, so that the later generations of time are somehow better off than the previous ones. If there is anything like a universal direction in this time-process, it is a movement downwards rather than upwards, a decline or degeneration rather than an evolution or progress. Such is the mythical concept of the successive world-epochs, as we find it in Hesiod, and a similar consequence might be drawn from Neoplatonic metaphysics.

The idea of evolution is, however, also entirely unknown within early Christianity. It is true that the basic conception of the coming kingdom of God includes the idea of a goal of history. It is also true that within this historical, temporal world a hidden germ of this kingdom of God is growing, intensively and extensively. Still, the idea of universal progress is impossible within this Christian conception because, alongside this growth of the kingdom, there is the concurrent growth of the evil powers and their influence within this temporal world. The tares are growing together with the wheat.[10] The opposition to the kingdom is growing at the same rate as the kingdom itself, so that the later generations are in no way better off than the earlier ones. On the contrary—it is in the last days that the conflict between good and evil forces reaches a climax. The goal of history is reached not by an immanent growth or progress, but by a revolutionary change of the human situation at the end of history, brought about not by man's action, but by divine intervention—an intervention similar to that of incarnation, namely the παρουσία, the advent of the Lord, the resurrection of the dead, the coming of the eternal world. That this end of human history is utterly distinct from continuity and immanent growth is most clearly expressed in the idea of the *dies irae*, the day of the Last Judgment, which puts an end to human history. The framework of this Universe is broken, death—"the last enemy," and the characteristic feature of the temporal world—is overcome and annihilated, and the eternal world is established. There is no room in this picture for the idea of universal progress and evolution.

On the other hand, the popular belief that the idea of evolution and progress was first worked out within natural science, and thence affected the conception of history, is false. The reverse is true: the idea has been transplanted from an evolutionary conception of history into natural science. Lamarck and Darwin are not the pioneers but the heirs of this modern idea. The real pioneers are men like Rousseau, Lessing, Herder, Hegel. The idea of progress and evolution is a child of the optimistic philosophy of the Enlightenment.

Its basis is an optimistic evaluation of human nature and, as its negative consequence, the repudiation of the fundamental Christian ideas of the Fall and of original sin. Human nature as such is good; at least, it is raw material fit to be shaped into something good, into true humanity. This anthropology seems to be based not on axiomatic speculation but on observation, on facts. History does begin with primitive man; he is the raw material out of which perfect humanity can be shaped. He it is whose mental capacities are not yet developed, whose cultural life has not yet begun. Civilisation and culture are acquired only in the course of a process extending through thousands of years, growing from generation to generation. It is this undeniable fact of the continuous growth of the benefits of civilisation, and of a progressive use of man's mental capacities, which is the backbone of the 18th-century idea of the universal progress of humanity.

This idea, however, is possible only by using a very dubious equation, *i.e.* the supposition that the more developed human life is in the cultural sense, the more human or good it is in the ethical sense; that moral evil is therefore only the primitive, the not-yet-developed; and that the good, the truly human is identical with the no-longer-primitive, the developed. Or—to express the same from the negative angle—the idea of universal progress is made possible only by denying the Christian conception of evil as sin, *i.e.* egoistic self-will and self-affirmation contradicting and opposing the will of God and the moral law. According to the Christian conception, there is continuity between the primitive state of mind and the developed one, but between the morally good and the morally evil there is no continuity but merely contradiction. Moral evil, understood as sin, is not that which is not yet good, but that which is no longer good. Sin is not undeveloped good, but spoilt and perverted good. It is not something which is not yet there, but it is a present reality of a negative character, the antagonism of men's will to the will of God. It is therefore only by substituting for the contradiction, for the Yes-and-No relation, the merely relative contrast of less and more, that the idea of universal progress is possible. As a consequence, the Christian idea of redemption is replaced by the idea of cultural development. The more man is trained to use his mental faculties, the more he gains power over the outside world and over his own forces, the more human he becomes, so the more evil disappears. This is the basic illusion of this favourite and most influential idea of modern man.

But where did 18th-century philosophy get the idea of a goal towards which history moves—an idea which was utterly foreign to rational philosophy in pre-Christian times? The answer, I think, is obvious, and the proof for it can easily be found in thinkers like Lessing and Herder. The idea of a universal goal of history is a Christian heritage, although completely transformed in context. Whilst, in the Christian view of history, this goal is transcendent in character, namely the world of resurrection and eternal life, it has now become immanent, being here identified with an imaginary terminus of the movement which leads from the primitive to civilised cultural life. In this fashion was formed that inspiring—not to say intoxicating—idea of idealistic progressivism which has taken hold of the best minds since the middle of the 18th century. It is the bastard offspring of an optimistic anthropology and Christian eschatology. Humanity as a whole is involved in a unique process, leading upwards from primitive beginnings, from a more or less animal start, to the loftiest peaks of true spiritual humanity, a process which is far from being finished, in which our generation is involved; one which perhaps will never be finished, but the end of which we are steadily approaching.[11]

It is this idea of evolution which modern natural science inherited and which it had only to supplement, to support and substantiate by its own means. From this idealistic conception Lamarck, Lyell and Darwin drew their ideas of an all-embracing evolution of life on this globe. The scientific evolutionism of the later 19th-century is composed of two elements: this idealistic idea of progress, combined with certain observations in the field of biology. What 18th-century philosophy had worked out in the limited field of human history was now brought into a much larger context. The history of the forms of organic life on our planet seemed to corroborate such an optimistic idea of a universal development. Was it not a fact that everywhere the primitive, undifferentiated forms precede the differentiated, the higher forms or organisation? Therefore it would appear that life is moving onward to unknown heights. Again, it was not seen that this naturalistic form of evolutionism is based on an unjustified identification, namely that the more "differentiated" in the biological sense is the "higher" in the human or spiritual sense.

But, once taken for granted, this idea of evolution seemed to give a new value to temporal becoming, which in the thought of the ancient world was a merely negative concept. In the course of becoming the perfect seems to emerge gradually.[12] The splendour of the idea of perfection, which in ancient philosophy had been identified with the transcendent and timeless world of ideas, and which in Christian thought had been reserved for the divine, supernatural sphere, then seemed to have shifted over to the historical world and to natural forces. From then on it seemed to be possible to believe in perfection on the basis of purely secular, natural, even material, principles. Since the idea of progress had come into the wide field of natural science, it seemed to have become independent of all metaphysical and religious presuppositions. It had become an instrument of natural explanation.

This was certainly not the conception of Rousseau, Lessing, Herder and Hegel. When they were speaking of evolution, they meant something which was at the same time immanent and transcendent, natural and divine. For them evolution was not merely a causal process of differentiation, but in the literal sense an evolution, i.e. the disclosure of something divine hidden in the natural. To them the time-process was at once both natural and supernatural and certainly, in any case, teleological and spiritual, not merely causal and material. But with Darwin's theory of selection, teleology seemed to be superseded. The one principle of causality was sufficient not only to explain a process as such, but to explain a progress, i.e. a process with a certain definite direction. Now it was possible to have finality without a principle of finality, to have teleology on the basis of causality, to have a direction of history by merely natural forces—in a word, automatic progress.

This new phenomenon—the idea of evolution and progress— is not only important from the point of view of becoming, but also as an element in that feature which we found so characteristic of our age, the temporalisation of existence. By means of the idea of evolution it seemed possible to repudiate eternity and still keep all those values which in previous times had been connected with the eternal. The eternal is no more necessary to give meaning to life.

Temporal life, interpreted in terms of evolution, had meaning, direction and finality in itself. For that reason evolutionism became one of the most potent factors of temporalisation, of radical repudiation of the idea of eternity within the conception of human existence.

But I am constrained to offer some observations which lead to a different conclusion:—

1. Even granted that the idea of universal progress is correct— which we never should admit—it is undeniable that the result of this progress means very little to the individual. One has to think in generations, in centuries. This means that the interest moves away from the personal to the collective. The individual and his fate, his future, become irrelevant. It is only the totality which counts; or rather it is an abstract humanity forming, so to say, the subject of this evolution.

2. Therefore this present existence has no meaning and value of its own. It is merely a point of transition, a rung on the ladder which leads upward. Its own value—if you ask for such estimate—must be left indefinite, and is therefore open to question.

3. But these factors lead in the direction which we have been calling the dwindling-away of time. The real, existing man appears to himself like a snapshot, a fraction of a large reel of film—a picture which, taken by itself, is as meaningless as a single frame cut from a movie strip and as absurd as a slow motion film. So this idea of evolution must—once its first intoxicating effect is over—take the whole substance away from life. It means that life is, as it were, eaten away from the inside.

Needless to say, this idea of a universal progress of such a natural upward movement is irreconcilable with Christian faith. This does not mean that the Christian cannot acknowledge certain aspects of the evolutionary theory of natural science. From the point of view of Christianity, there is no reason to deny that life on earth has a long history, spanning millions of years; that it has passed through many transformations; that the origins of mankind lie far back in prehistoric, primitive beginnings, presumably in animal forms. Within the limits which conscientious scientists have set for themselves, the evolutionist theory is not in conflict with Christian faith.

Two elements of this evolutionist thought, however, must be unconditionally rejected from the Christian point of view; first, the identification of moral evil or sin with the primitive; and, second, the assumption that the development of human intelligence, technical skill and cultural enrichment mean in themselves a progress in the sense of the truly human. The Christian conception of man includes the belief that the higher differentiation of intellectual powers, as well as the increase of the means of civilisation, is most ambiguous with regard to goodness and to the truly human. It can mean an increase of moral evil, of destructive inhumanity, just as much as the opposite. Civilised man, with the highest scientific and technical training, and commanding the accumulated wealth of ages of civilised life, may still be morally bad, even devilish, and if he is, he is so much the more dangerous. The highly developed human mind and the highly developed human civilisation may come to a point where they are capable of destroying all gains and goods in one frantic moment of diabolical madness.

This is why the modern identification of the idea of progress with the Biblical message of the kingdom of God is a demonstrable error which has most fatal effects. The idea of progress means a movement from here to there, from below to above, reaching more or less steadily towards a point in the far future, in which perfection is conceived of as materialised. The Christian message of the coming kingdom, however, means just the opposite movement—a movement coming down from above to below, from "heaven," *i.e.* from the transcendent, to earth. Where it reaches the historical plane, it breaks the framework of this temporal, earthly existence. That is what is meant by resurrection, *parousia,* eternal life. The New Testament knows nothing whatever of a kingdom of God which develops according to the idea of progress, slowly, immanently, from below upward. This so-called kingdom of God is simply an invention of the 19th century, read into the Bible, but not to be found there. It is a mixture of the New Testament message and modern evolutionism, out of which nothing good can come, but only illusion, disillusionment and final despair.

One last question has not yet been touched: From the point of view of Christian faith and hope, what is the result and value of the historical process? This question cannot be answered by a simple scheme. The Christian expectation of the coming kingdom first of all places everything historical under the radical negation of the divine judgment. All human history is flesh, taking the word in its Biblical sense. Therefore it is transient. From the texture of history the two dark threads of sin and death cannot be eliminated anywhere, from the beginning to the end. They belong to the picture of historic life. History in its process already performs part of this judgment upon its own creations. "Die Weltgeschichte ist das Weltgeriche." History devours its own children; whatever it brings forth passes away some day. This, however, is only one side of the picture. There is also continuity, there is tradition, there is historical heritage. Not every epoch begins anew from nothing. We all live from the stored-up wealth of previous ages. Eternal life is not only the negation, but also the fulfilment of this earthly life. It is not only a new world, but also the perfection of this world. Even our body, which seems to be particularly perishable and unfit to inherit the eternal, will be not simply destroyed, but transformed into a completely obedient organ and expression of the life of the spirit.

If, however, we ask whether there is any part of this reality, any element of our present experience, which as such shall be deemed worthy to enter into the perfect eternal existence, the answer must be, Yes indeed, there is one element which, whilst being an experience within the Christian life, will also be *the* element of eternal life, namely love in the New Testament sense of Agapé. Neither the State, nor culture and civilisation, nor even faith and hope, are that element which remains in eternity, but love alone. For God Himself is Love. That is why it is said that whilst all other things pass away, including faith, knowledge, language and hope, love alone remains, and this love is the principle of true humanity.

NOTES

1. Of course Bergson's idea of *durée réelle* was an attempt to overcome this spatialisation of time; just as, in a very different way, was Heidegger's conception of *Dasein* (*Sein und Zeit*). But both solutions of the time problem are very different

from that of Christianity, Bergson's *durée* being a pantheistic or mystical mixture of temporality and eternity, Heidegger's *Dasein*, on the other hand, being correlative to life-unto-death, without a Beyond. But it is highly important that the leading philosophers of our age are dealing with the problem of time much more intensively than any previous school of philosophy.

2. James i, 17.

3. Gal. iv, 4.

4. Eph. i, 9.

5. *Cf.* my article, "Das Einmalige und der Existenzcharakter," in *Deutsche Blätter für Philosophie,* 1929; and *Die christliche Lehre von Gott,* S. 285 ff.

6. Matth. xxv, 12.

7. Of course it is true that Augustine's *De Civitate Dei* is no *philosophy* of history as Troeltsch points out (*Der Historismus und seine Probleme,* S. 14 and note, S. 15). The question is whether anything which Troeltsch would have acknowledged as *philosophy* would be able to deal with that what a Christian would acknowledge as *history.*

8. Rom. viii, 38.

9. Rom. viii, 18.

10. Matt. xiii, 30.

11. The first idealist philosophy of history is Lessing's *Erziehung des Menschengeschlechts,* 1777 and 1780, soon followed by Herder's *Ideen zur Philosophie der Geschichte der Menschheit,* 1784–90. I do not know any system of philosophy of history, not even Hegel's, which shows more clearly the traits of this optimistic evolutionism than Schleiermacher's, embedded in his "philosophische Ethik."

12. The typical and most influential representative of this optimistic evolutionism is Auguste Comte in his *Cours de Philosophie Positive* and *Système de Politique Positive, ou traité de sociologie, instituant la religion de l'humanité, 1830–54.* Whilst in Comte's system the faith in science is combined with a spiritual, although entirely immanent element, Herbert Spencer's evolutionist philosophy has got rid even of this remainder of religion or idealism. Spencer puts his faith in evolution entirely on the natural process of "differentiation" and "integration" and on the rôle of utilitarian thinking. The more recent idea of "emergent evolution"—as, *e.g.* expounded in Laird's Gifford Lectures (*Theism and Cosmology*) is a combination of speculative idealism and naturalistic evolutionism following Bergson's neo-Schellingian idea of *évolution créatrice.*

RUDOLF BULTMANN

The relation between the history of redemption which the Bible reveals and the course of ordinary human history is a central question of a Christian view of history. Rudolf Bultmann (1884–1976), who was professor at the University of Marburg, offers an existentialist approach which sets him apart from what Dawson, Latourette, Niebuhr, and Brunner have said about the meaning and the direction of history.

The problem of history arose in Bultmann's New Testament studies. As he understands it, the Christ of salvation history does not come to us, in faith, as the Jesus of profane history. In *The Presence of Eternity: History and Eschatology* (1957) he claims that the real advent of Christ occurs in the preaching of the kerygma of the gospel when Christ addresses me and I respond with "the decision to accept a new life grounded in the grace of God." Accordingly, Bultmann believes, "in his faith the Christian is a contemporary of Christ, and time and the world's history are overcome." He concludes: "the meaning of history lies always in the present." By means of my present decision of faith I may draw upon the spiritual realm of eternity to change my attitude toward the fleshly realm of history in which I must remain. My present becomes thereby "eschatological," and I am, so to speak, a contemporary of the fulfillment of history as well.

Bultmann's views on faith, the kerygma, history, demythologizing, and hermeneutics came to dominate much of New Testament research after 1945. His *magnum opus* is *New Testament Theology* (2 volumes, 1952–55).

Christian Faith and History

(1) When we look back into the history of historiography and the different ways of understanding history we see a many-coloured picture. Indeed, history can be understood as political history as well as economic or social history, as the history of mind or ideas as well as the history of civilisations. All these views are legitimate, but they all are one-sided, and the question is whether there is a core of history from which history ultimately gains its essence and its meaning and becomes relevant. Otherwise it remains a meaningless play or a mere spectacle.

. . . [T]he question about meaning in history cannot be answered when we ask for the meaning of history as the entire historical process, as though it were like some human undertaking whose meaning we can recognise when we can survey it in its entirety. For meaning in history in this sense could only be recognised if we could stand at the end or goal of history and detect its meaning by looking backwards; or if we could stand outside history. But man can neither stand at the goal, nor outside of history. He stands within history. The question about meaning in history, however, can be put and must be put in a different sense, namely, as the question about the nature, the essence of history. And this brings us again to the question: What is the core of history? What is its real subject?

The answer is: man. . . . [T]his is the answer of Jacob Burckhardt: the historian has to deal with man as he is and was and ever shall be. . . . Toynbee's valuation of religion [also] leads of itself to the inference that the real subject of history is man. And the understanding of history by Dilthey, by Croce, and by Collingwood points in the same direction. Finally this answer is implicitly contained in the often repeated definition of history as the field of human actions. For to live in actions is the very essence of man.

We usually distinguish between history and nature. The course of both passes within time. But the difference is clear, for history is constituted by human actions. "Action is distinguished from natural events in so far as it does not merely happen, but has to be expressly performed, borne and animated by some kind of consciousness." [1] History as the field of human actions cannot, however, be cut off from nature and natural events. Geographical and climatic conditions are relevant for civilisations. The historical character of peoples is, although not determined, nevertheless still influenced by the cold or hot climate, by abundance or scarcity of water, by whether they live inland or on the coast, and so on. Natural events, such as change of climate, can bring about historical movements, such as migrations or wars. The reason for such events can also be the increase of population. And from this point of view even eating and drinking belong indirectly to history, although they are not historical actions, as Collingwood rightly stresses. Particular events in nature, such as natural catastrophes, can also become of historical importance, for instance when they call forth inventions. Or we may remember the thunder-clap which drove Luther into the monastery.

All these conditions and events within nature, so far as they are relevant for human life and history, may be called encounters (in German: "Widerfahrnisse") in contrast to human actions. Indeed, not only human actions but also human sufferings belong to history; in a certain sense they are also actions in so far as they are reactions.

(2) Now, when we reflect about human actions and when we consider that human actions are caused by purposes and intentions, then it becomes clear that human life is always directed towards the future. As long as man lives, he is never content with his present, but his intentions, his expectations, his hopes, and his fears are always stretched into the future. He can never, like Goethe's "Faust," say to the moment: "Stand still, thou art so

beautiful." That means: the genuine life of man is always before him; it is always to be apprehended, to be realised. Man is always on the way; each present hour is questioned and challenged by its future. That means at the same time that the real essence of all that man does and undertakes in his present becomes revealed only in the future as important or vain, as fulfilment or failure. All actions are risks.

But the fact that man can either gain his genuine life or miss it, includes the fact that this very thing which he is really aiming at, genuineness of life, is at the same time demanded from him. His genuine willing is at the same time his being obliged. The realisation of his genuine life stands before him as obligation as well as intention. The good which everyone aims at—as Socrates already saw—is at the same time the ethical law which he has to obey.

The concrete form of the demand is always determined by the present situation. Historicism is perfectly right in seeing that every present situation grows out of the past; but it misunderstands the determination by the past as purely causal determination and fails to see it as leading into a situation of questions, of problems. It does not understand the present situation as the situation of decision—a decision which, as our decision over against our future, is at the same time our decision over against our past concerning the way in which it is to determine our future. For our past has by no means one meaning only; it is ambiguous. In consequence of its misunderstanding of the present, historicism also misunderstands the future as determined by the past through causality instead of being open.

The concrete possibilities for human actions are, of course, limited by the situation arising from the past. Not all things are possible just as we wish them at every time. But the future is open in so far as it brings the gain or the loss of our genuine life and thereby gives to our present its character as moment of decision. Historicism in its traditional form overlooks the dangerous character of the present, its character of risk. The relativity of each present moment, rightly seen by historicism, is therefore not relativity in the sense in which any particular point within a causal series is a relative one, but has the positive sense that the present is the moment of decision, and by the decision taken the yield of the past is gathered in and the meaning of the future is chosen. This is the character of every historical situation; in it the problem and the meaning of past and future are enclosed and are waiting, as it were, to be unveiled by human decisions.

Croce and Collingwood saw rightly that the relativity of every moment and every historical phenomenon has a positive meaning. But, in understanding mind as acting reason, Croce does not take into account what I have called the encounters. According to him, the historian has not to deal with the irrational, with sufferings, catastrophes, and evils, or only in so far as they are occasions, incitements for human activity. But he does not see that reaction is a specific kind of action, that to suffer is not a purely passive kind of behaviour, but that it becomes activity in so far as it means to tolerate, to endure. To this extent it is an evidence of will and belongs to historicity. Croce ignores this because, according to him, the very essence of man is reason, not primary will. But though human will is in general not without reason, the will is to be esteemed as the determining factor, if it is correct that human life is lived through decisions. When Collingwood calls the actions, which the historian has to deal with, thoughts, it is not in the one-sided manner of Croce. As we have seen, thought for him includes purpose and intention; he recognises the unity of willing and thinking. But he fails to draw all the consequences of his conception. He rightly recognises that history is the history of problems and that every historical situation contains problems whose solution is the task of the responsible present. But, as with Croce, his view is directed only to the problem of actions, not to the problem of encounters, of suffering.

In looking back to Croce and especially to Collingwood we can say that the problem of historicism is solved, that the embarrassment into which historicism had led is overcome. First, *history is understood as the history of man*. It may well be said that history is the history of mind. But mind is not realised otherwise than in human thoughts, and human thoughts are ultimately intentions of individuals. The subject of history is therefore humanity within the individual human persons; therefore it may be said: The subject of history is man. Secondly, *the relativity of every historical situation is understood as having a positive meaning*.

Modern historicism, as we have seen, understood the his-

toricity of man in such a way that it saw man bound by the historical conditions of the time in question. In this way it had the merit
of awaking anew the question of the meaning of history, for just
this question became urgent for the individual who was taught
that he is at the mercy of history. Historicism has also the merit of
itself showing the way in which it is to be overcome. It has destroyed by implication the conception of the relation between historian and history as the relation between subject and object. The
historian cannot see history from a neutral stand-point outside history. His seeing of history is itself a historical event. So historicism
prepared the way for the deeper conception of historicity developed
by Croce and Collingwood. Historicity now gains the meaning of
responsibility over against the future, which is at the same time
the responsibility over against the heritage of the past in face of
the future. Historicity is the nature of man who can never possess
his genuine life in any present moment, but is always on the way
and yet is not at the mercy of a course of history independent of
himself. Every moment is the *now* of responsibility, of decision.
From this the unity of history is to be understood. This unity does
not consist in a causal connection of events, nor in a progress developing by logical necessity; for the historical process falls to the
responsibility of men, to the decisions of the individual persons. In
this responsibility, as responsibility over against the past as well as
over against the future, the unity of history is grounded. In this
sense it may be said, as Croce did, following the intention of
Hegel, that humanity is always a whole in each epoch and in each
human being.

(3) But does it follow from this that the entire course of history
is a field without heights and depths? That there are no differences in the historical phenomena, persons, and thoughts? Are
we not allowed to make distinctions, because the Sophists in
Athens were human beings as well as Socrates and Plato? Or
Cesare Borgia as well as Luther? Or an average author as well as
Milton or Goethe? Or because a Gothic cathedral and a railway sta-
tion in Gothic style are both expressions of human thought? By no
means.

Collingwood states clearly that the re-enactment of past
thought is a matter of evaluating and criticising, precisely because
of our responsibility. The events of the past cannot be established

by neutral perception as facts and events in nature can be. Historical facts and events are not to be perceived but to be understood, and understanding means at the same time evaluating.

But there remains one point which has not yet been considered, at any rate explicitly, either by Croce or by Collingwood. They are right in saying that knowledge of history is at the same time *self-knowledge*. Both of them understand this self-knowledge as the knowledge of oneself as historical and this means the knowledge of one's situation and of the problems, the tasks, and the possibilities which are contained within it. This formal definition of self is certainly correct, but I do not think it is sufficient. *The human person* is not completely recognised so long as it is not explicitly taken into account that in the decisions of the individual there is a personal subject, an *I*, which decides and which has its own vitality. This does not mean that the *I* is a mysterious substance beyond or beside the historical life. Life is always within the historical movement; its genuineness stands always before it in the future. But the subject of the ever-new decisions is the same, namely, the *I*, as an ever-growing and becoming, an ever-increasing, improving or degenerating *I*. Signs of this identity of the *I* within the flow of decisions are memory and consciousness and the phenomenon of repentance.

And we may also ask whether the decisions through which life runs are solely decisions demanded by historical situations and historical tasks. Decisions within personal encounters, decisions of friendship and love, or of indifference and hatred—can these be called answers to historical problems? Gratitude or personal fidelity, are they answers to historical problems? Choosing a career of life, prepared by one's gifts and personal encounters, can that be called decision about a historical problem? Certainly, all these decisions and kinds of behaviour may have consequences for history, but they are not in themselves decisions over against historical problems in the sense in which Croce and Collingwood speak about historical problems. Neither are patience and endurance in sufferings or joy in beauty answers to the questions of historical situations. Self-knowledge, arising from one's personal destiny, may concern blessings or distresses or the threatening nearness of death, but is this the same thing as the self-knowledge arising from historical reflection described by Croce and Collingwood?

It seems to me that the self in question has a further dimension which Croce and Collingwood neglect. We may call this the dimension of *Personality*. Its existence is recognised, in my opinion by Dilthey, when he tries to detect the experiences of the soul as the origin of historical works. And this is perhaps also intended by Jaspers when he seeks for the individual a stand-point beyond history. Following the hints of Dilthey, Heidegger says in his analysis of the human being as temporal-historical that the human being chooses its genuine existence by resolution and is thereby brought into the simplicity of its destiny.[2] Butterfield also seems to have personality in mind, but does not see clearly the historicity of the human being.

For it must be stressed that what we call *personality* is also temporal-historical and is constant only as a possibility which is ever to be realised. Personality is not a substance behind the decisions, a substance in relation to which the concrete historical decisions are only accidents. My self-understanding as personality depends on my decisions, which may for the most part be unconscious, made without reflection. As I have already said, the *I* is an ever-growing, ever-becoming, ever-increasing entity. Personality experiences its own history within the frame of universal history and interwoven within it, but nevertheless as a history which has its own meaning and is not merged into universal history.

This is the justification of autobiography, which plays no rôle either in Croce or in Collingwood. In autobiography the author gives an account of the personal history of his life. Certainly, autobiographies may gain an extraordinary importance for universal history as, for instance, the "Confessions" of Augustine or of Rousseau. But this clearly shows that history has a dimension not included in the concept of it as the history of problems, favoured by Croce and Collingwood. History is also moved by the personal self-understanding of the persons who are acting in history. Such personal self-understanding usually finds its expression in so-called *world-views* ("*Weltanschauungen*") and religions. Therefore history can also be viewed as the history of "Weltanschauungen," and Dilthey is justified in distinguishing types of "Weltanschauungen."

Now there can be no doubt that there is a reciprocal interaction between the so-called "Weltanschauungen" and the history of problems which Croce and Collingwood have in view, especially between "Weltanschauung" and science. At the basis of Greek science and philosophy lies a self-understanding of man which is in turn shaped by science. In Greek tragedy this self-understanding is questioned, most of all by Euripides, and it eventually broke down, at any rate for a great mass of people, in Gnosticism. In connection with Gnosticism, and at the same time in opposition to it, Christianity arose.

It seems to me one cannot explain such changes purely from the viewpoint of the history of problems any more than the changes from the Middle Ages to the Renaissance, to the Enlightenment, to Idealism and Romanticism, although in all these changes the history of politics, economics, and science was also relevant. This explanation is impossible because all these "Weltanschauungen" and religions are permanent possibilities of human self-understanding which once they have found expression in history remain as ever-present possibilities coming to life at different times in different forms. For fundamentally they are not answers to special historical problems in definite historical situations, but are expressions of personal self-understanding, of personality, however they may be stimulated by special historical situations.

But now one may ask whether the consequence is a complete relativism, whether all "Weltanschauungen" and religions are expressions of possible self-understanding. The question of truth seems to disappear, as, in fact, happens in Dilthey. Naturalistic theories then offer themselves to explain the peculiarities of the different "Weltanschauungen" and religions by reducing them to geographical and general-historical conditions.

But this conclusion is not justified. From the fact that there are different possibilities of self-understanding it does not follow that they are all equally right. On the contrary, the view of the different possibilities raises the question of legitimate self-understanding. How have I to understand myself? May self-understanding not go astray? Can the risk of human life be escaped by possession of a "Weltanschauung"?

In fact, the personal history of the individual clearly shows that this history has not always one consistent meaning, one straight direction. It may go through repentance, through doubt, yes, through despair. There are breaks, mistakes, and conversions.

A so-called "Weltanschauung" is genuine when it originates ever anew within changing historical situations and encounters. It cannot become an assured possession as can a result of scientific research. Mostly it is misconceived as scientific theory which can solve all the riddles of life. But it then cut off from the ground from which alone it can grow, from the personal life. In this misconception "Weltanschauung" is in reality a flight from historicity.

But with this we have gained a criterion for a legitimate human self-understanding. A "Weltanschauung," we may say, is the more legitimated the more it expresses the historicity of the human being. Self-understanding is the more astray the more it fails to appreciate historicity and flees from its own history. Gnostic self-understanding failed in this way and so did Stoicism so far as the Stoic ideal of life was consistently conceived, namely, as the behaviour of the man who shuts himself off from all encounters, good as well as evil, in order to preserve the calm of his interior, and who understands freedom only negatively as being untouched by all encounters, instead of as freedom for responsible acting.

I do not intend to review the different "Weltanschauungen" to discover in what measure the personality of man and his historicity is understood by them. But there can be no doubt that the radical understanding of the historicity of man has appeared in Christianity, the way being prepared in the Old Testament. This is proved by the fact that real autobiography arose for the first time within Christianity. From this origin the understanding of the human being as historical became effective in the West, and it remained vivid even when it was divorced from Christian faith and secularised as in the modern philosophy of existence which finds its extreme form in Sartre.

(4) But we have to ask: What is the peculiarity of *Christian* faith besides the fact that it understands the human being as historical? Christian faith believes that man does not have the freedom which is presupposed for historical decisions. In fact, I am always determined by my own past by which I have become what I am and of which I cannot get rid, of which in the last resort I am unwilling to be rid, although unconsciously. For everyone refuses to give himself up without reservation. Certainly everyone can be conscious of his responsibility and has a relative freedom in the moments of decision. But if he recognises that this freedom is only

a relative one, that means that his freedom is limited by himself as he is coined by his past. Radical freedom would be freedom from himself. The man who understands his historicity radically, that is, the man who radically understands himself as someone future, or in other words, who understands his genuine self as an ever-future one, has to know that his genuine self can only be offered to him as a gift by the future. Usually man strives to dispose over the future. And indeed, his very historicity misleads him to this attempt, because his historicity includes responsibility for the future. His responsibility awakes the illusion of having power of disposal. In this illusion man remains "the old man," fettered by his past. He does not recognise that only the radically free man can really take over responsibility, and that he is not allowed to look round for guarantees, not even the guarantees of a moral law, which take off or lighten the weight of responsibility, as it is expressed in Luther's famous words: *pecca fortiter*. Man has to be free from himself or to become free from himself. But man cannot get such freedom by his own will and strength, for in such effort he would remain "the old man"; he can only receive this freedom as gift.

Christian faith believes that it receives this gift of freedom, by which man becomes free from himself in order to gain himself. "Whoever will save his life shall lose it, but whoever will lose his life shall find it." The truth of this statement is not yet realised when it is only comprehended as general truth. For man cannot say this word to himself, it must be said to him—always individually to you and to me. Just this is the meaning of the Christian message. It does not proclaim the idea of the grace of God as a general idea but addresses and calls man and imparts to him the grace of God which makes him free from himself.

This message knows itself to be legitimated by the revelation of the grace of God in Jesus Christ. According to the New Testament, *Jesus Christ is the eschatological event,* the action of God by which God has set an end to the old world. In the preaching of the Christian Church the eschatological event will ever again become present and does become present ever and again in faith. The old world has reached its end for the believer, he is "a new creature in Christ." For the old world has reached its end with the fact that he himself as "the old man" has reached his end and is now "a new man," a free man.

It is the paradox of the Christian message that the eschato-logical event, according to Paul and John, is not to be understood as a dramatic cosmic catastrophe but as happening within history, beginning with the appearance of Jesus Christ and in continuity with this occurring again and again in history, but not as the kind of historical development which can be confirmed by any histo-rian. It becomes an event repeatedly in preaching and faith. Jesus Christ is the eschatological event not as an established fact of past time but as repeatedly present, as addressing you and me here and now in preaching.

Preaching is address, and as address it demands answer, *deci-sion*. This decision is obviously something other than the decisions in responsibility over against the future which are demanded in every present moment. For in the decision of faith I do not decide on a responsible action, but on a new understanding of myself as free from myself by the grace of God and as endowed with my new self, and this is at the same time the decision to accept a new life grounded in the grace of God. In making this decision I also decide on a new understanding of my responsible acting. This does not mean that the responsible decision demanded by the historical moment is taken away from me by faith, but it does mean that all responsible decisions are born of love. For love consists in unreserv-edly being for one's neighbour, and this is possible only for the man who has become free from himself.

It is the paradox of Christian being that the believer is taken out of the world and exists, so to speak, as unworldly and that at the same time he remains within the world, within his historicity. To be historical means to live from the future. The believer too lives from the future; first because his faith and his freedom can never be possession; as belonging to the eschatological event they can never become facts of past time but are reality only over and over again as event; secondly because the believer remains within history. In principle, the future always offers to man the gift of freedom; Christian faith is the power to grasp this gift. The free-dom of man from himself is always realised in the freedom of his-torical decisions.

The paradox of Christ as the historical Jesus and the ever-present Lord, and the paradox of the Christian as an eschatological and historical being is excellently described by Erich Frank: ". . . to the Christians the advent of Christ was not an event in that temporal process which we mean by history today. It was an event in the history of salvation, in the realm of eternity, an eschatological moment in which rather this profane history of the world came to its end. And in an analogous way, history comes to its end in the religious experience of any Christian 'who is in Christ.' In his faith he is already above time and history. For although the advent of Christ is an historical event which happened 'once' in the past, it is, at the same time, an eternal event which occurs again and again in the soul of any Christian in whose soul Christ is born, suffers, dies and is raised up to eternal life. In his faith the Christian is a contemporary of Christ, and time and the world's history are overcome. The advent of Christ is an event in the realm of eternity which is incommensurable with historical time. But it is the trial of the Christian that although in the spirit he is above time and world, in the flesh he remains in this world, subject to time; and the evils of history, in which he is engulfed, go on. . . . But the process of history has gained a new meaning as the pressure and friction operate under which the Christian has to refine his soul and under which, alone, he can fulfil his true destiny. History and the world do not change, but man's attitude to the world changes." [3]

In the New Testament the eschatological character of the Christian existence is sometimes called "sonship." F. Gogarten says: "Sonship is not something like an habitus or a quality, but it must be grasped ever and again in the decisions of life. For it is that towards which the present temporal history tends, and therefore it happens within this history and nowhere else." Christian faith just "by reason of the radical eschatological character of the salvation believed in never takes man out of his concrete worldly existence. On the contrary, faith calls him into it with unique sobriety. . . . For the salvation of man happens only within it and nowhere else." [4]

We have no time to describe how Reinhold Niebuhr in his stimulating book *Faith and History* (1949) endeavours to explain the relation between faith and history in a similar way. Nor have we time to dispute with H. Butterfield's thought, developed in his book *Christianity and History*. Although I do not think he has clearly seen the problem of historicism and the nature of historicity, his book contains many important statements. And I agree with him when he says: "Every instant is eschatological." [5] I would prefer, however, to say: every instant has the possibility of being an eschatological instant and in Christian faith this possibility is realised.

The paradox that Christian existence is at the same time an eschatological unworldly being and an historical being is analogous with the Lutheran statement *simul iustus, simul peccator*. In faith the Christian has the standpoint above history which Jaspers like many others has endeavoured to find, but without losing his historicity. His unworldliness is not a quality, but it may be called *aliena* (foreign), as his righteousness, his *iustitia* is called by Luther *aliena*.

We started our lectures with the question of meaning in history, raised by the problem of historicism. We have seen that man cannot answer this question as the question of the meaning in history in its totality. For man does not stand outside history. But now we can say: *the meaning in history lies always in the present,* and when the present is conceived as the eschatological present by Christian faith the meaning in history is realised.[6] Man who complains: "I cannot see meaning in history, and therefore my life, interwoven in history, is meaningless," is to be admonished: do not look around yourself into universal history, you must look into your own personal history. Always in your present lies the meaning in history, and you cannot see it as a spectator, but only in your responsible decisions. In every moment slumbers the possibility of being the eschatological moment. You must awaken it.

NOTES

1. Fritz Kaufmann, "Reality and Truth in History" [*Perspectives in Philosophy* (1953)], p. 43.

2. Martin Heidegger, *Sein und Zeit* [1927], p. 394.

3. Erich Frank, "The Role of History in Christian Thought" [*The Duke Divinity School Bulletin,* XIV (1949)], pp. 74, 75.

4. Friedrich Gogarten, "Zur Frage nach dem Ursprung des geschichtlichen Den kens," *Evangelische Theologie* (1954), p. 232.

5. [Herbert Butterfield, *Christianity and History* (London: Bell, 1949)], p. 121.

6. Cf. Ernst Fuchs, "Gesetz, Vernunft und Geschichte," *Zeitschrift für Theologie und Kirche* (1954), p. 258.

WOLFHART PANNENBERG

Pannenberg (b. 1928) finds Bultmann's solution of the problem of history unsatisfying. He contends in *Jesus—God and Man* (1968) that we must view Jesus "from below" from within history, and not "from above" outside history. In *Revelation As History* Pannenberg, with his colleagues, argues that history is the very mode of God's revelation of himself and his salvation. God tells Israel that he "is to be revealed in his acts in history." Later the prophets extend the horizon beyond Israel to a universal history which includes the totality of all events. "It is at the end of this chain of world events that God can for the first time be revealed with finality as the one true God," he writes. Jesus is the culmination of the process of revelation as history: "With the resurrection of Jesus, the end of history has already occurred, although it does not strike us in this way."

In this selection from *Revelation As History,* as well as in "Hermeneutic and Universal History" (1967), Pannenberg stresses the continuity of universal history which joins the history of Israel and Jesus with our own history. No further revelation of God occurs after Jesus, but by the proclamation of the revelation of God in Christ "the history after Christ bears his mark."

Pannenberg, a professor at the University of Munich, believes a renewal of the idea of the kingdom of God in history is needed but without the optimism of the social gospel. His ideas on the subject are given in *Theology and the Kingdom of God* (1969).

Revelation As History

THESIS 1: *The self-revelation of God in the biblical witnesses is not of a direct type in the sense of a theophany, but is indirect and brought about by means of the historical acts of God.*

In developing this thesis, I wish to draw together the results of the exegetical investigations and expand them with particular reference to the question of the indirectness (or directness) of revelation.

The Old Testament essay has shown that a decisive insight concerning revelation is found in the Israelite traditions, in which an understanding of Jahweh is obtained through his historical activity. The earlier traditions about appearances of Jahweh which were connected closely with Israel's cult and place of worship are suppressed and displaced by the thought that Jahweh is to be revealed in his acts in history. At first, this idea was linked most vividly with exodus from Egypt, which ancient Israel took as Jahweh's primal act of salvation. Statements to this effect can already be found in the Jahwistic tradition, which makes no significant distinction between the miracles of Moses in Egypt and Jahweh's own decisive act of judgment at the Reed Sea. Both are proofs of the deity and power of Jahweh. The writer sees the purpose of the Egyptian plagues in terms of their effect in causing Pharaoh to acknowledge the power of Jahweh and thus bring about the release

of the Israelites (Ex. 7:17; 8:16, 18; 9:14). At the end of the narra-
tion relating the escape through the Reed Sea and the destruction
of the Egyptians, the Jahwist says: "And Israel saw the great work
which the Lord did against the Egyptians, and the people feared
the Lord; and they believed in the Lord and his servant Moses"
(Ex. 14:31). According to this, faithful trust was effected by the
evidence of historical facts that brought about salvation and revealed Jahweh's deity and power.

In Deuteronomy, the attention is not on the single events, but
on the complex of exodus and occupancy of the land, all of which
is viewed as the self-vindication of Jahweh: "And because he loved
your fathers and chose their descendants after them, and brought
you out of Egypt with his own presence, by his great power, driving out before you nations greater and mightier than yourselves, to
bring you in, to give you their land for an inheritance, as at this
day: know therefore this day, and lay it to your heart, that the Lord
is God in heaven above and on the earth beneath; there is no
other. Therefore, you shall keep his statutes and his commandments, which I command you this day" (Dt. 4:37–40; compare
7:7–11). The last sentence shows that the authority of God's judgment is grounded in the historical self-vindication of Jahweh for
rescuing Israel from Egypt and for giving the land. This does not
mean that through this act Jahweh has proved that he is God in a
manner analogous to the confrontation with Pharaoh. In this action of rescuing and giving he has proved himself to be *their* God,
for he has acted on *their* behalf. The exodus and the occupancy of
the land are established as the decisive factor in the knowledge of
God, and this is so stated in Hosea and later in Jeremiah.[1]

The prophets, however, especially those of the time of the
exile, no longer took the events connected with the occupancy of
the land as the ultimate self-vindication of Jahweh. In Isaiah it is
clear that the election of Zion and the House of David were added
to the above in the tradition of Judah. Isaiah proclaims the fall of
the nation and the new activity of salvation anticipated in this as
the new self-vindication of Jahweh through which his deity will be
demonstrated before the eyes of the nations. Next to Ezekiel, it is
second Isaiah who has, more than anyone, proclaimed the proof of
the deity of Jahweh as the aim of the newly introduced and still-
imminent activity of salvation.[2] As was shown in the New Tes-

tament essay, the apocalyptic literature advanced this aspect of the
Old Testament's understanding of revelation. The apocalyptic writings expect the final and ultimate self-vindication of Jahweh in
connection with the end event, and envision his appearance in
glory. This expectation is also part of the apocalyptic horizon in the
proclamation of Jesus. But his appearance compressed the content
so that the sharp distinction between the times vanishes, and from
this springs the framework of apocalyptic theology. This is particularly evident in the first petition of the Lord's Prayer: "May your
name be kept holy." It is only within this tradition of prophetic and
apocalyptic expectation that it is possible to understand the resurrection of Jesus and his pre-Easter life as a reflection of the eschatological self-vindication of Jahweh.

An investigation of the New Testament's concept of the self-
revelation of God in the fate of Jesus does not depend solely on
terms that are used for revelation. If one proceeds from $\dot{a}\pi o\kappa a$-
$\lambda \dot{\upsilon}\pi\tau\epsilon\iota\nu$ and $\phi\alpha\nu\epsilon\rhoo\tilde{\upsilon}\nu$ alone, as H. Schulte has done, then one
finds no statement at all about God's self-revelation. An investiga-
tion of the christological titles does not carry us much further. On
the other hand, the conception of the *glory of God* often designates
with precision his becoming manifest. This is true in the New Testament as well as in the apocalyptic literature.

It is well known that the background of this New Testament
concept is many-sided.[3] The idea goes back to both Old Testament
and gnostic roots. As von Rad has demonstrated, the כבר יהוה in
the Old Testament is already connected with Jahweh's becoming
manifest.[4] Isaiah, for instance, saw such manifestations in all
earthly events (Is. 6). The manifestation of the glory of Jahweh is
generally bound up with his acts, especially those historical acts
connected with the emergence of Israel. The priestly document is
acquainted with an appearance of the glory in the exodus history
and in the institution of the cult. Since the time of the postexilic
prophets, the appearance (or the reappearance) of the glory has
become a future event (see Is. 43:1ff.), and an "established element of the eschatological hope" (v. Rad). We note especially the
expression of second Isaiah that speaks of the revelatory meaning
of the future unveiling of glory. The goal of second Isaiah's vision
about a highway in the wilderness, over which God will bring back
the exiles, is seen in Is. 40:5: "And the glory of the Lord shall be

revealed, and all flesh[!] shall see it together" (see 66:18f.). The priestly document expressly links the concept of glory with the formula of acknowledgment: "And the Egyptians shall know that I am the Lord, when I have gotten glory over Pharaoh, his chariots, and his horsemen" (Ex. 14:18). This is the priestly recension of the passage through the Reed Sea. Although formulated only in words, the glorification of Jahweh through his acts in history is clearly an expression pointing to the indirect revelation of his deity in those acts (see also Ex. 16:6). In this respect, it becomes clear just how far the apocalyptic hope in the future manifestation of present realities in salvation and judgment is also a matter of God revealing himself. Thus, in the apocalyptic theology, the revelation of the glory of God persists until the final event and in this the salvation of the elect is revealed.[5]

However, it is not only in the texts of the Old Testament and in the apocalyptic literature that the concept of glory plays an essential role.[6] This is also true for the gnostic texts. In the Magic Papyri from Egypt, the sorcerer prays to Isis: "Glorify me as I have glorified the name of your son Horos"—a formula very reminiscent of John 17. Naturally, in this text the historical event is not the means of the many-sided glorification and, particularly, it is not expected as a cosmic end event.

In comparison to the gnostic doxa-thought, the Pauline usage is closer to the Old Testament and apocalyptic conception of the glory of God. The glory of God is visible to Paul in the fate of Jesus, whom he emphatically proclaimed as the Crucified One (II Cor. 4:6). God is indirectly revealed in the fate of Jesus. The apocalyptic revelation of his glory in the end judgment has come to pass ahead of time in this fate. In Paul and other New Testament writings, the concept of $\delta\acute{o}\xi\alpha$ has its place in the terminological complex of $\alpha\pi o$-$\kappa\acute{\alpha}\lambda\upsilon\psi\iota\varsigma$ in much the same way as in the apocalyptic literature.[7] The revelation of God's glory is also part of the established content of the primitive Christian and apocalyptic expectation. Because the imminent *eschaton* has broken in with the fate of Jesus, the glory of God is already present in the proclamation of the gospel (II Cor. 3). Thus, the congregations united with Christ and living in the hope of their own resurrection already have the $\pi\nu\epsilon\hat{\upsilon}\mu\alpha$ $\tau\hat{\eta}\varsigma$ $\delta\acute{o}\xi\eta\varsigma$ (I Pet. 4:14), the "eschatological gift of the Spirit."[8] Because the Spirit is the specific form of reality in the new aeon, the event of

Christ is itself spiritual as the eschatological event, and the resulting participation in the Spirit mediated through the proclamation
of this event and faith in it (Gal. 3:2 and 14) is the earnest money
on the future glory (I Cor. 1:22, 5:2; Rom. 8:23). In this sense Paul
can give relatively free reign to the gnostic concept of the Spirit
and even say that the Spirit searches the depths of the deity (I Cor.
2:10). But we should not forget that for Paul himself such expressions are always related to the horizon of the eschatological future.
And since the past event of salvation, the future of the faithful, and
the present of the Spirit are all bound together in the eschatological nearness of God, the apportionment of weight to these three
elements is no problem for him. As Wilkens has shown, this was
altered in the case of the primitive Christian witnesses of the second
generation. They were the first to see the distinction between the
present moment and the fate of Jesus as a problem. For them, the
center of gravity in the revelation of God could only be in the past,
or in the present, or in the future. For Luke, it is in the past. The
eschatological future recedes into the undefined distance. It is
worth noting that, along with the recession of the eschatological
horizon, Luke does not explicitly characterize the event of salvation as revelation. In John the accent is on the present experience
of the Spirit. In this case, there are also gnostic lines of thought
that come to the fore in the conception of revelation. There is a
directness in the gnostic thinking about revelation that is in the
tradition that John draws on and that is expressed in the epiphany-
like nature of the Christ figure. This directness is broken in John
by his reshaping of the Christ event with a stress on its past character. Thus, the Christians of the second generation perceived the
glory of God in Christ only indirectly. The experience of the Spirit
in the Gospel of John is linked to the Christ of the past, who is consciously thought of as a figure in the past (John 16:14; cf. 14:26).
It is only with such a presupposition that one can come to anything like an understandable conception of John's gospel. It is of
course true that his presentation of the activity of Jesus himself is
still largely styled like a direct manifestation.

What is true for John holds also for Hebrews in many respects. Also, with Hebrews the relation to the past events of Jesus
is unbalanced. On the one hand, it is the point of departure for
faith, and on the other hand, it is contemporized by a gnostic styl-

ization (Heb. 2:14f.). However, the accent is different, for Hebrews points to the future of salvation. Thus John as well as Hebrews held fast to the past event of Jesus as the norm for the Christian participation in salvation, in spite of their gnostic characteristics. Hebrews stresses the future, and Luke, for his part, emphasizes the present participation of salvation in the Spirit. However, the stress on the past life of Jesus, which is not brought to a close, is carried out with more decisiveness by Luke than by the other two theologians. In this respect, they maintained a peculiar balance between present and past and thus brought the soteriological character of the Christ event to expression in a convincing way.

In this situation, the dogmatic conception of revelation must first of all orient itself to the chain of tradition, which runs from the Old Testament through the apocalyptic literature and on to the proclamation of Jesus found in the first community and in Paul. It must do this so that the specific theological motifs that lay at the base of the New Testament witnesses of the second generation will be kept in view. For one thing, the past character of the event of Jesus ought not be dissolved into a mere "that," but should also have the substance of a "what."

Also, the eschatological qualification of the present, by means of the Christ event and the future salvation, is not lost.

THESIS 2: Revelation is not comprehended completely in the beginning, but at the end of the revealing history.

The linking of revelation with the end of history is related to its indirect character. It follows directly out of the indirectness of the divine self-vindication, and without this presupposition revelation cannot be understood.

We have seen that the revelation of God is the defined goal of the present events of history. And only after their occurrence is God's deity perceived. Thus, placing revelation at the close of history is grounded in the indirectness of revelation.

This proves to be valuable knowledge if one is not involved with single revelatory events, but with a series of occurrences. We have already seen that the Old Testament's understanding of reve-

lation tended in this direction. In the development from the Jahwistic tradition to the apocalyptic literature, it is not just the extent
of events proving the deity of God that is increasing, but also the
content of revelation that is continually revising itself. What had
previously been the final vindication of God is now seen as only
one step in the ever-increasing context of revelation.

At first, individual events were credited with revealing Jahweh's deity, as, for instance, in the Jahwistic tradition. But in the
later words of the prophets, a much more comprehensive plan of
Jahweh's history is usually presupposed. Since the time of the
Deuteronomist, the total activity, which has a relatively extensive
horizon, becomes the means for the self-vindication of Jahweh. We
saw that Dt. 4:37ff. understood the deity of God as the result of a
whole complex of history, a historical complex that extended from
the promises to the fathers to the fulfilling of these in the occupancy of the land. It is not just through the single events of this
long history, but rather at the end, in the fulfillment of the promises to the fathers, that Jahweh's deity is proved. For the Deuteronomist, the occupancy of the land was the close of revelatory
history. After that event, one can look back to the revelation of
Jahweh as one would on a closed event.

All of this was altered with the fall of Judah and the exile from
the promised land. The prophets of the exile looked forward to the
decisive event of salvation, which now, for the first time, was in
the future. The decisive and ultimate revelation of Jahweh was
also removed to the future.

In apocalyptic thought, the spiritual situation is substantially
sharpened. Not only is the decisive event of salvation always in the
future, but the meaning of the present event is, in general, totally
hidden. Thus, the continuity from the present to the future is not
easily discerned. The two aeons stand in juxtaposition. For apocalyptic thought, the present is filled with tribulation. It is only in the
time of the eschatological inauguration of the new aeon that the
meaning of the present time is revealed. The destiny of mankind,
from creation onward, is seen to be the unfolding according to a
plan of God. The apocalyptic thought conceives of a universal history. Thus, the revelation of God and his glory is transferred to the
end of all events. That the end will make manifest the secrets of
the present is also the presupposition of primitive Christianity.

The history that demonstrates the deity of God is broadened to include the totality of all events. This corresponds completely to the universality of Israel's God, who is not only the God of Israel, but will be the God of all men. This broadening of the *Heilsgeschichte* to a universal history is in essence already accomplished in the major prophets of Israel in that they treat the kingdoms of the world as responsible to God's commands.[9] With the exception of the lists in Chronicles, this point of view is first carried through systematically in apocalyptic literature. Since the time of the Deuteronomist and the prophets of the exile, the God of Israel was known as the Lord of all. Correspondingly, the apocalyptic viewpoint conceived of Jahweh's Law as the ground of the totality of world events. It is at the end of this chain of world events that God can for the first time be revealed with finality as the one true God.

This concept of history determined the Western philosophy of history up to the time of Hegel and Marx. Both conceived of history with a view to its end. For Marx, the revolution of the proletariat will bring an end of all previous history and reveal the humanity of man. Of course Hegel firmly maintains that the Christ event is the one revelation of God; but insofar as he understood his own time and his own philosophy as the kairos for the universal comprehension of history, he also brings it into concurrence with the revelation of Christ.

Placing the manifestation of God at the end of history means that the biblical God has, so to speak, his own history. That is, the historical event of revelation cannot be thought of in an outward way as revealing the essence of God. It is not so much the course of history as it is the end of history that is at one with the essence of God. But insofar as the end presupposes the course of history, because it is the perfection of it, then also the course of history belongs in essence to the revelation of God, for history receives its unity from its goal. Although the essence of God is from everlasting to everlasting the same, it does have a history in time. Thus it is that Jahweh first becomes the God of all mankind in the course of the history that he has brought to be.

This is a history-of-religion statement, and it produces many consequences for the relation of theology to the science of religion. The beginnings of Israel develop only gradually out of the religious environment of the ancient Orient and in this way it has a distinct antecedent: even in its later stages Israel retains connections with this heritage. Israel is not to be artificially isolated from its environment by the assertion of a supernatural revelation that took place at the time of its beginnings. Such an assertion would be arbitrarily limited to the "sacred" region of a *Heilsgeschichte* (in its most disreputable sense). Such an assertion is unnecessary and meaningless if we understand that revelation does not have its place in the beginning, but at the end of history. The earliest appearances of Jahweh are to be understood as the appearance of a numinous being, not just from the phenomenological point of view, but theologically as well. This being may be a numinous being of a special type, but it is a special type known within the history of religion. It is only in the course of this history brought about by Jahweh that this tribal God proves himself to be the one true God. This proof will be made in the strict and ultimate sense only at the end of all history. However, in the fate of Jesus, the end of history is experienced in advance as an anticipation. As we now conceptualize more precisely—it is only in view of the end that we can say God has proved himself in the fate of Jesus as the one true God. It is not by chance that the salvation now is for the Gentile also. This is a necessity because in the fate of Jesus as the anticipation of the end of all history, God is revealed as the one God of all mankind who had been expected since the time of the prophets. The inclusion of the heathen belonged to the universality of the eschatological revelation of God. Thus, it is appropriate that the proclamation of the God who raised Jesus would be tested by means of Greek philosophy and its questions about God, for philosophy is that discipline that raises the question of the true form of God for all men. Where the eschatological self-revelation of the God of Israel was proclaimed as the one God of all men, this question could not be overlooked, although it would be answered in a way that could not have been foreseen by any Greek. It is from this perspective, namely, the explication of the Christ event as an event for all peoples, that it becomes clear that the father of Jesus Christ has always been the one God from the very beginnings of Israel and, indeed, from the beginning of the world. There is a fundamental validity about the way in which the theology of the ancient church developed through the assimilation of the Greek spirit.

With these last sentences, I have already touched upon the next thesis.

THESIS 3: *In distinction from special manifestations of the deity, the historical revelation is open to anyone who has eyes to see. It has a universal character.*

We are ordinarily urged to think of revelation as an occurrence that man cannot perceive with natural eyes and that is made known only through a secret mediation. The revelation, however, of the biblical God in his activity is no secret or mysterious happening. An understanding that puts revelation into contrast to, or even conflict with, natural knowledge is in danger of distorting the historical revelation into a gnostic knowledge of secrets.

In the Old Testament discussion about the self-vindication of Jahweh, it is his acts in history that were the events through which Jahweh proved his deity to all peoples, not just to Israel.[10] What Jahweh accomplished in history cannot be written off as the imagination of the pious soul, for its inherent meaning of revealing the deity of Jahweh is impressed on everyone.

In this way Paul can say: "By the open statement of truth we would commend ourselves to every man's conscience in the sight of God" (II Cor. 4:2). H. Schulte has noted with justice that Paul is not sharing a secret knowledge after the manner of the gnostics. "The Gospel is no dialectic play between the state of revelation and hiddenness, but is fully revealed." It is not without significance that Paul uses the philosophical term "conscience" in this passage.[11]

In a similar vein, Paul can speak of those who do not wish to see the truth that is manifest. The fact that some do not believe does not mean that the gospel is accessible to only a few, but that "the god of this world has blinded the minds of the unbelievers" (II Cor. 4:4) so that they cannot see the truth of the revelation of God in the fate of Jesus, a revelation that is available to all.[12] Nothing must mute the fact that all truth lies right before the eyes, and that its appropriation is a natural consequence of the facts. There is no need for any additional perfection of man as though he could not focus on the "supernatural" truth with his normal equipment for knowing. The event, which Paul witnessed, took place totally within the realm of that which is humanly visible. In particular, the Holy Spirit is not an additional condition without which the event of Christ could not be known as revelation. Bultmann has rightly insisted that Paul never describes faith as a gift of the Spirit, but rather that the Spirit is described as the gift received by means of faith,[13] in that which the gospel proclaims, which for its own part belongs to the sphere of the Spirit so long as it relates to the eschatological event. The paradox that there are persons who will not see this most evident truth does not absolve theology and proclamation from the task of stressing and showing the ordinary, and in no way supernatural, truth of God's revelation in the fate of Jesus. Theology has no reason or excuse to cheapen the character and value of a truth that is open to general reasonableness.

To say that the knowledge of revelation is not supernatural does not mean that man is only confirming what he already knows through the force of his own intellect. In this respect, no one comes to the knowledge of God by his own reason or strength. This is not only true about the knowledge of God, but about other experiences that we have. The divinely revealed events and the message that reports these events brings man to a knowledge he would not have by himself. And these events *do* have transforming power. When these are taken seriously for what they are, and in the historical context to which they belong, then they speak their own language, the language of facts. God has proved his deity in this language of facts. Naturally, these experiences are not to be treated as naked facts, but are to be seen in their traditio-historical context. If we are to take these facts seriously, nothing ought to be inserted so as to allow them to be seen in a way different from what would naturally emerge. That these and also other events are veiled from many men, indeed, from most men, does not mean that this truth is too high for them, so that their reason must be supplemented by other means of knowing. Rather, it means that they must use their reason in order to see correctly. If the problem is not thought of in this way, then the Christian truth is made into a truth for the in group, and the church becomes a gnostic community.

The history of Israel all the way to the resurrection is a series of very special events. Thus they communicate something that could not be gotten out of other events. The special aspect is the event itself, not the attitude with which one confronts the event. A person does not bring faith with him to the event as though faith were the basis for finding the revelation of God in the history of Israel and of Jesus Christ. Rather, it is through an open appropriation of these events that true faith is sparked.

This is not to say that faith is made superfluous by the knowledge of God's revelation in the events that demonstrate his deity. Faith has to do with the future. This is the essence of trust. Trust primarily directs itself toward the future, and the future justifies, or disappoints. Thus a person does not come to faith blindly, but by means of an event that can be appropriated as something that can be considered reliable. True faith is not a state of blissful gullibility. The prophets could call Israel to faith in Jahweh's promises and proclaim his prophecy because Israel had experienced the dependability of their God in the course of a long history. The Christian risks his trust, life, and future on the fact of God's having been revealed in the fate of Jesus. This presupposition must be as certain as possible to him. Otherwise who could expect to obtain a participation in the life that has been manifested in Jesus, if such a presupposition were not oriented to the future?

There is a consequence for the Christian proclamation from this point. The proclamation of Christ presents, for those who hear it, a fact (taken to be reasonably and reliably true) that in the fate of Jesus of Nazareth, God has been revealed to all men.[14] The proclamation of the gospel cannot assert that the facts are in doubt and that the leap of faith must be made in order to achieve certainty. If this sort of assertion were allowed to stand, then one would have to cease being a theologian and Christian. The proclamation must assert that the facts are reliable and that you can therefore place your faith, life, and future on them.

The knowledge of God's revelation in the history demonstrating his deity must also be the basis of faith. Faith does not need to worry that this knowledge has been altered because of shifts in historical research, just as long as this current image of the facts of history allows him to reassess and to participate in the events that are fundamental to it. This far-reaching independence of faith from the particular form of historical knowledge out of which it has come is founded on the fact that, in the act of trust, faith transcends its own picture of the event. The event has its own foundation in that it relies on the God who reveals himself in it. In the trusting surrender of his existence, the faithful man is thrust beyond his own theological formulations and open to new and better understandings of history, which are the basis for his life. It is through such faith that the patriarchs of Israel had a part in the fulfillment, in Jesus Christ of the promises given to them, a fulfillment very different from anything that they might have been able to imagine. Through such faith, men have a part in the same history of God even though their ideological formulations of the history of God are irreconcilable. Such men are not only reciprocally bound to each other through faithful participation in the one history, but are also bound to those men who have no understanding of what the two are arguing about. Nevertheless, only the knowledge of God's revelation can be the foundation of faith, no matter how confused or mixed with doubt such knowledge might be. It should also be emphasized that it is not knowledge, but the resulting faith in God that secures participation in salvation.[15]

To what extent is God manifest in the history of Israel and in Jesus of Nazareth? How does he prove his deity? The following theses will attempt to furnish answers to these questions.

THESIS 4: *The universal revelation of the deity of God is not yet realized in the history of Israel, but first in the fate of Jesus of Nazareth, insofar as the end of all events is anticipated in his fate.*

In the history of Israel, Jahweh had not proved himself to be a God for all men. He had only established himself as the God of Israel. This came about in a way that is quite understandable, although it is hardly applicable to us as non-Israelites. Jahweh had proved himself to be a powerful God in the eyes of Israel by delivering the land promised to Israel. And as long as Israel remained in possession of the land, the knowledge of being under the protection of his might enabled Israel to acknowledge the one to whom it was obligated for such possession. This kind of thinking is clearly understandable, and only the greatest superficiality would ignore the evidence of this complex. It would be a superficiality of a type that

would see all earthly developments as nothing but human arrangements and involvements. In any event, the occupancy of the land
is not proof for us of the deity of Jahweh in its fullest sense, since
we are heirs of the Greek philosophical tradition and can give the
name God in an unqualified way only to the one God of all men,
and can understand the gods of the religions as at best representations and analogies of the one God. From this point of view, to
understand the deity of Jahweh in any other way would be to allow
the divine figure of a religion to surpass the concept of God in philosophy. Israel's or Judah's faith in Jahweh was matured in crisis
through the loss of the land in the destruction of the year 587.
Only because the prophets had for a long time been sounding the
warning about just such a catastrophe could it later be understood
as the self-vindication of Jahweh. Thus, the faith of Israel survived
the collapse of its own national identity and the temporary loss of
the gifts of salvation and pointed to Jahweh's new proof of salvation. This understanding had been remarkably substantiated by
the prophets through the course of events that had already been
proclaimed.

In the times of Ezra and of the Maccabean revolt, when the
new salvation was thought of as in the present, it still appeared as
something strictly provisional.

Whenever the historical self-demonstration of Jahweh in his
acts was viewed as being definitive and lasting, this demonstration
still retained a provisional character. It is always surpassed with
new events, new historical activity in which Jahweh presents himself in new ways. Thus, we saw that it is only the end of all events
which could bring in the final self-manifestation of Jahweh, the
perfection of his revelation.

Through an extraordinary vision the apocalyptic writer sees
ahead to the end of all things. The historical plan of God was
disclosed to him ahead of time. However, wasn't the apocalyptic
view itself corrected by the further course of history? In contrast,
the witness of the New Testament is that in the fate of Jesus
Christ the end is not only seen ahead of time, but is experienced
by means of a foretaste. For, in him, the resurrection of the dead
has already taken place, though to all other men this is still something yet to be experienced.

If we allow the apocalyptic expectation of the end of the world to be linked with the general resurrection of the dead, then in these events the God of Israel has proved himself to be the one God of all men . . . Let us remember: The one and only God can be revealed in his deity, but only indirectly out of a totality of all events. This was also the lead thought regarding the true form of the divine in Greek philosophy. It is only that this philosophy did not understand the totality of reality as a history always open to the new contingency, but rather took it to be a world with unchangeable structures of order.[16] In this way, one could make inferences about the true form of the divine on the basis of the totality of phenomena that are known to every period of time. But, in the context of the history of thought, the Greek cosmos offered only a narrow conception of reality that was open to man's experience. The biblical experience of reality as history is more inclusive, since the contingency of the real event is included in this conception. Experience of the reality of history is superior to that connected with the contemplation of the cosmos. This is true both then and now because history can accept cosmic reflection as an element within it and make the regularity expressed in this cosmic reflection more realistic in structure and movement by providing it with a broader base of presuppositions. In such a situation, the God who is revealed out of the totality of history in this indirect way would also be the dominant answer to the philosophical question about God.[17]

Now the history of the whole is only visible when one stands at its end. Until then, the future always remains as something beyond calculation. And, only in the sense that the perfection of history has already been inaugurated in Jesus Christ is God finally and fully revealed in the fate of Jesus. With the resurrection of Jesus, the end of history has already occurred, although it does not strike us in this way. It is through the resurrection that the God of Israel has substantiated his deity in an ultimate way and is now manifest as the God of all men. It is only the eschatological character of the Christ event that establishes that there will be no further self-manifestation of God beyond this event. Thus, the end of the world will be on a cosmic scale what has already happened in Jesus. It is the eschatological character of the Christ event as the anticipation of the end of all things that alone can establish this development so that from now on the non-Jew can acknowledge the God of Israel as the one true God, the one whom Greek philosophy sought and the only one who could be acknowledged as the one true God from that time on. This is a point of view quite distinct from the self-vindication of Jahweh through the giving of the promised land to Israel. This acknowledgment, and the accompanying ratification of the universal revelation of God in the fate of Jesus, is itself a fact that became a part of world history through the absorption of the classical world into the ancient church.

In the fate of Jesus the God of Israel is revealed as the hidden God. The hiddenness and transcendence of the God who is revealed in the crucified Jesus surpassed the canon of the incomprehensibility of the philosophical concept of God. On the basis of the above-mentioned reasons, one can really know that the resurrection of the crucified one is the eschatological self-revelation of God. However, no one person can see everything or exhaust what is specifically contained in this self-manifestation of God. There are many concrete things that can be said about this, but at the same time there is an incomprehensible future that stands before us in the "then" and "there" of the Jesus event. We can speak of the resurrection, but we are not able to exhaust all the implications of what we say with that term, although what we appropriate from the event of the resurrection of Jesus, namely, our life's reality in the light of the final decision, does place us in a position to speak about the self-revelation of God and justifies such language even now. From the point of view of our comprehension, the inexhaustibility of the event of revelation as an eschatological event is very important. Otherwise one would easily misunderstand what has previously been said about the knowledge of the self-disclosure of God as a claim to knowing everything.

In the fate of Jesus, the God of Israel is revealed as the triune God. The event of revelation should not be separated from the being of God himself. The being of God does not belong just to the Father, but also to the Son. The Holy Spirit also shares in the being of God by virtue of his participation in the glory of God that comes to life in the eschatological congregation. Hegel and Barth are correct in the principle of grounding the doctrine of the Trinity in revelation. In all periods of history, one can experience with special force the incomprehensibility of God in that the dualism of the one and the many, which always guided Greek conceptualization of God, is here overcome. All of this is connected with the fact

that the doctrine of the Trinity formulates the concept of God as a
historically experienced revelation.

If the fate of Jesus Christ is the anticipation of the end, and
thus the revelation of God, then no further revelation of God can
happen. Of course, God is active even in the events after Christ,
and he also discloses himself in that time, but not in any fundamentally new way, but rather as the one who has already been
revealed in the fate of Jesus. This does not mean that nothing new
happens after Christ. The history after Christ bears his mark. Its
special motifs seem to become noticeable for the first time in the
thrust that is contained in the Christ event. The history after
Christ is determined in essence by the proclamation of the revelation in Christ. In the effects of this proclamation, new facts are
created in the history of the world. I would mention only two at
this point: the linking of the gospel with the Greek spirit and the
assumption of responsibility of civil justice during the Constantinian period on the basis of an understanding of the eschatological
congregation. The church is always tempted to play down the still-
impending future of the eschatological life and to forget that all
forms of Christian life in this world are provisional. This was also
true of the Constantinian era, and the result of the church's forget-
fulness had enormous consequences for the history of the world,
including the anti-Christian turns in the subsequent Christian history. But even this has a part in the unity of history by means of its
relation to the Christ event. To pursue all the particular connections would be the task of a theology of church history within the
necessary framework of a theology of history. But no new self-
disclosure of God would become evident in the extension of the
eschatological Christ event in the subsequent history.

If one is careful to note the eschatological character of the fate
of Jesus as the presupposition for the nature of God's revelation,
then the thought structures that plagued the concept of the historical revelation of God in German idealism are avoided. (1) While it
is only the whole history that demonstrates the deity of the one
God, and this result can only be given at the end of all history,
there is still one particular event that has absolute meaning as the
revelation of God, namely, the Christ event, insofar as it anticipates
the end of history. (2) So long as man is still under way toward the
still-open future of the *eschaton*, the Christ event is not overtaken

by any later event and remains superior to all other concepts as the anticipation of the end. Finally (against Rothe), it satisfies the eschatological character of the Christ event to see in it the self-revelation of God. Without that understanding of the event, a supplementary kind of inspiration must be presupposed.

NOTES

1. H. W. Wolff, "Wissen um Gott bei Hosea als Urform von Theologie," in *Ev. Theol.*, vol. 12, 1952/53, pp. 533–54, esp. p. 553.

2. W. Zimmerli, *Erkenntnis Gottes nach dem Buche Ezechiel*, 1954. In this book, the whole Old Testament tradition of this concept is investigated.

3. On this see G. Kittel, *TWNT*, II, pp. 242–55, and H. Kittel, *Die Herrlichkeit Gottes*, 1934.

4. *TWNT*, II, p. 242.

5. G. Kittel, *op. cit.*, pp. 242ff., and also D. Rössler, *Gesetz und Geschichte*, 1960, p. 61, note 4.

6. *TWNT*, II, pp. 252f.

7. Rom. 8:17f., II Thess. 1:7, I Pet. 1:7f. and 11, Luke 2:32.

8. This is the apt characterization of Bultmann concerning the whole of the primitive Christian thought about the Spirit, *Theology of the New Testament*, vol. 1, pp. 42f., 155ff., 337f.

9. Compare A. Alt, "Die Deutung der Weltgeschichte im Alten Testament," *ZThK*, 56, 1959, pp. 129ff.

10. See Is. 25:7, 11, 17; 26:6; 28:22ff.; 29:16, 21; 30:8, 19, 26, etc.; 36:23; 39:22, 27f. Further, second Isaiah 41:20, 23; 45:36; 49:23. In Israel's prayers concerning the help of Jahweh, the thought of the self-vindication of Jahweh had an established place in the structure and is in juxtaposition to the request: I Kg. 8:60; II Kg. 19:19; Bar. 2:15–31; Prayer of Asarjas 21. This list could be extended into the New Testament.

11. See G. Bornkamm, "Glaube und Vernunft bei Paulus," in *Studien zu Antike und Urchristentum*, 1959, pp. 119–37, esp. 129ff. and the presentation, pp. 133ff., in the important text I Cor. 14:1–25. His point is that Paul employs the rational argumentation and insight in proclamation so that he can express, in an understandable way, the truly unique form and conceptual development of the gospel.

12. The relationship of the event of revelation to the sin of man cannot be developed here in the particulars. The man turned in on himself by sin is closed off from God and also from reality, although he is continually living from newly experienced "realities." Wherever he was forced to appropriate a new experience or a new item that does not fit into the customary scheme of his life and world, then there always emerges, in opposition to the tendency of his own persistent self-will, the unavoid-

able reality of the facts of the case (or event) that confronts him. The same is the case with the activity that reveals God. The proclamation of this ought to urge the hearer to take this event seriously in its undeniable reality.

13. R. Bultmann, *Theology of the New Testament,* vol. I, #37; see p. 329 on Gal. 3.

14. Of course, the correlation of revelation and salvation cannot be discussed in detail here, since we are primarily concerned with the fundamental structure of revelation. However, the fact of this connection is presupposed throughout the development of these theses. For the man who is disposed to an openness toward God, revelation in its deepest sense means salvation, fulfillment of his destiny and his very being. All discussion about concrete benefits of salvation is faithful to salvation only insofar as they share indirectly in the nearness of God, and mediate fellowship with the end of everything. The revelation of God truly speaks to the sinner only as long as there is a possibility of new communion with God, which gives him the power to turn out of his closedness to himself to an openness to God. To this extent, the salvatory meaning of God's revelation is essentially linked with its proleptic character. The revelation of God at the end of all history in the judgment of the living and the dead means only damnation for the sinner who cannot repent. This is the end of his human destiny. The proleptic manifestation of the eschatological revelation of God has the character of a turn of events that was deliberately chosen. It is the character of the revelation that it brings about a still more real participation in salvation and in communion with God.

15. The connection between faith and knowledge (I am not speaking of understanding, but of knowledge in the comprehensive sense of insight) is so complicated that it cannot be presented here in all its aspects. Suffice it to say that there is an existential movement in which both are bound to each other in a variety of ways. The knowledge on which faith is grounded is the present result of a process of knowing that is always open-ended. Faith cannot stop the constant probing and investigation of its source. Thus, while faith is not brought into being by an external cause, verification of its sources strengthens it. Doubt questions the knowledge on which faith is grounded and also tempts faith itself. This temptation ought to become a stimulus to make faith deeper and more truly certain. Thus, faith assumes that the ongoing knowledge will not pull the rug out from under it, but will lead to results through which faith will have new insight into its own foundations. Thus, the process of knowledge in which faith firms up its foundation is normally held in process by faith that is marked by an assurance that anticipates the results of the process of understanding. This is not unusual, for all knowledge takes place in view of the anticipation of its results and receives its impulse from this, although the anticipated results that are to establish faith seem to have an undercurrent of an extremely self-critical testing. The Christian faith can indeed come through strengthened in the assurance that it can hold its ground in every critical test, even in those times when there is uncertainty about the validity of faith. But in such times faith can persevere in the anticipation that its truth will be established in a future and better insight. This tension between faith and knowledge cannot be covered up, or else the nerve of Christian existence is destroyed.

16. For the latter I refer to my essay in *ZKG,* 70. 1959, pp. 1–45: "Die Aufnahme des philosophischen Gottesbegriffs als dogmatisches Problem der frühchristlichen Theologie."

17. The assertion that the one God of all men and of all time is revealed in the fate of Jesus is not a philosophical reflection, but is rather one that must be constantly

confirmed in the everyday experience of reality in each generation. And the philosophical formulation of the concept of reality will also be related to this. This confirmation of the biblical God's deity in the whole of the present experience of reality (not after the manner of Pietism, in the experience of the conscience) is something that is later. This presupposes the self-revelation of God in the event of Jesus and the confirmation of this in the church of earlier generations. However, when the one God of past times would be manifest to our world and generation, then his deity must be confirmed subsequently in this world and in the life experience of the men of our time. It is the concern of a dynamic proclamation that this confirmation does function in an enlightening way.

GUSTAVO GUTIÉRREZ

Gutiérrez (b. 1928), a theologian from Lima, Peru, is disturbed by any suggestion of a disjuncture between salvation and ordinary history. His concern is to discover the relationship between God's work of salvation in Christ and human action, especially all acts of liberation from oppression and exploitation in sociopolitical life. His conviction is that history is one: ". . . there are not two histories, one profane and one sacred, 'juxtaposed' or 'closely linked.' Rather there is only one human destiny, irreversibly assumed by Christ, the Lord of history. His redemptive work embraces all the dimensions of existence and brings them to their fullness. The history of salvation is the very heart of human history."

Gutiérrez's *A Theology of Liberation: History, Politics, and Salvation* (1973) advocates a Christian understanding of political and social liberation from the economic, class, and foreign sources of oppression of the poor and powerless. His method is to reread the Old and New Testaments in the light of the experience of working for a just society in Latin America, "the only continent among the exploited and oppressed peoples where Christians are in the majority."

This is his conclusion: "salvation embraces all men and the whole man; the liberating action of Christ—made man in this history and not in a history marginal to the real life of man—is at the heart of the historical current of humanity; the struggle for a just society is in its own right very much a part of salvation history."

History Is One

What is the relationship between salvation and the process of the liberation of man throughout history? Or more precisely, what is the meaning of the struggle against an unjust society and the creation of a new man in the light of the Word? A response to these questions presupposes an attempt to define what is meant by salvation, a concept central to the Christian mystery. This is a complex and difficult task which leads to reflection on the meaning of the saving action of the Lord in history. The salvation of the whole man is centered upon Christ the Liberator.

SALVATION: CENTRAL THEME OF THE CHRISTIAN MYSTERY

One of the great deficiencies of contemporary theology is the absence of a profound and lucid reflection on the theme of salvation.[1] On a superficial level this might seem surprising, but actually it is what often happens with difficult matters: people are afraid to tackle them. It is taken for granted that they are understood. Meanwhile, new edifices are raised on old foundations established in the past on untested assumptions and vague generalities. The moment comes, however, when the whole building totters; this is the time to look again to the foundations. This hour has arrived for

Reprinted by permission of Orbis Books and SCM Press Ltd. from *A Theology of Liberation* (1973). The original chapter title is "Liberation and Salvation." The original Spanish edition was published in 1971.

the notion of salvation.[2] Recently various works have appeared attempting to revise and deepen our understanding of this idea.[3] These are only a beginning.

We will not attempt to study this criticism in detail, but will only note that a consideration of this question has revealed two focal points; one follows the other in the manner of two closely linked stages.

From the Quantitative . . .

The questions raised by the notion of salvation have for a long time been considered under and limited by the classical question of the "salvation of the pagans." This is the quantitative, extensive aspect of salvation; it is the problem of the number of persons saved, the possibility of being saved, and the role which the Church plays in this process. The terms of the problem are, on the one hand, the universality of salvation, and on the other, the visibile Church as the mediator of salvation.

The evolution of the question has been complex and fatiguing.[4] Today we can say that in a way this evolution has ended. The idea of the universality of the salvic will of God, clearly enunciated by Paul in his letter to Timothy, has been established. It has overcome the difficulties posed by various ways of understainding the mission of the Church and has attained definite acceptance.[5] All that is left to do is to consider the ramifications, which are many.[6]

Here we will briefly consider one important point and leave for later a treatment of the repercussions of this idea on ecclesiological matters. The notion of salvation implied in this point of view has two very well-defined characteristics: it is a cure for sin in this life; and this cure is in virtue of a salvation to be attained beyond this life. What is important, therefore, is to know how a man outside the normal pale of grace, which resides in the institutional Church, can attain salvation. Multiple explanations have attempted to show the extraordinary ways by which a person could be assured of salvation, understood above all as life beyond this one. The present life is considered to be a test: one's actions are judged and assessed in relation to the transcendent end. The perspective here is moralistic, and the spirituality is one of flight from this world. Normally, only contact with the channels of grace instituted by God can eliminate sin, the obstacle which stands in the way of reaching that life beyond. This approach is very understandable if we remember that the question of "the salvation of the pagans" was raised at the time of the discovery of people belonging to other religions and living in areas far from these where the Church had been traditionally rooted.

. . . *to the Qualitative.*

As the idea of the universality of salvation and the possibility of reaching it gained ground in the Christian consciousness and as the quantitative question was resolved and decreased in interest, the whole problem of salvation made a qualitative leap and began to be perceived differently. Indeed, there is more to the idea of the universality of salvation than simply asserting the possibility of reaching it while outside the visible frontiers of the Church. The very heart of the question was touched in the search for a means to widen the scope of the possibility of salvation: man is saved if he opens himself to God and to others, even if he is not clearly aware that he is doing so. This is valid for Christians and non-Christians alike—for all people. To speak about the presence of grace—whether accepted or rejected—in all people implies, on the other hand, to value from a Christian standpoint the very roots of human activity. We can no longer speak properly of a profane world.[7] A *qualitative and intensive* approach replaces a *quantitative and extensive* one. Human existence, in the last instance, is nothing but a yes or a no to the Lord: "Men already partly accept communion with God, although they do not explicitly confess Christ as their Lord, insofar as they are moved by grace (*Lumen gentium*, no. 16), sometimes secretly (*Gaudium et spes*, nos. 3, 22), renounce their selfishness, and seek to create an authentic brotherhood among men. They reject union with God insofar as they turn away from the building up of this world, do not open themselves to others, and culpably withdraw into themselves (Mt. 25:31–46)."[8]

From this point of view the notion of salvation appears differently than it did before. Salvation is not something otherworldly, in regard to which the present life is merely a test. Salvation—the communion of men with God and the communion of men among themselves—is something which embraces all human reality, transforms it, and leads it to its fullness in Christ: "Thus the center of God's salvific design is Jesus Christ, who by his death and resurrection transforms the universe and makes it possible for man to reach fulfillment as a human being. This fulfillment embraces every aspect of humanity: body and spirit, individual and society, person and cosmos, time and eternity. Christ, the image of the Father and the perfect God-Man, takes on all the dimensions of human existence." [9]

Therefore, sin is not only an impediment to salvation in the afterlife. Insofar as it constitutes a break with God, sin is a historical reality, it is a breach of the communion of men with each other, it is a turning in of man on himself which manifests itself in a multifaceted withdrawal from others. And because sin is a personal and social intrahistorical reality, a part of the daily events of human life, it is also, and above all, an obstacle to life's reaching the fullness we call salvation.

The idea of a universal salvation, which was accepted only with great difficulty and was based on the desire to expand the possibilities of achieving salvation, leads to the question of the intensity of the presence of the Lord and therefore of the religious significance of man's action in history. One looks then to this world, and now sees in the world beyond not the "true life," but rather the transformation and fulfillment of the present life. The absolute value of salvation—far from devaluing this world—gives it its authentic meaning and its own autonomy, because salvation is already latently there. To express the idea in terms of Biblical theology: the prophetic perspective (in which the Kingdom takes on the present life, transforming it) is vindicated before the sapiential outlook (which stresses the life beyond). [10]

This qualitative, intensive approach has undoubtedly been influenced by the factor which marked the last push toward the unequivocal assertion of the universality of salvation, that is, the appearance of atheism, especially in the heart of Christian countries. The nonbeliever is not interested in an other-worldly salvation, as are believers in other religions; rather he considers it an evasion of the only question he wishes to deal with: the value of earthly existence. The qualitative approach to the notion of salvation attempts to respond to this problem.[11]

The developments which we have reviewed here have allowed us definitively to recover an essential element of the notion of salvation which had been overshadowed for a long time by the question of the possibility of reaching it. We have recovered the idea that salvation is an intrahistorical reality. Furthermore, salvation— the communion of men with God and the communion of men among themselves—orients, transforms, and guides history to its fulfillment.

HISTORY IS ONE

What we have recalled in the preceding paragraph leads us to affirm that, in fact, there are not two histories, one profane and one sacred, "juxtaposed" or "closely linked." Rather there is only one human destiny, irreversibly assumed by Christ, the Lord of history. His redemptive work embraces all the dimensions of existence and brings them to their fullness. The history of salvation is the very heart of human history. The Christian consciousness arrived at this unified view after an evolution parallel to that experienced regarding the notion of salvation. The conclusions converge. From an abstract, essentialist approach we moved to an existential, historical, and concrete view which holds that the only man we know has been efficaciously called to a gratuitous communion with God. All reflection, any distinctions which one wishes to treat, must be based on this fact: the salvific action of God underlies all human existence.[12] The historical destiny of humanity must be placed definitively in the salvific horizon. Only thus will its true dimensions emerge and its deepest meaning be apparent. It seems, however, that contemporary theology has not yet fashioned the categories which would allow us to think through and express adequately this unified approach to history.[13] We work, on the one hand, under the fear of falling back again into the old dualities, and, on the other, under the permanent suspicion of not sufficiently safeguarding divine gratuitousness or the unique dimension of Christianity. Although there may be different approaches to understanding it, however, the fundamental affirmation is clear: there is only one history [14]—a "Christo-finalized" history.

The study of two great Biblical themes will allow us to illustrate this point of view and to understand better its scope. The themes are the relationship between creation and salvation and the eschatological promises.

Creation and Salvation

The Bible establishes a close link between creation and salvation. But the link is based on the historical and liberating experience of the Exodus. To forget this perspective is to run the risk of merely juxtaposing these two ideas and therefore losing the rich meaning which this relationship has for understanding the recapitulating work of Christ.

Creation: the First Salvific Act

The Bible does not deal with creation in order to satisfy philosophic concerns regarding the origin of the world. Its point of view is quite another.

Biblical faith is, above all, faith in a God who reveals himself through historical events, a God who saves in history. Creation is presented in the Bible, not as a stage previous to salvation, but as a part of the salvific process: "Praise be to God the Father of our Lord Jesus Christ. . . . In Christ he chose us before the world was founded, to be dedicated, to be without blemish in his sight, to be full of love; and he destined us—such was his will and pleasure— to be accepted as his sons through Jesus Christ" (Eph. 1:3–5).[15] God did not create only in the beginning; he also had an end in mind. God creates all men to be his children.[16] Moreover, creation appears as the first salvific act: "Creation," writes Von Rad, "is regarded as a word of Yahweh in history, a work within time. This means that there is a real and true opening up of historical prospect. No doubt, Creation as the first of Yahweh's works stands at the very remotest beginnings—only, it does not stand alone, other works are to follow." [17] The creation of the world initiates history,[18]

the human struggle, and the salvific adventure of Yahweh. Faith
in creation does away with its mythical and supernatural character. It is the work of a God who saves and acts in history; since
man is the center of creation, it is integrated into the history which
is being built by man's efforts.

Second Isaiah—"the best theologian among Old Testament
writers" [19]—is an excellent witness in this respect. His texts are
frequently cited as one of the richest and clearest expressions of
the faith of Israel in creation. The stress, however, is on the saving
action of Yahweh; the work of creation is regarded and understood
only in this context: "But now this is the word of the Lord, the
word of your creator, O Jacob, of him who fashioned you, Israel:
Have no fear; for I have paid your ransom; I have called you by
name and you are my own" (43:1; cf. 42:5–6). The assertion is
centered on the redemption (or the Covenant). Yahweh is at one
and the same time Creator and Redeemer: "For your husband is
your maker, whose name is the Lord of Hosts; your ransomer is
the Holy One of Israel who is called God of all the earth" (54:5).
Numerous psalms sing praise to Yahweh simultaneously as Creator and Savior (cf. Pss. 74, 89, 93, 95, 135, 136). But this is
because creation itself is a saving action: "Thus says the Lord,
your ransomer, who fashioned you from birth: I am the Lord who
made all things, by myself I stretched out the skies, alone I ham-
mered out the floor of the earth" (Isa. 44:24; cf. also Amos 4:12ff.;
5:8 ff.; Jer. 33:25 ff.; 10:16; 27:5; 32:17; Mal. 2:10). Creation is
the work of the Redeemer. Rendtorff says: "A more complete fu-
sion between faith in creation and salvific faith is unimaginable." [20]

Political Liberation: Self-Creation of Man

The liberation from Egypt—both a historical fact and at the same
time a fertile Biblical theme—enriches this vision and is moreover
its true source.[21] The creative act is linked, almost identified with,
the act which freed Israel from slavery in Egypt. Second Isaiah,
who writes in exile, is likewise the best witness to this idea:
"Awake, awake, put on your strength, O arm of the Lord, awake as
you did long ago, in days gone by. Was it not you who hacked the
Rahab in pieces and ran the dragon through? Was it not you who

dried up the sea, the waters of the great abyss, and made the
ocean depths a path for the ransomed?" (51:9–10) The words and
images refer simultaneously to two events: creation and liberation
from Egypt. Rahab, which for Isaiah symbolizes Egypt (cf. 30:7;
cf. also Ps. 87:4), likewise symbolizes the chaos Yahweh had to
overcome to create the world (cf. Pss. 74:14; 89:11).[22] The "waters
of the great abyss" are those which enveloped the world and from
which creation arose, but they are also the Red Sea which the
Jews crossed to begin the Exodus. Creation and liberation from
Egypt are but one salvific act. It is significant, furthermore, that
the technical term *bara*, designating the original creation, was
used for the first time by Second Isaiah (43:1, 15; cf. Deut. 32:6)
to refer to the creation of Israel. Yahweh's historical actions on
behalf of his people are considered creative (41:20; 43:7; 45:8;
48:7).[23] The God who frees Israel is the Creator of the world.

The liberation of Israel is a political action. It is the breaking
away from a situation of despoliation and misery and the beginning of the construction of a just and fraternal society. It is the
suppression of disorder and the creation of a new order. The initial
chapters of Exodus describe the oppression in which the Jewish
people lived in Egypt, in that "land of slavery" (13:3; 20:2;
Deut. 5:6): repression (1:10–11), alienated work (5:6–14), humilia-
tions (1:13–14), enforced birth control policy (1:15–22). Yahweh
then awakens the vocation of a liberator: Moses. "I have indeed
seen the misery of my people in Egypt. I have heard their outcry
against their slave-masters. I have taken heed of their sufferings,
and have come down to rescue them from the power of Egypt.
. . . I have seen the brutality of the Egyptians towards them.
Come now; I will send you to Pharaoh and you shall bring my people Israel out of Egypt" (3:7–10).

Sent by Yahweh, Moses began a long, hard struggle for the
liberation of his people. The alienation of the children of Israel was
such that at first "they did not listen to him; they had become impatient because of their cruel slavery" (6:9). And even after they
had left Egypt, when they were threatened by Pharaoh's armies,
they complained to Moses: "Were there no graves in Egypt, that
you should have brought us here to die in the wilderness? See
what you have done to us by bringing us out of Egypt! Is not this
just what we meant when we said in Egypt, 'Leave us alone; let us

be slaves to the Egyptians'? We would rather be slaves to the Egyptians than die here in the wilderness" (14:11–12). And in the midst of the desert, faced with the first difficulties, they told him that they preferred the security of slavery—whose cruelty they were beginning to forget—to the uncertainties of a liberation in process: "If only we had died at the Lord's hand in Egypt, where we sat round the fleshpots and had plenty of bread to eat!" (16:3). A gradual pedagogy of successes and failures would be necessary for the Jewish people to become aware of the roots of their oppression, to struggle against it, and to perceive the profound sense of the liberation to which they were called. The Creator of the world is the Creator and Liberator of Israel, to whom he entrusts the mission of establishing justice: "Thus speaks the Lord who is God, he who created the skies, . . . who fashioned the earth. . . . I, the Lord, have called you with righteous purpose and taken you by the hand; I have formed you, and appointed you . . . to open eyes that are blind, to bring captives out of prison, out of the dungeons where they lie in darkness" (Isa. 42:5–7).

Creation, as we have mentioned above, is regarded in terms of the Exodus, a historical-salvific fact which structures the faith of Israel.[24] And this fact is a political liberation through which Yahweh expresses his love for his people and the gift of total liberation is received.

Salvation: Re-Creation and Complete Fulfillment

Yahweh summons Israel not only to leave Egypt but also and above all to "bring them up out of that country into a fine, broad land; it is a land flowing with milk and honey" (3:8). The Exodus is the long march towards the promised land in which Israel can establish a society free from misery and alienation. Throughout the whole process, the religious event is not set apart. It is placed in the context of the entire narrative, or more precisely, it is its deepest meaning. It is the root of the situation. In the last instance, it is in this event that the dislocation introduced by sin is resolved and justice and injustice, oppression and liberation, are determined. Yahweh liberates the Jewish people politically in order to make them a holy nation: "You have seen with your own eyes what I did to Egypt. . . . If only you will now listen to me and

keep my covenant, then out of all peoples you shall become my
special possession; for the whole earth is mine. You shall be my
kingdom of priests, my holy nation" (19:4–6). The God of Exodus
is the God of history and of political liberation more than he is the
God of nature. Yahweh is the Liberator, the *goel* of Israel (Isa.
43:14; 47:4; Jer. 50:34). The Covenant gives full meaning to the
liberation from Egypt; one makes no sense without the other: "The
Covenant was a historical event," asserts Gelin, "which occurred
in a moment of disruption, in an atmosphere of liberation; the revolutionary climate still prevailed: an intense spiritual impulse
would arise from it, as often happens in history." [25] The Covenant
and the liberation from Egypt were different aspects of the same
movement,[26] a movement which led to encounter with God. The
eschatological horizon is present in the heart of the Exodus.
Casalis rightly notes that "the heart of the Old Testament is the
Exodus from the servitude of Egypt and the journey towards the
promised land. . . . The hope of the people of God is not to return
to the mythological primitive garden, to regain paradise lost, but to
march forward towards a new city, a human and brotherly city
whose heart is Christ." [27]

Yahweh will be remembered throughout the history of Israel
by this act which inaugurates its history, a history which is a re-
creation. The God who makes the cosmos from chaos is the same
God who leads Israel from alienation to liberation. This is what is
celebrated in the Jewish passover. André Neher writes: "The first
thing that is expressed in the Jewish passover is the certainty of
freedom. With the Exodus a new age has struck for humanity:
redemption from misery. If the Exodus had not taken place,
marked as it was by the twofold sign of the overriding will of God
and the free and conscious assent of men, the historical destiny of
humanity would have followed another course. This course would
have been radically different, as the redemption, the *geulah* of the
Exodus from Egypt, would not have been its foundation. . . . All
constraint is accidental; all misery is only provisional. The breath
of freedom which has blown over the world since the Exodus can
dispel them this very day." [28] The memory of the Exodus pervades
the pages of the Bible and inspires one to reread often the Old as
well as the New Testaments.

The work of Christ forms a part of this movement and brings

it to complete fulfillment. The redemptive action of Christ, the foundation of all that exists, is also conceived as a re-creation and presented in a context of creation (cf. Col. 1:15–20; 1 Cor. 8:6; Heb. 1:2; Eph. 1:1–22).[29] This idea is particularly clear in the prologue to the Gospel of St. John.[30] According to some exegetes it constitutes the foundation of this whole Gospel.[31]

The work of Christ is a new creation. In this sense, Paul speaks of a "new creation" in Christ (Gal. 6:15; 2 Cor. 5:17). Moreover, it is through this "new creation," that is to say, through the salvation which Christ affords, that creation acquires its full meaning (cf. Rom. 8). But the work of Christ is presented simultaneously as a liberation from sin and from all its consequences: despoliation, injustice, hatred. This liberation fulfills in an unexpected way the promises of the prophets and creates a new chosen people, which this time includes all humanity. Creation and salvation therefore have, in the first place, a Christological sense: all things have been created in Christ, all things have been saved in him (cf. Col. 1:15–20).[32]

Man is the crown and center of the work of creation and is called to continue through his labor (cf. Gen. 1:28). And not only through his labor. The liberation from Egypt, linked to and even coinciding with creation, adds an element of capital importance: the need and the place for man's active participation in the building of society. If faith "desacralizes" creation, making it the area proper for the work of man, the Exodus from Egypt, the home of a sacred monarchy, reinforces this idea: it is the "desacralization" of social praxis, which from that time on will be the work of man.[33] By working, transforming the world, breaking out of servitude, building a just society, and assuming his destiny in history, man forges himself. In Egypt, work is alienated and, far from building a just society, contributes rather to increasing injustice and to widening the gap between exploiters and exploited.

To dominate the earth as Genesis prescribed, to continue creation, is worth nothing if it is not done for the good of man, if it does not contribute to his liberation, in solidarity with all, in history. The liberating initiative of Yahweh responds to this need by stirring up Moses' vocation. Only the *mediation of this self-creation*—first revealed by the liberation from Egypt—allows us to rise above poetic expressions and general categories and to understand in a profound and synthesizing way the relationship between creation and salvation so vigorously proclaimed by the Bible.

The Exodus experience is paradigmatic. It remains vital and contemporary due to similar historical experiences which the People of God undergo. As Neher writes, it is characterized "by the twofold sign of the overriding will of God and the free and conscious consent of men." And it structures our faith in the gift of the Father's love. In Christ and through the Spirit, men are becoming one in the very heart of history, as they confront and struggle against all that divides and opposes them. But the true agents of this quest for unity are those who today are oppressed (economically, politically, culturally) and struggle to become free.[34] Salvation—totally and freely given by God, the communion of men with God and among themselves—is the inner force and the fullness of this movement of man's self-generation which was initiated by the work of creation.

Consequently, when we assert that man fulfills himself by continuing the work of creation by means of his labor, we are saying that he places himself, by this very fact, within an all-embracing salvific process. To work, to transform this world, is to become a man and to build the human community; it is also to save. Likewise, to struggle against misery and exploitation and to build a just society is already to be part of the saving action, which is moving towards its complete fulfillment. All this means that building the temporal city is not simply a stage of "humanization" or "pre-evangelization" as was held in theology up until a few years ago. Rather it is to become part of a saving process which embraces the whole of man and all human history. Any theological reflection on human work and social praxis ought to be rooted in this fundamental affirmation.

Eschatological Promises

A second important Biblical theme leads to converging conclusions. We refer to the eschatological promises. It is not an isolated theme, but rather, as the former one, it appears throughout the Bible. It is vitally present in the history of Israel and consequently claims its place among the People of God today.

Heirs According to the Promise

The Bible is the book of the Promise, the Promise made by God to men which is the efficacious revelation of his love and his self-communication; simultaneously it reveals man to himself. The Greek word which the New Testament uses to designate the Promise is *epangelía,* which also means "word pledged," "announcement," and "notification"; it is related to *evangelion.*[35] This Promise, which is at the same time revelation and Good News, is the heart of the Bible. Albert Gelin says that "this Promise lies behind the whole Bible, and it makes it the book of hope, the slight hope stronger than experience, as Peguy said, which persists through all trials and is reborn to greater strength after every set-back." [36] The Promise is revealed, appeals to man, and is fulfilled throughout history. The Promise orients all history towards the future and thus puts revelation in an eschatological perspective.[37] Human history is in truth nothing but the history of the slow, uncertain, and surprising fulfillment of the Promise.

The Promise is a gift accepted in faith. This makes Abraham the father of believers. The Promise was first made to him (cf. Gen. 12:1–3; 15:1–16) that he and his posterity would be, as St. Paul says in a vigorous and fertile expression, "the heirs of the world" (Rom. 4:13).[38] For this reason Jesus, John the Baptist (Luke 3:8; 13:16; 16:22; 19:9), and Paul (Gal. 3:16–29; Rom. 4; Heb. 11), place Abraham at the beginning of the work of salvation.[39] This Promise is "given to those who have such faith" in Jesus Christ (Gal. 3:22). The Promise is fulfilled in Christ, the Lord of history and of the cosmos. In him we are "the 'issue' of Abraham, and so heirs by promise" (Gal. 3:29). This is the mystery which remained hidden until "the fullness of time."

But the *Promise* unfolds—becoming richer and more definite—in the *promises* made by God throughout history. "The first expression and realization of the Promise was the Covenant." [40] The kingdom of Israel was another concrete manifestation. And when the infidelities of the Jewish people rendered the Old Covenant invalid, the Promise was incarnated both in the proclamation of a New Covenant, which was awaited and sustained by the "remnant," as well as in the promises which prepared and accompanied its advent. The Promise enters upon "the last days" with the proclamation in the New Testament of the gift of the Kingdom of God.[41]

The Promise is not exhausted by these promises nor by their fulfillment; it goes beyond them, explains them, and gives them their ultimate meaning. But at the same time, the Promise is announced and is partially and progressively fulfilled in them. There exists a dialectical relationship between the Promise and its partial fulfillments. The resurrection itself is the fulfillment of something promised and likewise the anticipation of a future (cf. Acts 13:23); with it the work of Christ is "not yet completed, not yet concluded"; the resurrected Christ "is still future to himself." [42] The Promise is gradually revealed in all its universality and concrete expression: it is *already* fulfilled in historical events, but *not yet* completely; it incessantly projects itself into the future, creating a permanent historical mobility. The Promise is inexhaustible and dominates history, because it is the self-communication of God. With the Incarnation of the Son and the sending of the Spirit of Promise this self-communication has entered into a decisive stage (Gal. 3:14; Eph. 1:13; Acts 2:38–39; Luke 24:29). But by the same token, the Promise illuminates and fructifies the future of humanity and leads it through incipient realizations towards its fullness.[43] Both the present and future aspects are indispensable for tracing the relationships between Promise and history. . . .

The conclusion to be drawn from all the above is clear: salvation embraces all men and the whole man; the liberating action of Christ—made man in this history and not in a history marginal to the real life of man—is at the heart of the historical current of humanity; the struggle for a just society is in its own right very much a part of salvation history. . . .

Christ the Liberator

The approach we have been considering opens up for us—and this is of utmost importance—unforeseen vistas on the problem of sin. An unjust situation does not happen by chance; it is not something branded by a fatal destiny: there is human responsibility behind it. The prophets said it clearly and energetically and we are rediscovering their words now. This is the reason why the Medellín Conference refers to the state of things in Latin America as a "sinful situation," as a "rejection of the Lord." [44] This characterization, in all its breadth and depth, not only criticizes the individual abuses on the part of those who enjoy great power in this social order; it challenges all their practices, that is to say, it is a repudiation of the whole existing system—to which the Church itself belongs.

In this approach we are far, therefore, from that naive optimism which denies the role of sin in the historical development of humanity. This was the criticism, one will remember, of the Schema of Ariecia and it is frequently made in connection with Teilhard de Chardin and all those theologies enthusiastic about human progress. But in the liberation approach sin is not considered as an individual, private, or merely interior reality—asserted just enough to necessitate a "spiritual" redemption which does not challenge the order in which we live. Sin is regarded as a social, historical fact, the absence of brotherhood and love in relationships among men, the breach of friendship with God and with other men, and, therefore, an interior, personal fracture. When it is considered in this way, the collective dimensions of sin are rediscovered. This is the Biblical notion that José María González Ruiz calls the "hamartiosphere," the sphere of sin: "a kind of parameter or structure which objectively conditions the progress of human history itself." [45] Moreover, sin does not appear as an afterthought, something which one has to mention so as not to stray from tradition or leave oneself open to attack. Nor is this a matter of escape into a fleshless spiritualism. Sin is evident in oppressive structures, in the exploitation of many by man, in the domination and slavery of peoples, races, and social classes. Sin appears, therefore, as the fundamental alienation, the root of a situation of injustice and exploitation.[46] It cannot be encountered in itself, but only in concrete instances, in particular alienations.[47] It is impossible to understand the concrete manifestations without understanding the underlying basis and vice versa. Sin demands a radical liberation, which in turn necessarily implies a political liberation.[48] Only by participating in the historical process of liberation will it be possible to show the fundamental alienation present in every partial alienation.

This radical liberation is the gift which Christ offers us. By his

death and resurrection he redeems man from sin and all its consequences, as has been well said in a text we quote again: "It is the
same God who, in the fullness of time, sends his Son in the flesh,
so that He might come to liberate all men from *all* slavery to which
sin has subjected them: hunger, misery, oppression, and ignorance, in a word, that injustice and hatred which have their origin
in human selfishness." [49] This is why the Christian life is a passover, a transition from sin to grace, from death to life, from injustice to justice, from the subhuman to the human. Christ introduces us by the gift of his Spirit into communion with God and
with all men. More precisely, it is *because* he introduces us into
this communion, into a continuous search for its fullness, that he
conquers sin—which is the negation of love—and all its consequences.

In dealing with the notion of liberation [we may distinguish]
three levels of meaning: political liberation, the liberation of man
throughout history, liberation from sin and admission to communion with God. In the light of the present chapter, we can now
study this question again. These three levels mutually effect each
other, but they are not the same. One is not present without the
others, but they are distinct: they are all part of a single, all-en-
compassing salvific process, but they are to be found at different
levels. [50] Not only is the growth of the Kingdom not reduced to
temporal progress; because of the Word accepted in faith, we see
that the fundamental obstacle to the Kingdom, which is sin, is also
the root of all misery and injustice; we see that the very meaning
of the growth of the Kingdom is also the ultimate precondition for
a just society and a new man. One reaches this root and this ultimate precondition only through the acceptance of the liberating
gift of Christ, which surpasses all expectations. But, inversely, all
struggle against exploitation and alienation, in a history which is
fundamentally one, is an attempt to vanquish selfishness, the
negation of love. This is the reason why any effort to build a just
society is liberating. And it has an indirect but effective impact on
the fundamental alienation. It is a salvific work, although it is not
all of salvation. As a human work it is not exempt from ambiguities, any more than what is considered to be strictly "religious"
work. But this does not weaken its basic orientation nor its objective results.

Temporal progress—or, to avoid this aseptic term, the liberation of man—and the growth of the Kingdom both are directed toward complete communion of men with God and of men among themselves. They have the same goal, but they do not follow parallel roads, not even convergent ones. The growth of the Kingdom is a process which occurs historically *in* liberation, insofar as liberation means a greater fulfillment of man. Liberation is a precondition for the new society, but this is not all it is. While liberation is implemented in liberating historical events, it also denounces their limitations and ambiguities, proclaims their fulfillment, and impels them effectively towards total communion. This is not an identification. Without liberating historical events, there would be no growth of the Kingdom. But the process of liberation will not have conquered the very roots of oppression and the exploitation of man by man without the coming of the Kingdom, which is above all a gift. Moreover, we can say that the historical, political liberating event *is* the growth of the Kingdom and *is* a salvific event; but it is not *the* coming of the Kingdom, not *all* of salvation. It is the historical realization of the Kingdom and, therefore, it also proclaims its fullness. This is where the difference lies. It is a distinction made from a dynamic viewpoint, which has nothing to do with the one which holds for the existence of two juxtaposed "orders," closely connected or convergent, but deep down different from each other.

The very radicalness and totality of the salvific process require this relationship. Nothing escapes this process, nothing is outside the pale of the action of Christ and the gift of the Spirit. This gives human history its profound unity. Those who reduce the work of salvation are indeed those who limit it to the strictly "religious" sphere and are not aware of the universality of the process. It is those who think that the work of Christ touches the social order in which we live only indirectly or tangentially, and not in its roots and basic structure. It is those who in order to protect salvation (or to protect their interests) lift salvation from the midst of history, where men and social classes struggle to liberate themselves from the slavery and oppression to which other men and social classes have subjected them. It is those who refuse to see that the salvation of Christ is a radical liberation from all misery, all despoliation, all alienation. It is those who by trying to "save" the work of Christ will "lose" it.

In Christ the all-comprehensiveness of the liberating process reaches its fullest sense. His work encompasses the three levels of meaning which we mentioned above. A Latin American text on the missions seems to us to summarize this assertion accurately: "All the dynamism of the cosmos and of human history, the movement towards the creation of a more just and fraternal world, the overcoming of social inequalities among men, the efforts, so urgently needed on our continent, to liberate man from all that depersonalizes him—physical and moral misery, ignorance, and hunger—as well as the awareness of human dignity (*Gaudium et spes*, no. 22), all these originate, are transformed, and reach their perfection in the saving work of Christ. In him and through him salvation is present at the heart of man's history, and there is no human act which, in the last instance, is not defined in terms of it." [51]

NOTES

1. This is clearly indicated by Piet Smulders, "La Iglesia como sacramento de la salvación," in *La Iglesia del Vaticano II*, ed. Guillermo Baraúna (Madrid: Juan Flors, 1966), 1:379; French version: "L'Église sacrement du salut," *L'Église de Vatican II* (Paris: Les Éditions du Cerf, 1966), 2:313–38. More recently Yves Congar has written, "There is a question on which very little has been written: What does it mean, for the world and for man, to be saved? In what does salvation consist?" (*Situation et tâches*, p. 80; see also p. 68); and in another place he writes, "It is necessary to ask ourselves again very seriously about our idea of salvation. There is hardly any other theological notion implying immediate consequences—very concrete and very important—which has been left so vague and which calls in a most urgent way for an adequate elaboration" ("Christianisme et libération de l'homme," *Masses Ouvrières*, no. 258 [December 1969], p. 8).

2. Even including the very term *salvation;* with its connotation of evasion it would seem more and more inadequate to express the reality in question.

3. See Juan Luis Segundo, "Intelecto y salvación," *Salvación y construcción del mundo*, pp. 47–91; Manaranche, *Quel salut?;* Christian Duquoc, "Qu'est-ce que le salut?" in *L'Église vers l'avenir*, ed. M. D. Chenu (Paris : Les Éditions du Cerf, 1969), pp. 99–102; and the interesting posing of the question in the recent article of Jean-Pierre Jossua, "L'enjeu de la recherche théologique actuelle sur le salut," *Revue des Sciences Philosophiques et Théologiques* 54, no. 1 (January 1970): 24–25. The old book of Congar, *The Wide World My Parish: Salvation and its Problems*, trans. Donald Attwater (Baltimore: Helicon Press, 1961) gathered together different studies on the notion of salvation and opened new paths which are still relevant. Moreover, we cannot forget in this regard the concerns and intuitions of Teilhard de Chardin.

4. For a historical study of this point, see the classic work of Louis Capéran, *Le probleme du salut des infidèles*, 2 vols. (Toulouse: Grand Séminaire, 1934); see also Angel Santos Hernández, *Salvación y paganismo* (Santander: Editorial Sal Terrae, 1960).

5. See the solid study of Hendrik Nys, *Le salut sans l'Évangile* (Paris: Les Éditions du Cerf, 1966); see also the article of Joseph Ratzinger, "Salus extra ecclesiam nulla est," in *Naturaleza salvífica de la Iglesia* (Barcelona: do-c, 1964); English mimeo published by do-c (Rome), research paper no. 88.

6. In the first place, for a theology of the Church and therefore for a theology of missionary activity, see the study done by the missionary periodical *Spiritus,* no. 24 (August–September 1965), and the position papers of the Thirty-fifth Missiology Week gathered in *Repenser la mission* (Louvain: Desclée de Brouwer, 1965); these are revealing examples of the crisis caused by this revision which has led to the clear and simple affirmation of the universality of salvation. See the state of the question of this revision in Boniface Willems, "Who Belongs to the Church?" in Concilium 1, pp. 131–51.

7. "For the orthodox tradition, the profane does not exist, only the profaned" (Olivier Clement, "Un ensayo de lectura ortodoxa de la constitución," in *La Iglesia en el mundo de hoy* (Madrid: Studium, 1967), p. 673. The same idea is found in Charles Moeller, "Renewal of the Doctrine of Man," *Theology of Renewal* (Montreal: Palm, 1968), p. 458.

8. *La pastoral en las misiones de América Latina,* conclusions of the meeting at Melgar organized by the Department of Missions of CELAM (Bogota, 1968), pp. 16–17. The same idea is found in another text which also presents an interesting theological reflection: "Men respond of their own free will to this salvation that is offered to them in Christ. They can respond to it somehow, even when they do not know Jesus Christ explicitly; they do so when, under the influence of grace, they try to move out of their egotism, to take on the task of constructing the world, and to enter into communion with their fellow men. . . . They fail to respond when they refuse to recognize this task of building the world and serving others in fellowship, thus committing sin" ("Working Draft of the Medellín Conference," in *Between Honesty and Hope, p. 189).

9. *Ibid.,* pp. 187–88.

10. In the interesting essay on the notion of salvation which we have already mentioned, Juan Luis Segundo notes a difference in focus between the thinking of Paul and the other authors of the New Testament, a difference parallel to the one we have just pointed out; Segundo concludes, "We can say then that Christianity, although like the religions of extraterrestrial salvation because of its absolute salvation, differs from them because it introduced this absolute value into the midst of the historical and apparently profane reality of the existence of man" ("Intelecto y salvación," p. 87).

11. Some years ago Christian Duquoc compared these two positions from another viewpoint: "What mattered then to the theologian was the way man worked in relation to his transcendent end; what matters to him today is what man does" ("Eschatologie et réalités terrestres," *Lumière et Vie* 9, no. 50 [November–December 1960]:5).

12. See [Gutiérrez, *A Theology of Liberation* (Maryknoll, N.Y.: Orbis, 1973), Chapter 5.]

13. In this regard see the effort of Jossua, "L'enjeu."

14. We will cite the testimony of two theologians considered rather moderate in their views. From a Biblical perspective, Pierre Grelot writes, "Profane history and sacred history are not two separate realities. . . . They are intertwined in each other. Concretely there is *only one* human history which develops *at the same time* on these two levels. The grace of redemption, whose mysterious itinerary constitutes sacred history, is at work in the very heart of profane history. . . . Sacred history integrates all of profane history, on which it confers, in the last instance, its intelligible meaning." Having said this, the author adds, "In the midst of profane history, which runs down through the centuries, sacred history has its points of emergence which enable us to establish its reality and know its essential aspects" (*Sens chrétien de l'Ancien Testament* [Tournai: Desclée & Cie, Éditeurs, 1962], p. 111). Nevertheless, the notion of "points of emergence" does not seem very clear. Do these have their own history in the midst of the general history of humanity? Are they necessary to establish the reality of sacred history? Or are they nothing more than the interpretation of history in the light of the Word of God?

For his part, Emile Rideau believes that "if the vocation of the world and of man is supernatural, there does not exist, in fact and in the deepest sense, anything but a supernatural reality. The profane world is nothing but an abstraction in relation to the supernatural world of faith" ("Y a-t-il un monde profane?" *Nouvelle Revue Théologique* 88, no. 10 [December 1966]:1080). This does not weaken for him the consistency of the temporal sphere, because we are before "a lively dialectic of the relationship between, on the one hand, a world that is not profane only because it is not perceived as divine and, on the other, a supernatural reality which seeks to assume it, to ransom it, to consecrate it, to divinize it" (*ibid.*, p. 1082).

The position of Karl Rahner, on the other hand, seems more ambiguous; see "History of the World and Salvation-history," in *Theological Investigations*, 5:97–114. See also Ovidio Pérez Morales, who clearly affirms the existence of a single history: *Fe y desarrollo* (Caracas: Ediciones Paulinas, 1971), p. 49.

15. See the comments of Heinrich Schlier, *Der Briefe an die Epheser* (Dusseldorf: Patmos-Verlag, 1958), pp. 37–48.

16. See the reflections of Piet Schoonenberg concerning the mutual implications of creation and the Covenant in *Covenant and Creation* (London: Sheed and Ward, 1968), pp. 141–49.

17. Gerhard Von Rad, *Old Testament Theology*, trans. D. M. G. Stalker (New York: Harper and Brothers, 1962), 1:139; see also Von Rad's, *Genesis*, trans. John H. Marks (London: SCM Press Ltd, 1961).

18. "With the creation of the world (the six-day schema) the dimension of history opens up. Only by referring history to the creation of the world could the saving action within Israel be brought into its appropriate theological frame of reference, because creation is part of Israel's etiology" (Von Rad, *Old Testament Theology* [New York: Harper & Row, Publishers, 1965], 2:341–42.

19. A. Jacob, *Théologie de l'Ancien Testament* (Neuchatel: Delachaux et Niestlé, 1953), p. 43. Regarding the message of Deutero-Isaiah, see the excellent article of A. Gamper, "Der Verkündigungsauftrag Israels nach Deutero-Jesaja," *Zeitschrift für Katholische Theologie* 91 (1969):411–29.

20. "Die theologische Stellung des Schöpfungsglaubens bei Deuterojesaias," *Zeitschrift für Theologie und Kirche* 51 (1954):10, cited by Walter Kern, "La creación como presupuesto de la Alianza," in *Mysterium Salutis* (Madrid: Cristiandad,

1969), 1:503; original German: *Mysterium Salutis* (Einsiedeln, Zurich, Cologne: Benziger Verlag, 1967).

21. As is well known the accounts of the creation are strongly marked by the experience of the Exodus and the Covenant. This is the case especially in the so-called *Yahwistic* narrative; Gen. 2:4–16 follows the outline of the Covenant pact.

22. See Jean Steinmann, *Le prophète Isaïe* (Paris: Les Éditions du Cerf, 1950), p. 221.

23. See Kern, "Creación como presupuesto."

24. In this regard see Rubem Alves, *A Theology of Human Hope* (Washington, D.C.: Corpus Books, 1969), p. 129. See also Arnaldo Zenteno, *Liberación social y Cristo* (Mexico, D.F.: Secretariado Social Mexicano, 1971).

25. Albert Gelin, "Moïse dans l'Ancien Testament," in *Moïse, L'homme de l'Alliance* (Paris: Desclée & Cie, Éditeurs, 1955), p. 39.

26. Regarding the central characteristic of the theme of the Covenant, see the short but interesting note of Beltrán Villegas, "El tema de la Alianza y el vocabulario teológico del A.T.," *Teología y Vida* 2, no. 3 (July–September 1961):178–82; and in a recent exegetical perspective, see the analysis of Paul Beauchamp, "Propositions sur l'Alliance de l'Ancien Testament comme structure centrale," *Recherches de Science Religieuse* 58, no. 2 (April–June 1970):161–93.

27. Cited by Congar in "Christianisme et liberation," p. 8.

28. *Moses and the Vocation of the Jewish People,* trans. Irene Marinoff (New York: Harper Torchbooks, 1959), pp. 136–37.

29. See the commentary on some of these texts in Franz Mussner, "Creación en Cristo," in *Mysterium Salutis,* 1:506–11.

30. See Charles Harold Dodd, *The Interpretation of the Fourth Gospel* (Cambridge [Eng.]: University Press, 1953), p. 269; Charles Kingsley Barrett, *The Gospel According to St. John* (London: S.P.C.K., 1955), pp. 125–32; and A. Feuillet, "Prologue du quatrième Évangile," *Supplément au Dictionnaire de la Bible,* fasc. 44, 1969, col. 623–88.

31. "With a little arrangement," writes M. E. Boismard, "we might say that St. John meant to divide Christ's life into seven periods of seven days, in seven weeks. We should do wrong to see in this mere puerile game on the part of the evangelist, or even a convenient or artificial frame in which to enclose the life of Christ. This structural scheme corresponds to the plan already indicated in the Prologue: to draw a parallel between the work of creation and the work of the Messias: the seven times seven days of Messianic ministry correspond to the seven days of creation" (*St. John's Prologue,* trans. Carisbrooke Dominicans [Westminster, Md.: Newman Press, 1957], p. 107).

32. See Severino Croatto, "La creación en la Kerygmática actual," in *Salvación y construcción del mundo,* pp. 95–104; A. Feuillet, *Le Christ sagesse de Dieu d'après les Épitres pauliennes* (Paris: J. Gabalda et Cie, 1966); regarding this work and this theme in general, see the perceptive observations of Juan Alfaro, *Hacia una teología del progreso humano* (Barcelona: Herder, 1969), p. 22, no. 22.

33. This was pointed out very clearly by Harvey Cox in *The Secular City.* But it should be clarified that this "desacralization" refers to something different from the

"sacred": it is not what is untouchable and separated from profane life, but rather something present and active in the heart of human history.

34. Frantz Fanon put it quite emphatically: "To educate the masses politically . . . means . . . to try, relentlessly and passionately, to teach the masses that everything depends on them; that if we stagnate it is their responsibility, and that if we go forward it is due to them too, that there is no such thing as a demiurge, that there is no famous man who will take the responsibility for everything, but that the demiurge is the people themselves and the magic hands are finally only the hands of the people" (*The Wretched of the Earth*, pp. 157–58).

35. In Hebrew there is no special term to signify *promise*. A combination of terms and expressions designate it: blessing, oath, inheritance, promised land. See Julius Schniewind and Gerhard Friedrich, "Epangelia," in *Theological Dictionary of the New Testament*, 2:576 ff.

36. *The Key Concepts of the Old Testament*, trans. George Lamb (New York: Sheed and Ward, 1955), pp. 36–37.

37. Jürgen Moltmann, *Theology of Hope*, pp. 139 ff.

38. Joseph Huby observes that "the object of the promise, 'to inherit the world,' is not found in this form in the passage from Genesis (15:1–7) to which Paul refers. 'This land' which God promised to Abraham was the land of Canaan. But in other texts (Gen. 12:3; 22:17–18) the promise was extended by the proclamation of blessings that would include all the families and nations of the earth. Therefore Jewish thought, according to certain of its representatives, was led to extend the boundaries of the land promised to Abraham until they were coterminous with the boundaries of the world" (*Saint Paul, Épitre aux Romains* [Paris: Beauchesne et ses Fils, 1957], p. 173).

39. In reality this is not an innovation. In the Old Testament the oath of God to the patriarchs is often recalled; see Deut. 1:8, 6:10, 18; 7:8; Ecclus. 44:19–23; Jer. 11:5; Mic. 7:20; Ps. 105:6–9.

40. Gelin, *Key Concepts*, p. 37.

41. "What we call the New Testament is the realization of the promise, and the actual taking possession of the inheritance" (L. Cerfaux, *The Church in the Theology of St. Paul*, trans. Geoffrey Webb and Adrian Walker [New York: Herder and Herder, 1959], p. 35). Incipiently we should say, to be exact. But what we are saying concerning the historical fulfillment of the promise should not make us forget the lesson of Exodus: the significance of the self-generation of man in the historical political struggle. On this point we are far from the position of Jürgen Moltmann (*Theology of Hope*) criticized perceptively by Rubem Alves (*Theology of Human Hope*, pp. 55–68); Moltmann would give the impression that he does not keep sufficiently in the mind the participation of man in his own liberation.

42. Karl Barth, *Kirchliche Dogmatik* 4/3, pp. 385 and 387, quoted by Moltmann, *Theology of Hope*, p. 87.

43. "The reason," Moltmann asserts, "for the overplus of promise and for the fact that it constantly overspills history lies in the inexhaustibility of the God of promise, who never exhausts himself in any historic reality but comes 'to rest' only in a reality that wholly corresponds to him" (*Theology of Hope*, p. 106).

44. See "Peace," nos. 1 and 14, in *Medellín*.

45. *Pobreza evangélica y promoción humana,* p. 29.

46. The religious resonances of Hegel's use of the term *alienation (Entäusserung et Entfremdong)* are well known. See George Cottier, *L'athéisme du jeune Marx* Paris: Librairie Philosophique J. Vrin, 1959), pp. 34–43; and Albert Chapelle, *Hegel et la religion, Annexes, Les textes théologiques de Hegel* (Paris: Éditions Universitaires, 1967), pp. 99–125.

47. See Christian Duquoc, "Qu'est-ce que le salut?," pp. 101–2.

48. Without overestimating its importance, it is interesting to recall here the comparison that Marx establishes between sin and private ownership of the means of production. Because of this private ownership the worker is separated, alienated, from the fruit of his work: "This primitive accumulation plays in political economy about the same part as original sin in theology. Adam bit the apple, and thereupon sin fell on the human race" ("Capital," Part 8, Chapter 26, in *Marx*, Great Books of the Western World, 50:354).

49. "Justice," no. 3, in *Medellín.* The italics are ours. See also the interesting reflections of Eduardo Pironio, *La Iglesia que nace entre nosotros* (Bogota: Indo-American Press Service, 1970).

50. This is what was implied, partially and in other terms, in the text of *Populorum progressio* which we have already quoted.

51. *La pastoral en las misiones de América Latina,* p. 16.

PAUL TILLICH

"History and the Kingdom of God" is the finale of Paul Tillich's (1886–1965) *Systematic Theology* (3 volumes, 1951–63). Because of Hitler Tillich lost his professorship at Frankfurt and was brought by Reinhold Niebuhr to teach at Union Theological Seminary in New York. He tells us that the impact of world-historical events from World War I to the nuclear age helped induce him to construct his theological system.

Tillich considers history to be the all-embracing dimension of life which holds the ambiguities of all aspects of life. He believes that the greatest human longing is for the unambiguous life beyond the dialectic, a life of fulfillment without inner contradictions and contrasts. The answer to ambiguity in the historical dimension is the "symbol" of the Kingdom of God, the most comprehensive symbol of Christian faith. This symbol refers our faith to the completely unambiguous life which is "the ultimate fulfillment toward which history runs." At the same time, it points to the struggle now against "the forces which make for ambiguity." For Tillich, the symbol of the Kingdom of God has a variety of connotations—political, social, personal, universal. It has both immanent and transcendent meaning, both of which must be received if imbalance is not to result.

The aim of much of his work was "to relate all cultural realms to the religious center." Many people regard his thought as a viable Protestant philosophical alternative to neo-Thomism. Throughout his career he advocated a "religious socialism" which sought to direct the power of the Christian gospel into historical action.

History and the Kingdom of God

THE QUEST
FOR UNAMBIGUOUS LIFE
AND THE SYMBOLS
OF ITS ANTICIPATION

In all life processes an essential and an existential element, created goodness and estrangement, are merged in such a way that neither one nor the other is exclusively effective. Life always includes essential and existential elements; this is the root of its ambiguity.

The ambiguities of life are manifest under all dimensions, in all processes and all realms of life. The question of unambiguous life is latent everywhere. All creatures long for an unambiguous fulfilment of their essential possibilities; but only in man as the bearer of the spirit do the ambiguities of life and the quest for unambiguous life become conscious. He experiences the ambiguity of life under all dimensions since he participates in all of them, and he experiences them immediately within himself as the ambiguity of the functions of the spirit: of morality, culture, and religion. The quest for unambiguous life arises out of these experiences; this quest is for a life which has reached that toward which it transcends itself.

Since religion is the self-transcendence of life in the realm of the spirit, it is in religion that man starts the quest for unambiguous life and it is in religion that he receives the answer. But the answer is not identical with religion, since religion itself is am-

biguous. The fulfilment of the quest for unambiguous life transcends any religious form or symbol in which it is expressed. The
self-transcendence of life never unambiguously reaches that toward which it transcends, although life can receive its self-
manifestation in the ambiguous form of religion.

Religious symbolism has produced three main symbols for
unambiguous life: Spirit of God, Kingdom of God, and Eternal
Life. Each of them and their relation to each other require a short
preliminary consideration. The Spirit of God is the presence of the
Divine Life within creaturely life. The Divine Spirit is "God
present." The Spirit of God is not a separated being. Therefore one
can speak of "Spiritual Presence" in order to give the symbol its
full meaning.

The word "presence" has an archaic connotation, pointing to
the place where a sovereign or a group of high dignitaries is. In
capitalizing it, we indicate that it is supposed to express the divine
presence in creaturely life. "Spiritual Presence," then, is the first
symbol expressing unambiguous life. It is directly correlated to the
ambiguities of life under the dimension of spirit although, because
of the multidimensional unity of life, it refers indirectly to all
realms. In it both "Spiritual" and "Presence" are capitalized, and
the word "Spiritual" is used for the first time in this part of *Systematic Theology*. It has *not* been used as an adjective from spirit with
a small "s," designating a dimension of life. This symbol will guide
our discussion in the fourth part of the system

The second symbol of unambiguous life is the "Kingdom of
God." Its symbolic material is taken from the historical dimension
of life and the dynamics of historical self-transcendence. Kingdom
of God is the answer to the ambiguities of man's historical existence but, because of the multidimensional unity of life, the symbol includes the answer to the ambiguity under the historical dimension in all realms of life. The dimension of history is
actualized, on the one hand, in historical events which reach out
of the past and determine the present, and on the other hand, in
the historical tension which is experienced in the present, but
runs irreversibly into the future. Therefore, the symbol of the
Kingdom of God covers both the struggle of unambiguous life with
the forces which make for ambiguity, and the ultimate fulfilment
toward which history runs.

This leads to the third symbol: unambiguous life is Eternal Life. Here the symbolic material is taken from the temporal and spatial finitude of all life. Unambiguous life conquers the servitude to the categorical limits of existence. It does not mean an endless continuation of categorical existence but the conquest of its ambiguities. This symbol, together with that of the Kingdom of God, will be the leading notions in the fifth part of the theological system: "History and the Kingdom of God."

The relation of the three symbols, "Spiritual Presence," "Kingdom of God," and "Eternal Life" can be described in the following way: all three are symbolic expressions of the answer revelation gives to the quest for unambiguous life. Unambiguous life can be described as life under the Spiritual Presence, or as life in the Kingdom of God, or as Eternal Life. But as shown before, the three symbols use different symbolic material and in doing so express different directions of meaning within the same idea of unambiguous life. The symbol "Spiritual Presence" uses the dimension of spirit, the bearer of which is man, but in order to be present in the human spirit, the Divine Spirit must be present in all the dimensions which are actual in man, and this means, in the universe.

The symbol Kingdom of God is a social symbol, taken from the historical dimension in so far as it is actualized in man's historical life. But the historical dimension is present in all life. Therefore, the symbol "Kingdom of God" embraces the destiny of the life of the universe, just as does the symbol "Spiritual Presence." But history's quality of running irreversibly toward a goal introduces another element into its symbolic meaning, and that is the "eschatological" expectation, the expectation of the fulfilment toward which self-transcendence strives and toward which history runs. Like Spiritual Presence, the Kingdom of God is working and struggling in history; but as eternal fulfilment of life, the Kingdom of God is above history.

The symbolic material of the third symbol of unambiguous life, Eternal Life, is taken from the categorical structure of finitude. Unambiguous life is Eternal Life. As with Spiritual Presence and Kingdom of God, Eternal Life is also a universal symbol, referring to all dimensions of life and including the two other symbols. Spiritual Presence creates Eternal Life in those who are grasped by it. And the Kingdom of God is the fulfilment of temporal life in Eternal Life.

The three symbols for unambiguous life mutually include each other, but because of the different symbolic material they use, it is preferable to apply them in different directions of meaning: Spiritual Presence for the conquest of the ambiguities of life under the dimension of the spirit, Kingdom of God for the conquest of the ambiguities of life under the dimension of history, and Eternal Life for the conquest of the ambiguities of life beyond history. Yet in all three of them we find a mutual immanence of all. Where there is Spiritual Presence, there is Kingdom of God and Eternal Life, and where there is Kingdom of God there is Eternal Life and Spiritual Presence, and where there is Eternal Life there is Spiritual Presence and Kingdom of God. The emphasis is different, the substance is the same—life unambiguous.

The quest for such unambiguous life is possible because life has the character of self-transcendence. Under all dimensions life moves beyond itself in the vertical direction. But under no dimension does it reach that toward which it moves, the unconditional. It does not reach it, but the quest remains. Under the dimension of the spirit it is the quest for an unambiguous morality and an unambiguous culture reunited with an unambiguous religion. The answer to this quest is the experience of revelation and salvation; they constitute religion above religion, although they become religion when they are received. In religious symbolism they are the work of the Spiritual Presence or of the Kingdom of God or of Eternal Life. This quest is effective in all religions and the answer received underlies all religions, giving them their greatness and dignity. But both quest and answer become matters of ambiguity if expressed in the terms of a concrete religion. It is an age-old experience of all religions that the quest for something transcending them is answered in the shaking and transforming experiences of revelation and salvation; but that under the conditions of existence even the absolutely great—the divine self-manifestation—becomes not only great but also small, not only divine but also demonic. . . .

INTERPRETATIONS OF HISTORY AND THE QUEST FOR THE KINGDOM OF GOD

1. The Nature and the Problem of an Interpretation of History

Every legend, every chronicle, every report of past events, every scholarly historical work, contains interpreted history. This is the consequence of the subject-object character of history. . . . Such interpretation, however, has many levels. It includes the selection of facts according to the criterion of importance, the valuation of causal dependences, the image of personal and communal structures, a theory of motivation in individuals, groups, and masses, a social and political philosophy, and underlying all this, whether admitted or not, an understanding of the meaning of the history in unity with the meaning of existence in general. Such understanding influences consciously or unconsciously all other levels of interpretation, and it, conversely, is dependent on a knowledge of historical processes, both specifically and universally. This mutual dependence of historical knowledge in all its levels and an interpretation of history should be realized by everyone who deals with history on *any* level.

Our problem is the interpretation of history in the sense of the question: What is the significance of history for the meaning of existence in general? In what way does history influence our ultimate concern? The answer to this question must be related to the ambiguities implied in the processes of life under the dimension of history, all of which are expressions of the basic antinomy of historical time.

How is an answer to the question of the meaning of history possible? Obviously, the subject-object character of history precludes an objective answer in any detached scientific sense. Only full involvement in historical action can give the basis for an interpretation of history. Historical activity is the key to understanding history. This, however, would lead to as many interpretations as there are types of historical activity, and the question arises: Which type provides the right key? Or, in other words, in which historical group must one participate to be given the universal view that opens up the meaning of history? Every historical group is particular, and participation in its historical activities implies a particular view of the aim of historical creativity. It is the vocational consciousness, referred to above, that decides upon the key and what it opens in the understanding of history. For example, the Greek vocational self-interpretation, as given in Aristotle's *Politics*, sees in the contrast between Greeks and barbarians the key to an interpretation of history, while the Jewish vocational self-interpretation, as given in the prophetic literature, sees such a key in the establishment of the rule of Jahweh over the nations of the world. More examples will be given later. At this point the question is: Which group and which vocational consciousness are able to give a key to history as a whole? Obviously, if we try to answer, we have already presuppposed an interpretation of history with a claim to universality; we have already used the key in justifying its use. This is an unavoidable consequence of the "theological circle" within which systematic theology moves; but it is an unavoidable circle wherever the question of the ultimate meaning of history is asked. The key and what the key opens are experienced in one and the same act; the affirmation of the vocational consciousness in a definite historical group and the vision of history implied in this consciousness go together. Within the circle of this theological system, it is Christianity in which key and answer are found. In the Christian vocational consciousness, history is affirmed in such a way that the problems implied in the ambiguities of life under the dimension of history are answered through the symbol "Kingdom of God." This, however, is an assertion which must be tested by contrasting this symbol with the other main types of understanding history and by reinterpreting the symbol in light of these contrasts.

The interpretation of history includes more than an answer to the question of history. Since history is the all-embracing dimension of life, and since historical time is the time in which all other dimensions of time are presupposed, the answer to the meaning of history implies an answer to the universal meaning of being. The historical dimension is present in all realms of life, though only as a subordinated dimension. In human history, it comes into its own.

But after it has come into its own, it draws into itself the ambiguities and problems under the other dimensions. In terms of the symbol of the Kingdom of God, this means that "Kingdom" includes life in all realms, or that everything that is participates in the striving toward the inner aim of history: fulfilment or ultimate sublimation.

Such an assertion, of course, is more than an answer to the question of the interpretation of history. It implies an interpretation; therefore, the question now is: How can this particular understanding of the inner aim of history, as it appears in the theological system, be described and justified?

2. Negative Answers to the Question of the Meaning of History

The ambiguities of history, as the final expression of the ambiguities of life under all its dimensions, have led to a basic split in the valuation of history and life itself. We have referred to it in the discussion of the New Being and its expectation by the two contrasting types of interpreting history—the non-historical and the historical. The non-historical type, our first subject of consideration, presupposes that the "running ahead" of historical time has no aim either within or above history but that history is the "place" in which individual beings live their lives unaware of an eternal *telos* of their personal lives. This is the attitude toward history for the largest number of human beings. One can distinguish three forms of such non-historical interpretations of history: the tragic, the mystical, the mechanistic.

The tragic interpretation of history receives its classical expression in Greek thought but is by no means restricted to it. History, in this view, does not run toward a historical or transhistorical aim but in a circle back to its beginning. In its course it provides genesis, acme, and decay for every being, each one at its time and with definite limits; there is nothing beyond or above this stretch of time which itself is determined by fate. Within the cosmic circle, periods can be distinguished which as a whole constitute a process of deterioration, starting with an original perfection and falling by degrees into a stage of utter distortion of what the world and man essentially are. Existence in time and space and in the separation of individual from individual is tragic guilt, which leads necessarily to self-destruction. But tragedy presupposes greatness, and in this view there is heavy emphasis on greatness in terms of centeredness, creativity, and sublimation. The glory of life in nature, nations, and persons is praised, and it is just for this reason that the shortness and misery and tragic quality of life are deplored. But there is no hope, no expectation of an immanent or transcendent fulfilment of history. It is non-historical, and the tragic circle of genesis and decay is its last word. None of the ambiguities of life is conquered; there is no consolation for the disintegrating, destructive, profanizing side of life, and its only resource is the courage which raises both hero and wise man above the vicissitudes of historical existence.

This way of transcending history points to the second type of the nonhistorical interpretation of history, the mystical. Although it appears also in Western culture (as, for example, in Neoplatonism and Spinozism), it is most fully and effectively developed in the East, as in Vedanta Hinduism, in Taoism, and in Buddhism. Historical existence has no meaning in itself. One must live in it and act reasonably, but history itself can neither create the new nor be truly real. This attitude, which demands elevation above history while living in it, is the most widespread of all within historical mankind. In some Hindu philosophies there is a speculation similar to that of Stoicism about cosmic cycles of genesis and decay and the deteriorization of historical mankind from one period to another up to the last in which we are living. But in general there is no awareness of historical time and of an end toward which it is running in this type of non-historical interpretation of history. The emphasis is on the individual and particularly on the comparatively few illuminated individuals who are aware of the human predicament. The others are objects of a pharisaic judgment about their *karma* for which they are responsible in a former incarnation, or they are objects of compassion and adaptation of the religious demands to their unenlightened stage, as in some forms of Buddhism. In any case, these religions contain no impulse to transform history in the direction of universal humanity and justice. History has no aim, either in time or in eternity. And again, the consequence is that the ambiguities of life under all dimensions are unconquerable. There is only one way to cope with them and that is to transcend them and live within them as someone who has already returned to the Ultimate One. He has not changed reality but he has conquered his own involvement in reality. There is no symbol analogous to that of the Kingdom of God. But there is often a profound compassion for the universality of suffering under all dimensions of life—an element often lacking under the influence of historical interpretations of history in the Western world.

Under the impact of the modern scientific interpretation of reality in all its dimensions, the understanding of history has undergone a change, not only in relation to the mystical interpretation of history, but also in relation to the tragic interpretation. Physical time controls the analysis of time so completely that there is little place for the special characteristics of biological, and even less of historical, time. History has become a series of happenings in the physical universe, interesting to man, worthy to be recorded and studied, but without a special contribution to the interpretation of existence as such. One could call this the mechanistic type of non-historical interpretation of history (where the term "mechanistic" is used in the sense of a "reductionistic naturalism"). Mechanism does not emphasize the tragic element in history as the classical naturalism of the Greeks did. Since it is intimately related to the technical control of nature by science and technology, it has in some cases a progressivistic character. But it is also open to the opposite attitude of cynical devaluation of existence in general and of history in particular. The mechanistic view usually does not share the Greek emphasis on the greatness and tragedy of man's historical existence, and it shares to an even lesser extent the interpretation of history from the point of view of an inner-historical or transhistorical aim toward which history is supposed to run.

3. Positive but Inadequate Answers to the Question of the Meaning of History

In some cases the mechanistic interpretation of history is allied with "progressivism," the first type of a historical interpretation of history that will be discussed. In it "progress" is more than an empirical fact (which it also is); it has become a quasi-religious symbol. In the chapter on progress we discussed the empirical validity and empirical limitations of the concept of progress. Here we must look at its use as a universal law determining the dynamics of history. The significant side of progressivistic ideology is its emphasis on the progressive intention of every creative action and its awareness of those areas of the self-creativity of life in which progress is of the essence of the reality concerned, for example, technology. In this way the symbol of progress includes the decisive element of historical time, its running ahead toward an aim. Progressivism is a genuinely historical interpretation of history. Its symbolic power was in some periods of history as strong as any of the great religious symbols of historical interpretation, including the symbol of the Kingdom of God. It gave impetus to historical actions, passion to revolutions, and a meaning to life for many who had lost all other faith and for whom the eventual breakdown of the progressivistic faith was a spiritual catastrophe. In short, it was a quasi-religious symbol in spite of its inner-historical aim.

One can distinguish two forms of it: the belief in progress itself as an infinite process without an end, and the belief in a final state of fulfillment, for example, in the sense of the concept of the third stage. The first form is progressivism in the proper sense; the second form is utopianism (which requires separate discussion). Progressivism, as the belief in progress as progress without a definite end, has been produced by the idealistic wing of the philosophical self-interpretation of modern industrial society; Neo-Kantianism was most important for the development of the idea of infinite progress. Reality is the never finished creation of man's cultural activity. There is no "reality in itself" behind this creation. Hegel's dialectical processes have the element of infinite progress in their structure and that element is the driving power of negation, which, as Bergson has strongly emphasized, requires an infinite openness for the future—even in God. The fact that Hegel stopped the dialectical movement with his own philosophy was incidental to his principle and has not prevented his becoming one of the most powerful influences for progressivism in the nineteenth century. The positivistic wing of nineteenth-century philosophy—as Comte and Spencer show—could accept progressivism on its own terms; and this school has given a large amount of material for a scientific justification of progress as a universal law of history, appearing under all dimensions of life but becoming conscious of itself only in human history. The progressivistic belief was undercut by the experiences of our century: the world-historical relapses to stages of inhumanity supposed to have been conquered long ago, the manifestation of the ambiguities of progress in the realms in which progress takes place, the feeling of the meaninglessness of an infinite progress without an end, and the insight into the freedom of every newborn human being to start again for good and evil. It is astonishing to notice how sudden and radical the breakdown of progressivism was, so radical that today many (including this writer) who twenty years ago fought against the progressivistic ideology now feel driven to defend the justified elements of this concept.

Perhaps the sharpest attack on the belief in infinite progress came from an idea which originally has grown out of the same root—the utopian interpretation of history. Utopianism is progressivism with a definite aim: arrival at that stage of history in which the ambiguities of life are conquered. In discussing utopianism it is important to distinguish, as in the case of progressivism, the utopian impetus from the literally interpreted symbol of utopia, the latter being the "third stage" of the historical development. The utopian impetus results from an intensification of the progressive impetus, and is distinguishable from it by the belief that present revolutionary action will bring about the final transformation of reality, that stage of history in which the *ou-tópos* (no-place) will become the universal place. This place will be the earth, the planet which in the geocentric world view was farthest removed from the heavenly spheres and which, in the heliocentric world view, has become a star among the others, of equal dignity, equal finitude, and equal internal infinity. And it will be man, the microcosm, the representative of all dimensions of the universe, through whom the earth will be transferred into the fulfilment of what in paradise was mere potentiality. These ideas of the Renaissance lie behind the many forms of secular utopianism in the modern period and have given incentive to revolutionary movements up to the present day.

The problematic character of the utopian interpretation of history has been clearly betrayed in the developments of the twen-

tieth century. Certainly, the power and truth of the utopian impetus has become manifest in the immensity of success in all
those realms in which the law of progress is valid, as foreseen in
the Renaissance utopias; but at the same time, there has appeared
a complete ambiguity between progress and relapse in those
realms in which human freedom is involved. Realms involving
human freedom were also envisaged in a state of unambiguous
fulfilment by the utopianists of the Renaissance and all their successors in the revolutionary movements of the last three hundred
years. But these expectations were disappointed with that profound disappointment which follows every idolatrous reliance on
something finite. A history of such "existential disappointments"
in modern times would be a history of cynicism, mass indifference,
a split consciousness in leading groups, fanaticism, and tyranny.
Existential disappointments produce individual and social diseases
and catastrophes: the price for idolatrous ecstasy must be paid. For
utopianism, taken literally, is idolatrous. It gives the quality of ul-
timacy to something preliminary. It makes unconditional what is
conditioned (a future historical situation) and at the same time dis-
regards the always present existential estrangement and the ambiguities of life and history. This makes the utopian interpretation
of history inadequate and dangerous.

A third form of inadequate historical interpretation of history
could be called the "transcendental" type. It is implicit in the eschatological mood of the New Testament and the early church up
to Augustine. It was brought to its radical form in orthodox Lutheranism. History is the place in which, after the Old Testament
preparation, the Christ has appeared to save individuals within the
church from bondage to sin and guilt and to enable them to participate in the heavenly realm after death. Historical action, especially in the decisive political realm, cannot be purged from the
ambiguities of power, internally or externally. There is no relation
between the justice of the Kingdom of God and the justice of
power structures. The two worlds are separated by an unbridgea-
ble gap. Sectarian utopian and Calvinistic theocratic interpretations of history are rejected. Revolutionary attempts to change a
corrupt political system contradict God's will as expressed in his
providential action. After history has become the scene of saving
revelation, nothing essentially new can be expected from it. The

attitude expressed in these ideas was quite adequate to the predicament of most people in the late feudal period of central and eastern Europe, and it contains an element which is relevant to the situation of innumerable individuals in all periods of history. In
theology it is a necessary counterbalance to the danger of secular
as well as religious utopianism. But it falls short of an adequate
historical interpretation of history. Its most obvious shortcoming is
the fact that it contrasts the salvation of the individual with the
transformation of the historical group and the universe, thus separating the one from the other. This error was sharply criticized
by Thomas Muenzer, who in his criticism of Luther's attitude
pointed to the fact that the masses have no time and strength left
for a spiritual life, a judgment which was repeated by Religious Socialists in their analysis of the sociological and psychological situation of the proletariat in the industrial cities of the late nineteenth
and early twentieth centuries. Another shortcoming of the transcendental interpretation of history is the way in which it contrasts
the realm of salvation with the realm of creation. Power in itself is
created goodness and an element in the essential structure of life.
If it is beyond salvation—however fragmentary the salvation may
be—life itself is beyond salvation. In such consequences the Mani-
chaean danger of the transcendental view of history becomes visible.

Finally, this view interprets the symbol of the Kingdom of God
as a static supranatural order into which individuals enter after
their death—instead of understanding the symbol, with the biblical
writers, as a dynamic power on earth for the coming of which we
pray in the Lord's Prayer and which, according to biblical thought,
is struggling with the demonic forces which are powerful in
churches as well as empires. The transcendental type of historical
interpretation, consequently, is inadequate because it excludes
culture as well as nature from the saving processes in history. It is
ironical that this happened in that type of Protestantism which—
following Luther himself—has had the most positive relation to nature and has made the greatest contribution to the artistic and cognitive functions of culture. But all this remained without decisive
consequence for modern Christianity because of the transcendental attitude toward politics, social ethics, and history in Lutheranism.

It was the dissatisfaction with the progressivistic, utopian, and transcendental interpretations of history (and the rejection of the non-historical types) that induced the Religious Socialists of the early 1920's to try a solution which avoids their inadequacies and is based on biblical prophetism. This attempt was made in terms of a reinterpretation of the symbol of the Kingdom of God.

4. The Symbol "Kingdom of God" as the Answer to the Question of the Meaning of History

a) The characteristics of the symbol "Kingdom of God."—In the chapter on the three symbols of unambiguous life we have described the relationship of the symbol "Kingdom of God" to the symbols "Spiritual Presence" and "Eternal Life." We found that each of them includes the other two but that, because of the differences in the symbol materials, we are justified in using Spiritual Presence as the answer to the ambiguities of the human spirit and its functions, Kingdom of God as the answer to the ambiguities of history, and Eternal Life as the answer to the ambiguities of life universal. Nevertheless, the connotations of the symbol of the Kingdom of God are more embracing than those of the two others. This is a consequence of the double character of the Kingdom of God. It has an inner-historical and a transhistorical side. As inner-historical, it participates in the dynamics of history; as transhistorical, it answers the questions implied in the ambiguities of the dynamics of history. In the former quality it is manifest through the Spiritual Presence; in the latter it is identical with Eternal Life. This double quality of the Kingdom of God makes it a most important and most difficult symbol of Christian thought and—even more—one of the most critical for both political and ecclesiastical absolutism. Because it is so critical, the ecclesiastical development of Christianity and the sacramental emphasis of the two Catholic churches has pushed the symbol aside, and today, after its use (and partial secularization) by the social gospel movement and some forms of religious socialism; the symbol has again lost in power. This is remarkable in view of the fact that the preaching of Jesus started with the message of the "Kingdom of Heaven at hand" and that Christianity prays for its coming in every Lord's Prayer.

Its reinstatement as a living symbol may come from the encounter of Christianity with the Asiatic religions, especially Buddhism. Although the great India-born religions claim to be able to receive every religion as a partial truth within their self-transcending universality, it seems impossible that they can accept the symbol of the Kingdom of God in anything like its original meaning. The symbolic material is taken from spheres—the personal, social and political—which in the basic experience of Buddhism are radically transcended, whereas they are essential and never missing elements of the Christian experience. The consequences of this difference for religion and culture in East and West are world-historical, and it would seem that there is no other symbol in Christianity which points to the ultimate source of the differences as clearly as the symbol "Kingdom of God," especially when it is contrasted with the symbol "Nirvana."

The first connotation of the Kingdom of God is political. This agrees with the political sphere's predominance in the dynamics of history. In the Old Testament development of the symbol, the Kingdom of God is not so much a realm in which God rules as it is the controlling power itself which belongs to God and which he will assume after the victory over his enemies. But, although the kingdom as realm is not in the foreground, it is not altogether absent, and it is identical with Mount Zion, Israel, the nations, or the universe. Later in Judaism and in the New Testament the realm of the divine rule becomes more important: it is a transformed heaven and earth, a new reality in a new period of history. It results from a rebirth of the old in a new creation in which God is everything in everything. The political symbol is transformed into a cosmic symbol, without losing its political connotation. The word "king" in this and many other symbolizations of the divine majesty does not introduce a special constitutional form into the symbol material, against which other constitutional forms, such as that of a democracy, must react; for "king" (in contrast to other forms of rule) has since earliest times been a symbol in its own right for the highest and most consecrated center of political control. Its application to God, therefore, is a generally understandable double symbolization.

The second characteristic of the Kingdom of God is social.

This characteristic includes the ideas of peace and justice—not in contrast to the political quality and, therefore, not in contrast to power. In this way the Kingdom of God fulfils the utopian expectation of a realm of peace and justice while liberating them from their utopian character by the addition "of God," for with this addition the impossibility of an earthly fulfilment is implicitly acknowledged. But even so the social element in the symbol is a permanent reminder that there is no holiness without the holy of what ought to be, the unconditional moral imperative of justice.

The third element implied in the Kingdom of God is the personalistic one. In contrast to symbols in which the return to the ultimate identity is the aim of existence, the Kingdom of God gives eternal meaning to the individual person. The transhistorical aim toward which history runs is not the extinction but the fulfilment of humanity in every human individual.

The fourth characteristic of the Kingdom of God is its universality. It is a kingdom not only of men; it involves the fulfilment of life under all dimensions. This agrees with the multidimensional unity of life: fulfilment under one dimension implies fulfilment in all dimensions. This is the quality of the symbol "Kingdom of God" in which the individual-social element is transcended, though not denied. Paul expresses this in the symbols "God being all in all" and "the Christ surrendering the rule over history to God" when the dynamics of history have reached their end.

b) *The immanent and the transcendent elements in the symbol "Kingdom of God."*—The symbol "Kingdom of God," in order to be both a positive and an adequate answer to the question of the meaning of history, must be immanent and transcendent at the same time. Any one-sided interpretation deprives the symbol of its power. In the section on inadequate answers to the question of the meaning of history we discussed the utopian and transcendental interpretation, adducing examples for both of them from the Christian-Protestant tradition. This indicates that the mere use of the symbol "Kingdom of God" does not guarantee an adequate answer. Although its history gives all the elements of an answer, the same history shows that each of these elements can be suppressed and the meaning of the symbol distorted. Therefore it is important to point to the emergence of these elements in the basic development of the idea of the Kingdom of God.

The emphasis in the prophetic literature is inner-historical-

political. The destiny of Israel is the revelatory medium for the prophetic understanding of Jahweh's character and actions, and
Israel's future is seen as the victory of the God of Israel in the
struggle with her enemies. Mount Zion will become the religious
center of all nations, and although the "day of Jahweh" is first of
all judgment, it is also fulfilment in a historical-political sense. But
this is not the whole story. The visions about judgment and fulfilment include an element which could hardly be called inner-historical or immanent. It is Jahweh who wins the battle against
enemies infinitely superior in numbers and power to Israel. It is
God's holy mountain that, in spite of its geographical insignifi-
cance, will be the place to which all nations come to worship. The
true God, the God of justice, conquers a concentration of partly political, partly demonic, forces. The Messiah, who will bring about
the new eon, is a human being with superhuman traits. The peace
between the nations includes nature, so that the most hostile species of animals will live peacefully beside each other. These transcendent elements within the predominantly immanent-political
interpretation of the idea of the Kingdom of God point to its double
character. God's Kingdom cannot be produced by the inner-historical development alone. In the political upheavals of Judaism
during the Roman period, this double character of the prophetic
anticipation was almost forgotten—which led to the complete destruction of the national existence of Israel.

Experiences such as this, long before the Roman period,
brought about a change in emphasis from the immanent-political
to the transcendent-universal side in the idea of the Kingdom of
God. This was most impressive in the so-called apocalyptic literature of the intertestamental period, with some predecessors in the
latest parts of the Old Testament. The historical vision is enlarged
upon and superceded by a cosmic vision. The earth has become
old, and demonic powers have taken possession of it. Wars, disease, and natural catastrophes of a cosmic character will precede
the rebirth of all things and the new eon in which God will finally
become the ruler of the nations and in which the prophetic hopes
will be fulfilled. This will not happen through historical developments but through divine interference and a new creation, leading
to a new heaven and a new earth. Such visions are independent of
any historical situation and are not conditioned by human activi-

ties. The divine mediator is no longer the historical Messiah, but the Son of Man, the Heavenly Man. This interpretation of history was decisive for the New Testament. Inner-historical-political aims within the Roman empire were beyond reach. The empire has to be accepted according to its elements of goodness (Paul), and it will be destroyed by God because of its demonic structure (Revelation). Obviously, this is far removed from any inner-historical progressivism or utopianism; nevertheless, it is not without immanent-political elements. The reference to the Roman empire—sometimes seen as the last and greatest in a series of empires—shows that the vision of the demonic powers is not merely imaginary. It is related to the historical powers of the period in which it is conceived. And the cosmic catastrophes include historical events within the world of nations. The final stages of human history are described with inner-historical colors. Again and again in later times people have found their own historical existence described in the mythical imagery of the apocalyptics. The New Testament adds a new element to these visions: the inner-historical appearance of Jesus as the Christ and the foundation of the church in the midst of the ambiguities of history. All this shows that the emphasis on transcendence in the symbol "Kingdom of God" does not exclude inner-historical features of decisive importance—just as the predominance of the immanent element does not exclude transcendent symbolism.

These developments show that the symbol "Kingdom of God" has the power to express both the immanent and the transcendent sides, though one side is normally predominant. . . .

ARNOLD TOYNBEE

A *Study of History* (12 volumes, 1934–61) has undoubtedly generated more discussion and thought than any other history writing in our century. The abridgment in two volumes even became a bestseller among non-academic readers. The breadth of Toynbee's (1889–1975) learning is boggling. His feeling in the 1920's that western civilization could well be in an advanced stage of breakdown led him to undertake his monumental study of the genesis and disintegration of civilizations.

He was not a historical determinist; something could be done to renew western civilization. Toynbee felt that the experience of our troubled times cried out, "See with your own eyes what happens to a building from which Religion has been left out." The cue for salvation, he writes in a characteristic phrase, "may still be given us by the message of Christianity and the other higher religions." Christianity, in Toynbee's view, is not the answer for the renewal of Islamic and Buddhist civilizations—Islam and Buddhism are. But for western civilization Christianity is *the* answer. On this point he was willing to evangelize. The article given here comes from a group of essays by Anglicans who believed Christianity offered the best answer to communism in the West.

Typically Toynbee works comparatively. He discloses that the uniqueness of a Christian view of history lies in the Incarnation of Christ, that central belief which makes Christianity "the historical religion *par excellence*." Christians—that includes Toynbee—believe "that the human founder of the Christian Church is God Himself incarnate." Through the Incarnation God affirms humanity, the world, and history. History receives its meaning, direction, and purpose, and life is freed from mere cycle. We can come to understand suffering in history and see beyond it. The closing sentence summarizes Toynbee's belief: "Christianity's last word will be that mankind has nevertheless been given a chance of salvation from the nemesis of its own sinful acts in being enabled, in virtue of Christ's passion, to seek this salvation by praying for God's grace."

The Christian Understanding of History

In a brief discussion of a vast subject—the relation between Christianity and history—perhaps the best plan will be to concentrate on three points. If we are looking for light on what the distinctive relation of Christianity to history may be, we must begin by considering the likenesses and differences, in their relation to history, between Christianity and other religions. We can then go on to look, in turn, at history in the light of Christianity, and at Christianity in the light of history.

When we take a bird's-eye view of the higher religions and philosophies that have made their appearance in the world since the rise of the first civilisations some five or six thousand years ago, we see that they fall into two broad groups, the "historical" and the "mythical." The historical group includes philosophies like Platonism, Aristotelianism, Stoicism, Epicureanism, Hīnayānian Buddhism, and Confucianism and religions like Judaism, Zoroastrianism, Christianity, and Islam. The mythical group includes religions like the worships of Tammuz and Ishtar, Osiris and Isis, Attis and Cybele, Jupiter Dolichênus and Mithras, all of which were Christianity's competitors in a contest for winning the allegiance of the population of the Roman Empire, and this second

Reprinted by permission of Macmillan, London and Basingstoke, from *Christian Faith and Communist Faith: A Series of Articles by Members of the Anglican Communion* (1953), edited by D. M. MacKinnon.

group also includes religions like Neoplatonism and Mahāyānian Buddhism, which are transmutations of philosophies.

The philosophies and religions in the historical group are "historical" in two senses. In the first place, they all owe their existence to human founders who lived in times and places that lie in the full light of history, and whose lives are intertwined with historical events whose authenticity is not questioned by the critics who do question the authenticity of some of the acts, powers, and characteristics that have been ascribed to the founders of these religions and philosophies by their followers. The second sense in which these philosophies and religions are historical is that their founders all established schools or churches which came to play prominent parts on the stage of history. On the whole, these institutions founded for spiritual purposes have shown a greater survival power than the civilisations, and a very much greater survival power than any states or empires. Out of the ten that we have cited, six are still alive today, when even the youngest of them, Islam, is already in its fourteenth century; and, though the Hellenic philosophical schools were suppressed by a Christian Roman Government in A.D. 529, much of their doctrine and practice had by then already been incorporated into Christianity.

By contrast, the Mahāyāna is the only one of the seven "mythical" religions on our list that has not by now become extinct, and both its survival and the disappearance of the other six are significant. The mythical religions have, of course, also played their part on the stage of history, but they differ from the historical religions and philosophies in neither basing their claims to acceptance on the authority of historical founders nor attaching importance to the interaction between their histories and the course of mundane historical events; and this is because they are chiefly concerned with "timeless" aspects of life and existence which cannot be caught in the meshes of history's web and can only be conveyed in a myth which, like a fairy story, is the expression of a truth that is true without being historical.

Five out of the six extinct mythical religions on our list were concerned with mankind's relation to the powers of physical nature in the material environment of human life on this planet. They arose at a time when mankind was still at nature's mercy, and when human beings therefore saw in her a divinity to be propitiated; but the history of civilisation has been the history of mankind's progressive conquest of physical nature, and this conquest had gone far enough to make us physical nature's masters, instead of leaving us still her slaves, long before the recent unprecedented acceleration in the pace of technological progress in the Western world. Man's conquest of physical nature took the sheen of divinity out of her, and therefore it is not surprising that those five forms of nature-worship should have been abandoned long ago—except in so far as they have been incorporated, like the Hellenic philosophies, into Christianity and other still living historical religions and philosophies.

There is, however, another "timeless" aspect of existence and life which mankind has so far signally failed to master, and that is the psychic nature of the human soul. There has been no cumulative growth in the wisdom, virtue, or holiness of the human race *pari passu* with the cumulative and ever accelerating growth in our scientific knowledge and technical skill; and this constantly widening gap between mankind's mastery of its external environment and our perpetual defeat by "Original Sin" has been making the material nemesis of spiritual failure more and more serious for us. It is not that men and women have become more wicked on the average since the successive inventions of the war-chariot, the crossbow, gunpowder, and the atomic bomb; what has happened is that these more and more effective lethal tools have put a more and more powerful driving-force into still unregenerately foolish and wicked human actions. The still unmastered demonic forces of the soul's inner spiritual world are thus a more serious menace to us, and therefore a more pressing problem for us, than they have ever been; and that is one reason why the Mahāyānian form of Buddhism, which has inherited a concern with the psychic universe from the Hīnayānian Buddhist philosophy, still has a meaning and a value in an age of history in which mankind's mastery over external nature has broken the spell of a sun-worship, weather-worship, and vegetation-worship that were once in the forefront of mankind's religious interests. Another reason—at least in a Christian observer's estimation—why the Mahāyāna is still a great spiritual force in the world today is that the path along which it has diverged from the older Hīnayānian Buddhist philosophy points in a Christian direction. Whereas the model sage according

to the Hīnayāna is the ascetic who has saved himself by extin-
guishing his self, the hero according to the Mahāyāna is the
aspirant to buddhahood who, like the Buddha Gautama, has voluntarily postponed his own entry into his rest in the unconscious,
passionless, will-less state of Nirvāna in order to save, not himself,
but his fellow living beings by guiding them along the path that he
himself has traversed.

While Christianity shares with a number of other religions
and philosophies the characteristic of being "historical" in its setting and its outlook, it has one central feature which it seems to
share only with Judaism, of which it is an offshoot, and with Islam,
which is another religion of Judaic origin. The Judaic religions'
distinctive mark is that they see the meaning of existence, and the
heart of religion, in personal encounters between human beings
and a God who is likewise a person (whatever else He may be besides); and they also agree with one another in believing that these
encounters take the form of historical acts and events in this
world—or, as a modern physical scientist would put it, on the face
of this planet. In the belief of these Judaic religions, God as well as
mankind is at work in history in this world, though this world is
only one part of the field of God's activity.

Their belief in God's epiphany in terrestrial history is the
ground for the significance that history has in the Judaic religions'
eyes. In the sight of the other historical religions and philosophies,
history does not have the absolute importance and value that it
must have for anyone who believes that it is one of God's chosen
fields of operation. The Confucian school, for example, treasures
the history of the classical period of the Chinese civilisation for the
utilitarian purpose for which an English barrister keeps a library of
law reports. They find in history a store-house of precedents to
serve as guides for current ethical and political practice. As for the
Hīnayānian Buddhist and the Hellenic philosophers, they could
not help being implicated in history by their pious veneration for
their historical human founders; but in their eyes man's historicity, like his sexuality, his mortality, and his exposure to physical and spiritual suffering, was one of the humiliating circumstances of unsophisticated human life from which every wise man
would do his best to liberate himself by cultivating philosophy. The
Greek and Indian philosophers' ideal standards of perfection,

which the humiliating facts of unsophisticated human life fell so far below, were unchangingness, deathlessness, and impassibility. These would be the characteristics of divinity, if God should prove to be a reality; and it was the business of philosophy to bring a spiritual *élite* of the human race as near as possible to attaining to this god-like state. In this disdainful withdrawal from a humiliating implication in the evils of unsophisticated human life, Hīnayānian Buddhism excelled the Hellenic philosophies in the intellectual clarity with which it perceived the consequences of its convictions, and in the moral courage with which it acted on its insight. Buddhism told its followers that the only effective way of getting rid of suffering was to get rid of consciousness and will.

The Buddhist philosophers' conclusion is, on a Christian view, as stultifying as it is courageous and correct on Buddhist premises; and here we come to a point in which Christianity seems, at least in Christian eyes, to be unique in differing even from its sister Judaic religions; for, on the touchstone of their attitude towards suffering, both Judaism and Islam seem to a Christian to be less akin to Christianity than they are to the Hellenic philosophies and to the Hīnayāna. The non-Christian Judaic religions seem to regard suffering simply as an evil to which God's miserable creatures are subject but from which Almighty God Himself is exempt; and, though neither of them declares that God is Power without adding that He is also Mercy and Compassion, neither Judaism nor Islam has entertained the idea that this divine compassion and mercy could move God, for the sake of His creatures' salvation, voluntarily to "empty Himself" of His power and expose Himself to the suffering to which His creatures are subject. The distinctive turn which Christianity seems, as Christians see it, to have given to the Judaic view of the nature of God and the character of His relations with human beings is the declaration that God is Love as well as Power; that this divine love has been manifested in an unique encounter between God and mankind in the shape of Christ's Incarnation and crucifixion; and that God's revelation of Himself as Love is more significant than His revelation of Himself as Power, though God's love (whatever Marcion may say) is so far from being incompatible with His omnipotence that the infiniteness of His power is the only plummet by which the infiniteness of His love can be fathomed. It will be seen that the characteristic and central belief of Christianity makes Christianity the historical religion *par excellence* (however vigorously Confucianism may dispute this claim); for this central belief—"to the Jews a stumbling-block, to the Greeks folly"—is that the human founder of the Christian Church is God Himself incarnate. And the Incarnation is an encounter between God and all men in which God does not intervene *de haut en bas,* like the *deus ex machina* who descends to produce the *dénouement* at the end of a Greek play without being affected by the tragedy of the human *dramatis personae.* In the Incarnation, so Christians believe, God has revealed His nature by making an epiphany in history in which He has humbled Himself by becoming one of these human actors in the tragedy, and has voluntarily suffered for the sins of others the pains of physical agony and the sharper spiritual pains of seeing, as a dying man, His mission on earth ending, as it must have seemed to His human mind, in failure.

What does history look like in the light of this central Christian belief? In the first place, a world that has not only been created by God but has also been the scene of God's suffering as a human actor on the stage of history must be an integral part of God's Kingdom. It cannot be just an unsuccessful experiment in creation which the Creator has ruthlessly scrapped after writing it off as a failure; and *a fortiori* it cannot be a realm of Chaos and Ancient Night altogether outside God's jurisdiction. If this world were not both an integral and a precious part of the Kingdom of God, God would not have redeemed it at the price which Christians believe that He has paid on account of His love for it. The world's need for redemption was evident before the preaching of the Gospel; the Greeks did not have to wait for Christianity to become aware of that. The belief which was new in Christianity, and which to Greek minds was a new folly, was the belief that the world was in fact redeemable and that God had now actually redeemed it through the Incarnation and passion of Christ. A world which had been the scene of that divine event was manifestly a battleground between Good and Evil, as the Iranian prophet Zarathustra had already declared this world to be; but, if Christianity was the truth, this must be a battleground which lay within God's Kingdom and a province which, though spiritually rebellious and cruelly devastated by the ravages of sin, must be as valuable as other provinces, inaccessible to human beings in this life, in which God's sovereignty had never been challenged. The Incarnation must be a guarantee of the value of this world in God's eyes—and consequently a guarantee that the tragedy of human life on Earth has a value for the human actors in it likewise.

If the Incarnation is evidence that this world has an intrinsic and an absolute value as the scene of the suffering through which God has shown His love for His creatures, it is at the same time an event which gives history not only a meaning but also a direction and a purpose; and this transfiguration of history by the Incarnation makes all the difference to our outlook on life, because it liberates us from the domination of a cyclical rhythm which runs through the fabric of the universe in our experience.

There are, of course, levels of existence on which this cyclic rhythm in the universe seems beneficent and reassuring. Ever since mankind became conscious, we have lived in faith that day will follow night and spring follow winter, and that each revolution of the year will bring with it new crops and new lambs; but our joy in the birth of a new generation is tempered on the human level by our grief at the death of their elders; and this grief is aggravated by a bewilderment at the discrepancy between the brevity of human life and our endowment with gifts of intellect and will whose potentialities so far out-range the staying-power of our physique. The dismay that this tragic discrepancy inspires in us is magnified when we face the truth that mortality is the fate, not only of individual men and women, but of mankind's supra-personal collective achievements, including institutions—arts, sciences, states, civilisations, and churches—whose longevity seems almost godlike by comparison with the brevity of their human makers' personal life-spans, yet which, in the event, have always proved, sooner or later, to share the mortality of the creatures that have made them. In this perspective, life does indeed look like a tale signifying nothing; and, when we train our telescope on the stellar universe, we feel the positive fright to which Pascal has confessed, at the spectacle of cosmic cycles whose immensity makes their vain repetitions all the more fatuous. When we think of an infinite series of an infinite host of nebulae each taking its aeon of aeons to make the same transit from primaeval gas to eventual cinders, and when we gaze, from the cramped surface of this planet, at the immense residue of physical nature's domain, which mankind has small hopes of ever subjugating by technological applications of the science through which this cosmos has been apprehended by the human intellect, we are almost constrained to fall back into the pre-scientific fallacy of personifying these cosmic powers and beholding them to be very malignant. On this astronomical scale the cyclic rhythm in the universe becomes both terrifying and repulsive; for the anthropocentric view of the universe into which we have been deluded by our terrestrial technology is here brutally refuted by the science of which our technology is a by-product. The Incarnation liberates us from these alien and demonic powers and principalities by assuring us that, in virtue of God's suffering and death on this infinitesimally trivial speck of dust, the whole physical universe is theocentric; for, if God is Love, man can feel himself at home in any environment in which God is in power.

In the third place—and this is perhaps the brightest of all the new light thrown on history by Christianity—Christ's passion gives a meaning to human suffering that can reconcile us to the tragedy of our life on Earth; for it assures us that this tragedy is neither the meaningless and pointless evil that it has been declared to be by the Buddha and by Epicurus, nor the inexorable punishment for inveterate sin that is its explanation according to non-Christian schools of Judaic theology. The light thrown by the Passion on suffering is the revelation that suffering is necessary because it is a necessary means of redemption and creation under the temporal and temporary conditions of life on Earth. Suffering is neither an evil in itself nor a good in itself, nor meaningless in itself nor significant in itself. It is a means to an end, and its purpose is to give human beings an opportunity of sharing in Christ's work and thereby realising their potentiality of being God's children in virtue of being Christ's brethren.

If Christianity throws this light on history, what light does history throw on Christianity? History's light on Christianity has been notably increased in recent times by two extensions of our historical knowledge. In the first place, the recent unification of the whole habitable world through "the annihilation of distance" by modern Western technology has made it possible today, for the first time in history, for mankind to pool all its local historical records. In the second place, the recent discoveries of archaeology have recovered for us the lost record of temporarily forgotten passages of human history, while geology and cosmology have carried the history of mankind back to before the dawn of civilisation; the history of life on earth back to before the emergence of the human race; the history of the planet back to before the epiphany of life, and the history of the physical cosmos back to before the generation of this planet, this solar system, and this galaxy. What is more, these vast new vistas of the past have been matched by no less vast vistas of a future.

In this perspective, Christianity in company with the other higher religions—for, on this titanic time-scale, all the higher religions are virtually coeval—appears to have come into the world only the other day. Even if we measure the age of the higher religions, not by that of Christianity, but by the age of the oldest representatives of the species—say the worship of Tammuz and Ishtar and the worship of Osiris and Isis, which made their first appearance as long ago as the third millennium B.C.—we find that all the higher religions are things of yesterday compared even with the civilisations, and still more so when compared with the antiquity of primitive man and with the far longer time-span of pre-human history. This is a revolution in our vista of history that has overtaken us since the dawn of modern Western science; for in the darkness before the dawn, little more than three centuries ago, Archbishop Ussher, diligently studying, combining, and taking at their face value, as revealed truth, the chronological data in the Bible, calculated that the world must have been created in the year 4004 B.C. The revolution brought about by science's subsequent overthrow of Ussher's initial date in favour of an antiquity of an altogether different order of magnitude is not simply a revolutionary revision of a chronological reckoning; it is also a revolution in our idea of the historical relation between the beginning of the Christian era and our own age. In Voltaire's time, before the advent of geology, it seemed to be a very obvious and very damaging criticism of Christianity to point out that by that time Christianity had been in existence for the best part of two thousand years without having so far succeeded (so its critics could plausibly maintain) in making any appreciable difference to the general climate of moral and spiritual life in long-since nominally Christian countries. The progress of science has now turned the laugh against these would-be scientific critics of Christianity by showing that the time-scale on which their argument was based was fantastically wide of the mark. These disbelievers in revelation had in fact inadvertently been taking their stand on a chronology that had been constructed from scriptural materials on the warrant of a Christian belief that the Scriptures were divinely inspired. According to Archbishop Ussher's chronology, the interval between the beginning of the Christian era and, say, the year A.D. 1751 did, indeed, amount to more than 34.364 per cent of the total length of time that, by this date, had elapsed since the world's genesis on a biblical computation; and, on this time-scale, those first 1751 years of the Christian era might reasonably be reckoned as a long time for Christianity to have taken in producing a so far hardly appreciable effect. But on our post-Voltairean scientific time-scale the first 1951 years of the Christian era have to be reckoned as so infinitesimally brief a period that it would be difficult to make so minute an interval visible on a cosmic time-chart, drawn to scale, without having to make the chart itself quite unmanageably too large for the use of a standard-size human reader. If we can place ourselves, in imagination, at the standpoint of a historian compiling a handy select chronology of the principal events of history up to date, at a date, say, a million million years later than A.D. 1951, we may venture today to guess that our distant successor will be likely still to give the date of the epiphany of Christianity a place in his table; but if we could borrow H. G. Wells's time-machine and look over that distant future chronologist's shoulder we might be startled to find that the next entry in his table after the birth of Jesus Christ in 4 B.C. was some event in, let us say, the eleventh or twelfth millennium of the Christian era, which, in this year A.D. 1951, is still utterly beyond our chronological horizon. On this hypothetical but rationally credible distant future time-scale, the time-interval between our own day and the date of Christ's life and ministry on Earth would be only infinitesimally greater than zero. If we can accustom ourselves to thinking on this scale, we shall find ourselves thinking of the Incarnation, not as something that happened yesterday, but as something that has been happening "right now"—to use an apt archaic American idiom.

When we have digested this idea that the advent of Christianity and the other higher religions is, not ancient history, but contemporary, and indeed current, history, we may go on to enquire whether history can tell us why all the representatives of this group of religions chose the particular fraction of a cosmic second that they did choose for making their virtually contemporaneous first appearance. This historic minim of time is comprised, as we have seen, between the third millennium B.C., which saw the epiphany of the worships of Tammuz and Ishtar and of Osiris and Isis, and the seventh century of the Christian era, which saw the epiphany of Islam. On the cosmic time-scale these three millennia amount to no more than the twinkling of an eye. Why (to speak in old-fashioned religious language) did God choose precisely that moment in history for giving mankind this spiritual enlightenment? This is a question to which history suggests an answer if we take as our clue the Christian intuition of the pre-Christian Hellenic poet Aeschylus that, on the plane of our spiritual experience (as contrasted with our science and technology), "learning comes through suffering."

With this Aeschylean clue in our hands we shall find that every one of the philosophies and higher religions has made its appearance in the world at a time and place at which mankind's perennial suffering has been intensified by the harrowing experience of living through the breakdown and disintegration of a mundane civilisation. The worship of Tammuz and Ishtar came to flower among the ruins of a Sumerian civilisation; the worship of Osiris and Isis among the ruins of Egyptian civilisation; the Buddhist philosophy among the ruins of an Indian civilisation; Judaism and Zoroastrianism among the ruins of a Babylonian and a Syrian civilisation; the Greek philosophies, Mithraism, and Christianity among the ruins of an Hellenic civilisation; and, if we were to follow out this historical enquiry into details for which there is no room in this essay, we should find that the circumstances in which the Mahāyàna and Islam came to birth were the same.

When once we have observed the fact that the falls of civilisations have been the occasions of the rises of higher religions, the psychological explanation of this historical fact is not far to seek. These occasions offered opportunities for spiritual truths to gain access to human minds and for divine commandments and precepts to gain a hold on human hearts because, in these particularly tragic passages of history, hearts and minds had been opened for the entry of the Holy Spirit by their bitter disillusionment over the collapse of mundane institutions whose imposing appearance of durability and grandeur had moved their human makers, beneficiaries, and servants to put their trust in them and to devote their lives to their service. Such disillusionment, born of suffering, with the achievements of this world is, of course, in itself no more than a negative predisposing condition for the reception of divine grace; and the occasion may remain barren or may bring forth what, in Christian eyes, is Dead Sea fruit, in the shape of a philosophy which draws from suffering only the lesson that it is expedient to get rid of suffering even at the price of having, in the process, also to divest oneself of will and consciousness. Yet this disillusionment with the vanities of this world is also the experience that has inspired other suffering human souls to respond to a call to have life, and have it more abundantly, by putting their treasure in a Kingdom of God that is to come on Earth as well as in Heaven.

If history has thrown this light upon the epiphany of Christianity and the other higher religions, has it also thrown light on their future by opening up a vista of the future that is as immeasurably long as history's vista of the past?

Our modern science's expectation of an immensely long future for human life and human institutions on Earth is, of course, in sharp contradiction with the expectations of the first generation of Christians, and with the beliefs on which those expectations were founded. The primitive Christian Church held the belief, inherited by Archbishop Ussher, that the world was not more than a few thousand years old; and against the background of this belief they cherished an expectation and a hope which, by Ussher's time, had been disappointed by the Church's experience in the meanwhile, though the Church had not then, and has not now, ever explicitly abandoned the original Christian outlook. The members of the primitive Church took Christ's coming to signify that their generation had been born at the end of time; and they lived in the hope and expectation that the Second Coming of Christ was so imminent that some among them would live to see it. As time went on, however, the Church, without ever repudiating the doctrine that the Last Things might descend on the world at any moment, began to act as if it had to prepare itself for a long future of militancy in this world. The action implying this tacit shift of the

Church's chronological horizon into a more distant future was the far-sighted building up of systematic Christian institutions. We have already noticed, in passing, that, of all human institutions, the ecclesiastical have so far been apt to be the longest lived, and a student of living human institutions in the twentieth century of the Christian era would probably single out the Roman Catholic Church as the corporate body which habitually took the longest views in making decisions of policy. By comparison with the Vatican (our observer would probably pronounce), contemporary governments, firms, trades unions, academies, and laboratories were all living from hand to mouth. In other words, the Christian Church had been acting on the unformulated hypothesis that mankind had an immensely long time on Earth ahead of it for some seventeen centuries before his hypothesis received the *imprimatur* of modern Western science.

Science has now pronounced that the survival of life on this planet will continue to be a physical possibility for perhaps a million million years beyond the present date; but, like the Christian Church, this post-Christian science has taken action that runs counter to its own expectations and hopes; for science has gone into action in technology, and technology has placed in human hands (if science is not mistaken in some of her most recent pronouncements) the means of bringing life on earth to an end as soon, at as short notice, as completely and as inexorably as God was expected, according to an old-fashioned Christian mythology, to act when He gave the signal for the sounding of the Last Trump.

There is, though, one crucial point of difference between a traditional Christian expectation and the latest scientific bulletin; and in this point science strikes a more Christian note than the Apocalypse; for while, according to the Apocalypse, the future sudden liquidation of World, Life, and Time will be an act of God in which mankind will have no say, science has proclaimed that this irretrievable physical catastrophe will come, if it does come, through mankind's wantonly bringing it upon themselves by suicidal human action. In thus pronouncing that the wages of sin is death, science is speaking with an authentic Christian voice; but, if Christianity is to be given a hearing again, there is, of course, more than this to be said. Christianity will go on to declare the still more appalling truth that human nature is prone to choose death instead of life by choosing evil instead of good whenever the human heart follows its own devices; but Christianity's last word will be that mankind has nevertheless been given a chance of salvation from the nemesis of its own sinful acts in being enabled, in virtue of Christ's passion, to seek this salvation by praying for God's grace.

THE NATURE
OF HISTORY
AND CULTURE

HERBERT BUTTERFIELD

Are there laws or regularities in history, and if so, what are they? Secular analytic philosophy has turned the question over incessantly and come up with different answers of yes and no. Marxist philosophy has no doubt there are historical laws and knows rather clearly what they are. Christian philosophy has usually held that there are such laws or at least regularities, based on the notion that God has created a reality of order, sometimes called the natural law. How such natural law relates to God's Providence and to human freedom Christians have never agreed upon.

Herbert Butterfield (b. 1900), as a historian, comes to the matter from the bottom up, so to speak, and gives a good introduction to the topic. He states his position as an affirmation which he does not work out in detail. There are, he believes, three different and compatible ways or levels of looking at an event in history. Each one tells us something completely true about the event, and can be taken by itself. If, however, we add a second way, then the third, our understanding of the event becomes more profound.

At the first level, history is the result of human decisions and actions which are taken in freedom and for which people are held responsible. Biography opens this way up to us. Looked at on a different level, these free actions are perceived as part of longer-range processes and tendencies which are "in a certain sense reducible to law." We can detect these processes in retrospect by means of historical, scientific examination, carried out with Christian charity. At another level, which Christian religion discloses, history can be seen as the action of the Providence of God "in whom we live and move and have our being." God is at work in our freedom and the larger processes of history judging our sin and blessing our good works. This we see especially in the conjunctures of history where our individual decisions pass out of our hands and the results of history transcend our plans.

God in History

Of all the factors which have operated to the disadvantage of religion and the undermining of the religious sense in recent centuries, the most damaging has been the notion of an absentee God who might be supposed to have created the universe in the first place, but who is then assumed to have left it to run as a piece of clockwork, so that he is outside our lives, outside history itself, unable to affect the course of things and hidden away from us by an impenetrable screen. This idea has had unfortunate effects upon religion and religious life even within the bosom of the Church itself. It has helped to discourage many people who were not really unfriendly to religion—helped to push them away on to the fringe of Christianity and into the position of friendly neutrals, sitting on the fence, but not quite convinced that there is anything very much that they can do about religion. Some of them believe in God but, since he is an absentee God, shut out from the events of this world, he might as well not be there—one can't really have a deep or a vivid kind of religion in relation to such a God. Indeed such a God does harm by giving people a comfortable general feeling of optimism about the universe, combined with a feeling that there is not very much point in troubling oneself about religion. And if God cannot play a part in life, that is to say, in history, then neither can human beings have very much concern about him or very real relationships with him. Nothing is more important for the cause of religion at the present day than that we should recover the sense and consciousness of the Providence of God—a Providence that

From *Steps to Christian Understanding,* edited by R. J. W. Bevan and published by Oxford University Press, London (1958), pp. 105–21. Reprinted by permission of the publisher.

acts not merely by a species of remote control but as a living thing, operating in all the details of life—working at every moment, visible in every event. Without this you cannot have any serious religion, any real walking with God, any genuine prayer, any authentic fervour and faith.

It is clear that one of the reasons why people have lost their way in regard to this question is due to the effects of science, the effects of what I should call popular science rather than of the scientific mind or the scientific method as such. Partly this is the result of the fact that men have forgotten how the modern scientific method came into existence and the terms on which it came to be developed—have forgotten just what are the limits of what can be achieved by observing a blade of grass more and more microscopically or by looking at the stars through bigger and bigger telescopes. Partly people are over-awed by the things which we call "laws of nature," thinking of them as laws in the sense that Acts of Parliament are laws, when rather they are hypotheses—they represent our mode of understanding nature, our ways of formulating to ourselves the movements and processes that we observe to be taking place in the universe. And, if we make a mistake about this, our view of life and the world is apt to be very mechanical. In the old days they would teach musical composition by the use of mechanical rules, and the student had to do exercise after exercise until he had mastered the rules. The rules themselves were all taken from an analysis of the works of successful composers—it was possible to show that on the whole successful music did in fact conform to these particular rules. Everybody knew, however, that the great composers actually writing music never wrote it to rule in this way—the rules were things which you discovered when you subjected good music to mechanical analysis afterwards. It would be a wild error to imagine that the composer created his music in the way in which students analysed it after it had been written. And similarly one must not imagine that God created the universe in the way in which we analyse it—more likely he resembled the composer who, we might say, was just out to create a beautiful thing. Above all one of the effects of this misunderstanding of the scientific method has been to give people a too mechanical and too abstract idea of God—one which fails to do justice to his fullness and richness. In particular we forget those significant words which St. Paul declared to the men of Athens when they, also, were worshipping an unknown God, too remote, too far removed from human life and history. St. Paul said: "He giveth to all life, and breath, and all things. . . . he is not far from every one of us; for in him we live and move and have our being." If we grasp those words properly and see all the world lying in the hollow of God's hand—see ourselves as living and moving only in him—then it becomes less difficult to imagine how intimately all Nature and History lie in the Providence of God.

Concerning the events that take place in nature and in history and in life there are three ways that we can have of looking at them—it might be said perhaps that we can imagine them at three different levels and with three different kinds of analysis. And because they are taken at different levels they can all be true at the same time, just as you could have three different shapes of the same piece of wood if you took three different cross-sections. If you go on a journey, and at the end of it I ask: Why are you here now? you may answer: "Because I wanted to come"; or you may say: "Because a railway-train carried me here"; or you may say: "Because it is the will of God"; and all these things may be true at the same time—true on different levels. So with history: we may say at the first level of analysis that men's actions make history—and men have free will—they are responsible for the kind of history that they make. But, then, secondly, at a different level, we find that history, like nature itself, represents a realm of law—its events are in a certain sense reducible to laws. However unpredictable history may be before it has happened it is capable of rational explanation once it has happened; so much so that it becomes difficult sometimes to imagine that it ever had been possible for anything else to have happened or for history to have taken any other course. Now these two things are difficult enough to reconcile in themselves—first of all the free will of human beings and secondly the reign of law in history. But they are reconcilable—and historians can discover large processes taking place in society for a hundred years to produce a French Revolution and an Industrial Revolution; and yet at the same time the historian will treat the French revolutionaries themselves or the nineteenth-century capitalists as subjects of free will, capable of making one decision rather than another, and even blamable for certain decisions that they actually made. We can even work out the laws and conditioning circumstances which have made the twentieth century an epoch of colossal world-wars; and those laws are so clear that some people were predicting their ultimate results nearly a hundred years ago. Some people in the nineteenth century, analysing the processes that were taking place in their time, predicted that the twentieth century would be a period of stupendous warfare and of still more prolonged war-strain. Yet, looking at the story from a different angle, we do not say that nobody is to blame for the outbreak of war in Europe in July 1914. The men who made disastrous decisions in July 1914 are still responsible and blamable for the decisions that they made.

But besides the freedom of the human will and besides the reign of law in history, there is a further factor that is operative in life and in the story of the centuries—one which in a sense includes these two other things—namely the Providence of God, in whom we live and move and have our being. And in part the Providence of God works through these two other things—it is Providence which puts us in a world where we run all the risks that follow from human free will and responsibility. It is Providence which puts us into a world that has its regularities and laws—a world therefore that we can do something with, provided we learn about the laws and the regularities of it. It would be wrong for us to picture God as interfering with the motion of the planets, stopping one of them arbitrarily, hurrying another of them along by sheer caprice—for we cannot imagine God as working by mere caprice. Indeed, centuries ago (before modern science had come into existence) men were looking for the laws and regularities in nature because they felt sure that God would not act by mere caprice. God is in all the motion of the planets—just as he is in all the motions of history. He is not interfering with the stars in their rotations—he is carrying them round all the time and in him they live and move and have their being. In his Providence he continues the original work of Creation and keeps the stars alight, maintains his world continually; we ought to feel that if he stopped breathing it would vanish into nothingness. It is like the case of the people you see in dreams—when you stop dreaming they no longer exist; and when God stops his work of creating and maintaining this universe we ourselves and all this fine pageantry of stars and planets simply cease to exist any longer. Those people are right who praise God every morning for the rising of the sun, and who see in this not merely a Providence which operated at the creation of the solar system millions of years ago, but evidence of his continuing care, his ever-present activity. It is not meaningless to praise God for the coming of the spring or for bringing us safely through to another day. It is because God is in everything, in every detail of life, that people so easily think that they can cancel him out. The world comes to do its thinking as though he did not exist.

Now that is the real affirmation that we as Christians have to make about life before the world at the present day—a world that is like something derelict and disinherited because it has lost touch with a really present God, with the real immediacy of God. It means that the Providence of God is at work in the downfall of Nazism, in the judgements that come on the British Empire for its own sins, in the present prosperity of the United States, and in our own individual daily experiences. That is what we see with the higher and more royal parts of our minds, when we make our highest judgements about life—our real valuations about events. And that is what we ought to say when we have our national joys, or our national victories or our national problems or our national dangers. We have to say: Providence has put us in this predicament—what can it mean? what moral good can we get out of it? what does God intend us to do when he puts this problem before us? what sins did we commit as a nation to merit this response from God and from history?

For let us make sure of one thing—in the long run there are only two alternative views about life or about history. Here is a fact which was realized thousands of years ago and it is still as true as ever. Either you trace everything back in the long run to sheer blind Chance, or you trace everything to God. Some of you might say that there is a third alternative—namely that everything just happens through the operation of the laws of nature. But that is not an explanation at all and the mind cannot rest there, for such a thesis does not tell us where the laws themselves can have come from. Either we must say that there is a mind behind the laws of nature—there is a God who ordered things in that particular way—or we must say that in the infinity of time all possible combinations of events are exhausted by the blind work of Chance, which produces amongst all the planets of the sky at any rate one where vegetation is possible and where animal life develops, and where in human beings matter itself acquires the quality of mind. There was one historian who outshone all others in regarding history as a science and historical events as subject to law. He was the Regius Professor of History in my University, a very famous scholar, Professor Bury, and in his Inaugural Lecture he stated in its most rigid form the scientific view of the course of history. But as he grew older he became greatly puzzled by the fact that he could explain why a Prime Minister happened to be walking down a street, and he could explain the scientific laws which loosened a tile on a roof so that it fell down at a particular moment; but he could not explain the conjuncture of the two—the fact that the Prime Minister should just be there to be killed by the falling tile—and yet it was just this *conjuncture* of the two things which was the most important feature of the story. What was more significant still—he found that all history was packed with these conjunctures—you can hardly consider anything in history without coming across them—so that this rigid believer in the firmness of scientific laws in history turned into the arch-prophet of the theory that Chance counted most of all. In his view the whole of the world's history was altered, for example, by the shape of Cleopatra's nose. Similarly he said that the Roman Empire fell in the West because of a handful of separate events which unfortunately happened to be taking place at the same time. Any single one of these events could be explained and reduced to law, but it was their conjuncture that mattered, and this Bury could only account for as the effect of Chance. Indeed when you go on analysing historical events further and further you find that the final problem of all—the really big thing that you have to solve—is this problem of the conjuncture. You can explain why each separate thing happened; but the important thing is the combination—the Prime Minister's path crossing the path of the tile at a given moment. If Hitler had been executed in 1925 or if Churchill had been killed in the Boer War we can be sure that all our history in this present year would have been different, though we should still have been able to work out scientifically the laws which help to explain how things came to happen in that way. Chance itself, or some equivalent of it, seems to have its part to play in historical explanation, therefore. And the historical process is much more subtle and flexible than most people seem to understand.

So, when we are considering historical events, there are three ways in which we can look at them. The first I would call the biographical way—we can see human beings taking their actions and decisions and operating with a certain amount of freedom so that they can be held responsible for the decisions they make; and in this sense men do make their own history and can blame themselves when their history goes wrong. The Christian would always have to be very emphatic about the free will of men and their moral responsibility—more emphatic I believe than anybody else; and he must come to the conclusion that all men are sinners—even all the statesmen of 1914 would have been wiser if they had had less egotism, less fear for their vested interests. The second way of looking at historical events is what I should really call the historical way rather than the biographical one—because it is the scientific examination of the deep forces and tendencies in history—the tendencies for example which had been making for war in Europe for fifty years before 1914, almost before the statesmen of 1914 were born—deep forces and tendencies which were working in fact for generations to help to make the twentieth century an era of colossal warfare. In this sense there is a part of men's history which the men themselves do not make—a history-making that goes on over their heads—helping to produce a French Revolution or an Industrial Revolution or a great war. And in this aspect of history we are much less inclined to blame the human beings concerned, and we see how much we have to be sorry for them. A Christian again must be most emphatic in his demand for this kind of history, this scientific kind of history, which examines the deep processes behind wars and revolutions and even tries to reduce them to law. And here is the great opportunity for Christian charity in history—here is why the Christian has to go over the past making no end of allowances for people—no end of explanations—we might almost say that he cannot read history without being a little sorry for everybody. So you have free will in history, and the statesmen of 1914 are blamable for unloosing the horses of war. But also you have the operation of laws and processes in history; and the statesmen of 1914 are not as blamable as they might have seemed at first sight, perhaps not more blamable than you yourself might have been if you had been in the same historical predicament—perhaps not more blamable than you yourself have often been at moments when the disaster was only reduced because you did not happen to be a statesman responsible for the welfare of millions of people. Thirdly, however, you have to think of another aspect. Either you must say that Chance is one of the greatest factors in history and that the whole of the story is in the last resort the product of blind Chance, or you must say that the whole of it is in the hands of Providence—in him we live and move and have our being—even the free will of men and even the operation of law in history, even these are within Providence itself and under it. But if you say that it is Providence, you must not imagine that Providence can act merely in a chancy and capricious way— Providence is acting in all that part of history which is subject to law as well as in all that part of history which men otherwise tend to attribute to Chance. And if you hold this view, then there is a further way of looking at the war of 1914—you must regard that war as itself a judgement of God on certain evils of our civilization which could not be rooted out in any other way. And if you look at the question in this light you can even discover what those evils actually were. Indeed we know what the moral diseases of the pre-1914 world were, which led to the outbreak of a European war.

Of course it is possible to read history and study the course of centuries without seeing God in the story at all; just as it is possible for men to live their lives in the present day without seeing that God has any part to play. I could not go to people and say that if they studied nearly two thousand years of European history this would be bound to make them Christian; I could not say that such a stretch of history would prove to any impartial person that Providence underlies the whole human drama. You can learn about the ups-and-downs of one state and another in one century and another, you can learn about the rise of vast empires and the growth of big organizations and the evolution of democracy or the development of modern science—and all this will not show you God in history if you have not found God in your daily life. When we seek to know how God is revealed in history we do not make a chart or a diagram of all the centuries and try to show to what future great world-empires are tending or to what end great human organizations are moving. Russia, the United States, England—these are only names on a map, and if we know anything we know that some time in the far future men will be asking what was this thing

called England, just as we ask about Assyria and Tyre and Sidon—
some day the archaeologists will be rummaging amongst the ruins
of London just as we excavate for Nineveh and hunt for ancient
Troy. If we wish to know how God works in history we shall not
find it by looking at the charts of all the centuries—we have to
begin by seeing how God works in our individual lives and then we
expand this on to the scale of the nation, we project it on to the
scale of mankind. Only those who have brought God home to
themselves in this way will be able to see him at work in history,
and without this we might be tempted to see history as a tale told
by an idiot, a product of blind Chance. If a great misfortune comes
on us we may just feel how unlucky we are when compared with
all our other friends who had previously seemed to be in a condition similar to ours. We need not adopt this attitude, however;
there are some people who bring their sins home to themselves
and say that this is a chastisement from God; or they say that God
is testing them, trying them in the fire, fitting them for some more
important work that he has for them to do. Those who adopt this
view in their individual lives will easily see that it enlarges and
projects itself on to the scale of all history; it affects our interpretation of national misfortunes as well as private ones. And when we
reach this point in the argument we realize that we are adopting
the biblical interpretation of history.

The way that God reveals himself in history is in fact the great
theme of the Bible itself. And if you want to ask: "How does God
reveal himself in ordinary secular history?" then it is exactly this
which is the particular theme of the Old Testament. The Old Testament is the history of a people whose fate and vicissitudes were
uncommonly like those of most other states—even modern ones. If
the history was peculiar, it was perhaps in being worse and more
violent than that of other states; for the ancient Hebrews lived in a
tiny country with vast empires rising on either side of them and
they retained their political independence only for a moment, only
for a tiny fraction of their history. Afterwards, down till the twentieth century their land remained under the heel of vast empires,
the Assyrian, the Babylonian, the Persian, the Roman, the Arabian,
and the Turkish Empire in turn. Where they differed from other
nations was in the way in which they interpreted their history—in
fact it was their way of interpreting their history that was their

chief contribution to the development of civilization. Because of that, they are remembered today and hold a high place in the world's story, even though they were no bigger than Wales and retained their political independence for so short a period.

They saw God as being essentially the God of History, and the result was that first and foremost they regarded history as based on the Promise. And although they took this Promise in a purely nationalistic way, all Christians must regard history as based finally on the Promise—it is never permitted to a Christian to despair of Providence. But the Children of Israel sinned, and theirs is the only national history I ever remember reading which proclaimed the sinfulness of the nation—proclaimed its own nation even to be worse than the other pagan nations round about them. And because of this, history at the second stage of the argument appeared to this people in its aspect as Judgement. When colossal national disaster came upon them they saw the tragedy as the effect of a Judgement from Heaven. At the next stage, however, they saw that God's Judgement does not cancel his Promise—if God judged the nation it was only in order to save it—for God is Love and it is always dangerous to think of the power of God without also thinking of his love. Even when their distresses were at their greatest and God seemed to be chastising them most severely, they came to what I think is the ultimate picture of God in History—God looking upon this world of cupidity and cross-purposes, of violence and of conflict—and pulling upon it like a magnet—drawing men with his loving-kindness. Judgement might fall heavily upon them but they were undefeatable in one respect. They saw that the Judgement did not cancel the Promise.

The Children of Israel had actually come in sight of the Promised Land—their spies had actually entered it and brought samples of its rich fruits—when they met an unexpected enemy whom God told them they must fight before they could actually enter the Promised Land—and they rebelled against him for putting them to this further trial. God brought us out of the land of Egypt because he hated us, they said—he brought us here only to entrap us. Let us go back to the land of Egypt, back to the House of Bondage. Let us make a captain and let us return to Egypt, they said. And God was so angry that he said they should not see the Land of Promise—their carcasses should fall in the wilderness. But in spite

of the Judgement he kept his Promise to the Children of Israel—
for though these people themselves were not to enter the land of
Canaan, he decreed that their children should come into it later.
He did not take hope away from the world.

And much later than that, when in the days of the prophets
Judgement came upon the Kingdoms that the Children of Israel
had established, and Jerusalem itself was razed to the ground—
still once again the Judgement did not cancel the Promise—God
said that he would make a new covenant with his people. He said
that even his sending them into exile was meant for their further
good—and we know that these particular experiences deepened
the religion of the Children of Israel in many remarkable ways, so
that this period of defeat and anguish was one of their great creative moments. Just at this time they gave a new development to
the history of religion and religious thought. It proved to be an immortal moment for them.

But even now they sinned through excessive nationalism and
worldly-mindedness, and when God made a new Covenant with
them, they took it to mean a promise of new worldly success, victory in war, glory for their kingdom, dominion on earth. After this
date the ancient Hebrews committed some terrible and wilful mistakes because they believed that God was to be on their side in
battle and was to bring their nation to the top of the world—they
even believed that the promised Messiah was to be a warrior-
leader, a military saviour. Again their punishment was terrible and
tragedy after tragedy came upon their endeavours; but the Judgement did not cancel the Promise. The trouble was that God's
Promise to them was a higher thing than they knew, a better thing
than they had imagined. They had been construing God's Promise
in too worldly a way. And, though they were wrong, the Promise
was not cancelled.

The greatest of the Old Testament Jews came to realize that
God's Promise was not one of luxury and worldly success—it was a
Promise that the nation should have a mission—a mission that
should give meaning to its very disasters—and it was through that
mission that it was to have a great role in history, an immortal
name amongst men. Its mission was to teach the nations of the
world about God—to spread to the rest of mankind the special revelation it had had—the knowledge of God as revealed in history.

Through the very sufferings of Israel the world was to be carried to a higher religious life. It was the final mark of their mission that Christ was to come into the world as a member of this stricken, oppressed subject-nation—a Messiah who was to bring them greater glory and fame, a greater place in history than any warrior-leader ever could have done. It was a sign of the blindness of even this nation at the crucial moment that it rejected the Messiah when the Messiah actually came. That is the history of a nation whose stories of violence and conflict, treachery and war, of world-liness and cupidity, could be told just like the story of any other nation. The one difference was that the ancient Jews interpreted their history differently and saw the hand of God in it—they had the same experiences as other nations but they turned those experiences into spiritual experiences and because of that their history did become different—because of that they achieved creative things. For the greatest triumph of spirit over matter is when people can turn even their defeats and distresses into a creative moment like that.

We must imagine Providence as doing the best that the wilfulness of men allows it to do. For all of us History is the Promise and we need never despair—but it is a Promise punctuated by acts of Judgement. Even the great disasters of history, like the Jewish Exile, or the downfall of the Roman Empire, or the Norman Conquest of England can turn out to appear in history as a colossal benefit to mankind, and Providence can draw even good out of evil. It can even use our past sins to serve its future purposes. The Judgement of God may come upon an old world only to make way for a new one. Perhaps it is the only way in which on occasion the world in general can be induced to rise higher.

KARL BARTH

Karl Barth (1886–1968), professor at Basle, and the most influential theologian of our century, comes to the question of philosophy of history from the top down. His emphasis is all upon God. "Christ is the absolutely new from above; the way, the truth, and the life of God among men," he proclaimed prophetically in 1919. His monumental *Church Dogmatics* (13 volumes, 1936–69) elaborates this confession of the primacy of God. His is a neoorthodox alternative to the then prevailing emphases on immanentism, historicism, social action, and the idea of progress.

His views on Providence and philosophy of history are indicative of his whole line of thought. What matters to Christians, says Barth, is that God is the Lord of history and that the whole of history, and its details, "proceeds under the fatherly care of God the Creator, whose will is done." The history of God's glory "takes place in, with and under the history of creation." It is a hidden history. No human conception of the process of history, not even a Christian view of history, has more than very limited worth. Not our philosophies of history, but the *belief* in Providence gives a light on our path so that we may see something of the hidden history of God's will and purpose in specific events and relationships.

Barth does not rule out the task of studying a philosophy of history; he merely puts it in its humble place. His attitude toward philosophy of history is summarized by his comment in 1958 on the new quest for the historical Jesus—he does not think it impossible or unnecessary, but it is "a search in which I now as before prefer not to participate."

The Christian Belief in Providence

THE DOCTRINE OF PROVIDENCE, ITS BASIS AND FORM

The doctrine of providence deals with the history of created being as such, in the sense that in every respect and in its whole span this proceeds under the fatherly care of God the Creator, whose will is done and is to be seen in His election of grace, and therefore in the history of the covenant between Himself and man, and therefore in Jesus Christ.

1. The Concept of Divine Providence

. . . The simple meaning of the doctrine of providence may thus be summed up in the statement that in the act of creation God the Creator as such has associated Himself with His creature as such as the Lord of its history, and is faithful to it as such. God the Creator co-exists with His creature, and so His creature exists under the pre-supposition, and its implied conditions, of the co-existence of its Creator. God does this as His free will normative in its creation, and His wisdom, goodness and power therein displayed, remain the same. He does it as He is always to the creature the One He was when it did not exist and came into being, as He continually acts as such towards and with the creature which He has called to life, as He sovereignly exercises His lordship over His

Reprinted by permission of T. & T. Clark Limited from *Church Dogmatics*, III, Part 3 (1960). The original chapter title is "The Creator and His Creature."

work and possession in new acts and revelations of His free will, wisdom, goodness and power, and therefore as He causes the history of the creature to be the history of His own glory. He does it as—far from leaving the creature to itself and its own law or freedom, its dissatisfaction or self-satisfaction—He causes it to share in His own glory, namely by the fact that it may serve Him in His immediate presence and under His immediate guardianship and direction, thus fulfilling its own meaning and purpose, having its own honour and existing to its own joy. Hence whatever may take place in the history of the creature, and however this may appear from the standpoint of its own law and freedom, it never can nor will escape the lordship of its Creator. Whatever occurs, whatever it does and whatever happens to it, will take place not only in the sphere and on the ground of the lordship of God, not only under a kind of oversight and final disposal of God, and not only generally in His direct presence, but concretely, in virtue of his directly effective will to preserve, under His direct and superior co-operation and according to His immediate direction. In this history, therefore, we need not expect turns and events which have nothing to do with His lordship and are not directly in some sense acts of His lordship. This Lord is never absent, passive, non-responsible or impotent, but always present, active, responsible and omnipotent. He is never dead, but always living; never sleeping, but always awake; never uninterested, but always concerned; never merely waiting in any respect, but even where He seems to wait, even where He permits, always holding the initiative. In this consists His co-existence with the creature. This is the range of the fact that in the act of making it He has associated Himself with the creature. He co-exists with it actively, in an action which never ceases and does not leave any loopholes. And so the creature co-exists with Him as the reality distinct from Him, and in its own appropriate law and freedom, as He precedes it at every turn in His freedom of action and with His work—He its Creator, who as such must no less necessarily precede it than it must follow Him as His creature, and be directly upheld by Him in its own existence, and stand under His direct and superior co-ordination, and be directly ruled by Him. Again, it is the majestic freedom of the Creator in face of His creature which is as such the guarantee of the faithfulness and constancy with which He is over and with it. . . .

2. *The Christian Belief in Providence*

Belief in God's providence is the practical recognition that things are as we have said. It is the joy of the confidence and the willingness of the obedience grounded in this reality and its perception. In the belief in providence the creature understands the Creator as the One who has associated Himself with it in faithfulness and constancy as this sovereign and living Lord, to precede, accompany and follow it, preserving, co-operating and overruling, in all that it does and all that happens to it. And in the belief in providence the creature understands itself as what it is in relation to its Creator, namely, as upheld, determined and governed in its whole existence in the world by the fact that the Creator precedes it every step of the way in living sovereignty, so that it has only to follow. And in the belief in providence this does not have the character of idle speculation, just as God's providence is not the idle onlooking of a divine spectator, but takes practical shape in the fact that the creature which enjoys this recognition may always and in every respect place itself under the guidance of its Creator, recognise its higher right, and give it its gratitude and praise. . . .

In the light of this statement several sharp delimitations are indispensable.

1. The Christian belief in providence is faith in the strict sense of the term, and this means first that it is a hearing and receiving of the Word of God. The truth that God rules, and that the history of existent creation in its given time is also a history of His glory, is no less inaccessible and inconceivable, no less hard for man to grasp, than the truth of the origin of creation in the will and power of the Creator. In regard to the former there is as little to discover, comprehend and maintain, as little to conceive and postulate, as little room for pious or impious, practical or theoretical ventures, as there is in the latter. In both we find ourselves in the sphere of the confession which is possible only as the confession of faith or not at all. It is quickly said, and apparently easy to understand, that the history of created being takes place in every respect and in its whole range under the lordship of God. But we have only to consider one little portion of this history of created being even in outline, let alone in its concrete differentiations and details, and honesty forces us to ask whether these are not empty

words. We start back from what we say, for it obviously goes far beyond what we know from our own experience and conviction, and what we can see and know and say responsibly falls far short of what is said with this confession. Indeed, it is better not to say it if in and in spite of this hesitation we do not have to say it as we confess our faith. Sincerely? Yes, if this sincerity consists in the fact that we are directed to say it by the Word of God, but not if it rests only on our own experiences and convictions. And we have only to ask how far, i.e., how little what we say with this confession squares with a corresponding heartfelt trust and obedience, to be honestly arrested afresh by the question whether it is not a cheap and unimpressive saying because we have never really answered it with our lives, and never will. If in spite of this more serious hesitation we do not have to say it as we confess our faith; if we do not know that we can say it only to our own shame, it is better not to say it. In this matter too, Christian faith begins where the sincerity of our own experiences and convictions reaches its limit with faith, where the measure of our corresponding trust and obedience obviously does not suffice, where we must completely abandon any self-confidence. It begins where we can cling only to the Word of God, where we may cling to this Word, but may do so with the indisputable certainty which is legitimate and obligatory and even self-evident when a man looks away from himself to God, when he has to do with His gift, when he makes use of the possibility which is created by the free work of the Holy Spirit within him, within his despondent heart, his foolish and fickle thoughts, his sinful life. In this faith, man must say what a Christian has to say concerning the providence of God. If it is a confession of this faith, it is *eo ipso* a solid confession, because *eo ipso* one which has reference to this objective content and derives from the revelation of this objective content.

The notion against which we have to delimit ourselves at this point is that which regards the Christian belief in providence as an opinion, postulate or hypothesis concerning God, the world, man and other things, an attempt at interpretation, exposition and explanation based upon all kinds of impressions and needs, carried through in the form of a systematic construction, and ventured as if it were a pious outlook which has a good deal in its favour and may be adopted if we ourselves are pious. We can formulate and

adopt opinions, postulates and hypotheses of this type, and sometimes abandon them again. But it is important to remember that
even in the form of belief in providence Christian faith is grounded
on the Word of God, and can draw its life from this alone. On this
basis alone we can be sure, and on this basis we must, that it is not
a non-obligatory and ultimately insecure view, and that the lordship of God over the history of created being is not therefore a
problem, but an objective fact which is far more certain than anything else we think we know about this history or even ourselves.
We can and must understand that the knowledge of this lordship
of God can be compared only to the category of axiomatic knowledge, and that even in relation to this category it forms a class
apart. If the Christian belief in this lordship were a view which ultimately had behind it only the thinking, feeling, choosing and
judging human subject, both it and its confession would always be
unstable. But it is not such a view. It consists in a realization of the
possibility which God gives to man. It is the freedom which God
Himself has given to man for God. And as such it cannot vacillate.
The matter itself, God's lordship over the history of creaturely
being, has spoken in the Word of God as in His revelation to man,
and it no longer permits him even hypothetically to think as
though it were not present and this history took place under no
lordship at all, or that of another. Man has not elected himself, but
is elected, to believe in the lordship of God. He has thus no option
but to believe in it, and to confess this faith. In this sense the statement concerning providence is a statement of faith. We shall have
to take pains to understand and assert it as such in all its details.
We shall have to avoid the temptation of slipping back from the
level of faith to the level where there can be only interpretations,
opinions, postulates and hypotheses which it would be difficult to
establish dogmatically. . . .

2. The Christian belief in providence is also faith in the strict
sense to the extent that, with reference to its object, it is simply
and directly faith in God Himself, in God as the Lord of His creation watching, willing and working above and in world-occurrence. The consolation and impulse of faith is that it points man
to God in respect of the whole history of created being including
his own. The man who lives by his faith may know that in everything which may happen to him he has to do with God. And

beyond his own personal situation and history, as a near or distant witness and participant in all world-occurrence in all its dimensions, he may realise and count on it that God Himself not only has a hand in it all, but is in the seat of sovereign rule, so that no other will can be done than His. Whatever the distance, the heights or depths, they are all bounded by the horizon that God exists as and where His creatures exist, and that His existence as such controls theirs. God's disposing is the kernel by which faith in His providence is nourished, to which it always strives and must continually return. Much may vary in the sphere of the divine disposing. In it there is a place for prosperity and adversity, victory and defeat, peril and protection, life and death, angels and demons, even human sin and human liberation. God is Lord in all these things. He is so in very different ways. But properly and in the last resort exclusively it is He who is always Lord. And this reference to Him is the meaning and power of the belief in providence. In face of all the variations of world-occurrence the trust and obedience of this belief always have Him in view as Helper, Commander, Judge and King. They look always to His mercy, holiness, faithfulness and omnipotence. Belief in providence depends on God and God alone: on God as the One who works all in all; but only on Him and on the fact that He is Lord of all.

It does not depend, therefore, on creatures and the different determinations proper to them in the world of His control, whether in detail, so that this or that good and fine and beautiful or in some way illuminating creaturely being is its true object, or as a whole so that even though we say God we really mean creation and its life and their goodness or beauty or some other distinction. God is not creation. Neither in detail nor as a whole is He a determination of creation. To be sure, in its various determinations creation is, in the fine phrases of Luther, the mask of God, namely to the extent that its history is also the history of the glory of its Creator. But it is only His mask and never His face, so that in it and its determinations in detail or as a whole we never have to do with God Himself. For as the history of God's glory takes place in, with and under that of creation, it is a hidden history, which is neither felt, seen, known or dialectically perceived by man, but can only be believed on the basis of this Word of God. We do not now speak of the divine manifestations, particularly that which fulfilled all others as the incarnation of the Word, the becoming creature of the Creator. In divine manifestation it is a matter of the establishment of faith in which the glory of God breaks through its concealment and man finds himself in direct confrontation with God. Even here the acting subject and therefore the basis of faith is God Himself and not His creaturely appearance in itself and as such. Even as the person of Jesus Christ it is the eternal Son of the Father, and only in unity with Him the man in whom this glory is revealed. Our present reference is to faith in God's more general presence and lordship in world-occurrence. Of this it falls to be said that it is real, and takes place in the world, but is concealed in world-occurrence as such, and therefore cannot be perceived or read off from this. Its revelation is not world-occurrence itself, but the Word of God, Jesus Christ. On the basis of this Word, in the freedom created by it, it may be believed, but prior to the consummation of the time of the world it can never be seen. Hence the object of the belief in providence can only be God Himself, as God Himself in His revelation in Jesus Christ is its only basis. The object of this belief cannot, then, be a creature, or any of its variable and varied determinations, instead of God. How could this belief stand if God were to it only what this or that glorious or apparently glorious creature is, or if He were only the Lord of the good and beautiful, of light and love and life, in the cosmic process, in a process which obviously stands so largely and we might often think totally under opposite determinations? If He is not the Lord in the latter, He is not in the former, and this is not the Christian belief. The Christian belief is not directed to any creature, or any modification or aspect of the creature, but to the Creator who is the Lord of His creature in all its modifications and aspects.

But this means—and here we come to the decisive point in this delimitation—that no human conception of the cosmic process can replace God as the object of the belief in providence. Man makes such conceptions. It is inevitable that he should do so, for otherwise he would not be capable of any practical orientation and decision. It is difficult to see how to forbid this. It belongs to his very life and that of his nearest fellow; a picture of his own or someone else's life-work as it has so far developed and will do so, or should or should not do so, according to his insight, understanding and judgment. His particular notion of those different determinations of creaturely being, of good and evil, of right and wrong, weal and woe, etc., will naturally play an important part in this. Such pictures may have a wider reference. They may be pictures of the life-process of a society, e.g., the Church, or a particular form of the Church, or a nation, or group of nations, or the whole human history. Some standards, moral or amoral, technical, cultural, political or economic, will dominate the one who forms them, leading him to assert progress or decline, formation, reformation or deformation, and determining both his assessment of the past and his expectations, yearnings and fears for the future. And such pictures, always on the same assumptions on the part of the one who forms them, may have an even wider reference. They may embrace the whole of being known to man, perhaps as a kind of history of evolution, perhaps more modestly as an analysis and description of the eternal movement of all being and its laws and contingencies, possibly including or defiantly or gaily excluding the good God, who at bottom, subject to what the one who forms them thinks concerning Him, might well be able to call some place his own within this total picture. There is no objection to man making these small and great conceptions of the course of things. Indeed, there is much to be said for it. It is itself quite definitely part of the world-process, and therefore of the history of creaturely or at any rate human being, that there should always be such conceptions, which whether small or great can never be conceived as mere pictures of history, but raise the claim, and can always make it good in some depth and breadth, to shape and actually make history. Our present point is that no such conception can replace God as the object of the belief in providence. No such picture can come in question as a picture of God. The belief in providence does not rule out such conceptions. It can allow them their specific place and right as necessary expressions and media of human life. In certain circumstances it can take them very seriously. It can sometimes, transitorily and with a particular application, see its object in the similitude of such pictures. But it will realise that even in them, on the strict sense of the concept, it has to do only with the masks of God, or more accurately with the masks through which man—not without divine appointment, will and permission—can see these masks of God, and behind which he usually hides himself from God and his fellows (under the name and pretext of an "ism"). The belief in providence embraces these conceptions, but it also limits them. It reckons with the truth which they contain. It also reckons with the distinctive dynamic with which they do not merely reflect but shape history. But it remains free in face of them. It does not rest on any of them. It cannot do this. For it is faith in God and His dominion and judgment to which all history, even that of the spirit, even that of human conceptions of human history, is wholly subject. It cannot, then, become belief in a human system of history invented by man, even when this system is the one to which the believer himself would give the preference and his heartiest approval. When a man believes, he will understand and apply even his own system, his own more or less distinct picture of history, only as a working hypothesis, and thus maintain the humility, the humour and the freedom to modify or abandon it as occasion may demand. He will treat it as an instrument which he has fashioned or taken over from others, which he uses so long as it can be used, but which he may see himself compelled and authorised to alter or to set aside and replace by another. He may give it much *fides humana,* but he will not give it any *fides divina.* He will be seriously convinced of its relative truth and goodness, but he will not believe in them. He will believe in God's providence, and not in his own as documented in his system. In all that follows we must beware of any aberration in this respect.

What we have to avoid is the equation of the belief in providence and its confession with a philosophy of history.

To see clearly at this point, we must refer back to our first contention that the belief in providence is not an opinion, postulate, hypothesis or world-view of the believing subject, but his freedom born of the Word of God. It is as God Himself tells man that He is the Lord of history, and man hears and accepts this from God Himself, that he believes in the providence of God. He thus believes in God. To be sure, he also reads in the book of history, whether of his own life or of the narrower or wider historical contexts in which it is lived. He makes some sense of what he reads and thinks he understands there. He forms his own opinion of it. On the basis of this opinion he sees himself forced to certain postulates. He thus works with certain hypotheses. And therefore independently, or stimulated and taught by others, he fashions with some degree of comprehension and accuracy a kind of philosophy of history. Why should he not do this? Again, and rightly again, he hazards the supposition that the rule of

God's providence corresponds in some degree to his philosophy of history. But he will not think that he can really read the rule of God's providence from the book (or his own little booklet) of history. He will listen to the Word of God, and not to the inner voice which suggests that he should regard this or that historical picture as perhaps the most accurate. For in the providence of God he does not have to do with a picture but with the reality of history. And in the belief in providence he does not have to do with a tenable or probable knowledge, but with the true knowledge of this reality. If he believes in the providence of God, he does not believe in himself. He does not rely on or appeal to his own eyes which he uses to read the book of history, nor the inner voice which seems to suggest the best interpretation of what he reads, but the ears which God has given him to hear His Word. He believes in God, and therefore in the voice of truth, and therefore in the revelation and reality of history. He believes in the divine providence itself, not in an assertion or estimation, however well-founded, of what he thinks is perhaps its previous course, or present *kairos*, or future purpose, in short its plan.

But this entails a further step. As man believes in God, even in the form of his belief in providence he can believe only in God, and only God. This object cannot be confused with any other. As no philosophy of history can be the basis of the belief in providence, none can be its object. This faith believes that God is the Lord who rules over and in all things, not that history is the unfolding of a specific process, the execution of a specific schema, the development of a specific programme. Sometimes with all seriousness we can regard it as probable that all or many things have previously come to pass in a particular interconnexion which we think we see, that they now stand in a particular crisis, and that they will develop in a particular direction. But no matter how firmly we are convinced of this, we cannot believe in it, nor live by it, nor find comfort in it. We may receive from it our penultimate, but not our ultimate and proper directives. We cannot believe, as Lessing did, in an education of the human race, played out in history, to a moral and religious rationality to be attained in time or eternity. Nor can we believe, as Hegel did, in a self-development of the absolute spirit to be realised in history and more or less attained in 1830. Nor can we believe, as Karl Marx did, in a purpose of history worked out in the clash and counter-clash of the economic classes culminating in the victory and liberation of the economically oppressed. Nor can we believe, as did Treitschke and his contemporaries, in the conflict of nations which reached its most important phase with the rise of a united Germany. Nor can we believe, as did Spengler, in history as the evolution and conflict, the rise and fall, of different cultures. Nor can we believe, as did J. Burckhardt, in history as the mounting and tragic crisis of humanity, and therefore in the pathology of world history. We can think we see many of these things. We can be very seriously determined in practice by some such view. But while we may quietly or enthusiastically accept these constructs, and count on their validity, we cannot believe in them. We cannot think that to see them is to see God. The identification of the leading principles of such pictures with the God of the Old and New Testaments has never been possible. On the contrary, their inventors and champions have usually been wise enough to refrain from claiming such things for them, preferring to deny this God either directly or indirectly, and to give their principles another name (or no name at all) in accordance with their character. The fact is that we cannot believe in these principles. Unfortunately we can offer them false worship as what the Bible would call alien and false gods. But we cannot really impose them upon ourselves or others. We can absolutise them. But they can never be more than relative absolutes. We cannot really rest on them. They are not capable of any genuine faithfulness or reliable direction. They have their own dynamic. But they can reign only in part and for a time (whether a thousand years or only twelve). And at bottom they can do so only in appearance. In their place and time they, too, are naturally objects of the divine providence. But they can be confused with this providence only if we have very poor sight. We may add by way of warning that all that we have said applies fully to Christian or supposedly Christian views of history constructed with the aid of the Bible, like those championed by Gottfried Arnold or J. A. Bengel.

And now we must take a third step. In faith in God's providence man will certainly consider history with very open, attentive and participating eyes. How could it be otherwise? He exists in it, and as he does so—how else?—he has to live out and exercise his faith in the ruling God, and to show his little trust and obedience. The history of created being in its great and little consequences and connexions is the sphere over and in which there takes place the mighty and penetrating sway of this ruling God. It is in it that there is fulfilled secretly but very really the history of His glory. And so the belief in God's providence undoubtedly consists in the fact that man is freed to see this rule of God in world-occurrence, this secret history of His glory. This does not mean that faith becomes sight. It will know how to separate itself from a supposed and arrogant and certainly deceptive sight. Yet this does not mean that it is blind. It would not be faith if it were not knowledge in this respect, relative, provisional and modest knowledge in need of correction, yet true and thankful and courageous knowledge. When a man believes in God's providence, he does not know only *in abstracto* and generally that God is over all things and all things are in His hand, but he continually sees something of the work of this hand, and may continually see God's will and purpose in very definite events, relationships, connexions and changes in the history of created being. He notes in this history disposings and directions, hints and signs, set limits and opened possibilities, threats and judgments, gracious preservations and assistances. He knows how to distinguish between great and small, truth and appearance, promise and threat. He knows how to distinguish between necessary waiting and pressing on, speech and silence, action and passion, warfare and peace. He perceives always the call of the hour, and acts accordingly. He is free for this intercourse with the divine providence.

But it is not a philosophy of history which gives him this freedom. Perhaps he has such a philosophy. Perhaps he is constructing one. And we repeat that there is no reason why he should not do so. But even at best such a philosophy cannot free him for this thankful and courageous recognition of the sway of providence. On the contrary, if he were under the delusion that in it he possessed the key to this knowledge, he could only be hampered. For it would then be a serious matter that it is only his own idea and invention or that of some other man, and that as such it may serve as a non-obligatory guide, but cannot give knowledge of the ways of God. If it fills and dominates his vision, it thus blinds him to God and makes him unfit for that intercourse with His providence.

No, "thy word is a lamp unto my feet, and a light unto my path" (Ps. 119:105). Our attempts to orientate ourselves in the dark, in the great movement of the masks of God which we call history, are necessary, right and good. But when it is a matter of receiving and having light in this darkness—and faith in God's providence does receive and have light in the darkness—we are forced back upon the Word of God, and this alone is to be received. To believe is to believe only in God and only God, we have maintained. But to believe in God in this twofold sense means concretely to believe in the Word of God and to believe the Word of God. This is the light which when and as we see it shines over history and causes us to see at various points in its course the sway of the Creator, disclosing the masks of God as such. It is not the case, however, that the Word of God in which he believes, and which he believes, can as such cause him to see something of God's rule, not His universal plan or total view, but God Himself at work at various points, and always and in every respect enough to give the man's faith in Him the character of a knowledge in which he may genuinely and rightly live by his faith. It is thus the case that when and as a man accepts the Word of God he does not have to interpret the cosmic process of himself, or according to the patterns given him by others, but that even while he does this he may also hear the infallible voice of his Lord, and cleave to it.

In faith in God's providence what is needed is the relationship to history of which we have an exemplary form in the Old Testament prophets. What makes them prophets is not that they can rightly perceive and publicly appraise past and present and future history, but that the hand of the Lord seizes them (cf. Is. 8:11), that He says something to them which in relation to the thoughts of their contemporaries and even their own is always new and strange and unexpected and even unwanted, a "burden" laid upon them (Hab. 1:1), a fire kindled and burning in them (Jer. 20:9), even a superabounding joy filling them (Jer. 15:16). It is not that they had or acquired a particular insight into the things which happened, but that these things, far from happening by chance or according to an immanent law which man could and should divine, were done by the Lord God, who does nothing "but he revealeth his secret to his servants the prophets" (Amos 3:7). Hence it is not from history or their own view of history but into history, apart from and even against their own view, that a very definite light is given to the prophets in the form of concretely directed and fashioned perceptions which are not only clear to themselves, but have to be shown by them to others, in individual assertions, in agreements and repudiations, in threats and promises, in particular decisions, and also in more or less connected and far-ranging historical pictures. Basically and structurally this prophetic relationship to history is also that of belief in providence. It consists in the fact that the man who is apprehended and freed by the Word of God is not without light and therefore always sees light in the obscurity of world-occurrence.

It is to be noted again that this is not the light in which all things are open to God. It is not the revelation and contemplation of *the* mystery, *the* history. But it is light, and as much light as God thinks necessary and salutary for the believer in his time and place, and will therefore give him.

It is to be noted further that in the knowledge of God's providence by faith there can never be any question of speculation or theory. The seeing of the ways of God can never be an end in itself. It can never be a matter of aesthetic contemplation. It is always a matter of the practical insights necessary and salutary for man at specific points. What man can receive through the Word of God in this respect is knowledge for life. It is daily bread, manna from heaven, which must be gathered and eaten but not kept. We cannot boast of having it, or become complacent. If it is not to be given in vain, we can only live with it, stretching out our hands for a further gift that we may always have it afresh.

It is to be noted further that in this knowledge even a practical principle is not given to man in the sense of a constant programme. The continuity and consistency of this knowledge rest with God who will give it to man by His Word. It arises for man only as he listens openly and attentively to what God will say to him in His Word, not as he reduces what is already said to inflexible rules. The relationship of the Old Testament prophets to the history of their time never took the form of a programme. Hence a vitally self-renewing knowledge of faith in this matter, as its object is the faithfulness and constancy of God, can never be rigid, or clearly enough distinguished from an obstinate clinging to insights already won, a sterile repetition of a position already adopted. That history necessarily repeats itself, and that pictures once seen must be regarded as necessary to-day, is the very last thing to be expected by the man who believes in the providence of God. Hence he will not allow even a sound view of the historical process to become a strait-jacket. Indeed, he will not allow even the best view, even and especially when he believes that at the time he did not adopt it out of human caprice but in obedience to the Word of God. It will not be his concern—and in this respect the different attitudes of Luther to such problems of his age as the Turkish War, the Peasants' War and the Jewish question are formally at least important models—to try to give his view and attitude a particular character or aspect by the rigid insistence upon a certain line. He will not be ashamed if it can be shown that he once thought or spoke otherwise. The man who believes in the providence of God is distinguished from the man who does not, but rests instead upon his own prudence, by the fact that he is not too proud to be a continual learner. If he is under the instruction of the Word of God he need have no fear that his way will not finally have and show far more line and character than the ways of those who so wish to be true to themselves that they cannot really be true to God.

It is to be noted further that it belongs to this knowledge of God's providence by faith that although it refers to the infallible Word of God it is a human and, as such, a fallible knowledge. Not everything which the serious believer seriously listening to the Word of God regards as such is in fact a divine disposing and directing in history, a hint and sign of providence. He might have misunderstood what God has really said to him. We surely have such a misunderstanding when Eusebius of Caesarea, the father of Church history, saw in the emperor Constantine a second Moses, and in his kingdom a kind of definitive revelation of the kingdom of God. That he did not take this from the Word of God but his own judgment may be seen from the fact that he could make nothing of the Apocalypse, which would surely have warned him in this respect, but wanted to see it demoted from the true Canon. A similar misunderstanding arose when the great J. A. Bengel, who was much too cocksure in his understanding of the Apocalypse, thought that he could fix on 1836 as the date of the defeat of the beast from the abyss. For the rest, Bengel had so clear a vision of his time and the then future that in spite of this blunder—or accepting the fact that there could be this admixture of error—we may adduce him as an outstanding example of the fact that, even though an only too human misunderstanding of the Word of God may disturb in detail the knowledge of God's providence by faith, it cannot prevent it in general (and therefore also in detail). We have to remember that there are fruitful as well as unfruitful misunderstandings of the Word of God. If the believer's understanding is false in one respect, it is perhaps so much the better in others. And in any case it is better to misunderstand the Word of God than not to understand it at all. We may well say that not only is it no *pudendum,* but it belongs to the very best in the Old Testament, to the character of Holy Scripture as human witness to the revelation of God, that in the history of its prophecy there should obviously be some clear historical errors and prophecies either unfulfilled or fulfilled in a very different sense from that of the prophets. The lesson to be drawn for the doctrine of providence from this side of the matter can consist only in the affirmation that since man is so capable of error in relation to God it must not rest on any of its achievements. It must be free to withdraw in all its detailed insights. It must be continually ready to receive new and better instruction, and to that extent to censure itself. In short, it must be willing as a movement of knowledge to take part in the great movement of reality which is its theme, the co-existence of the Creator with His creature in which the Creator constantly increases and the creature decreases, in which the Creator always precedes and the creature can only follow. Only, but always, as it takes part in this movement is it the faith for which man is given freedom in this matter.

It is to be noted finally that in the upshot the knowledge peculiar to the belief in providence can consist in its decisive content only in the knowledge of God Himself. It is a matter of God in His quality as the Lord of all lords and King of all kings, of His world government, and therefore of the concrete knowledge related to the course of great and small world-occurrence and filled out and shaped accordingly. It is not a matter of a dead knowledge of God's lordship over all things, to which there might correspond a blindness for the details. It is a matter of the living seeing of the living Lord in the details of history. Hence it is not a theoretical seeing but a practical, not a programmatic but a free, not an infallible but one which stands in need of correction. The unconditioned and constant element in this seeing will not consist, therefore, in something that man sees in the course of the world as such, but in what he sees in the course of the world of God Himself as its Lord and Ruler. The Word of God continually places the history of creaturely being in its light in order that God Himself, who speaks to man, may be the better known by him. God Himself is what is necessary and wholesome for man. God Himself is the goal and measure of human action in the world. God Himself is the free One in face of whom man cannot entrench himself in any programme. God Himself is the true One who speaks infallibly even when man is deceived as to what He has really said. That God Himself is known as Lord is the decisive difference between the belief in providence and every philosophy of history as stated in this second delimitation.

3. We now come to the third and most important delimitation. In its substance the Christian belief in providence is Christian faith, i.e., faith in Christ. The Word of God which it believes, in which it believes and which sets it in the light in which it may see the lordship of God in the history of creaturely being, is the one Word of God beside which there is no other—the Word which became flesh and is called Jesus Christ. And the history of creaturely being is—secretly but really—the history of the glory of God in the fact that it does not merely run alongside the history of Jesus Christ and therefore the history of the covenant of grace between God and man, but has its meaning in this, is conditioned and determined by it, serves it, and in its reflected light (and shadow) is the place, the sphere, the atmosphere and medium of its occurrence and revelation.

Hence the belief in providence is not a kind of forecourt, or common foundation, on which the belief of the Christian Church may meet with other conceptions of the relationship of what is called "God" with what is called "world." The lordship of God over world-occurrence which is its theme is not a general form which might have a very different content. It is not a genus comprehending not only the lordship of the Father of Jesus Christ, the God of the election and covenant of grace, but also the sway of any other deities freely selected by religion or philosophy. In virtue of its relation to what God has done once for all in Jesus Christ, it is a happening *sui generis*. . . .

The Christian belief in providence is given its content and form, and therefore its distinction from other views apparently similar, by the fact that the lordship of God over the world which is its object is not just any lordship, but the fatherly lordship of God. And this "fatherly" does not mean only "kind" and "friendly" and "loving." It means all this, yet not abstractly, but on a specific basis. Similar attributes of the supreme ruler of principle of the world are to be found elsewhere, but only in a way which is nonobligatory, contingent and problematical. In the language of the Christian belief in providence, "fatherly" means first of all, quite apart from any such predicates and as their solid foundation, that the God who sits in government is "the eternal Father of our Lord Jesus Christ." The Christian belief does not gaze into the void, into obscurity, into a far distance, height or depth, when it knows and confesses God as the Lord of the history of created being. It really knows this God, and therefore His rule. Under our second point we have established that it knows Him as it receives His Word. But His Word is not empty. It is not the references to a supreme being which is supposed to have certain qualities. It is He Himself. But it is He Himself in a way in which He can be accepted by man. It is His person as a human person, His Word in the flesh, His eternal Son born in time as the Son of Mary, and crucified and raised for us. This "God with us" and "God for us" is God in eternity, the Son. And no other, but this God, is also "God over us," the eternal Father of this eternal Son. In the belief in providence it is a matter of "God over us," of God the Creator in His majesty, transcendence and lordship over His creature. But God the Creator is one God. The One who is for us as the Son is over us as the Father. As God has elected to be for us in His Son, He has elected Himself our Father and us His children. We are not in strange hands, nor are we strangers, when He is over us as our Creator and we are under Him as His children. We are His children for the sake of His Son and with Him (in whom He is so really for us that He becomes one with us). And it is as such that we are creatures in His fatherly hand. This fatherly hand is the divine power which

rules the world. We can know no divine power over us, nor is there
any such power, which is not this fatherly hand. As and because it
is this fatherly hand, it is kind and friendly and loving. It has these
qualities as the grace with which the same God who elected Himself our Father in His Son is also over us as our Creator. He is over
us in a way which corresponds to this election of grace, to this
eternal "for us" in His Son. Even as our Creator He is not alien or
ungracious, but gracious. He is gracious as a Father to His children. And in this connexion we have to remember that the truth of
this relationship is not to be found in what might take place between a human father and his children, but in what has taken
place from all eternity and then in time, between God the Father
and the Son. He is our heavenly Father, in a way which surpasses
all that we can see or think. We are thus warned in advance that
we cannot make what we think we know as fatherly or any other
kindness, friendliness and love the measure and criterion of His. It
is a matter of the eternal fatherly fidelity which we can only try to
see and grasp where it is revealed to us. "He that hath seen me
hath seen the Father" (John 14:9). It is here that the Christian
belief in providence sees the Father, and therefore God over us,
and therefore the Lord of the world-process. It is here that the will
which rules the history of created being is not concealed. It looks
to the history of the covenant which is fulfilled in the mission, in
the person and work of the incarnate Son, of the "God for us." And
through and beyond this it looks to the divine election of grace.
And it thus sees the Father, the "God over us," as it sees the Son.
As it sees Him it hears the Word of God, and as it hears the Word
of God it receives the light on God's rule in the world beside which
there is no other. The light which it receives and by which it lives
will thus consist always in the fact that it may there perceive not
only the will of an unknown Lord, not only the lines of an order
and consistence, not only the stages of a process, but the demonstration of the Lord who is our Father for the sake of His Son, of
the Lord of the covenant of grace, of the God of the eternal election
of grace. In very general terms this is the specific and incomparable element in the Christian belief in providence.

C. S. LEWIS

C. S. Lewis (1898–1963), fellow of Magdalen College, Oxford, and later professor of Medieval and Renaissance English at Cambridge University, was a man of many talents: Christian apologist, writer of fantasy, literary historian, critic. Some of his books are widely read: *The Screwtape Letters* (1942), *Mere Christianity* (1952), *The Four Loves* (1960), the Narnia stories for children (1950–56).

This article draws upon his various gifts. It is an affirmation and a denial. He believes without question that human history is "a story written by the finger of God." But he adamantly rejects all claims to know the inner meaning and patterns of history by means of mere rational observation of the historical process. Writing history is worthwhile, but philosophy of history, which he calls "Historicism," is an illusion, often harmful, and at best a waste of time. He has in mind the grand constructs of Hegel, Marx, and the idea of cultural progress, as well as Christian views of history like Augustine's and Dante's. He writes: "If by one miracle, the total content of time were spread out before me, and if, by another, I were able to hold all that infinity of events in my mind and if, by a third, God were pleased to comment on it so I could understand it, then, to be sure, I could do what the Historicist says he is doing. I could read the meaning, discern the pattern. Yes; and if the sky fell we should all catch larks."

Lewis wants instead to affirm trust in God and openness to that "primary history" in which God reveals himself in the moment by moment experience of life to each one who seeks him.

Historicism

He that would fly without wings must fly in his dreams.
—Coleridge.

I give the name *Historicism* to the belief that men can, by the use of their natural powers, discover an inner meaning in the historical process. I say *by the use of their natural powers* because I do not propose to deal with any man who claims to know the meaning either of all history or of some particular historical event by divine revelation. What I mean by a Historicist is a man who asks me to accept his account of the inner meaning of history on the grounds of his learning and genius. If he had asked me to accept it on the grounds that it had been shown him in a vision, that would be another matter. I should have said to him nothing. His claim (with supporting evidence in the way of sanctity and miracles) would not be for me to judge. This does not mean that I am setting up a distinction, to be applied by myself, between inspired and uninspired writers. The distinction is not between those who have and those who lack inspiration, but between those who claim and those who do not claim it. With the former I have at present no concern.

I say *an inner meaning* because I am not classifying as Historicists those who find a "meaning" in history in any sense whatever. Thus, to find causal connections between historical events, is in my terminology the work of a historian not of a historicist. A historian, without becoming a Historicist, may certainly infer unknown events from known ones. He may even infer future events from past ones; prediction may be a folly, but it is not Historicism.

Reprinted by permission of *The Month* from *The Month*, new series, IV (1950), 230–43. (114 Mount Street, London W1Y 6AH.)

He may "interpret" the past in the sense of reconstructing it imaginatively, making us feel (as far as may be) what it was like, and in that sense what it "meant," to a man to be a twelfth-century villein or a Roman *eques*. What makes all these activities proper to the historian is that in them the conclusions, like the premises, are historical. The mark of the Historicist, on the other hand, is that he tries to get from historical premises conclusions which are more than historical; conclusions metaphysical or theological or (to coin a word) atheo-logical. The historian and the Historicist may both say that something "must have" happened. But *must* in the mouth of a genuine historian will refer only to a *ratio cognoscendi:* since A happened B "must have" preceded it; if William the Bastard arrived in England he "must have" crossed the sea. But "must" in the mouth of a Historicist can have quite a different meaning. It may mean that events fell out as they did because of some ultimate, transcendent necessity in the ground of things.

When Carlyle spoke of history as a "book of revelations" he was a Historicist. When Novalis called history "an evangel" he was a Historicist. When Hegel saw in history the progressive self-manifestation of absolute spirit he was a Historicist. When a village woman says that her wicked father-in-law's paralytic stroke is "a judgment on him" she is a Historicist. Evolutionism, when it ceases to be simply a theorem in biology and becomes a principle for interpreting the total historical process, is a form of Historicism. Keats's *Hyperion* is the epic of Historicism, and the words of Oceanus,

> 'tis the eternal law
> That first in beauty should be first in might,

are as fine a specimen of Historicism as you could wish to find.

The contention of this article is that Historicism is an illusion and that Historicists are, at the very best, wasting their time. I hope it is already clear that in criticizing Historicists I am not at all criticizing historians. It is not formally impossible that a Historicist and a historian should be the same man. But the two characters are in fact very seldom combined. It is usually theologians, philosophers and politicians who become Historicists.

Historicism exists on many levels. The lowest form of it is one that I have already mentioned: the doctrine that our calamities (or more often our neighbours' calamities) are "judgments"; which here means divine condemnations or punishments. This sort of Historicism sometimes endeavours to support itself by the authority of the Old Testament. Some people even talk as if it were the peculiar mark of the Hebrew prophets to interpret history in this way. To that I have two replies. Firstly, the Scriptures come before me as a book claiming divine inspiration. I am not prepared to argue with the prophets. But if any man thinks that because God was pleased to reveal certain calamities as "judgments" to certain chosen persons, he is therefore entitled to generalize and read all calamities in the same way, I submit that this is a *non sequitur*. Unless, of course, that man claims to be himself a prophet; and then I must refer his claim to more competent judges. But secondly, we must insist that such an interpretation of history was not the characteristic of ancient Hebrew religion, not the thing which sets it apart and makes it uniquely valuable. On the contrary, this is precisely what it shares with popular Paganism. To attribute calamity to the offended gods and therefore to seek out and punish the offender, is the most natural thing in the world and therefore the world-wide method. Examples such as the plague in *Iliad A* and the plague at the opening of the *Oedipus Tyrannus* come at once to mind. The distinctive thing, the precious peculiarity, of Scripture is the series of divine rebuffs which this naïve and spontaneous type of Historicism there receives; in the whole course of Jewish history, in the Book of Job, in Isaiah's suffering servant (liii), in Our Lord's answers about the disaster at Siloam (*Luke* xiii. 4) and the man born blind (*John* ix. 13). If this sort of Historicism survives, it survives in spite of Christianity. And in a vague form it certainly does survive. Some who in general deserve to be called true historians are betrayed into writing as if nothing failed or succeeded that did not somehow deserve to do so. We must guard against the emotional overtones of a phrase like "the judgment of history." It might lure us into the vulgarest of all vulgar errors, that of idolizing as the goddess History what manlier ages belaboured as the strumpet Fortune. That would sink us below the Christian, or even the best Pagan, level. The very Vikings and Stoics knew better.

But subtler and more cultivated types of Historicism now also claim that their view is especially congenial to Christianity. It has

become a commonplace, as Fr. Paul Henri lately remarked in his
Deneke lecture at Oxford, to say that Judaic and Christian thought
are distinguished from Pagan and Pantheistic thought precisely by
the significance which they attribute to history. For the Pantheist,
we are told, the content of time is simply illusion; history is a
dream and salvation consists in awaking. For the Greeks, we are
told, history was a mere flux or, at best, cyclic: significance was to
be sought not in Becoming but in Being. For Christianity, on the
other hand, history is a story with a well-defined plot, pivoted on
Creation, Fall, Redemption, and Judgment. It is indeed the divine
revelation *par excellence,* the relevation which includes all other
revelations.

That history in a certain sense must be all this for a Christian,
I do not deny. In what sense, will be explained later. For the
moment, I submit that the contrast as commonly drawn between
Judaic or Christian thought on the one hand and Pagan or Pantheistic on the other is in some measure illusory. In the modern
world, quite plainly, Historicism has a Pantheistic ancestor in
Hegel and a materialistic progeny in the Marxists. It has proved so
far a stronger weapon in our enemies' hands than in ours. If Christian Historicism is to be recommended as an apologetic weapon it
had better be recommended by the maxim *fas est et ab hoste
doceri* than on the ground of any supposedly inherent congeniality.
And if we look at the past we shall find that the contrast works
well as between Greek and Christian but not as between Christian
and other types of Pagan. The Norse gods, for example, unlike the
Homeric, are beings rooted in a historical process. Living under
the shadow of Ragnarok they are preoccupied with time. Odin is
almost the god of anxiety: in that way Wagner's Wotan is amaz-
ingly true to the Eddaic original. In Norse theology cosmic history
is neither a cycle nor a flux; it is irreversible, tragic epic marching
deathward to the drum-beat of omens and prophecies. And even if
we rule out Norse Paganism on the ground that it was possibly influenced by Christianity, what shall we do with the Romans? It is
quite clear that they did not regard history with the indifference, or
with the merely scientific or anecdotal interests, of the Greeks.
They seem to have been a nation of Historicists. I have pointed out
elsewhere that all Roman epic before Virgil was probably metrical
chronicle; and the subject was always the same—the coming-to-be

of Rome. What Virgil essentially did was to give this perennial theme a new unity by his symbolical structure. The *Aeneid* puts forward, though in mythical form, what is precisely a reading of history, an attempt to show what the *fata Jovis* were labouring to bring about. Everything is related not to Aeneas as an individual hero but to Aeneas as the Rome-bearer. This, and almost only this, gives significance to his escape from Troy, his *amour* with Dido, his descent into Hades, and his defeat of Turnus. *Tantae molis erat;* all history is for Virgil an immense parturition. It is from this Pagan source that one kind of Historicism descends to Dante. The Historicism of the *De Monarchia,* though skilfully, and of course sincerely, mortised into the Judaic and Christian framework, is largely Roman and Virgilian. St. Augustine indeed may be rightly described as a Christian Historicist. But it is not always remembered that he became one in order to refute Pagan Historicism. The *De Civitate* answers those who traced the disasters of Rome to the anger of the rejected gods. I do not mean to imply that the task was uncongenial to St. Augustine, or that his own Historicism is merely an *argumentum ad hominem.* But it is surely absurd to regard as specifically Christian in him the acceptance of a *terrain* which had in fact been chosen by the enemy.

The close connection which some see between Christianity and Historicism thus seems to me to be largely an illusion. There is no *prima facie* case in its favour on such grounds as that. We are entitled to examine it on its merits.

What appears, on Christian premises, to be true in the Historicist's position is this. Since all things happen either by the divine will or at least by the divine permission, it follows that the total content of time must in its own nature be a revelation of God's wisdom, justice, and mercy. In this direction we can go as far as Carlyle or Novalis or anyone else. History is, in that sense, a perpetual Evangel, a story written by the finger of God. If, by one miracle, the total content of time were spread out before me, and if, by another, I were able to hold all that infinity of events in my mind and if, by a third, God were pleased to comment on it so that I could understand it, then, to be sure, I could do what the Historicist says he is doing. I could read the meaning, discern the pattern. Yes; and if the sky fell we should all catch larks. The question is not what could be done under conditions never vouchsafed us *in via,* nor even (so far as I can remember) promised us *in patria,* but what can be done now under the real conditions. I do not dispute that History is a story written by the finger of God. But have we the text? (it would be dull work discussing the inspiration of the Bible if no copy of it had ever been seen on earth).

We must remind ourselves that the word *History* has several senses. It may mean the total content of time: past, present, and future. It may mean the content of the past only, but still the total content of the past, the past as it really was in all its teeming riches. Thirdly, it may mean so much of the past as is discoverable from surviving evidence. Fourthly, it may mean so much as has been actually discovered by historians working, so to speak, "at the face," the pioneer historians never heard of by the public who make the actual discoveries. Fifthly, it may mean that portion, and that version, of the matter so discovered which has been worked up by great historical writers. (This is perhaps the most popular sense: *history* usually means what you read when you are reading Gibbon or Mommsen, or the Master of Trinity.) Sixthly, it may mean that vague, composite picture of the past which floats, rather hazily, in the mind of the ordinary educated man.

When men say that "History" is a revelation, or has a meaning, in which of these six senses do they use the word *History?* I am afraid that in fact they are very often thinking of history in the sixth sense; in which case their talk about revelation or meaning is surely unplausible in the extreme. For "history" in the sixth sense is the land of shadows, the home of wraiths like Primitive Man or the Renaissance or the Ancient-Greeks-and-Romans. It is not at all surprising, of course, that those who stare at it too long should see patterns. We see pictures in the fire. The more indeterminate the object, the more it excites our mythopoeic or "esemplastic" faculties. To the naked eye there is a face in the moon; it vanishes when you use a telescope. In the same way, the meanings or patterns discernible in "history" (Sense Six) disappear when we turn to "history" in any of the higher senses. They are clearest for each of us in the periods he has studied least. No one who has distinguished the different senses of the word *History* could continue to think that history (in the sixth sense) is an evangel or a revelation. It is an effect of perspective.

On the other hand, we admit that history (in Sense One) is a story written by the finger of God. Unfortunately we have not got it. The claim of the practising Historicist then will stand or fall with his success in showing that history in one of the intermediate senses—the first being out of reach and the sixth useless for his purpose—is sufficiently close to history in the first sense to share its revealing qualities.

We drop, then, to history in Sense Two: the total content of past time as it really was in all its richness. This would save the Historicist if we could reasonably believe two things: first, that the formidable omission of the future does not conceal the point or meaning of the story, and, secondly, that we do actually possess history (Sense Two) up to the present moment. But can we believe either?

It would surely be one of the luckiest things in the world if the content of time up to the moment at which the Historicist is writing happened to contain all that he required for reaching the significance of total history. We ride with our backs to the engine. We have no notion what stage in the journey we have reached. Are we in Act I or Act V? Are our present diseases those of childhood or senility? If, indeed, we knew that history was cyclic we might perhaps hazard a guess at its meaning from the fragment we have seen. But then we have been told that the Historicists are just the people who do not think that history is merely cyclic. For them it is a real story with a beginning, a middle, and an end. But a story is precisely the sort of thing that cannot be understood till you have heard the whole of it. Or, if there are stories (bad stories) whose later chapters add nothing essential to their significance, and whose significance is therefore contained in something less than the whole, at least you cannot tell whether any given story belongs to that class until you have at least once read it to the end. Then, on a second reading, you may omit the dead wood in the closing chapters. I always now omit the last Book of *War and Peace*. But we have not yet read history to the end. There might be no dead wood. If it is a story written by the finger of God, there probably isn't. And if not, how can we suppose that we have seen "the point" already? No doubt there are things we can say about this story even now. We can say it is an exciting story, or a crowded story, or a story with humorous characters in it. The one thing we must not say is what it means, or what its total pattern is.

But even if it were possible, which I deny, to see the significance of the whole from a truncated text, it remains to ask whether we have that truncated text. Do we possess even up to the present date the content of time as it really was in all its richness? Clearly not. The past, by definition, is not present. The point I am trying to make is so often slurred over by the unconcerned admission "Of course we don't know *everything*" that I have sometimes despaired of bringing it home to other people's minds. It is not a question of failing to know everything: it is a question (at least as regards quantity) of knowing next door to nothing. Each of us finds that in his own life every moment of time is completely filled. He is bombarded every second by sensations, emotions, thoughts, which he cannot attend to for multitude, and nine-tenths of which he must simply ignore. A single second of lived time contains more than can be recorded. And every second of past time has been like that for every man that ever lived. The past (I am assuming in the Historicist's favour that we need consider only the human past) in its reality, was a roaring cataract of billions upon billions of such moments: any one of them too complex to grasp in its entirety, and the aggregate beyond all imagination. By far the greater part of this teeming reality escaped human consciousness almost as soon as it occurred. None of us could at this moment give anything like a full account of his own life for the last twenty-four hours. We have already forgotten; even if we remembered, we have not time. The new moments are upon us. At every tick of the clock, in every inhabited part of the world, an unimaginable richness and variety of "history" falls off the world into total oblivion. Most of the experiences in "the past as it really was" were instantly forgotten by the subject himself. Of the small percentage which he remembered (and never remembered with perfect accuracy) a smaller percentage was ever communicated even to his closest intimates; of this, a smaller percentage still was recorded; of the recorded fraction only another fraction has ever reached posterity. *Ad nos vix tenuis famae perlabitur aura*. When once we have realized what "the past as it really was" means, we must freely admit that most—that nearly all—history (in Sense Two) is, and will remain, wholly unknown to us. And if *per impossibile* the whole were known, it would be wholly unmanageable. To know the whole of one minute in Napoleon's life would require a whole minute of your own life. You could not keep up with it.

If these fairly obvious reflections do not trouble the Historicist that is because he has an answer. "Of course," he replies, "I admit that we do not know and cannot know (and, indeed, don't want to know) all the mass of trivialities which filled the past as they fill the present; every kiss and frown, every scratch and sneeze, every hiccup and cough. But we know the important facts." Now this is a perfectly sound reply for a historian: I am not so clear that it will do for the Historicist. You will notice that we are now already a long way from history in Sense One—the total story written by the finger of God. First, we had to abandon the parts of that story which are still in the future. Now it appears we have not even got the text of those parts which we call "past." We have only selections; and selections which, as regards quantity, stand to the original text rather as one word would stand to all the books in the British Museum. We are asked to believe that from selections on that scale men (not miraculously inspired) can arrive at the meaning or plan or purport of the original. This is credible only if it can be shown that the selections make up in quality for what they lack in quantity. The quality will certainly have to be remarkably good if it is going to do that.

"The important parts of the past survive." If a historian says this (I am not sure that most historians would) he means by "importance" relevance to the particular inquiry he has chosen. Thus, if he is an economic historian, economic facts are for him important: if a military historian, military facts. And he would not have embarked on his inquiry unless he had some reason for supposing that relevant evidence existed. "Important" facts, for him, usually do survive because his undertaking was based on the probability that the facts he calls important are to be had. Sometimes he finds he was mistaken. He admits defeat and tries a new question. All this is fairly plain sailing. But the Historicist is in a different position. When he says "Important facts survive" he must mean by the "important" (if he is saying anything to the purpose) that which reveals the inner meaning of History. The important parts of the past must for a Hegelian Historicist be those in which Absolute Spirit progressively manifests itself; for a Christian Historicist, those which reveal the purposes of God.

In this claim I see two difficulties. The first is logical. If history is what the Historicist says—the self-manifestation of Spirit, the story written by the finger of God, the revelation which includes all other revelations—then surely he must go to history itself to teach him what is important. How does he know beforehand what sort of events are, in a higher degree than others, self-manifestations of Spirit? And if he does not know that, how does he get his assurance that it is events of that type which manage (what a convenience!) to get recorded?

The second difficulty is obvious, if we think for a moment of the processes whereby a fact about the past reaches, or fails to reach, posterity. Prehistoric pottery survives because earthenware is easy to break and hard to pulverize; prehistoric poetry has perished because words, before writing, are winged. Is it reasonable to conclude either that there was no poetry or that it was, by the Historicist's standard, less important than the pottery? Is there a discovered law by which important manuscripts survive and unimportant perish? Do you ever turn out an old drawer (say, at the break-up of your father's house) without wondering at the survival of trivial documents and the disappearance of those which everyone would have thought worth preservation? And I think the real historian will allow that the actual *detritus* of the past on which he works is very much more like an old drawer than like an intelligent epitome of some longer work. Most that survives or perishes survives or perishes by chance: that is, as a result of causes which have nothing to do either with the historian's or the Historicist's interests. Doubtless, it would be possible for God so to ordain these chances that what survives is always just what the Historicist needs. But I see no evidence that He has done so; I remember no promise that He would.

The "literary" sources, as the historian calls them, no doubt record what their writers for some reason thought important. But this is of little use unless their standards of importance were the same as God's. This seems unlikely. Their standards do not agree with one another nor with ours. They often tell us what we do not greatly want to know and omit what we think essential. It is often easy to see why. Their standard of importance can be explained by their historical situation. So, no doubt, can ours. Standards of historical importance are themselves embedded in history. But then, by what standard can we judge whether the "important" in some high-flying Hegelian sense has survived? Have we, apart from our Christian faith, any assurance that the historical events which we

regard as momentous coincide with those which would be found
momentous if God showed us the whole text and deigned to comment? Why should Gengis Khan be more important than the patience or despair of some one among his victims? Might not those
whom we regard as significant figures—great scholars, soldiers,
and statesmen—turn out to have their chief importance as giving
occasion to states of soul in individuals whom we never heard of? I
do not, of course, mean that those whom we call the great are not
themselves immortal souls for whom Christ died, but that in the
plot of history as a whole they might be minor characters. It would
not be strange if we, who have not sat through the whole play, and
who have heard only tiny fragments of the scenes already played,
sometimes mistook a mere super in a fine dress for one of the protagonists.

On such a small and chance selection from the total past as
we have, it seems to me a waste of time to play the Historicist. The
philosophy of history is a discipline for which we mortal men lack
the neccessary data. Nor is the attempt always a mere waste of
time: it may be positively mischievous. It encourages a Mussolini
to say that "History took him by the throat" when what really took
him by the throat was desire. Drivel about superior races or immanent dialectic may be used to strengthen the hand and ease the
conscience of cruelty and greed. And what quack or traitor will not
now woo adherents or intimidate resistance with the assurance
that his scheme is inevitable, "bound to come," and in the direction which the world is already taking?

When I have tried to explain myself on this subject in conversation I have sometimes been met by the rejoinder: "Because historians do not know all, will you forbid them to try to understand
what they do know?" But this seems to me to miss the whole
point. I have already explained in what sense historians should attempt to understand the past. They may infer unknown events
from known, they may reconstruct, they may even (if they insist)
predict. They may, in fact, tell me almost anything they like about
history except its metahistorical meaning. And the reason is surely
very plain. There are inquiries in which scanty evidence is worth
using. We may not be able to get certainty, but we can get probability, and half a loaf is better than no bread. But there are other
inquiries in which scanty evidence has the same value as no evi-

dence at all. In a funny anecdote, to have heard all except the last
six words in which the point lies, leaves you, as a judge of its
comic merits, in the same position as the man who has heard none
of it. The historian seems to me to be engaged on an inquiry of the
first type; the Historicist, on one of the second. But let us take a
closer analogy.

Suppose a lost Greek play of which fragments totalling six
lines survive. They have survived, of course, in grammarians who
quoted them to illustrate rare inflexions. That is, they survive because someone thought them important for some reason, not because they were important in the play as a play. If any one of them
had dramatic importance, that is simply a lucky accident, and we
know nothing about it. I do not condemn the classical scholar to
produce nothing more than a bare text of the fragments any more
than I condemn the historian to be a mere annalist. Let the scholar
emend their corruptions and draw from them any conclusions he
can about the history of Greek language, metre or religion. But let
him not start talking to us about the significance of the play as a
play. For that purpose the evidence before him has a value indis-
tinguishable from zero.

The example of a defective text might be used in another way.
Let us assume a mutilated MS., in which only a minority of passages are legible. The parts we can still read might be tolerable evidence for those features which are likely to be constant and evenly
distributed over the whole; for example, spelling or handwriting.
On such evidence a palaeographer might, without excessive boldness, hazard a guess about the character and nationality of the
scribe. A literary critic would have much less chance of guessing
correctly at the purport of the whole text. That is because the
palaeographer deals with what is cyclic or recurrent, and the literary critic with something unique, and uniquely developing
throughout. It is possible, though not likely, that all the torn or
stained or missing leaves were written by a different scribe; and if
they were not, it is very unlikely that he altered his graphic habits
in all the passages we cannot check. But there is nothing in the
world to prevent the legible line (at the bottom of a page)

Erimian was the noblest of the brothers ten

having been followed on the next and now missing page, by something like

As men believed; so false are the beliefs of men.

This provides the answer to a question which may be asked: Does my canon that historical premises should yield only historical conclusions entail the corollary that scientific premises should yield only scientific conclusions? If we call the speculations of Whitehead or Jeans or Eddington "scienticism" (as distinct from "science") do I condemn the scienticist as much as the Historicist? I am inclined, so far as I can see my way at present, to answer No. The scientist and the historian seem to me like the palaeographer and the literary critic in my parable. The scientist studies those elements in reality which repeat themselves. The historian studies the unique. Both have a defective MS. but its defects are by no means equally damaging to both. One specimen of gravitation, or one specimen of handwriting, for all we can see to the contrary, is as good as another. But one historical event, or one line of a poem, is different from another and different in its actual context from what it would be in any other context, and out of all these differences the unique character of the whole is built up. That is why, in my opinion, the scientist who becomes a scienticist is in a stronger position than the historian who becomes a Historicist. It may not be very wise to conclude from what we know of the physical universe that "God is a mathematician": it seems to me, however, much wiser than to conclude anything about His "judgments" from mere history. *Caveas disputare de occultis Dei judiciis,* says the author of the *Imitation.* He even advises us what antidotes to use *quando haec suggerit inimicus.*

It will, I hope, be understood that I am not denying all access whatever to the revelation of God in history. On certain great events (those embodied in the creeds) we have what I believe to be divine comment which makes plain so much of their significance as we need, and can bear, to know. On other events, most of which are in any case unknown to us, we have no such comment. And it is also important to remember that we all have a certain limited, but direct, access to History in Sense One. We are allowed, indeed compelled, to read it sentence by sentence, and every sentence is labelled *Now.* I am not, of course, referring to what is commonly called "contemporary history," the content of the newspapers. That is possibly the most phantasmal of all histories, a story written not by the hand of God but by foreign offices, demagogues, and reporters. I mean the real or primary history which meets each of us moment by moment in his own experience. It is very limited, but it is the pure, unedited, unexpurgated text, straight from the Author's hand. We believe that those who seek will find comment sufficient whereby to understand it in such degree as they need; and that therefore God is every moment "revealed in history," that is, in what MacDonald called "the holy present." Where, except in the present, can the Eternal be met? If I attack Historicism it is not because I intend any disrespect to primary history, the real revelation springing direct from God in every experience. It is rather because I respect this real original history too much to see with unconcern the honours due to it lavished on those fragments, copies of fragments, copies of copies of fragments, or floating reminiscences of copies of copies, which are, unhappily, confounded with it under the general name of *history*.

JACQUES MARITAIN

At the end of the nineteenth century Pope Leo XIII stimulated a revival of Thomistic philosophy as a Christian alternative to the idealistic and naturalistic philosophies then available. Two generations later the prolific work of two Frenchmen, Etienne Gilson and Jacques Maritain (1882–1973), established neo-Thomism on a firm systematic basis. Maritain carried on his work as professor at the Pontifical Institute of Medieval Studies, Toronto, and later at Princeton University, and for years lectured annually at the University of Chicago and Columbia.

Neo-Thomism, following Thomas Aquinas, paid only marginal attention to philosophy of history until the appearance of Maritain's *On the Philosophy of History* in 1957. Like Barth, Maritain places definite limits on what philosophy of history can do, and like C. S. Lewis, he finds Hegel, Comte, and Marx deluded. But he also believes, unlike Lewis, that the search for laws in historical development is valid and, unlike Barth, that it is worth his efforts when using Christian philosophical ideas.

For Maritain, historical laws do not necessitate or explain history; they merely help interpret it in certain general ways. They have to do primarily with the order of nature and the world as contrasted with the order of grace and the church. One discovers such laws via an inductive process of drawing out observed relationships and connections from the individual and unique facts of history, and then verifying them by rational analysis based on a previously acquired knowledge of human nature. Historical laws are of two kinds. Axiomatic laws deal with general characteristics of history, such as that good and evil tend to develop together and antagonistically, rather than that good tends to obliterate evil. Typological, or vectorial, laws, the ones discussed in this selection, pertain to periodization and the stages of history. For example, history, viewed as a whole, and in spite of reversals, tends to move from magical to rational states, from sacred to secular phases, and from authoritarian to democratic casts of mind.

Laws in the Historical Development of Mankind

1. These [typological] formulas or [vectorial] laws manifest the variety of ages or aspects in human history. They relate to what may be called *vectors of history*—I mean given segments determined in extent and direction and in significance. They relate also to the relationship between one vector and another, given a certain perspective or line of consideration.

I would suggest that the inductive process has a still greater part to play in this kind of law than in the axiomatic laws. One of our examples will be the distinction to be made between the *magical* and the *rational* states or regimes of human thought and culture. Here induction appears preponderant. Given the data of anthropology, we are confronted with the inductive fact that there is some big difference between the way of thinking of primitive man and our own way of thinking (so much so that the primitive man's way of thinking was first described as *"pre-logical* mentality").[1] But we cannot rest on this purely inductive notion. Furthermore, it must be re-elaborated, re-stated, if it is to be correctly conceptualized. For this we have to call upon some philosophical notions or insights—for instance, the knowledge of certain "natures" like imagination and intellect, and the knowledge of their relationship and connection in the progress of human knowing. A certain uni-

Reprinted by permission of Charles Scribner's Sons from *On the Philosophy of History* by Jacques Maritain. Copyright © 1957 Jacques Maritain. The original chapter title is "Typological Formulas or Vectorial Laws."

versal idea will then emerge, grouping and giving account of the various characteristics of primitive mentality and civilized mentality—what I call *imagination-ruled regime or state,* on the one hand, and *intellect-ruled regime or state,* on the other. And given this notion, which is not a simple induction but rather a rational insight quickening induction, we perceive that there is a certain internal necessity for a historic transition from one state to the other.

The Theological Notion of the Various "States" of Human Nature

2. Let us first turn our attention to data which have nothing to do with induction, because they are theological data, but which are particularly illuminating and suggestive for the philosopher of history, because they provide him with a basic framework and basic indications about the direction of human history. This is in keeping with, and indeed a particular instance of, the significance these data have for the moral philosopher.

I have in mind the theological notions of the "state of pure nature," the "state of innocence or integrity," the "state of fallen nature," and the "state of redeemed nature." As we know, according to Catholic theology the state of pure nature never existed—it is a mere possibility; and the state of fallen nature and the state of redeemed nature are to be distinguished, but they are not in succession—because God never abandoned fallen nature to itself, divine grace never ceased being at work in mankind; in other words, fallen nature was to be redeemed either by virtue of Christ's passion *to come* or by virtue of Christ's passion *already come.* Now I would simply propose here a few remarks on two questions suggested by this theological distinction of the states of human nature.

A first question is: can the fact of the original fall of man be proved, demonstrated by reason, brought out by some inductive process? It seems that Pascal would answer in the affirmative. He seems to have thought that given the contradiction, on which he insisted so much, offered by human nature—unheard-of misery, on the one hand, unheard-of grandeur, on the other—there must have been in the human past some catastrophe which will account for this contradiction. And therefore the original fall would appear to him as rationally proved by the analysis of human nature in the condition in which it can be observed by us.

I do not believe that it is possible to prove such a thing. It depends on a revealed datum; it does not pertain to the philosophical realm. The original sin, however, did not only deprive human nature of the supernatural gifts proper to the state of adamic innocence; it also *wounded* human nature. That is a theological datum on which St. Thomas lays particular stress. And these wounds of our nature are a reality always present in the human race. Hence, it appears that if the fact of the Fall cannot be demonstratively inferred, nevertheless there should be signs—for instance the very ones emphasized by Pascal—which cause reason to conclude in a *probable* manner that such an event took place at the dawn of our history. Here we have a problem which is of great import for moral philosophy and the philosophy of history in their own fields.

I have no intention of discussing it here (though, in my opinion, the question should be answered in the affirmative). I would prefer to submit a few remarks connected with the problem.

We might first observe that what we experientially know of man has to do with the real and concrete man, man in the state of fallen and redeemed nature—better to say, for our present purposes, in the state of wounded nature—whereas we have no experiential knowledge of what the state of pure nature might have been; we can only depict it ourselves in an abstract and imaginary manner, on the basis of our concept of human nature. As a result, a special difficulty arises in the discussion of the problem under consideration because we are liable to have our experience of the real man influence too much our very idea of the state of pure nature, so that we shall run a risk of minimizing the difference between the state of wounded nature and what the state of pure nature would have been.

Yet, on further consideration, I would rather believe that the difficulty—and the risk—in question occur in a reverse way. It is rather, it seems to me, in terms of our abstract notion of human nature that we have a tendency spontaneously to conceptualize our very experience of the real man, of man in the state of wounded nature, thus making our idea of this state resemble too much what man in the state of pure nature might have been. This is, I think, a deeper view of the matter. I understand in this way the paradoxical fact that, more often than not, when we are confronted in concrete experience with what man really is, we are suddenly astonished to find him, in actual fact, either much worse or much better—and, in certain cases, much worse and much better at the same time—than our image of him was. Thus it is that those who have the more articulate and elaborated abstract knowledge of man, namely, the moral philosopher and the moral theologian, are often like infants when it comes to dealing with man in real life and with his resources in goodness and in perversity. Neither philosophers nor theologians, but great sinners and great saints truly know man in the actual state of his nature.

A second question has to do with the notion of moral philosophy adequately taken. To my mind, it seems clear that moral philosophy must take into account these theological data relating to the various states of human nature. For, in fact, as a result of the present state of human nature, man has more propensity to evil than the man of pure nature by reason of the original sin and of the concupiscence which remains even in the just; and, on the other hand, he has incomparably stronger weapons for good, by reason of divine grace, with the organism of internal energies and the change in moral climate involved. Therefore, if the moral philosopher is to deal with the existential, the *real* man, he has to take this situation into account. He must not deal only with a man of pure nature—the man of pure nature is a mere possibility, an abstract possibility; he is not the man who actually *is*.

The Theological Notion of the Various "States" in the Historical Development of Mankind

3. Here again, as in the next section also, we are learning from theology; yet, this time, we are coming closer to the subject matter

of the philosophy of history. For we have to do no longer with the
various states of human nature with respect to sin and to divine
grace, but with the various *historical* states of the existential man,
as theology sees them: the "state of nature," for instance, the state
of Abraham—that is, the moral regime or state of human kind
before the written law; the "state of the Ancient Law"; and the
"state of the New Law." The second state concerned especially the
Jewish people, the two others have a universal bearing. The distinction between these three historical states, which is rooted in
St. Paul's teachings, and ,in which mediaeval theologians were
deeply interested, refers to the theology of history. We may say
that St. Paul was the founder of the theology of history, especially
with his basic doctrine (Rom., 3, 4) on the transition from the state
of the Law (the Ancient Law) to the state of Gospel freedom (the
New Law.)

To sum up St. Paul's teaching:[2] the Law is holy because it is
the revealed expression of the wisdom of God. But while the Law
makes us know evil, it does not give us the strength to avoid evil.
And by making evil known, the Law is, for evil, an occasion for
tempting us; and the wages of evil is death. In short, the Law is
holy but it bears death with it. And Christ has freed us of the *regimen* of the Law because His grace, which makes us participate in
the very life and sanctity of God, has now become revealed and
manifested. We are no longer held to the multitude of ceremonial
precepts nor to the juridical rules of the Mosaic Law; we are held to
other ceremonial precepts less onerous and less numerous. And
while we are ever held to the moral precepts of the Law, we are
held thereto as to the requirements of the very life and freedom
which are within us, not as to requirements which (as long as only
the Law, and not Christ's grace, is relied upon) do us violence and
exceed our capacity. Thus the New Law is less burdensome than
the Old Law, though it prescribes a more difficult purity and holiness. If the New Law requires many less things beyond the pre-
scriptions of the natural law, and many less ceremonial obser-
vances than the Old Law, in return it requires that which is the
most difficult of all: purity in the hidden movements and internal
acts of the soul. (And it demands that we nurture the *spirit* of the
counsels of the Gospel.) But love makes light the yoke of this
higher perfection.

Thus it must be said that we are no longer "under the Law," which is to say that we are quit of the regimen of the Law. We are quit of that condition of humanity wherein the government of its actions had, as its basic rule, no longer the natural light and the internal promptings of conscience, as in the days of the Patriarchs, and not as yet the promulgation of the Gospel, as after Christ's coming, but the promulgation of the written law transmitted by Moses. We have passed under the regimen of the New Law, which is a law of freedom.

This is the teaching of St. Paul. And it is the first great teaching—a divinely inspired teaching—about the direction and meaning of the historical development of mankind. . . .

The False Hegelian and Comtian Laws of Various States or Stages

6. Both Hegel and Auguste Comte made use of this notion of states or stages which I employed above. Though their views relate, in my opinion, to a false philosophy of history, I would at least mention them here, for we can be instructed by wrong views, too.

According to Hegel, there are the three stages of the objective mind or spirit—the stage of abstract right; the stage of morality of conscience or subjective morality (*Moralität*); and the stage of social morality (*Sittlichkeit*) or of the advent of the State. Now, of course, for Hegel these three stages are more metaphysical than historical. They don't refer essentially to historical succession. Yet such dialectical progress is revealed or manifested in the consciousness of mankind in a particularly significant manner at certain moments of the historical evolution. For instance, abstract right was typically manifested at the time of the Roman Empire; the morality of conscience or subjective morality in the centuries of Catholicism, and still more in the eighteenth century Enlightenment; whereas the third and final stage, the stage where all antinomies are resolved, appears in history when the German Protestant community takes political form, and the State emerges as the objectivation of the Divine—of that Divine which the young Hegel contemplated in Napoleon, the old Hegel in the Prussian State.

Another erroneous notion of the various states in human history—a notion which was quite famous during the nineteenth century—is Auguste Comte's notion of what he called "la loi des trois états," the law of the three stages or states. For Comte, mankind and the human mind passed successively through the *theological,* the *metaphysical,* and the *positive* state. In the theological state, everything was explained by supernatural beings and wills; in the metaphysical state, abstract occult causes took the place of supernatural beings, and everything was referred to vital forces, substantial forms, etc.; and finally, in the positive state, science is the unique rule—everything is to be understood in the light of sense-verified science, and both "wills" and "causes" must be replaced by "laws" or invariable relations between phenomena.

I would merely remark that this is indeed a quite interesting false generalization: on the one hand it was possible to find inductively (as regards the ways in which the human mind endeavored to interpret the phenomena of nature and to decipher sense-experience) some indications for such a construction; but, on the other hand, any inductive result was understood and conceptualized in the light of an erroneous philosophy, namely, positivist philosophy, for which *"everything is relative,* this is the only absolute principle,"* and there is *no other knowledge* than the knowledge of phenomena and the deciphering of sense-experience. From a genuinely historical point of view the *loi des trois états* is, even in the field of the knowledge of phenomena, a questionable and oversimplified generalization. But it is pure sophistry to claim that theology and metaphysics are done away with because a thunderbolt is not to be explained as an effect of some supernatural anger or of some "occult qualities."

The Law of the Passage from the "Magical" to the "Rational" Regime or State in the History of Human Culture

7. This distinction, which I simply indicated at the beginning of this chapter, refers—at least, I think so—to a genuine philosophy

of history. It is a philosophical distinction founded on, and interpreting, inductive data afforded by anthropology.[3] In an essay on *Sign and Symbol*,[4] written many years ago, I submitted that a distinction should be made between the *logical* sign, which speaks primarily to the intellect, and the *magical* sign, which speaks primarily to the imagination. My working hypothesis was the notion of functional condition or existential state, in the sense in which I have used the term "state" in this book. I was pointing to a fundamental distinction between the state of our developed cultures and another state or existential condition in which, for psychic and cultural life as a whole, the last word rests with the imagination, as the supreme and final law. In this latter state, the intellect is doubtless present, and with all its inherent principles and laws, but in a way it is not *free*—it is tied up, bound to the imagination. That is the state I am calling the *magical* regime or state of psychic and cultural life.

I would note that this working hypothesis succeeded in reconciling opposed points of view in a particularly controversial field. A few years before his death, Professor Lévy-Bruhl was so kind as to write and express his agreement with me on this point: "as you put it quite rightly, primitive mentality is a *state* of human mentality, and I can accept the characteristics through which you define it."

Allow me to quote now the testimony of the great Polish anthropologist, Bronislaw Malinowski: "I have chosen to face the question of primitive man's rational knowledge directly: watching him at his principal occupations, seeing him pass from work to magic and back again, entering into his mind, listening to his opinions. The whole problem might have been approached through the avenue of language, but this would have led us too far into questions of logic, semasiology, and theory of primitive languages. Words which serve to express general ideas such as *existence, substance,* and *attribute, cause* and *effect,* the *fundamental* and the *secondary;* words and expressions used in complicated pursuits like sailing, construction, measuring and checking; numerals and quantitative descriptions, correct and detailed classifications of natural phenomena, plants and animals—all this would lead us exactly to the same conclusion: that primitive man can observe and think, and that he possesses, embodied in his language, systems of methodical though rudimentary knowledge."

And Malinowski continues: "Similar conclusions could be drawn from an examination of those mental schemes and physical contrivances which could be described as diagrams or formulas. Methods of indicating the main points of the compass, arrangements of stars into constellations, coordination of these with the seasons, naming of moons in the year, of quarters in the moon—all these accomplishments are known to the simplest savages. Also they are all able to draw diagrammatic maps in the sand or dust, indicate arrangements by placing small stones, shells, or sticks on the ground, plan expeditions or raids on such rudimentary charts. By co-ordinating space and time they are able to arrange big tribal gatherings and to combine vast tribal movements over extensive areas. . . . The use of leaves, notched sticks, and similar aids to memory is well known and seems to be almost universal. All such 'diagrams' are means of reducing a complex and unwieldy bit of reality to a simple and handy form. They give man a relatively easy mental control over it. As such are they not—in a very rudimentary form no doubt—fundamentally akin to developed scientific formulas and 'models,' which are also simple and handy paraphrases of a complex or abstract reality, giving the civilized physicist mental control over it?" [5]

The intellect in primitive man is of the same kind as ours. It may even be more alive in him than in some civilized men. But the question with which we are concerned is that of its existential conditions, the existential regime or state under which it operates. In primitive man the intellect is in a general way involved with, and dependent on, the imagination and its savage world. This kind of mental regime is one in which acquaintance with nature is experienced and lived through with an intensity and to an extent we cannot easily picture. . . . [I]n passing from the myths of the primitive man to our rational or logical regime there were surely losses, compensating for the greater gains achieved by such a progress.

The magical state is a state of inferiority, but it is by no means despicable. It is the state of mankind in its infancy, a fertile state through which we have had to pass. And I think that anthropologists should recognize that under this regime humanity enriched itself with many vital truths, which were known by way of dream or divinatory instinct, and by actual participation in the thing known—not in a conceptual, rational manner. It is extremely difficult for us to imagine now what can have been the functioning of the human mind in such a state. It is a difficulty analogous to that which we experience when we try to penetrate the mental life of animals. Whatever *we* picture to ourselves is in fact bathed in intelligence, and in intelligence which is free, which has the upper hand over imagination. Therefore we have great trouble in depicting to ourselves any state in which—in the case of primitive man—imagination had the upper hand over the intellect; or in which—in the case of the animal—there is knowledge, but merely sensitive knowledge: knowledge by way of the senses, which admittedly are capable, in superior vertebrates, of *resembling* intelligence to a great extent. It is really impossible for a man to imagine how a dog is "thinking." But nevertheless there is a dog-knowledge which exists as a matter of fact, and is the object of the psychology of animals. We experience a similar difficulty when it comes to the magical state proper to the mental activity of the primitive man, a state utterly different from our logical state, and in which the imagination was the queen of the human mind. We might call our present state a daylight or solar state because it is bound up with the luminous and regular life of the intellect. And the magical state might be called a nocturnal state, because it is bound up with the fluid and twilight life of the imagination.

8. Here I would like to propose some remarks on positivism and Comte's law of the three states. From the positivist point of view one is led to say that the mathematical and physico-mathematical sciences, and all the multifarious sciences of phenomena, constitute the only function of truth and real knowledge in human thought, and that, therefore, religion, mystical experience, metaphysics, and poetry are, in the civilized mind, an inheritance from the primitive and "pre-logical" mentality. This is a major tenet in the positivists' philosophy of history. These types of mental activity are but metamorphoses of ancient magic—perhaps justifiable in the practical and emotional order, but directly opposed, as is magic itself, to the line of science and truth.[6] The era of science has succeeded to the era of magic, and magic and science are essentially inimical and incompatible.

For Bergson, I may add, magic and science are similarly inimical and incompatible. "Magic is the reverse of science," he wrote in *The Two Sources* because, for Bergson, also, science consists entirely in the mathematical explanation of matter. Yet in Bergson's view, science, at least science in the process of being born, always co-existed with magic. And science does not exhaust the function of truth and real knowledge in human thought. Other functions—religion, mystical experience, metaphysics, and poetry—are also functions of truth, and more profound ones. But for Bergson, as for the positivists, these things are at right angles to the line of science, and they spring from the same vital centre as magic. Magic and religion have a common origin, from which they developed in opposite directions—magic in the direction of illusion, myth-making, and laziness; and religion (what Bergson called "dynamic religion") in the direction of heroism and of truth.

Now the distinction which I have proposed between the magical and the rational states of the human mind and culture differs at once from the positivist and from the Bergsonian positions. To my mind, our modern science of phenomena is only one of the possible forms of science, only one of the degrees of knowledge. Moreover, science, philosophy, metaphysics, like religion and mysticism, and like poetry, are destined to grow up together. In the nocturnal state, the magical state of the primacy of the dream and of the imagination, they were inchoate, more or less fused or confused, but they were there. Once the threshold of the daylight state of the primacy of the intellect and the Logos was passed, they became more and more differentiated from each other. It is not true that "the era of science has succeeded the era of magic"— what is true is that the state of Logos has succeeded the state of Magic—for all the mental and cultural functions of the human being existed in the state of magic, and they now exist in the state of logical thought. Science, like religion, existed in the nocturnal state before it existed in the daylight state. So, one cannot say that there is nothing in common between magic and science, and that magic is the reverse of science. One can only say that the magical state of science—of that rudimentary science of the tribal man which was alluded to in Malinowski's remarks quoted above—is in opposition to the logical state of civilized man's science.

Thus my point is that all human thought, with its great and at first undifferentiated primordial ramifications, passes through a diversity of existential conditions or states. The science of the primitive man was science, and it was such in the state of magic—primitive man had a certain knowledge of nature, real and workable, though different from ours. This knowledge made use of certain connections of physical causality, and it formulated them in an intelligibly manageable manner, all the while immersing them in a kind of sacral empiricism, and in a general way of thinking dominated by the magical sign. Science left this condition when it passed over the threshold of the Logos-dominated regime of thought and of culture. Now, in our civilized times, the residues of magical knowing are taken over, by virtue of a process of abnormal integration, by a pseudo-science—the occultism, or the occult "sciences," of civilized man—utterly different from the magic of primitive man, and which will carry with it certain pathological characteristics for intellectual life (as happens for affective life in certain cases of infantile retrogression among adults).

Similar observations may be made with respect to religion. Religion was at first in a magical or nocturnal state, and then it passed under a new regime, the daylight state of human thought and culture. The religion of civilized humanity crossed the threshold of this daylight state either by a transformation into more or less rationalized mythology (as in Greece), or by a process of metaphysical elaboration (as in India), or by forms of revelation adapted to such a state (as in Judaeo-Christian monotheism). And, just as in certain forms of pseudo-knowledge, so in certain pseudo-religious phenomena to which the civilized man is liable to fall prey, residues of the magical state will appear, taken over, by virtue of a process of abnormal integration, by superstitious notions and imagery, wherein the part played by pathology is far greater than in magical religion itself.

The Law of the Progress of Moral Conscience

9. I consider this to be a most important law in the philosophy of history. In its essence and even in its value, the rectitude and purity of moral conscience are independent of the explicit knowledge of all particular moral laws. We realize this if we think, for ex-

ample, of the three states distinguished by theology in the history of mankind. Abraham was a great saint, a saint of incomparable stature. But he did not know that certain actions which we condemn today were prohibited by natural law. Hence we must conclude that mankind's state of nature was not a state in which natural moral laws were perfectly known and practised.[7] As a matter of fact, the precise knowledge of these natural moral laws—with the exception of the self-evident primary principle, *good is to be done and evil to be avoided*—is acquired slowly and with more or less difficulty. I would say that the equipment necessary to know the particular precepts of natural law exists within us—it is made up of the essential tendencies and inclinations of our nature. But a very long experience is required to have the corresponding knowledge through connaturality take actual form.

In other words, our knowledge of moral laws is progressive in nature. The sense of duty and obligation was always present, but the explicit knowledge of the various norms of natural law grows with time. And certain of these norms, like the law of monogamy, were known rather late in the history of mankind, so far as it is accessible to our investigation. Also, we may think that the knowledge of the particular precepts of natural law in all of their precise aspects and requirements will continue to grow until the end of human history.

I think that this progress of moral conscience as to the explicit knowledge of natural law is one of the least questionable examples of progress in mankind. Allow me to stress that I am not pointing to any progress in human moral behavior (or to any progress in the purity and sanctity of conscience, for Abraham, again, was a very great saint, with an absolutely pure heart). I am pointing to a progress of moral conscience as to the *knowledge* of the particular precepts of natural law.[8] This progress in knowledge can take place at the same time as a worsening in the conduct of a number of men, but that is another question. Take, for instance, the notion of slavery. We are now aware that slavery is contrary to the dignity of the human person. And yet there are totalitarian States which enslave the human being. But, nevertheless, they would not like to acknowledge this fact—that's why propaganda is so necessary—because there is a common awareness in mankind today that slavery is contrary to the dignity of man.

We may cite a few of the other examples of this progress in moral conscience. One is the notion of the treatment to be given to prisoners of war. For many, many centuries, and even Christian centuries, it was considered quite normal to kill prisoners of war. No difference was recognized between an enemy soldier in combat and one who had been taken prisoner. If a prisoner of war was granted life, this was considered a favour which was legitimately paid for by slavery. But now we have a completely different view of our obligations towards prisoners of war. Another example is the notion of child labour. At the beginning of the industrial age, child labour was considered quite legitimate. But now we have other ideas about this matter, and they are surely more conformable to natural law. Still another example is the notion of human labour itself. The notion that human labour is impossible without the whip of destitution—a notion quite widespread in the nineteenth century—seemed at that moment to be in accordance with natural law. Even religion and a misreading of Adam's punishment in *Genesis,* were made to contribute to this notion. But now we realize the great error in such a conception. And again: the notion that authority cannot be exercized without a lot of ruthlessness, and without the suppression of any human fellowship between the one who commands and the one who obeys, is another notion which seemed obvious at one time, and which is now considered wrong by a progress in our awareness of what human nature basically requires in our mutual relations and in the moral atmosphere of our living together. Finally, may I say that we probably are still in the dark about the part normally to be played in temporal and political matters themselves by laws which deal directly with spiritual life, such as the law of mutual forgiveness.

10. So much for the progress in our awareness of the more and more particular requirements of natural law. If it is a question, on the other hand, of a certain primal, extremely general and undifferentiated knowledge of the basic precepts of natural law, we have to elaborate in connection with anthropology the notion of what I would call the *fundamental dynamic schemes* of natural law, the meaning of which is highly undetermined. They are but general tendential forms or frameworks, such as can be obtained by the first, the "primitive" achievements of knowledge through inclination. We may think, for instance, of such general and undif-

ferentiated principles as: to take a man's life is not like taking
another animal's life; the family group has to comply with some
fixed pattern; sexual intercourse has to be contained within given
limitations; we are bound to look at the Invisible; we are bound to
live together under certain rules and prohibitions. I think that
these five general regulations correspond to the basic inclinations
of which St. Thomas speaks in his treatise on natural law.[9] And
they are subject, I would submit, to a much more universal
awareness—everywhere and in every time—than would appear to
a superficial glance. It is true that there is an immense amount of
relativity and variability to be found in the particular rules, cus-
toms, and standards in which, among all peoples of the earth,
human reason has expressed its knowledge of these most basic
aspects of natural law. But if we consider the dynamic schemes in
their entire generality we see that they were always recognized in
one way or another.

And now, as a corollary to my reflections on the progress of
moral conscience, I would emphasize that moral philosophy presupposes moral experience, the historical experience of mankind.
Moral philosophy, as indeed all philosophical knowledge, comes
about through concepts and judgments. It supposes a developed
rational knowledge. It entails a scientific justification of moral values by a demonstrative determination of what is consonant with
reason, and of the proper ends of the human essence and of
human society. But it is a kind of after-knowledge. The moral philosopher submits to critical examination, elucidates, sorts out, justifies, re-interprets, formulates in a more systematic or more
pungent manner the natural morality of mankind, I mean the
moral standards and regulations which are spontaneously known
to human reason in such or such an age of culture. As a result, it
is rather infrequent that a moral philosopher is in advance with respect to his time.

In other words, moral philosophy is a reflective knowledge,
and in this we have a token of its difference from metaphysical
knowledge. Metaphysics is not a reflective knowledge—it is not a
reflection on common sense. It states its own truths, and nobody
can judge a metaphysician, except in the name of a higher wisdom. But any kind of virtuous man, even one completely ignorant
in philosophy, can judge a moral philosopher, if the moral philoso-

pher teaches something wrong. I see in this a sign that moral philosophy is a reflective knowledge. And therefore, while it can happen, of course, that a moral philosopher may have broader horizons than the common people of his time, and may see things that they do not see, nevertheless, in general, the work of theoretical reflection cannot replace in moral matters the slow advance of consciousness, conscience, and experience in mankind. And this means not only an advance in rational knowledge, but primarily an advance in our lived awareness of our basic inclinations—an advance which may be conditioned by social changes. Thus for many centuries moral philosophers and common consciousness stressed the obligations of man prescribed by natural law. But there are also rights of man, which were, of course, implicitly recognized, especially by Christian thinkers. Yet it seems to me that it was necessary to wait until the eighteenth century, and the related social changes in human history, to have the basic inclinations on which an explicit awareness of these rights depends liberated in us—a fact which had an impact both on the common consciousness of mankind and on the rational consideration of moral and social philosophers.

The Law of the Passage from "Sacral" to "Secular" or "Lay" Civilizations

11. The distinction between "sacral" and "secular" civilizations has a universal bearing. Yet—by reason of the very distinction between the things that are Caesar's and the things that are God's—it is with Christianity that this distinction has taken its full historical importance. It is, therefore, but natural that in the present discussion I should refer to sacral Christian civilization and to secular Christian civilization. There was a sacral age, the age of mediaeval Christendom, mainly characterized, on the one hand, by the fact that the unity of faith was a prerequisite for political unity, and that the basic frame of reference was the unity of that social body, religio-political in nature, which was the *respublica Christiana;* and, on the other hand, by the fact that the dominant dynamic idea was the idea of fortitude at the service of justice. The modern

age, on the contrary, is not a sacral but a secular age. The order of temporal society has gained complete differentiation, and full autonomy in its own sphere, which is something normal in itself, required by the Gospel's distinction between God's and Caesar's domains. But that normal process was accompanied—and spoiled—by a most aggressive and stupid process of insulation from, and finally rejection of, God and the Gospel in the sphere of social and political life. The fruit of this we can contemplate today in the theocratic atheism of the Communist State.

Yet the fact remains that, as a result of the process of differentiation I just alluded to, the dominant dynamic idea of modern civilization is not the idea of fortitude at the service of justice, but rather the idea of the conquest of freedom and of social conditions conformable to human dignity. On the other hand, the root requirement for a sound mutual cooperation between the Church and the body politic is no longer the unity of a religio-political body, as the *respublica Christiana* of the Middle Ages was, but the very unity of the human person, simultaneously a member of the body politic and of the Church. And the unity of religion is not a prerequisite for political unity. Men subscribing to diverse religious or non-religious creeds have to share in and work for the same political or temporal common good.

This distinction between sacral and secular civilizations is a quite simple distinction. But once it has been formulated in rational terms, it provides us with a key to interpret the life and cultural standards of the Middle Ages in comparison with our own ways of life and cultural standards.[10] In other books (especially *True Humanism* and *Man and the State*) I have laid stress on its importance with respect to a correct interpretation of the relation between Church and State in our times, and to a correct formulation of the concrete historical idea appropriate to the coming age of civilization.

I would suggest that the same distinction could also serve as a key to the discussion of other areas of civilization. Thus, if we were dealing with a complete philosophy of history, we should consider in what sense Indian civilization is a sacral civilization. This is a great problem. Another great problem—one with practical as well as theoretical implications—is whether a sacral civilization like the Moslem one can become secular. Is it possible to have the same kind of development or evolution in the Moslem world as in the Christian world? Still another problem, which has already been touched upon, has to do with the State of Israel. As a State, a modern and democratic State, it cannot be sacral. But, on the other hand, to be a Jew means essentially to belong to a certain religious tradition, which is still at work hiddenly—even in those who have repudiated any definite creed—and which will probably take some kind of new vitality in many of the Jews who are now re-grouped in the Promised Land. Now, how will the State of Israel solve this question? Can it be at the same time Jewish and secular? What kind of freedom will the Israelian citizens who have embraced the Christian faith enjoy in such a State? This is a big question, and one that relates both to the philosophy of history and to political practice.

Finally, I think that the distinction we just discussed may help us in our approach to antiquity. We know that in antiquity there was no distinction between the things that are Caesar's and the things that are God's. Religion was embodied in the gods of the city. So we cannot speak of Greek civilization, for instance, as a secular civilization. Nor was it sacral in the strict sense of this word. It was sacral, I would say, in a different though analogical sense, peculiar to polytheism, and moreover rather difficult to characterize. Some writers, for instance Henri Marrou,[11] are apt to speak of the early Greek conception of the city, even of the Platonic utopia, as "totalitarian." To my mind, this is an erroneous wording. I think that we should coin a special concept—Greek civilization was neither "totalitarian," nor "secular," nor "sacral" in the Christian or Moslem sense, but rather, I suggest, "hieropolitical." It was hieropolitical because, on the one hand, the body politic was supreme in dignity (though bound to venerate the unwritten wisdom embodied in the cosmos), and, on the other hand, there was something sacred, something hieratic in the very notion of the political city, which was itself in charge of religious functions. This is but another example of the kind of questions which are within the province of the philosophy of history.

The Law of the Political and Social Coming of Age of the People

12. This law, which I shall point to in a brief manner (because in order to be fully elucidated it would require an entire book) deals with the progressive passage of the people in the course of modern history, from a state of subjection to a state of self-government in political and social matters, in other words, to a regime of civilization characterized by the democratic cast of mind and democratic philosophy.

The change in question is, I think, still in its first phases and in relation to it nations which are *de facto* contemporaneous find themselves at quite diverse historical stages. It was but natural that it should appear in political life before extending step by step to social life. Moreover, a normal development, called for by deep aspirations in human nature, was there preyed upon by a lot of wrong or perverse ideas which finally instigated the very opposite of democracy—the totalitarian State—and which imperil the democratic principle itself as long as it does not free itself completely of them.

The remark I wish to submit is that, considered in its normal and essential features, the political and social coming of age of the people was in itself a natural development—I mean, one which answered deep-seated demands of the order of nature, and in which certain requirements of natural law came to the fore; but in actual fact it is only under the action of the Gospel leaven, and by virtue of the Christian inspiration making its way in the depths of secular consciousness,[12] that the natural development in question took place. Thus it is that the democratic process, with its genuine, essential properties, and its adventitious ideological cockle, appeared first in that area of civilization which is the historical heir to mediaeval Western Christendom—and it was the more genuine, and is now the more live, where the temporal life of the community remains to a larger extent Christian-inspired.

But once the democratic process had appeared and prevailed in the area in question, it spontaneously spread, and keeps on spreading, over all other areas of civilization (except in those places where it is blocked by totalitarianism.) [13] Such a spontaneous universal spreading of the democratic process is an obvious sign of its basically natural character, in the sense I pointed out a moment ago.

NOTES

1. Lucien Lévy-Bruhl, who coined this expression (I was a student of his at the Sorbonne, and I always liked this scrupulously sincere and fair-minded positivist), first seemed to hold the intellect of the primitive man and its laws of functioning as different in *nature* from our civilized intellect. Later on he came to other conclusions and accepted the interpretation founded on the notion of *state*.

2. See my book *The Living Thoughts of St. Paul* (New York: Longmans, Green, 1941).

3. I would stress that no philosophy of history can be complete without anthropology—anthropology is a basic consideration for the philosopher of history.

4. See *Quatre essais sur l' esprit dans sa condition charnelle* (1939; Paris: Alsatia, 1956, new ed.), Chapter II; *Redeeming the Time* (London: Geoffrey Bles, 1943), Chapter IX.

5. Bronislaw Malinowski, *Magic, Science and Religion* (Anchor Books), pp. 33–34. See also Pierre Lecomte du Noüy's *Human Destiny* (Signet Books), Book III, especially pp. 79–80.

6. I remember that Lévy-Bruhl sent a copy of his first book on primitive mentality to a friend of his, the Belgian poet Verhaeren. Verhaeren wrote to Lévy-Bruhl that he was delighted to read the book because he found in it a complete description of his own mentality. Well, this was more of a criticism than a compliment.

7. See Raïssa Maritain, *Histoire d'Abraham ou les premiers âges de la conscience morale* (Paris: Desclée De Brouwer, 1947); Engl. trans.: *Abraham and the Accent of Conscience*, in *The Bridge*, vol. I (New York: Pantheon Books, 1955).

8. I would recall here St. Jerome's comment in reference to the patriarchs and the limited knowledge of natural law which prevailed in their time (with particular reference to polygamy): "Abraham was much holier than I am," he said, "but my *state* is better." (I quote St. Jerome from memory; there is a similar remark in St. Augustine, *De bono conjugali*, XXIII, n. 28.)

9. "In man there is, first of all, an inclination to good in accordance with the nature which he possesses in common with all substances: inasmuch as every substance tends to preserve its own being, according to its nature. . . . Secondly, there is in man an inclination to things which appertain to him more specially according to the nature that he shares with the animals: and in virtue of this inclination, those things are said to belong to the natural law 'which nature has taught all animals,' such as sexual intercourse, education of offspring, and so forth. Thirdly, there is in man an inclination to good, according to the nature of his reason, which nature is

proper to him. Thus, man has a natural inclination to know the truth about God, and to live in society." *Summa theol.* I–II, 94, 2.

10. I was most gratified to see this distinction used and emphasized by Msgr. Charles Journet in his great work, *L'Eglise du Verbe Incarné* (Paris: Desclée De Brouwer, 1941). See Vol. I, pp. 269–425 (Eng. tr., *The Church of the Word Incarnate*, Vol. I, London and New York: Sheed and Ward, 1955, pp. 214–330). It is good to have a notion elaborated in the field of the philosophy of history thus sanctioned by a theologian. Again, there must be cooperation between the philosophy of history and the theology of history. They are distinct, but they must not be separated.

11. See his excellent *Histoire de l'éducation dans l'antiquité* (Paris: Editions du Scuil, 1948), especially Parts I and II.

12. See my book *Christianity and Democracy* (London: Geoffrey Bles, 1945).

13. And still the fact remains that willy-nilly, Communism, in the very use it makes of the phrase "people's democracy," cannot help paying tribute to the moral power of the democratic principle.

HERMAN DOOYEWEERD

Herman Dooyeweerd (1894–1977), professor of the philosophy of law at the Free University of Amsterdam, developed a comprehensive theory in which his philosophy of history is central. His *A New Critique of Theoretical Thought* (4 volumes, 1953–58) is a major systematic philosophy in the Christian tradition, and corresponds in kind with the work of Tillich and Maritain. This selection comes from his own summary of his philosophy, *In the Twilight of Western Thought* (1960), first presented during a lecture tour of the United States, beginning at Harvard.

Dooyeweerd looks upon "laws" in historical development not as necessities but as "norms" which people ought to follow if they are to experience well the rich possibilities of God's created reality. He detects these norms empirically by observation of regularities in the historical process, as approached from the perspective of the biblical ideas of creation, fall, and redemption. He takes these ideas as an integral ground-motive, rejecting thereby the Thomist division of reality into an order of nature and an order of grace.

Dooyeweerd associates the term "historical" with the human function of cultural formation which he sees as a specialized mode or aspect of human activity. Via cultural form-giving, people induce a process of development whereby various undisclosed features of life are opened up to human experience. This "opening process," when healthy, follows the norms or "laws" of differentiation, individuation, integration, and continuity. A prime characteristic of an "advanced" society, compared with a "primitive" one, in other words, is not moral or cultural superiority, but the presence of highly differentiated social relationships and institutions—e.g., church, state, industry, social clubs, families, friendships, universities.

History and Cultural Development

If in the pre-scientific attitude of experience, we try to answer the question: "What is history?" we usually say: "That which has happened in the past." From this non-theoretical experiential attitude this answer is doubtless correct. Here we do not reflect on the particular historical mode of our experience, but we give our attention exclusively to the concrete *what*, which is experienced in this way. And so we refer to the concrete events that have occurred in the past.

But if we wish to acquire an insight into the historical viewpoint, which in principle delimits the scientific field of research in historiography, there is no use in referring to the concrete *what*, that is experienced in the historical way. We are then much rather interested in this particular mode of experience itself, that is to say, in the historical aspect of our experience as such. . . .

But what is the historical aspect of the facts concerned? . . .

Now, all modern philosophical attempts at delimiting the proper historical scientific viewpoint from that of the genetic natural sciences, resulted in accepting the notion of culture as the central criterion. . . .

We shall . . . replace the noun *culture* with the adjective *cultural*, in order to emphasize that it is only a modal aspect of our temporal world which is meant. Taken in this modal sense, the term "cultural" means nothing but a particular (experiential) mode of formation, or moulding, which is fundamentally different from all modes of formation found in nature and conceived in the phy-

Reprinted by permission of the Presbyterian and Reformed Publishing Company from *In the Twilight of Western Thought* (1960). The original chapter title is "The Sense of History and the Historicistic World and Life View—II."

sico-chemical or biotic aspects of experience. It is a controlling mode whereby form is given to a material according to a freely elaborate and variable plan.

A spider spins its web with faultless precision; but it does so after a fixed and uniform pattern prescribed by the instinct of the species. It lacks free control or dominion over its material, which is the very condition of the variability of all cultural formation. Thus the cultural mode of formation must receive its specific qualification through freedom of control, domination or power. This is why the great cultural commandment given to man at creation reads: "Subdue the earth and have dominion over it."

And if the genuine historical viewpoint of historiography is that of the cultural development of humanity, it follows that formative power or control must also be the modal kernel of the historical aspect. It is this nuclear moment which alone can give the analogical or multi-vocal concept of development its proper historical sense. The historical development of mankind means in principle, then, the development of its formative power over the world and over its societal life.

The cultural mode of formation reveals itself in two directions, which are closely connected with each other. On the one hand it is a formative power over persons unfolding itself by giving cultural form to their societal existence; on the other, it appears as a controlling manner of shaping natural materials, things, or forces to cultural ends.

The Germans speak of *Personkultur* and *Sachkultur*. Since all cultural phenomena are bound to human society in its historical development, the development of *Sachkultur* is in principle dependent on that of *Personkultur*. For the cultural formation of natural materials or forces can only occur by human persons, who must learn it by socio-cultural education, given in a socio-cultural form to their minds. In addition, both *Personkultur* and *Sachkultur* presuppose the leading ideas of a project, which leading figures or groups in history seek to realize in a human society. Therefore, the formative power of these leading figures and groups always implies an intentional relation to such ideas.

These ideas cannot be realized according to the merely subjective conception of those who propagate them. They must assume a socio-cultural form so that they themselves may be able to exercise formative power in the relationships of society. By way of example, I refer to the cultural influence of the ideas of natural law, especially the idea of the innate human rights, or to the cultural influence of the technological ideas of great inventors, of the aesthetic ideas of great artists, of the moral ideas of the preachers of new moralities, et cetera. Such ideas are not of a cultural historical significance in themselves; but they acquire a historical significance as soon as they begin to exercise formative power in human society. They can be realized only in typical total structures of societal relationships which in principle function in all aspects of our experiential horizon, such as a state, an industrial community, a school, a religious community, and so forth. The empirical reality of a human society can, therefore, never be exhausted in its cultural-historical aspect, as Historicism assumed. All that is real or that really happens in human society is more than merely historical.

. . . [T]he nuclear moment of the historico-cultural mode of development, namely, formative power, has itself a normative sense, since it implies a normative cultural vocation and task, committed to man at creation. Even the most terrible misuse of cultural power in our sinful world cannot make power itself sinful, nor can it detract from the normative sense of man's cultural vocation.

Until the cultural historical aspect of a human society discloses the anticipatory moments of its meaning, it shows itself to be in a rigid and primitive condition. Primitive cultures are enclosed in undifferentiated organized communities, which display a strong tendency towards isolation. As long as such primitive societies maintain their isolation in history, there can be no question of cultural development in the sense in which it is understood in historiography proper.

They display a totalitarian character, since they include their members in all the spheres of their personal life, and the temporal existence of the individual is completely dependent on membership of the family or sib, respectively, and of the tribal community. There is no room as yet for a differentiation of culture in the particular spheres of formative power, those, namely, of science, fine arts, commerce and industry, of state and church, and so forth. Since such undifferentiated communities fulfill all the tasks for which, on a higher level of civilization, particular organizations are formed, there is only one single undifferentiated cultural sphere. A rigid tradition, often deified by a pagan belief, and anxiously guarded by the leaders of the group, has the monopoly of formative power. The development process by which such cultural communities are formed shows only analogies of the biotic phases of birth, ripening, adolescence, age and decline. The duration of their existence is dependent on that of the popular and tribal communities by which they are sustained. They may vanish from the scene without leaving any trace in the history of mankind. This is how radical Historicism conceived the course of every civilization and thus Spengler predicted the inescapable decline of Western culture.

But the situation is quite different in the historical development of cultures that are opened up. From the ancient cultural centers of world-history, such as Babylon, Egypt, Palestine, Crete, Greece, Rome, Byzantium, essential tendencies of development passed over into medieval and modern Western civilization. They fertilized the Germanic and Arabian cultures and this fertilization has given rise to new forms of civilization. This opened-up cultural development has been freed from rigid dependence upon the living conditions of small popular or tribal communities. It does not move within the narrow boundaries of a closed and undifferentiated cultural group. But, like a fertilizing stream, it is always seeking new channels along which to continue its course.

The process by which the cultural aspect of a society is opened up always occurs in a conflict between the guardians of tradition and the propounders of new ideas. The formative power of tradition is enormous, for, in a concentrated form it embodies cultural treasures amassed in the course of centuries. Every generation is historically bound to former generations by its tradition. We are all dominated by it to a much higher degree than we realize. In a primitive closed civilization its power is nearly absolute. In an opened up culture, tradition is no longer unassailable, but it has the indispensable role of guarding that measure of continuity in cultural progress without which cultural life would be impossible.

In the struggle with the power of tradition the progressive ideas of so-called molders of history have themselves to be purged of their revolutionary subjectivity and adjusted to the norm of historical continuity. Even Jacob Burckhardt, that great disciple of

Leopold von Ranke, although strongly affected by the historicistic relativism, held to the norm of continuity as a last guarantee against the decline of all civilization.

The opening-up process of cultural life is characterized by the destruction of the undifferentiated and exclusive power of primitive communities. It is a process of cultural differentiation which is balanced by an increasing cultural integration. It is effected by the bursting of the rigid walls of isolation which had enclosed the primitive cultural life. This is achieved by submitting the latter to fruitful contact with civilizations which already have burst the bonds of tradition and had been opened up to outside influences.

Since August Comte and Herbert Spencer the criterion of differentiation and integration has been accepted by many sociologists to distinguish more highly developed from primitive societies. The process of differentiation was viewed as a consequence of the division of labor, and an attempt was made to explain it in a natural scientific manner in analogy to the increasing differentiation of organic life in the higher developed organisms. But I do not understand the term "cultural differentiation" in this pseudo-natural scientific sense.

Much rather I have in mind a differentiation in the typical structures of the different social relationships presenting themselves in a human society. A primitive sib or clan displays mixed traits of an extended family, a business organization, a club or school, a state, a religious community, and so forth. In a differentiated society, on the other hand, all these communities are sharply distinguished from one another, so that each of them can reveal its proper inner nature, notwithstanding the fact that there are all kinds of interrelations between them. Each of these differentiated communities has its own typical historico-cultural sphere of formative power, whose inner boundaries are determined by the inner nature of the communities to which they belong.

The typical structures of these communities are really structures of individuality, since they are typical structures of an individual societal whole. With the exception of the natural communities such as marriage and family, which have a typical biotical foundation, they are all typically founded in historico-cultural power formations, which presuppose the process of cultural differentiation and integration. Consequently, although they cannot be realized before this historical process has started, their typical structures can no more be variable than the modal structures of their different aspects, since they determine the inner nature of the differentiated communities. As such, they must be founded in the order of creation, which has determined the inner nature of all that presents itself within our temporal world. And they are not to be traced in a natural scientific way, since they are structural norms, which may be violated by man.

In the temporal world-order norms are only given as principles which need a formation by man in accordance with the level of historical development of a society. The societal forms which they assume in this way, are consequently of a variable character; but the structural principles, to which these forms give a variable positive content, are not variable historical phenomena, since they alone make all variable formations of the societal communities possible. Neither the inner nature of marriage, nor that of the family, the state, the church, an industrial community, and the like, are variable in time, but only the social forms in which they are realized.

The Historical school stressed the absolute individuality of any national community. But it overlooked the typical structures of individuality which determine the inner nature of the different communities, inclusive of the national one, which as such cannot be of a merely historical character. Nevertheless, it is true that the process of cultural differentiation and integration is at the same time a process of increasing individualization of human cultural life; for it is only in an opened up and differentiated civilization that individuality assumes a really historical significance.

It is true that in primitive, closed cultural areas individuality is not altogether lacking. But in consequence of the rigid dominance of tradition this individuality retains a certain traditional uniformity, so that from generation to generation such closed cultures display in general the same, individual features. It is for this reason that historiography in its proper sense takes no interest in these cultural individualities.

As soon, however, as the process of differentiation and integration commences, the historical task of individual cultural dispositions and talents becomes manifest. Every individual contribution to the opening up of the cultural aspect of human society becomes in the course of time a contribution to the cultural development of *mankind*, which has a world-wide perspective. Accordingly, the individuality of cultural leaders and groups assumes a deepened historical sense.

It is the opening-up process of human culture also which alone can give rise to *national* communities. A nation, viewed as a socio-cultural unit, should be sharply distinguished from the primitive, ethnical unit, which is called a popular or tribal community. A real national cultural whole is not a natural product of blood and soil, but the result of a process of differentiation and integration in the cultural formation of human society. In a national community all ethnical differences between the various groups of a population are integrated into a new individual whole, which lacks the undifferentiated totalitarian traits of a closed and primitive ethnic unit as a tribe or folkship. The different peoples of the United States of America are doubtless united in a national community, but how different are the ethnical components which are integrated into this national whole.

It was, therefore, an unmistakable proof of the reactionary character of the myth of blood and soil propagated by German Nazism that it tried to undermine the national consciousness of the Germanic peoples by reviving the primitive ethnic idea of *Volkstum*. Similarly, it is an unmistakable proof of the retrograde tendency of all modern totalitarian political systems that they attempt to annihiliate the process of cultural differentiation and individualization by a methodical mental equalizing (*Gleichschaltung*) of all cultural spheres; for this equalizing implies a fundamental denial of the value of the individual personality in the unfolding (opening-up) process of history.

So we may posit that the norm of cultural differentiation, integration and individualization is really an objective norm of the historical unfolding process of human society. It is founded in the divine world-order, since it indicates the necessary conditions of this prospective unfolding process, without which mankind cannot fulfill its historical task committed to it by the great cultural commandment. Furthermore, it provides us with an objective criterion to distinguish truly progressive from reactionary tendencies in history.

The unfolding or opening-up process of the cultural-historical aspect occurs in the anticipatory or prospective direction of the temporal order; it must, therefore, be possible to indicate the anticipatory moments in its modal structure by which the inner coherence of meaning of the historical process of development with the subsequently arranged normative aspects of our temporal horizon of experience reveals itself. Historicism is not able to do so, since it has reduced these normative aspects to mere modalities of the historical process of development. Consequently, it denies their irreducible character and meaning.

To begin with, the progressive unfolding process of history is characterized by the disclosure of a symbolic, or linguistic anticipation in the historical mode of experience. The linguistic aspect of our experiential horizon is that of communication by medium of signs which have a symbolical meaning. These signs may be words or other symbols and they play an essential role in our social experience. In the opening-up process of historical development that which really has an historical significance begins to separate itself from what is historically insignificant. This gives rise to a symbolical signifying of historical facts in order to preserve the memory of them.

Hegel and von Ranke held that history proper did not start before the need arose to preserve the memory of historical events by means of chronicles, records and other means. The so-called *Kulturkreislehre* in ethnology, which seeks to trace genetic continuity in the cultural evolution of mankind from the so-called primeval cultures of pre-history to civilizations at the highest level of development of civilization, has denied that the presence of memorials can be of any essential importance for the delimitation of this historical field of research. As its founder, Frobenius, has said, "History is action, and in comparison with this, how unessential is its symbolical recording." The truth is, however, that the rise of such memorials is an unquestionable criterion of the cultural unfolding of a society in a progressive sense. Consequently, a depreciation of the rise of historical memorials with respect to their significance for the historical development of mankind, testifies to a lack of insight into the modal structure of the historical aspect of experience in its opening-up process. The fact that historical memorials, or at least, reliable oral historical informations are lacking in primitive society and that only mythological representations of the genesis and development of their cultural life are found, cannot be unessential. The relatively uniform course of their process of development has not yet given the Muse of history any material worth recording as memorable in a really historical sense. An as yet closed historical consciousness clings to the biotic analogies in cultural development and inclines to a mythological interpretation of its course under the influence of a primitive religion of organic life.

The disclosure of the symbolic or linguistic anticipation in the unfolding process of the historical aspect of experience is indissolubly linked to a disclosure of cultural intercourse between different nations, which are caught up in the stream of world history. Cultural intercourse between different nations in this international sense is an anticipatory moment in the process of historical development referring forwards to the opening up of the modal aspect of conventional social intercourse.

Since the process of cultural differentiation leads to an increasing typical diversity of cultural spheres, there is a constant danger that one of these spheres may try to expand its formative power in an excessive manner at the expense of the others. Indeed, since the dissolution of the ecclesiastically unified culture which prevailed in medieval European civilization, there has been a running battle between the emancipated cultural spheres of the state, of natural science, of industry and commerce, and so forth, to acquire the supremacy one over the other.

In the progressive unfolding process of history, therefore, the preservation of a harmonious relationship between the differentiated cultural spheres becomes a vital interest of the entire human society. But this cultural harmony can be guaranteed only if the process of historical development complies with the normative principle of cultural economy. This principle forbids any excessive expansion of the formative power of a particular cultural sphere at the expense of the others. Here the aesthetic and economic anticipations in the historical mode of experience reveal themselves in their unbreakable mutual coherence. Both principles, that of cultural economy and that of cultural harmony, appeal to the inner nature of the differentiated cultural spheres as determined by the typical structures of individuality of the spheres of society to which they belong. Thus they, too, are well founded in the divine world-order. In the unfolding (opening-up) process of human culture, as soon as the natural bounds of the different cultural spheres are ignored through an excessive expansion of one of them, disastrous tensions and conflicts arise in human society. This may evoke convulsive reactions on the part of those cultural spheres which are threatened, or it may even lead to the complete ruin of a civilization, unless counter-tendencies in the process of development manifest themselves before it is too late and acquire sufficient cultural power to check the excessive expansion of power of a particular cultural factor.

It is in such consequences of the violation of the principles of cultural economy and harmony in the historical unfolding-process that the juridical anticipation in history comes to light. At this point we find ourselves confronted with the Hegelian adage: *"Die Weltgeschichte ist das Weltgericht."* I do not accept this dictum in the sense in which Hegel meant it; but rather in the sense that the violation of the normative principles to which the unfolding process of the cultural historical aspect of human society is subject is avenged in the course of world-history. This may be verified by observing the consequences of such violations.

When, finally, the question is asked concerning the deepest cause of disharmony in the unfolding process of history, we come face to face with the problem concerning the relationship between faith and culture and with the religious basic motives which operate in the central sphere of human life.

The disharmony in question belongs, alas, to the progressive line of cultural development, since it can only reveal itself in the historical unfolding process of cultural differentiation.

The conflicts and tensions which are particularly to be observed in modern Western civilization, cannot occur in a primitive, closed culture. Since any expansion of the formative power of mankind over the world gives rise to an increasing manifestation of human sin, the historical opening-up process is marked by blood and tears. It does not lead to an earthly paradise.

What, then, is the sense in all this extreme endeavor, conflict, and misery to which man submits in order to fulfill his cultural task in the world? Radical Historicism, as it manifested itself in all its consequences in Spengler's *Decline of the West*, deprived the history of mankind of any hope for the future and made it meaningless. This is the result of the absolutization of the historical aspect of experience; for we have seen that the latter can only reveal its sense in an unbreakable coherence with all the other aspects of our temporal experiential horizon. This temporal horizon itself refers to the human ego as to its central point of reference, both in its spiritual communion with all other human egos and in its central relationship to the Divine Author of all that has been created.

Ultimately, the problem of the meaning of history revolves around the question: "Who is man himself and what is his origin and his final destination?" Outside of the central biblical revelation of creation, the fall into sin and redemption through Jesus Christ, no real answer is to be found to this question. The conflicts and dialectical tensions which occur in the process of the opening-up process of human cultural life result from the absolutization of what is relative. And every absolutization takes its origin from the spirit of apostasy, from the spirit of the *civitas terrena*, the kingdom of darkness, as Augustine called it.

There would be no future hope for mankind and for the whole process of man's cultural development if Jesus Christ had not become the spiritual center and his kingdom the ultimate end of world-history.

This center and end of world-history is bound neither to the Western nor to any other civilization. But it will lead the new mankind as a whole to its true destination, since it has conquered the world by the divine love revealed in its *self-sacrifice*.

T. S. ELIOT

T. S. Eliot (1888–1965) aims in this essay, like the others in the
end-of-war collection from which it comes, to contribute to the
reconstruction of culture along Christian lines. This leads him to
reflect on the nature of culture as well as on the "relation" between culture and religion. A revised version of the essay became
the first chapter of *Notes toward the Definition of Culture* (1948).

Eliot presents a philosophy of cultural development that, not
unlike Dooyeweerd's, joins "culture" and "history" via a theory of
differentiation and integration. As societies develop there emerges
a diversity of groups and classes of peoples and functions, which in
turn supports the cultural development of individuals. The failure
to achieve cultural integration in this process is a mark of modern
western society. Groups and individuals are isolated from each
other, as well as from general society, and people's lives are often
one-sided. The theme echoes some of his most famous poems, *The
Waste Land* (1922) and *The Four Quartets* (1944), and his play,
The Cocktail Party (1950).

Religion and culture are, perhaps, different aspects of the
same thing. Religion is not, properly speaking, "related" to culture,
nor "identified" with it, since "culture (is), essentially, the incarnation, so to speak, of a religion in a particular people." Our belief is
revealed in the creeds we formulate *and* in our whole cultural
behaviour. This notion, says Eliot, "gives . . . an importance to
our most trivial pursuits." It also can help us in finding a way of
life which is more consistently reflective of Christian belief.

Cultural Forces in the Human Order

The word *culture* cannot be precisely defined: that is to say, no definition can be given which would be of much use to anyone previously unacquainted with the word itself or with what it designates. Furthermore, although the word cannot be taken as exactly synonymous with *civilization*, the meanings of the two words certainly overlap, and can be in some contexts identical; so that any attempt either to identify or to keep quite separate the meanings of the two words is certain to be stultified in practice. The difficulties to which the use of the word *culture* gives rise, however, are due not to obscurity of meaning, but to our failure to keep apart, and consequently to relate properly, a number of meanings which the word from time to time conveys. It is desirable therefore to begin by indicating the main distinct contexts in the mind of the author of this paper.

The term *culture* has different associations according to whether we have in mind the development of A an individual, of B a group or class, or of C a whole society. As it is a part of my thesis that the culture of the individual is dependent upon the culture of a class or group, and that the culture of a class or group is dependent upon the culture of the society to which that class or group belongs, sense C will be the fundamental one. At first sight, however, sense C would appear to be the one which has the least relation to the biological sense of the word *culture,* that which we use in speaking of the bacteriologist's work, or of *agriculture:* for in

Reprinted by permission of Faber and Faber Ltd., being an essay entitled "Cultural Forces in the Human Order" by T. S. Eliot which first appeared in *Prospect for Christendom: Essays in Catholic Social Reconstruction* (1945), edited by M. B. Reckitt. This edition © Mrs. Valerie Eliot/1977.

this we have in mind the conscious manipulation of living organism and its environment. The culture of a class or group, and still more the self-culture of an individual, may be to a considerable extent the fruit of a conscious purpose to attain "culture" (though the use of the term itself in this way is relatively modern); but we cannot regard the culture of a people or race as the result of any such deliberate purpose. Nevertheless, the use of the term in sense C is cognate and proper, inasmuch as the culture of a people may be considered as the pattern formed by a number of activities each of which realizes a purpose.

This third, or anthropological sense of the term *culture*, as used by E. B. Tylor in the title of his book *Primitive Culture*, was developed independently of the two other senses: but if we are considering highly developed societies, and especially contemporary society, we have to settle the relationship of the three areas. It is at this point, precisely, that anthropology passes into sociology. Amongst men of letters and moralists, it has been common enough to discuss the first two senses, and especially the first, without relation to the third. The most notable example of this selection is Matthew Arnold's *Culture and Anarchy*. Arnold is concerned almost entirely with the individual and the kind of "perfection" at which he should aim. It is true that in his famous classification of "Barbarians, Philistines, Populace" he concerns himself with a criticism of classes: but this criticism is confined to an indictment of the shortcomings of his three classes, and does not proceed to consider what should be the proper function or "perfection" of each class as a class. The effect, therefore, is of an exhortation to the individual who would attain the peculiar kind of "perfection" which Arnold calls "culture" to rise superior to the limitations of any class, rather than to incarnate its highest attainable ideals.

The effect of thinness—I hesitate to say superficiality—which Arnold's abstract culture makes upon a modern reader, is partly due to the absence of social background to his picture, and to the falsification or distortion of reality by this culture in a vacuum. But it is also due, I think, to a failure to take account of another distinction of senses in which we use the term "culture," besides that already mentioned. There are at least three kinds of attainment which we may have in mind in different contexts. We may be thinking of *refinement of manners*—of *urbanity:* if so, we probably

indicate a *social class* as the repository of them. We may be thinking of *learning* and a close acquaintance with the accumulated
wisdom of the past: if so, our man of culture is the scholar. We
may be thinking of *philosophy* in the wildest sense—an interest in,
and some ability to manipulate, abstract ideas: if so, we may mean
what can be called the intellectual. Or we may be thinking of the
arts: if so, we mean the artist and the amateur or dilletante. But
what we very seldom have in mind, when we speak of culture, is
all of these things at the same time. We do not find, for instance,
that an understanding of music or painting, or indeed a purely aesthetic appreciation of anything, figures explicitly in Arnold's account of the cultured man: yet no one will deny that these attainments play a part in culture. Similarly, Mr. Herbert Read, in his
excellent but very wilfully named little essay *To Hell With Culture,*
means by "culture" only an antiquarian piety towards the works of
plastic art of the past—Baedeker culture.

If we look at the several activities of culture listed in the preceding paragraph, we must conclude that no perfect achievement
in any one of them, to the exclusion of the others, can confer culture on anybody. We know that good manners, without education,
intellect, or sensibility, is mere automatism; that learning without
good manners or sensibility is pedantry; that intellectual ability
without the more human attributes is admirable in the same way
as the brilliance of a child chess prodigy; and that the arts without
intellectual meaning are vanity. And if we do not find culture in
any one of these activities alone, so we must not expect any one
person to be accomplished in all of them; and we shall come to
infer, that the wholly cultured individual is a phantasm; and we
will look for culture, not in any one individual or in any one group
of individuals, or in any one social class, but in the pattern of society as a whole—or at least, at this stage, in the upper levels of it.
This seems to me a very simple conclusion: but it is one very
frequently overlooked. People are always ready to consider themselves persons of culture, on the strength of one proficiency or
another, when they are not only lacking in others, but blind to
those which they lack. It is further worth mentioning that an artist
of any kind, even a great artist, is not necessarily a man of culture
merely on the strength of his art: artists are not only, very
frequently, insensitive to other arts than those which they practise,

but sometimes have very bad manners or very meagre intellectual gifts. The person who contributes to culture, however important his contribution may be, is not always a "cultured person."

It does not follow from this that there is no meaning in speaking of the culture of an individual, or of a group or class. We only mean that we look to the society as a whole for something to give significance to these meanings. On the other hand, we do not mean that in a society, of whatever grade of culture, the groups concerned with each activity of culture will be numerically distinct and exclusive: on the contrary, it is only by an overlapping and sharing of interests, by participation and mutual appreciation, that the cohesion necessary for culture can obtain. A religion requires not only a body of priests who know what they are doing, but a body of worshippers who know what is being done.

It is obvious that among the more primitive communities the several activities of culture are inextricably interwoven. The Dyak who spends the better part of a season shaping, carving, and painting his barque of the peculiar design required for the annual ritual of head-hunting, is exercising several cultural activities at once— artistic, religious, and military. As civilization advances greater occupational specialization may evince itself: in the "stone age" New Hebrides, Mr. John Layard says that certain islands specialize in particular arts and crafts, exchanging their wares, and displaying their accomplishments, to the reciprocal satisfaction of the members of the archipelago. But while the individuals of a tribe, or different islands or villages, may have separate functions—of which the most peculiar are those of the king and the witch-doctor—it is only at a much further stage that religion, science, politics, and art become abstractly conceived apart from each other. And just as the functional activities of individuals tend to become hereditary, and hereditary function tends to harden into class or caste distinction, and class distinction leads to conflict, so do religion, politics, science, and art reach a point at which there is a conscious struggle between them for dominance or autonomy. This friction is, at some stages and in some situations, highly creative: how far it is the result, and how far the cause, of increased consciousness need not here be considered. The tension within the society may be also a tension within the mind of the more conscious individual: the clash of duties in the *Antigone* (which is not simply a clash between piety and civil obedience, or between religion and politics, but between conflicting laws within what is still a political-religious complex) represents a very advanced stage of civilization: for the conflict must have taken place in society before it could be made articulate by the dramatist and receive from the audience the response which the dramatist's art requires.

As a society develops towards functional complexity and differentiation, we may expect the appearance of several cultural levels: in short, meaning B, the culture of class or group, will present itself. It will not, I think, be disputed that in any future society, as in every highly civilized society of the past, there will be several cultural levels. I do not think that the most ardent champions of social equality dispute this: the only difference of opinion turns upon whether the transmission of culture B must take place by inheritance—that is, whether the cultured class must propagate itself—or whether it can be hoped that some scheme of automatic selection can be found, so that every individual will in due course take his place at the highest cultural level for which his natural aptitudes fit him. This question, which few persons are able to argue dispassionately, must be excluded, with many others equally relevant, from the scope of the present paper. What is pertinent here is the fact that the emergence of more highly cultured groups does not leave the rest of society unaffected: it is itself part of a process of change of that total society. And it is certain—and particularly obvious when we are concerned with the arts—that as new values appear, as thought, sensibility and expression become more elaborate, other values vanish. This is only to say that you cannot expect to have all stages of development at once; that you cannot simultaneously produce great folk poetry at one cultural level and *Paradise Lost* at another. Indeed, the one thing that time is ever sure to bring about is the loss: the possibility of gain or compensation is almost always conceivable but can never be assured.

While it appears that progress towards higher civilization will bring into being the higher cultural levels, and the more specialized culture groups such as those which I mentioned, we must expect this development, in its later stages, to be attended with perils. Cultural disintegration is perhaps the most radical kind of disintegration which can affect a society. It is not the only kind, or not the only aspect under which disintegration can be considered;

but whatever be cause and whatever be effect, the disintegration of culture is the most serious and the most difficult of repair. It must not be confused with another malady, that of a kind of ossification into caste, as in India, of what was originally a hierarchy of functions: even though (paradoxically in appearance) the two maladies may both have some hold upon British society to-day. Cultural disintegration may be pronounced to be present, when the culture of two or more social strata becomes so divergent that these approximate to having different cultures; and also when culture B tends itself to be broken into the fragments each of which represents one cultural activity alone. If I am not mistaken, some disintegration of the classes in which culture is, or should be, most highly developed, has already taken place—as well as cultural separation between one level of society and another. Religious thought and practice, philosophy, and art each tend to become an isolated area cultivated by different groups in no communication with each other. The artistic sensibility is impoverished by its separation from the religious sensibility, the religious by its separation from the artistic, and the vestige of *manners* may be left to those who, having their sensibility untrained either by religion or by art, and their minds unfurnished with the material for witty conversation, will have no context in their lives to give meaning to their behaviour. And deterioration at this level is a matter of concern, not only to the limited group which is visibly affected, but to the whole people.

The causes for the decline of culture (in the total sense which I have tried to suggest) are as complex as the evidences of it are various. Its history, indeed, is not so much the history of a particular subject, as the history of this country and of the world, in recent times, from a particular point of view—I say "particular," but indeed it might be considered more "general" than any other. It may be traced in the accounts given . . . of the causes of more tangible social ailments; and the remedy, if there be any, must consist largely of the application of the right remedies to these other disorders. But our being able to see the situation from this point of view, which is in a way more comprehensive than any of the others, should introduce an element of criticism and judgement which may affect our directions. To illustrate all the ways in which the problem of culture enters in to other problems would be itself a work of considerable scope. For it would mean reviewing almost every major problem with this aspect in mind. It should enter into our consideration of the relation of the great nations, regarded as individual "cultures," to each other; of the relation of the great nations to the smaller nations, and their future political and economic pattern; [1] of the relation of parent nations to colonial nations; of the relation of the more advanced to the less developed, as in Africa; of the policy to be adopted towards those districts, such as some of the West Indies, where economic compulsion or inducement have brought together a number of people of different races, in a situation in which their ancestral cultures disappear without prospect of being replaced by a new composite culture. It affects our whole policy of education— or should affect it, by giving us a scale of values, for I see very little evidence of its presence in current discussions of educational reform. If we take culture seriously, we must see that a people does not merely need enough to eat, but needs a proper *cuisine:* one symptom of the decline of culture in Britain is the indifference to the art of preparing food. Culture may even be described, as what makes life worth living. And it is what makes it possible for other peoples and generations to say, in retrospect, that it was worth while for an extinct civilization or a past generation to have existed.

My excuse for giving so much space to a kind of description or suggestion, of what I mean by culture, without mentioning religion, or the Christian Faith, or Christendom, is the confusion into which we are apt to fall through not examining the meanings of the term. In proceeding from this point, we must caution ourselves about the difference of two points of view, between which we are liable to waver dangerously; that from which we consider the relation of culture to "religion" regarded from the outside, and the relation of culture to a particular religion which we do not call religion because for us it is the Christian Faith. And even in discussing culture in relation to Christianity, we are in danger of slipping into the assumption that the Christian Faith is circumscribed by European culture.

Even when I speak of a "relation" between culture and religion, I must withdraw the word "relation." The assumption of a *relationship* between culture and religion is perhaps the most fundamental error of Matthew Arnold in the essay which I mentioned at the beginning of this paper. In *Culture and Anarchy,* as it is not a piece of reasoning from carefully defined premises, we find not only unexamined assumptions but also conclusions of which the author may not have been aware. Certainly he gives me the impression (and his operation is largely the giving of impressions) that Culture (as he uses the term) is something more comprehensive than religion; that the latter is merely a necessary element, providing ethical structure and some emotional colour, to Culture which is the highest value. And there is another point of view which, though perfectly sound, must be distinguished from that which I shall try to express. Brother George Every, in his admirable essay *Christian Discrimination,* is concerned with the more limited aspect of culture which is good taste in the arts and especially in the art of literature. He is, certainly, tackling what I have already mentioned as one of the symptoms of decline, the separation of artistic and religious sensibility. It is right that this ailment should be diagnosed and prescribed for in this way; just as it is right and desirable both that we should have better ecclesiastical art and architecture, and that Christians should be able to apply, in the right way, Christian criteria to secular literature. But what I am here trying to get at, lies at another level.

It may have struck the reader that what I have said about the development of culture, and about the danger of disintegration of a developed culture, may apply also in the history of religion. The development of culture and the development of religion, in a society uninfluenced from without, cannot be clearly distinguished from each other: and it will be a question of the bias of the particular observer, whether an advancement of culture is held to be the cause of a higher stage of religion, or whether a progress in the development of the religious sense is held to bring about a refinement of culture. It is probably the history of the penetration of the Graeco-Roman culture by the Christian Faith, a penetration which had profound effects both upon this culture and upon the forms of the Faith and the direction of theological thought, that inclines us to assume a distinct and separate life of religion and of culture. But the culture with which Christianity came into contact (as well as that of the environment in which it began) was itself a religious culture in decline. So while we believe that the same religion may inform a variety of differing cultures, we may ask whether any culture can either come into being, or maintain itself, without a religious basis. We may go further, and ask whether what we call the culture, and the religion, of a people are not different aspects of the same thing: the culture being, essentially, the incarnation, so to speak, of a religion in a particular people.

As a society develops, a greater number of degrees and kinds of religious capacity and function, as well as of other capacities and functions, will make their appearance. (I am not here concerned with how far these differences may be due to differences in individual ability, and how far to opportunities of education and environment.) It is to be noticed that in some religions the differentiation has been so great that there have been in effect two religions—one for the populace and one for the adepts. The evils, and resulting abuses, of this "two nations" situation in religion are obvious. Christianity, at least until the end of the Middle Ages, showed an exceptional resistance to this disease. The schisms of the sixteenth century, and the subsequent appearance of other sects, can be studied either as the history of division of religious doctrine, or as a struggle between opposed social groups—as the disintegration of culture, or as the variation of doctrine. Yet, while the Faith cannot admit of wide divergencies of belief on the same level, it must find room for many *degrees* and varieties of imaginative and emotive reception of the same doctrines, just as it must embrace many variations of order and ritual. The Christian Faith also, *psychologically* considered—as a system of beliefs and attitudes in particular living embodied minds—will have a history: though it would be the grossest of errors to suppose that the sense in which it can be spoken of as developing and changing, implies the possibility of any greater sanctity or divine illumination being attainable at a more developed stage. (We do not assume that there is *progress* even in art, or that "primitive" art is necessarily inferior to the more sophisticated.) But one of the features of advanced development, whether we are taking the religious or the cultural point of view, is the appearance of *scepticism*—by which, of course, I do not mean infidelity or destructiveness (still less the unbelief which springs from mental sloth) but a habit of examining evidence, and a capacity for delayed decision. Scepticism is a highly civilized faculty, but one of which society can die: for the abuse of scepticism is pyrrhonism. Where scepticism is strength, pyrrhonism is weakness, the inability to endure the strain of doubt and decision: and it is a malady from which we suffer to-day culturally as well as in religion.

The conception of culture and religion as being—when each term is taken in the right context—different aspects of the same thing, is one which requires a good deal of explanation. But I should like to suggest first, that it provides us with the means of combating two complementary errors. The one—at present the commoner of the two—is that held by people who hope that culture can be preserved, extended, and developed in the absence of religion. This error may be held by the Christian in common with the infidel, and its refutation would require an historical analysis of considerable fineness, because the truth is not immediately apparent to superficial inspection. A culture may linger on and indeed produce, for a time, some of its most brilliant artistic and social successes when the religious faith has fallen into extreme decay: so that to accept the point of view here taken requires standing a long way off from the object. The other error is the belief that the preservation and maintenance of religion need take no account of the preservation and maintenance of culture: a belief which may even lead to the rejection of the products of culture as frivolity and obstruction to the spiritual life. To be in a position to reject this error also means standing afar from the object, refusing to accept the easy conclusion, when the culture that we see is culture in decline, that culture is dispensable. And I must add that to see the unity of culture and religion in this way neither implies that all the products of art can be accepted uncritically, nor provides a criterion immediately utilizable by everybody, for distinguishing between them: aesthetic sensibility must be extended into spiritual perception, or spiritual perception focused by aesthetic sensibility and practised taste, before we are able to pronounce upon either decadence or diabolism or nihilism in art; or before we can perceive that, in the end, the judgement of a work of art by either religious or aesthetic standards will come to the same thing.

The way of looking at culture and religion which I am trying to indicate is one so difficult that I am not sure that I grasp it myself except in flashes, or that I understand all its implications. It is also one which entails the risk of error at every moment, by

some unperceived alteration of the meaning which either term has
when the two are coupled in this way, into some meaning which
either has when taken alone. For instance, it is easy to draw the
false inference, because we do not meet culture in the abstract,
but only the cultures of particular peoples and groups of peoples,
that there is a European religion, or even an English religion. It is
in the aspect in which we see a religion as the whole *way of life* of
a people, from birth to the grave, from morning to night and even
perhaps in sleep, that we see that a religion must be incarnated in
particular peoples; but, looking at it the other way round, we see
that a culture which is the actualization of a religion which is also
actualized in other cultures—a *universal* religion—is at least potentially a higher culture than that of an exclusive, racial, or state
religion. This does not separate culture and religion; for just as the
Christian Faith could be the spirit informing an infinite variety of
human cultures, so there is also an abstract identity in culture, an
element of identity which makes it possible for us to respect alien
cultures, however remote. If there was no meaning to the word in
the singular there would be no meaning to it in the plural.

The reader must constantly remind himself, as the writer of
this paper has constantly to do, of how much is here embraced by
the term *culture*. It includes not merely the kind of activity and interest which is considered the specific attribute of the persons involved by meaning B, but all the characteristic activities and interests of a people: to allow, at this point, a few pictures to pass
through the mind, such as Derby Day, Henley Regatta, Cowes, the
twelfth of August, a cup final, the dog races, the pin table, the dart
board, a Wensleydale cheese, boiled cabbage cut in sections, will
deflect the mind from a misleading concentration on perpendicular
Gothic and the music of Elgar. But before drawing any conclusions from this comprehensiveness, a qualification must be introduced. The actual religion of no people at any time has so far
been purely Christian, or indeed purely anything else, though the
faith of Israel, immediately after one of its periodic house-clean-
ings, may have approximated more closely to purity than any
other. There are, in fact, always bits and traces, more or less absorbed, of more primitive faiths; there is also a tendency for para-
sitic beliefs to flourish to a dangerous degree; and also perversions,
as when patriotism, which pertains to natural religion and is there-

fore licit and even encouraged by Christianity, becomes hyper-
trophied into a caricature of itself. Nor is the total religion of a
people—or the total culture—ever completely unified: it is only too
possible for a people to maintain contradictory beliefs, and to propitiate antagonistic powers. Apart from the fact that as cultures of
different peoples differ, the culture of individuals of the same people can differ, and not only in degree.

The reflection that what we believe is not merely what we
formulate and subscribe to, but that behaviour is also belief, and
that even the most conscious and developed of us live also at the
level at which belief and behaviour cannot be differentiated, is one
that may, once it is animated by the imagination, have disconcerting consequences. It gives, of course, an importance to our most
trivial pursuits, to the occupation of our every minute, which most
of us cannot contemplate long at a time without the horror of
nightmare. When we consider the extent of the integration implied, for the cultivation of the spiritual life, we must remember
the possibility of grace and the exemplars of sanctity in order not
to abandon the attempt and sink into despair. And when we turn
to the problem of evangelization, to the building of a Christian society, this also gives reason to quail. To believe that *we* are religious people and that the other people are without religion and
must be converted, is a belief which can be endured with some
complacency. But to ask whether the people have not a religion already, a religion of which part of the ritual is (or was) Derby Day
and the dog track, is as unpleasant as to suggest that part of the
religion of a higher ecclesiastic is gaiters and the Athenaeum. It is
at least inconvenient to find that as Christians we do not believe
enough, and that other people—and we among them—believe in
too many things. And to suggest that the perfection of faith for a
man of flesh and blood, is not to be found in the mind only, or in a
special and separate exercise of the emotions only, or in obser-
vance of the Law only, but is, so to speak, in the body also, is to
suggest a considerable readjustment for most of us.

The reader will perhaps be impatient on finding this essay
concerned rather with definition and analysis, than with prescription; and if he expects to find . . . some easily apprehended
plan of action for the period immediately succeeding this war,
he will be disappointed by this essay. I might have fulfilled his

expectations better, if I had occupied the space with designs for the establishment of municipal theatres, provincial orchestras, and modern art galleries, or suggestions for applying religious criteria to literature. All of these are serious subjects: but it seemed to me that the question of what culture is, from a religious point of view, and what the Christian faith means, from a cultural point of view, had a certain priority. Several assumptions have been questioned. It is commonly assumed that culture exists, but that it is the property of a small section of society; and from this assumption it is quite usual to proceed to one or the other of two conclusions—either that culture can only be the concern of a small number, and that therefore there is no place for it in the society of the future; or that in the society of the future the culture which has been the possession of the few must be put into the possession of everybody. This assumption and its consequences are parallel to those involved in the attack on the ascetic life and the monastic principle: for just as culture which consists of practices only possible for a small number of people is now deprecated, so was the enclosed and contemplative life contemned by extreme Protestantism, and celibacy disapproved almost as a perversion. As we tend to identify culture with some part of culture, so we tend to identify the religious life with the religious life of some part of society. Many people will admit either that our culture ought to be Christianized, or that our fragment of Christendom ought to be refined by more culture: but as I do not accept the kind of separation which they take for granted, so I do not find satisfactory the kind of unification which they advocate. If my definition has anything to commend it, then it is a point from which to start, and will affect our views of what is to be done in the matter of religious education, and in that of re-union of the churches, and in many other problems which otherwise would seem still more remote.

I hesitate to attempt to illustrate the application of this view in any particular areas of practical activity, for the reason that in considering these, and in suggesting lines of action, it is always possible that I may introduce fresh premises; and personal opinions which, whether right or wrong, are not strictly deducible as a consequence of the foregoing account, and may, by presenting some unpalatable doctrine, jeopardize my hope of commanding assent to what I have already said. On the other hand, I should not like to leave the reader under the impression that the questions with which I have been occupied have no bearing whatever upon action. If we must, then, supply some evidence of applicability, it is impossible to evade the problem of education: but I shall confine myself to the few remarks most likely to win the assent of anyone who has not already rejected what precedes. I have assumed throughout, that in any civilized society there must be different, distinguishable cultural levels, according to the increasing complexity of interdependent functions. The present agitation for educational equality is mostly impelled, I take it, not by a belief that everyone should have the same degree of education, but by a belief that what is considered superior education should be bestowed upon those who have the native ability to profit by it, rather than merely on those whose financial advantages make it possible. To this belief, stated in this way, I do not see how anyone can take exception. But there are two dangers, one or the other of which I have found latent in many recent public statements. One is a *Liberal* tendency, to regard education, and Culture B so far as it is attainable by education, in terms of material wealth or its equivalent in power or in social prestige; to emphasize, in consequence, opportunity for the individual rather than the benefit of the community as a whole. Just as it was once assumed that the man who made a fortune was incidentally conferring a benefit upon the community, so we may be in danger of assuming that the individual whose intellectual brilliance, unaided by parental fortune, gains him the highest academic awards is thereby benefiting society also. The other danger is the tendency to assume that it is more important that everyone should be educated, than that the highest standards of education for the few should be maintained: acting upon this impulse, we are likely to take the easy course of relaxing the admission requirements of the universities, rather than the more difficult one of adapting the tuition in the schools to the requirements of the universities.

A parallel appears in the matter of religious education. No one would maintain that the higher levels of religious knowledge should be accessible only to those of a certain social or economic position. The notion that religious instruction should be reserved for those who want it—that is, for young children whose parents want it—and that others may remain in ignorance, is still held. But the view that is likely to prevail, is that a uniform and "undenominational" religious instruction should be given in schools, to all pupils whose parents do not take the trouble to object. On the obvious advantages and disadvantages of this uniformity in comparison with the actual religious instruction in schools on religious foundations I shall not touch, for this is not a question which has been overlooked. But on the view of culture and religion which has here been advanced, we cannot afford to neglect any level; and if we are seriously concerned about the quality of the education provided for the individuals representing Culture B, we must ask what is to be done on this level for religious education also. For the great majority, whose religious life will remain largely on the plane of behaviour, instruction up to the age of fifteen or sixteen might suffice. But those who are capable of profiting by further education, should be provided with the opportunity of further religious education as well. We cannot look back on any past period which will provide an exact pattern for a future Christendom; and we have to take thought, in considering the maintenance and development of the different religious-cultural levels in future society, of matters which our ancestors left to look after themselves. Our problems of general education are much more complex than theirs, and we find ourselves obliged to lay much heavier burdens upon the educational system than they did. We cannot afford to be content to provide a religious education of the elementary kind which was adequate three hundred years ago, and which only appears modern because it now takes account of the results of textual criticism and archaeological exploration. We need, in fact, if we are to renew a Christian culture, to supply our Culture B with a laity (to say nothing of the priesthood) of men and women whose intellect and sensibility qualify them for a higher religious education than is at present, for the laity, obtainable. The Christendom of the future cannot afford to do without an *élite* among the laity; and if we really mean Christendom, and not merely a body of cultivated church people, these will be the same people in whose guardianship will repose Culture B in the secular sense, for it will, necessarily, be the same culture. As to what part the educational institutions can play in this education I have no suggestions to offer. I do not envisage an identical *curriculum* for every individual, but one variable according to the peculiar apti-

tudes and interests of individuals—historical, philosophical, sociological, ascetic, legal, or artistic—so as to have the closest bearing
upon each person's other studies and activities. For whereas it is
more practical in dealing with children to provide religious instruction as a separate study (inasmuch as at this stage of consciousness the greater part of their religious *education* is being received
unconsciously from their family and their environment and the
culture of the society to which they belong), for those of more
adult years a process of conscious re-integration of religion and
culture is appropriate. Our thinking about religious education
seems to me a century behind our thought about other educational
matters. And there would follow, I think, as an effect of the establishment of higher standards of training of the religious intellect and sensibility among the laity, a higher standard of culture
among the priesthood.

To proceed in a straight line is not the only method of exposition; and there is sometimes something to be said for leaving the
reader to draw mistaken inferences if he will, and returning to correct them afterwards. I think that some readers will have drawn
the conclusion, at an earlier stage, that I have *identified* religion
with culture; that I am, like Matthew Arnold, more interested in
the preservation and development of culture than I am with the
truths of the faith which I . . . profess.

I spoke at one point of the culture of a people as an *incarnation* of its religion; and while I am aware of some temerity in
employing such an exalted term, I cannot think of any other
which, used in this way metaphorically, would better express my
intention to avoid slipping into the error of *identification*. The
truth, partial truth, or falsity of a religion neither consists in the
cultural achievements of a people which professes that religion,
nor can it be exactly tested by them. From what a people may as a
whole be said to believe, as shown by its *behaviour,* is, as I have
said, always something more, and a great deal less, than its pro-
fessed faith in its purity. Furthermore, a people whose culture has
been formed by a religion of partial truth, or one which has not
received the full revelation, may live that religion (at some period
in its history, at least) with greater fidelity than another people
which has had the true light. It is only when we contemplate our
culture as it ought to be, if our society were a really Christian soci-

ety, that we can speak of Christian culture as the highest culture; it is only in referring to one or another development of it, at different periods in the past, and not by referring to any one epoch as a whole, that we can affirm that it is a higher culture than any other in history. In comparing our culture at the present day to that of some non-Christian peoples, we must be prepared to confess, in one respect or another, shameful inferiority. I do not overlook the possibility that Britain, if it consummated its actual apostasy by reforming itself according to the tenets of some secular religion, might produce a culture superior to what we can boast today. This would not be evidence—though everyone, at that stage, would take it as such—that the new religion was the Truth and that Christianity had been disproved. It would merely prove that any religion, while it lasts, and on its own level, gives a meaning to life, and preserves the mass of humanity from that boredom which ends as despair.

NOTES

1. This is touched upon, though without any discussion of the meaning of "culture," by E. H. Carr, *Conditions of Peace*, Part I, ch. iii. "In a clumsy but convenient terminology which originated in Central Europe, we must distinguish between 'cultural nation' and 'state nation.' The existence of a more or less homogeneous racial or linguistic group bound together by a common tradition and the cultivation of a common culture must cease to provide a *prima facie* case for the setting up or the maintenance of an independent political unit." But Mr. Carr is here more concerned with the problem of political unity, than with the preservation of cultures, or the question of whether they are worth preserving, in the political unity.

THE WORLD COUNCIL OF CHURCHES

This Faith and Order paper of the World Council of Churches is different in kind from every other entry in this anthology. It is a church document and the product of a lengthy and complex cooperative process of composition. Hendrikus Berkhof (b.1914), professor at the University of Leiden, prepared the first draft and guided it through several stages of revision over a period of years. It does retain the distinctive imprint of Berkhof's thought as found in his *Christ the Meaning of History* (Dutch 1958, English 1966). But it also underwent careful scrutiny by groups in various parts of the world, by theologians, natural scientists, and historians gathered at Geneva, and by the Faith and Order Commission itself at Bristol in 1967.

The document in a remarkable way touches most of the themes so far discussed, and thus may serve as a fitting conclusion of parts one and two. One important new element is the theme of nature in relation to a Christian view of history and culture. God's work within Israel's history, the document states, radically altered human understanding of nature and, with that, human cultural behaviour. In the Jewish and, subsequently, Christian view, we are liberated from subservience to the forces of nature. In our new freedom we can engage in the human task of transforming nature culturally. We do it in health when we respect the integrity of the non-human world in its place before God. The whole of creation, including non-human reality, thus gradually came to be understood as historically dynamic, moving toward the consummation of history.

The document is not merely a statement of ideas and beliefs, but throughout is a vehicle calling Christians to historical action which serves our neighbors by fighting "against hunger, suffering, poverty, discrimination, and oppression, and for welfare, freedom, equality and brotherhood."

God in Nature and History

I. Introduction

Without any deliberate choice on his part, modern man has entered into a new experience and understanding of nature and history. For many centuries there was a general tendency to consider non-human nature as an entirely earthbound static reality, this planet being conceived as the stage for the drama of human life. In European culture, history was thought of as covering a short period of but a few thousand years, and also as a basically static reality, within which Fall, Incarnation and Consummation were seen as three incidents, of which the second and the third aimed at the restoration of a supposedly perfect beginning.

This world-view underwent a gradual disintegration in the period succeeding the Renaissance. The process speeded up about 1850. Now, since 1950, the quick destruction of its last remnants has become manifest, as it has given way to a radically new and dynamic concept of nature and history.

For modern man nature is thus no longer a static, geocentric, limited entity, but a process in an indeterminate space and an almost endless time. The earth is a tiny satellite of a little star in one of the many galaxies discovered by terrestrial telescopes. The process of development of this earth began about four billion years ago. That process went on through all kinds of events, in a chequered career, as matter, then life, and then conscious life came to be, through ever higher and more complex unities, characterized by a gradually increasing possibility of freedom—until about 2 or 1 million years ago the phenomenon of man emerged.

Reprinted by permission of the World Council of Churches from *New Directions in Faith and Order: Bristol 1967* (1968).

According to the now dominant theory of evolution, man is the product of age-long natural development, moved forward by the forces of heredity and selection. Since the days of Darwin, there has been a latent temptation to use this theory as the basis of a materialistic and monistic ideology. Science itself, in virtue of its nature and limits, refuses to make this extrapolation, yet on account of its important role in modern society, cannot help creating for countless people an atmosphere which makes them feel like elements in a powerful and irresistible evolutionary process. For some this feeling results in optimism, because they believe themselves driven towards a future of greater freedom and welfare. Others, on the contrary, fear that this freedom, as expressed in the power of nuclear fission, of keeping alive the congenitally weak, etc. will in the long run destroy the human race.

The Christian Church shares in the bewilderment created by this new experience and understanding. For centuries the Bible has been thought of as witnessing to a small geocentric and static world, governed by a wise and almighty God, whose main interest is to help man, the crown of his creation, to his eternal destiny. Now, however, man looks insignificant indeed against the background of the vast dimensions of time and space. The question must arise whether the God of the Bible has any relation to the modern scientific world-view, or has anything to say to the feelings of either optimism or pessimism which it creates in the hearts of contemporary men.

Christendom, embarrassed by these facts and questions, has often given evasive answers to this new challenge. These answers have either denied the clear facts of science (fundamentalism) or the essentials of the Christian faith (modernism), or else have tried to separate the realms of faith and of science, by limiting God's work to the inner life and to existential decision, and by denying his relations to the visible realities of nature and history (pietism, theological existentialism). We may nevertheless acknowledge with gratitude that the Christian Church in its rich tradition has preserved many precious insights which can help us in this situation.

We feel the obligation to look for such answers, and to seek a new and better mutual relationship between the Christian message and the modern view of life and of the world. In trying to ac-

cept that obligation, this paper will start from the biblical side, aiming at a fresh understanding of what the Old and the New
Testaments teach about God's active presence in nature and history.

This subject is so closely connected with all the major themes
of Christian faith that we shall be in constant danger of losing
sight of the specific issue, unless we limit ourselves to it as strictly
as possible. Our readers will in consequence miss the consideration of many problems intimately related with the subjects of our
different chapters. We must keep in mind, however, that we are
writing, not a treatise on Christian dogmatics as a whole, but on
one specific question. We must therefore invite our readers themselves to integrate the insights given here into the whole of their
Christian faith. This limitation has also its implications for the way
in which, in the following chapters, we shall be reading the Bible.
We are aware of the fact that in this study we approach the Bible
with a specific pre-understanding which former generations did
not have to the same extent. We are not ashamed of it. We believe
that the biblical message comes alive in a special way when we
direct our existential questions to it. The abiding truth of the Bible
is manifested in its power to give relevant and decisive answers to
the life-questions which every age poses to it. It does so under the
condition that we are ready, if necessary, to correct and widen our
questions in light of the biblical answers. Whether we are on a
fruitful way with our pre-understanding must be proved by the extent to which the biblical message becomes alive and visible along
the way on which we approach it. We must never forget that this
is not more than one way among many others, all of which are
complementary to one another. On the one hand, we cannot abso-
lutize our approach. On the other hand, we believe that our approach is meaningful, because it is the same God who speaks in
the Bible and who under the pressure of our time urges us to ask
the questions expressed here. Finally, we must admit that we are
aware of the limitations of our work in yet another way. This study
has no pretention of being our contribution to the dialogue of the
Church with modern scientific man. We are not yet prepared for
that dialogue. What we have to do first is to have a conversation
within the Church itself. We have to help one another to discover
the relations between the biblical message and modern world-

view. The modest intention of this study is to contribute to that primary and urgent task. We express the hope that it will help many to overcome in their hearts and minds the gap between their Christian faith and their expectations and embarrassments as modern men.

II. The God of History As the God of Nature.

The heart of Israel's faith, as set forth in the Old Testament, was that God has made Himself known in some special decisive events of history. This was a radically new idea and experience in the world of religions. For the primitive and ancient religions of the Middle East, God or the gods are mainly revealed in nature. Nature is the external aspect of divine reality. God is as nature is— blessing and harming, ambiguous, capricious. And history is primarily a part of nature, partaking in the same divine natural reality, obeying the same laws as the seasons, the stars and the weather.

Through Moses, Israel encountered this God of History. She met Him at that great turning-point in her story when she was rescued from her life in Egypt, the "house of bondage." This new God was nameless. He called Himself "I am I." This meant a refusal to give a name by which He could be conjured. It meant at the same time a strong promise: you will experience My presence as you need it; "I shall be with you in the way in which I shall be with you." This God goes before his people through the desert, leading the way to the future, to the promised land. This does not mean that his way is always evident to the faithful. Mostly his guidance and purposes are hidden. "Thy footprints were unseen" (Ps. 77:19). Time and again, however, when his people in disobedience and distress need it, He speaks in judgment and in grace through the events of history. Then Israel sees anew, repentant and encouraged, her way ahead through history. And she knows that this same God in a hidden way is the Lord of all history, both of Israel's and also of that of all the nations.

History for Israel was no longer a part of nature. Unlike nature, it is directed towards a goal. This goal is higher and wider than Israel itself. It embraces all the nations. The history of Israel is the preparation for a universal history, for in Israel "all the families of the earth will be blessed" (Gen. 12:3).

In worshipping a God of history, Israel inevitably developed an attitude to history different from that of religions of the nations around; but her attitude to nature was also different. In earlier stages, the encounter with God again and again took place in phenomena of nature (burning bush, Mount Sinai), but always so that the revelation in these phenomena pointed to God's purpose in history. In a later stage, nature loses this role. More and more history becomes the vehicle of revelation. Therefore the old nature-feasts which Israel inherited from her neighbours, the feast of unleavened bread, the feast of the first-fruits and the feast of booths, were in the course of Israel's history turned into memorial feasts of God's historical deeds (cf. Ex. 23:14–17 with Deut. 16:1–17). Nature is not so much the realm where God is revealed to man, as the realm in which man, created in God's image, has to realize God's purpose for his creation (Gen. 1:26–30). This does not imply that Israel had a negative attitude towards nature. On the contrary, she believed and confessed that the God of history is also the last secret of nature. God is one, and his creation is one. History and nature therefore are governed by the same will. When history is believed to be the realm of the covenant-God, and the way towards his kingdom, then nature also must serve Him and his goal. The whole earth responds to his glory (Is. 6), and the fertility of the promised land is the expression of his covenant-love. So the creation of nature is conceived of as the opening act of history. In the ancient religions, history is naturalized; in Israel nature is historicized. In her scriptures, particularly in the Psalms, nature plays a great role, but almost without exception in connection with God's acts in history and his covenant with Israel, to which nature also bears witness and responds (cf. Psalms 19, 29, 65, 67, 74, 75, 89, 96, 104, 136, 147 and 148). After God's character in his historical deeds is discovered, this character can also be discerned and these deeds seen prefigured in the processes of nature, and nature can be invested with the same grace as history discloses. The order of nature can now be interpreted as a prefiguration, on the one hand,

and a confirmation, on the other, of God's steadfast truth and loyalty towards his people (cf. Is. 42:5 f., Jer. 31:35–37).

Thus for Israel, history came first in the order of knowledge.
Israel experienced God's deliverance at the Red Sea and trusted
him as her covenant God long before her prophets and teachers
formulated a clear understanding of God as creator of heaven and
earth. One of the first of such formulations appears in the second
creation story (Gen. 2:4b-25), where nature in general, and the
Garden of Eden in particular, are the stage-setting of human history, with its challenges and failures. Through her further historical experiences, not least through the tragedy of the exile, Israel
learned more deeply that if her God were to be trusted at all, he
must be a God who completely controls the world. The second
Isaiah in particular confesses this belief with impressive elo-
quence. For him, God's work in creation is the presupposition and
reflection of his redeeming work in history (Is. 40:21 ff., 42:5 ff.,
44:24 ff., 45:12 f., 51:9 f.). In the same period, the writer of Gen. 1
delineated creation as the week-long opening phase of the history
of mankind and of Israel. History and creation were thus joined
together in Israel's faith in God and her commitment to serve him
alone.

It is also clear that history cannot be an end in itself, but must
have an end beyond itself. God's creative and redemptive work will
not be complete until all the powers of darkness are definitely
brought beneath the rule of the God who wants the whole earth to
be full of the glory of his covenant. So creation is the beginning of
a chain in which nature, history and consummation are inseparable links. This continuum can be seen in its true character and
unity, however, only from the middle of God's revelatory deeds in
history, whence both a backward and a forward look are possible.

A good illustration of this faith is Psalm 75. It starts with the
praise of God's "wondrous deeds" in history. Then the poet hears
God say that He maintains and continues in history the work
which He began in creation: "It is I who keep steady the pillars of
the earth," even "when the earth totters and all its inhabitants."
This conviction fills the poet with boldness. He now turns to God's
enemies and reminds them of God's sovereignty over history. "It is
God who executes judgment, putting down one and lifting up
another." The poet looks forward to the moment when "all the

wicked of the earth" shall be defeated. Then the promise of creation, of the God who makes steady the pillars of his earth, will be completely fulfilled.

So Israel believed in the ultimate significance of her historical encounter with God; she believed that in this encounter the final reality was disclosed, and that this reality is the key to the understanding of all things, in nature and history, from creation to consummation.

III. Christ, the Agent of Redemption and Creation

The New Testament witnesses to the fact that in the life, death and resurrection of Jesus Christ, God has finally reconciled the world to himself. The event of Jesus Christ is thus a new disclosure event, in which all the meaning of past disclosure events is gathered up, the human situation is exposed in all its potentiality for good and evil, and the final achievement of God's purpose for the world affirmed beyond all that evil and mortality can do to frustrate it. This Christ-event surpasses previous disclosure events (such as the Exodus) for the following reasons:

a) The Christ-event is both the confirmation and the turning-point of the covenant-relation. Jesus Christ is both the fulfilment of God's action in wrath and grace, and the true covenant-partner, who acts vicariously on behalf of his people, in his life, teaching and sacrifice.

b) In his resurrection and in the outpouring of his Spirit, the great eschatological future is anticipated. Consequent upon these events, the Church comes into being, and the message of the radical justification of the godless and of the renewal of life is proclaimed.

c) The finality of this event is shown in the wiping out of the boundaries between the Chosen People and the nations, and in the spreading of the Gospel and the growth of the Church over all the earth, as the foretaste of the Kingdom in accordance with the eschatological expectancy of the prophets.

This involves a complex relationship between the Christ-event and the preceding revelations, a relationship which can be set out only under several heads—parallelism, cohesion and confirmation, as well as renewal, deepening and surpassing, and at times even contradiction. It is important to see how the framework of the unity of creation, nature, history and consummation is maintained, and how at the same time this whole concept is deepened and elaborated through the experience of God's incomparable action in history in Jesus Christ. The same order will here be taken as in chapter 2, that of history, creation and consummation. The specific application of all this to the problems of nature will follow in a later chapter.

The deepest driving powers of *history* are revealed in the double event of cross and resurrection. The witnesses see history as the battlefield of God with the powers of guilt and destruction. They see his rescuing initiative, as well as human resistance and rebellion. They see how God seemingly yields to this rebellion, but in reality uses it and gears it to his redemptive purpose. They see how God overcomes the resistance and makes grace and life triumph over sin and death. From this centre and perspective the witnesses look back to the history of Israel, which they see as a continuous struggle between the covenant-God and his resistant people (Matt. 21:33–39, Acts 7:1–53, Rom. 7:7 ff.), and to the history of the nations, which they regard as being governed by the patience of God (Acts 14:16, 17:30, Rom. 3:25 f.) but subjected to the consequences of Adam's sin (Rom. 5) and to "the elemental spirits of the universe" (Gal. 4:3). At the same time, the witnesses look forward and see future history, under the influence of the Gospel, as a continuous and increasingly wide and intense display of the mystery of the cross and resurrection, of the struggle between the powers of the Spirit and powers of darkness, and of the final victory of Christ's kingdom (II Thess. 2, the Book of Revelation). New Testament scholars have pointed to the analogy and connection between the Passion-story and the eschatological passages (Mark 13, at the opening of the Passion-story) and to the parallels between christological and eschatological events (persecution, darkening of the sun, appearance of the Son of Man, resurrection).

To take seriously the final events in Christ, must also mean that he is confessed as the ultimate secret of *creation*. The key to the understanding of history must at the same time be the key to the understanding of creation, since both are essentially one. This confession of Christ as the agent of creation is found in a particularly articulated form in three traditions, in John 1, Col. 1 and Heb. 1. All these passages make use of expressions borrowed from the popular Hellenistic philosophy of their time (probably in its turn influenced by Jewish Wisdom-speculations) about an intermediary hypostasis between the Most High God and the created world. Without interruption, however, they pass from the work in creation to the work in history (cf. Col. 1:17 f. and Heb. 1:3). In John it is almost impossible to say where the one ends and the other begins. In all these passages both actions are ascribed to the same Person, called the Word (John), the Son (Hebrews), the Son of His Love (Colossians). Moreover in all these passages the main emphasis is on the historical work of the revelation of God's glory (John), of atonement and restoration (Colossians), and of purification for sins (Hebrews). Apparently this historical work is considered as the consequence and completion of his creative work. Compared with similar passages in Hellenistic philosophy, these authors are not interested in a separate Logos-substance in creation and nature. They point to history as the only realm where the secret of creation is revealed and fulfilled. On the other hand, we must also say that what is revealed in history is no unrelated incident, but the realization of a condition which had been God's purpose from the very beginning. The crucified and risen Jesus of Nazareth is the key to the understanding of the meaning of the whole created world. One should notice the way in which Colossians plays with the word "first" (15c, 17a, 18b; a play unfortunately obscured in various translations). This close connection of what God meant in creation and what he accomplished in Christ was expressed by these writers, using contemporary patterns of thought, in the confession that the world was created in and through Jesus Christ. God's creation of the first Adam was effected with the last Adam in view, and the latter had to complete creation and to rescue the world from its incompleteness and estrangement. Just as in the Old Testament creation is described in terms of the Exodus (God's deliverance from chaos, darkness and flood), so in the New Testament it is described as the first revelation of Christ, the new man, the true image of God.

Here arises an old argument in Christian theology, concerning the motives of the Incarnation. Most classical theologians believed that the only motive was God's purpose to rescue a sinful and lost mankind. They saw the Incarnation as the great emergency-measure by which God decided to bring the world back to its original perfection. A minority, however, maintained that Christ is more than that, that he is also the crown of creation, the new man for which creation has been waiting from the beginning (Antiochene School, Duns Scotus, several forms of liberal theology, Barth). The consequence drawn is that Christ would have come anyway, apart from the fall and sin. The question was usually treated in this form. This is an unhappy way of posing the question, because it presupposes something unreal. Nevertheless, when a choice has to be made, the decison has to be in favour of the second doctrine, because the first cannot give a satisfactory explanation of the three passages in the New Testament which deal with Jesus Christ as mediator of creation.

All this leads also to a renewed concept of the *consummation*. For Israel the future is the crown of history, as the victory of Yahweh over all the rebellious powers and the elevation of Israel as the centre of the nations. In the New Testament we find basically the same approach to eschatology: the future is seen as the complete and radical display of God's victorious work in history. To those who had witnessed the resurrected Jesus, the outpouring of the Spirit and the beginning of the world-wide mission, the consummation could be nothing other than the glorious revelation of this Jesus, a world-wide resurrection, the judgment of all men according to their attitude towards his first appearance, and the ordering and renewal of the world according to his new humanity. That is what the New Testament confesses, nothing less, nothing more. "We are God's children now; it does not yet appear what we shall be, but we know that when he appears, we shall be like him, for we shall see him as he is" (I John 3:2).

Both the doctrine of Jesus as the agent of creation and what is traditionally called the doctrine of his "second" coming (though he was never absent; he also came in the Spirit!) point to the finality of his historical appearance as disclosing the ultimate meaning of the whole indivisible process of creation, nature and history.

The consequence of all that has been said is that *consummation is a far higher work than creation,* far more than only the restoration of an original situation. If it were that—as traditional conservative theology presents it—history would in the end be conceived of as not more than a circular movement (paradise lost and paradise regained), not essentially different from the concept in naturalistic cultures. Christ is, however, the new man who leads the process of history to its ultimate goal. Genesis 2 does not picture a perfect state but a point of departure. Rev. 20 and 21 do not present a repetition of the Garden of Eden, but a city, symbol of culture. In this context particular attention should be paid to the passage I Cor. 15:44b-49; here Christ is compared, not with the fallen Adam (as is often supposed), but with the first created Adam, who is "from the earth, a man of dust"; the latter is nothing but "a living being," far surpassed by the last Adam, since he comes "from heaven" and is "a life-giving spirit." The old adamic humanity was the starting-point of history; a new pneumatic humanity, built around the new man, the resurrected Christ, is the goal of history. At the same time, with regard to John 1, Col. 1 and Heb. 1, it must be said that the last Adam is the original one, meant and implied in the creation of the first. All this gives us the image of one great movement from lower to higher, going through estrangement and crises, but also through atonement and salvation, and so directed towards its ultimate goal, a glorified humanity, in full communion with God, of which goal the risen Christ is the guarantee and the first-fruits.

IV. "Nature," "Creation," "World," "The Universe," "History"

Before these biblical insights can be elaborated and applied, terminology must first be clarified. The word *nature* has already been used several times, connoting the totality of non-human reality. This use of the word has no equivalent in Scriptures—for two reasons: 1) It makes a separation between man and this reality, which surrounds and bears him, and of which he himself also partakes; yet such a separation is unknown in biblical thinking. 2) This word in its Latin and also in its Greek meanings (*natura, phusis*) suggests something centred in itself, with an immanent origin and growth; dependence on the Creator God cannot be expressed by it.

The New Testament, instead of nature, uses the word *creation* (*ktisis*) and even more the verb *create,* which includes the notions that are missing from "nature," as can clearly be seen in Rom. 8:18–25, where creation includes both man and non-human nature (the popular interpretation that Paul thinks mainly of the sufferings of animals and the disasters of nature presupposes a modern romantic concept, which is absent in Paul; man is primarily meant, and non-human nature is included in his fate). According to those passages, creation is entirely in the hand of the Creator God; it goes through a history of groaning and longing, until in the end it partakes of the glorious liberty of the children of God. In the Old Testament even the word "creation" is absent. There such expressions are found as "heaven and earth," "the earth," "all that lives," "all things." A predilection is shown for this last word in the Epistle to the Ephesians, where *ta panta* is often translated as *the universe.* The translation could mislead us into thinking mainly of outer space, planets and galaxies. The main emphasis lies on our well-known earthly realities. The *earth* (*eretz*) in the Old Testament often means the nations, as over against Israel. The same may be the case in Ephesians, where so much emphasis is laid on the unity between Israel and the Gentiles. "The universe" does not at any rate point to cosmic speculations, but to an earthly human historic process (see Eph. 1:9–14). We must, however, also say that the use of the word *ta panta* in a world of cosmological speculations implies that this historic process has its consequences also for the non-human world.

The word *world* (*kosmos*) has a similar meaning. It is used especially by Paul and John, sometimes in a neutral way, but even then in the sense of "human world." For the most part it expresses man's rebellion against God and God's saving love for this rebellious world.

This terminology supports what has been already stated: the

unity of non-human and human reality, the emphasis on man's place in God's creation, the unity of creation and redemption and the historical connotation of all the words used. The world is a creation, never without relation to the Creator God. Man is the junction, where all the lines between God and his earthly creation come together. The world view is geocentric, not because the existence of other beings is denied (think of the angels!), but because revelation is addressed to man, and man bears no responsibility except for his own world.

The word *nature* will continue to be used in this paper, because it would seem impossible to abolish it from ordinary speech. Modern man is accustomed to making a stricter distinction between human and non-human reality than does the Bible. In itself this is not objectionable. Such a distinction can help to illuminate the Christian message concerning this realm of reality. Nevertheless, it must not be forgotten that this reality does not subsist in itself, but exists because of God's continuous preservation, and that it is regarded as being the stage-setting for the history of God's dealings with mankind.

The word *history* has different meanings. It can be the name for all that happened in the past; or for the records and the study of the past; or for the total field of human responsibility, for man's acting as a subject, as well as for the results of these actions. In this study, the word indicates mainly the totality of human events in past, present and future, as governed by God and directed towards his goal.

V. The Biblical and the Modern World-View

Deepened understanding of the world of biblical speech, and an ever more sophisticated understanding of the nature and self-limitation of scientific speech, make it possible in our time for faith and natural science to begin a quite fresh conversation about our understanding of the world. This is so for the following reasons:

a) Creation is the first history, and nature is part of this pre-history. The word "generations" (*toledoth*) is used in Genesis not only for the succession of human generations, but also for the history of creation: "These are the generations of the heavens and the earth when they were created" (Gen. 2:4). Both Israel and modern science have a radically historicized conception of creation and nature.

b) Creation and nature are pre-history, directed towards man. Man is rooted in this pre-history. At the same time this history comes in man to a new decisive phase.

c) According to this, creation as the opening act of history is not complete. When we read that "God saw that it was (very) good" (Gen. 1), we should understand the word "good" in the sense not of being perfect, but of being fit and suitable for its function, for the goal it has to serve—in this case, for the history of God and man, for which it has to serve as a stagesetting.

d) God reveals Himself through his words and deeds in history. Looking back from this work of God, man can recognize also in his stagesetting work some traces of his being (e.g. his majesty, his power, his inscrutability).

e) The process of God's creative work has not yet come to an end. New developments are still to be expected. Living in a great historical process means looking constantly forward, believing in an open future.

Now the question arises: supposing all this is to be true, why then did it remain hidden for so long? Why did the Church so strongly resist the historicizing of nature in modern evolutionary theories? Why was the Church, which by her preaching led the ancient world out of a naturalistic life-concept into God's history, so reluctant to draw the consequences of her own convictions? Why did she cling for so many centuries to a static, unhistorical concept of life?

The reason is that for centuries the Church in Western Europe not only preached the Christian message, but also saw it as her duty to preserve and develop the Graeco-Roman scientific heritage, embodied in works such as those of Ptolemy of Alexandria.

This was a heritage of static conceptions about nature and history. The Christian message was thus framed in a static world-concept, which was handed down with the same ecclesiastical authority. Since the Enlightenment, this concept has been attacked. Both attackers and defenders have seen the attack as an assault upon Christianity. This misunderstanding could easily arise and be maintained, because the attack often used mechanistic and deterministic categories unsuitable for the Christian faith, whereas Christians tried to refute it on the basis of a literal acceptance of the creation narrative in Genesis. So in the nineteenth century, one was urged to make an unnecessary choice between a static Christian conception of creation and history and the modern idea of evolution. This situation lasted until the middle of this century, when the conviction gained ground on both sides that the alternative was a false one.

This does not mean that the Christian faith can identify itself with the modern world-view. Science is a specialized range of techniques, applied to the study of defined ranges of phenomena and problems by persons specially trained for this work. Some believe that science suggests a more general world outlook applicable to the whole of human life; but such suggested "scientific" world-outlooks are lacking in the vigour and precision of science itself. Moreover, science frequently finds itself unable to make assertions on a higher level, such as assertions of purpose, goal or meaning, about the phenomena which it describes. Scientists who sometimes try to make such assertions appear to assume the role of philosophers and theologians, and have to accept criticism by the procedures of philosophy and theology. Christians believe that some such higher level assertions have to be made, and that these higher level assertions must take account of the encounter with God in history, centered in Jesus Christ.

Thus Christian faith is not identical with modern science or any world-view claiming to depend upon it. But it is deeply indebted to modern science, because the scientific approach and its results have compelled Christians to re-examine their convictions and to free their faith from elements which, though long supposed to be integral to the Christian message, are now seen not to be so. Christians should therefore be grateful for the way in which God has used science to clarify and deepen the insights of faith. The growth of science has elements in common with, or parallel to, the assertions of faith in its growth of consciousness against the background of the ancient world-views. The next chapters will elaborate these biblical insights along different lines.

VI. Nature and Man

The full marvel of human existence in the midst of nature is perhaps best indicated by the fact that two almost contradictory statements are equally true. Now as never before, man has it in his power through technology to assume responsibility for nature, and to release himself from the supposedly inherent limitations nature has imposed on him. Yet it is equally true that today, as never before, we recognize the abiding continuity of man, even in his most spiritual activities, with the energy particles and the behavioural mechanisms that constitute material and animal nature. Christians, reflecting on God's presence in nature and history, must take into account the astonishing fact that our condition is equally well described in both ways. Therefore the following elements may be mentioned:

1. *Man is part of nature.* This is not only the thesis of a materialistic world-view, but of the Bible as well (cf. Gen. 2:7, I Cor. 15:47). One should particularly notice the structure of Genesis 1, where creation is recounted as a single history, proceeding from lower to higher realities and crowned by the appearance of man. This, of course, is not identical with the evolutionary causalistic conception. Here is no immanent process, but a God who acts. Nevertheless there is more analogy here than between Gen. 1 and the older static view about the world. In Gen. 1 man is rooted in nature. According to Genesis 2 his first companions are the animals. This line of thought in the Bible reminds one of the thinking of men like Marx, Darwin and Freud, who strongly reacted against the way in which philosophical idealism had detached man from nature. Until recently, Christian anthropology has leaned upon idealism and spiritualism in a way which finds no support in biblical thinking. And now man is in danger of surrendering himself to a kind of existentialism which, not unlike idealism, or even more

than that, detaches him from nature and one-sidedly stresses his standing over against nature. It should not be forgotten that even the most specifically human characteristics, like mobility, freedom and consciousness, have a foreshadowing and analogy in non-human nature.

2. *Man is nurtured by nature.* According to Genesis, man is given plants and trees, and later on even animals, for his food. Without nature man cannot exist; and not only so, but nature nurtures man in many other aspects of his life. It offers him aesthetic delight, meditation, companionship (esp. the animals), consolation, and inspiration (poets and painters). In times of inner crisis, nature helps man to come to himself. Man today lives in a culture in which he is in danger of underestimating this highly important role of nature in human life. Nature has become so much his servant that he forgets that she is also his sister. His desire for holiday-camps does not really help him, nor his modern vacation techniques in general. These aim more at transporting his daily conveniences to other, and often crowded, spots, rather than at making possible a deep and quiet encounter with nature. Here the Church should not only lift her finger warningly, but also help out short-sighted generations to a new experience of the beneficient riches of our sister nature.

To this end, Christians should support all those responsible for nature conservation in various countries in their long-standing struggle against the pollution of air and water, in their demand for an afforestation which counteracts the denudation and erosion of vast regions, and in their plea for a policy of habitation which takes into consideration the much endangered biological balance of many areas. What these groups claim for biological reasons, the Church has to support for basic theological reasons.

3. *Man is threatened and challenged by nature.* Nature is ambiguous. She is man's mother and his enemy. She brings forth thorns and thistles. Hers are the hurricanes, the floods, the droughts, the earthquakes, the famines, the abortions. When man does not resist nature, she can swallow and suffocate him.

4. *Man is made by nature.* By compelling man to offer resistance, nature makes man into what he should be—more than a part of nature: a controller of nature; the only being who refuses

"to take life as it is"; an inventor, a fighter, a builder. This leads us on to recognize that

5. *Man guides and transforms nature.* This is an unparalleled event in the age-long history of evolution: the product becomes the leader. Since the appearance of man, nature has become more and more domesticated. Her own unconscious ends are now submitted to man's conscious planning. This is the great turn that can be observed in the history of evolution. We now live more and more in an unnatural nature, reshaped by man, a world of concrete and plastic, of parks and medicines.

6. *Man is the master of nature.* When Gen. 1:27 says that God created man in his own image, the whole passage 1:26–28 makes it clear that what is mainly thought of is man's dominion over nature. As God is the Lord over his whole creation, so He elects man as his representative to exercise this lordship in God's name over the lower creation. This was an unprecedented insight in the ancient world. As long as man believed nature to be the external manifestation of divine powers, he was more or less doomed to passivity. Every deeper change in the course of nature was an act of Promethean recklessness. That is why the primitive and ancient cultures in general limited themselves to cattle-raising and agriculture; and even these were surrounded by magical practices in order to propitiate the envious gods. According to Genesis 1 and Psalm 8, Gods stand no longer on the side of nature over against man, but on the side of man over against nature. Man is encouraged and even instructed by God to dominate the world.

7. *Nature's meaning surpasses man's understanding.* God has also his own relation with nature. The pedestrian way in which the Enlightenment tried to prove that all phenomena in nature are there for man and for man only, has served to prove just the opposite. The very fact that so many phenomena are meaningless and imcomprehensible to man, is extremely meaningful, in so far as it teaches him the limits of his knowledge and task. That is the way in which nature appears in the mighty chapters 38–41 of Job. The abundancy and inexhaustibility, the absurdities and irrationalities of nature (i.e. what man calls so, from his limited viewpoint) reflect, in their own way, the majesty and inscrutability of the Creator.

Finally, this conception of man's relation to nature excludes two others:

a) The conception which sees man as essentially an "outsider" in the world, through the fact that he is the bearer of "existence." In that case man's existential attitude is the only thing which counts; nature and history are meaningless. This radical separation between existence and the world in which it is grounded is, in our conviction, incompatible both with biblical faith and with modern science. Man's existence is embedded in nature. Lower and higher form a unity. Body and soul belong together. An artificial isolation of existence impoverishes man's faith and makes his life in the world ghostly.

b) The conception which sees man almost exclusively as a product of nature, to the extent of biologizing man and naturalizing history. Out of the process of evolution a unique phenomenon emerges, which brings a decisive turn, and not only continues evolution, but also takes the lead. Moreover man makes life risky by his freedom, which he can use in different ways. This is an entirely new element, and forbids the view that man is only a continuation of nature.

VII. Nature, Man, Sin and Tragedy

The use of the word "sin," and even more the use of the word "fall," suggests an interruption, a disruption, and discontinuity in the great nature-history process to which many are unable to give a place in their thinking. This attitude may be due to a mythological conception of sin and fall, but is in itself unnecessary. To begin with, evolution in nature is a road full of risks, detours, frustrations and deadlocks. It has nothing to do with a mechanistic, smooth and straightforward causality. The reality which is the outcome of this process is, statistically speaking, of the highest improbability. At no stage was there the slightest guarantee that the way of natural development would go steadily upwards. It did not need so to do, nor did it do so. Now that it is possible to look back, however, this road can be seen to be a way towards ever more complicated, higher, and more mobile entities. The highest level is reached with man as a being endowed with freedom. Here nature stops acting merely spontaneously and unconsciously. In the phenomenon of man, nature starts to act consciously and responsibly. In that very fact the terrible possibility of sin is given. This is, however, the reverse side of the possibility of acting freely and responsibly. This open possibility is one of the greatest steps forward in the evolutionary process. This does not imply a naturalization of sin. Sin is not natural. Man's nature as distinct from lower nature means that man is no longer bound to act merely naturally. He can transcend his nature in either the right or the wrong direction. When he does the latter, he acts "unnaturally," he becomes guilty. There is no excuse for guilt. The possibility of becoming guilty is however man's high privilege, the counterpart of his being created in the image of God. Genesis 2 and 3 belong together. Their togetherness does not mean a temporal succession. At the same time, these chapters are distinct from one another, indicating that sin is not a logical consequence of creation, but something unnatural. At the same time, we have to face the fact that this misuse of freedom is far more than an accident; it is an enigmatic distortion of our created nature.

There is yet a second and even more serious reason to see a cleavage between the biblical and the modern world-view on this point. That is the way in which sin, according to the Bible, affects human and non-human nature, by introducing evil and suffering, thorns and thistles, and human death. Passages like Genesis 3 and Romans 5 give the impression of a "fallen creation." In modern scientific thinking, however, there is no place for the conception that an alteration and deterioration took place in man's physical nature, and in the biological world around him, as a consequence of his culpability. According to our experience, death is inherent in all life. Strife and suffering belong to nature. Floods and earthquakes are part of the same reality to which majestic mountains and fertile valleys belong. In Scripture, an identifiable connection between sin and suffering is sometimes definitely denied (Job, Luke 13:1-5, John 9:3), but more often it is strongly posited. In the latter case, the biblical writers—basing themselves on the world-view, and using the common mythological language, of their

time—tried to express something which is as near to modern man
as it was to them: the unity of man and nature and of soul and
body, and the decisive role which man plays in the process of nature. Man, who is in fact sinful man, on the one hand is rooted in
nature and, on the other hand, transforms nature. He lives in three
relations: as child of God, as his neighbour's partner, and as master of nature. If one relation is distorted, it also affects the others.
When man, as the master of nature, fails to put his mastery to the
service of God and of his neighbour, he denies the true purpose of
his dominion, and thereby harms nature. Again, when man does
not feel himself sheltered in the Fatherhood of God over his life,
nature becomes to him a threat and an enemy. What Genesis 3
expressed in terms of substance (nature under a curse) is better
expressed today in terms of relation. This applies to human death
also. Death in itself is natural. But there is no such thing as
"death-in-itself," only the death of this or that kind of being. Man
is not nature. It is his nature to transcend his nature. So his death
is not natural, but personal, existential. It differs widely from animal death. It is the end of a life of responsibility and guilt. Man by
the very fact of his transcendence of nature, rebels against death.
To him it is more than a fate. As soon as man is confronted with
the revelation of God, this general anthropological observation is
deepened and understood as part of a new pattern. Death then
becomes the sign and seal of the imperfect and preliminary state
in which the sons of the "first Adam" still dwell. Fresh attention
must be paid in this connexion to Romans 8:18–25. The longing
and groaning creation is in the first place mankind outside the
Church, without the knowledge of salvation. Man is longing, but
he does not know for what. His groaning is the sign that God has
destined him for a far higher form of existence than the bondage
to decay (v. 21) in which he now lives, namely for liberty (v. 21)
and the redemption of his body (v. 23, i.e. his total existence).
Therefore his groaning is a "groaning in travail" (v. 22); out of this
preliminary existence a new world will be born, of which mankind
in its rebellion against bondage and decay is dimly aware, and
which the Christian community of the resurrected Jesus has to
explain. In the light of Christ human death is seen as a preliminary stage belonging to the "first things" which will "pass away"
(Rev. 21:4). The same holds good for sin. That is why Paul takes

them together in a "causal" relation in Romans 5. We are, however, unable to follow him in affirming this connexion. This "creation" in Romans 8 also includes non-human nature, which, since man appeared, depends on him for its situation and for its future. Paul, who points to the future of man with the words "liberty" and "resurrection," makes no attempt to describe what this future will mean for non-human nature.

These considerations bring to our mind what is often called the "tragic" element in God's creation. Much evil and suffering, death included, cannot be explained either as a consequence of man's sin or as an expression of God's providence. The process of God's work in nature and history has also its deep dark sides. Man can partly remove them, but can never overcome them. They belong to the "futility" and the "dust" which are inherent in this first creation (Rom. 8:20, I Cor. 15:47). To us they seem to be inconsistent with the love of God as revealed in Jesus Christ. They remind us of the fact that the Kingdom has not yet come, and that accordingly our knowledge is also only "in part." We are not able to find meaning in the evil of the world. We are not called upon to explain the tears, but to hope for a future in which God will wipe them away.

VIII. Nature in God's History with Man

God's work in history deals directly with man and indirectly with nature; its aim is the salvation of man. The work upon history and the work upon nature, however, cannot be completely separated. The degree to which God, in his history with man, uses events on a natural level appears to vary between one stage and another of the process, as the biblical narrative depicts it. In early stages of Israel's life, and from time to time in the prophetic tradition, any natural phenomenon can be seen as dependent on God and is used as an instrument of his revealing, judging and rescuing will: winds, thunderstorm, famine, rain, etc. The deliverance of Israel from Egypt is depicted in categories of natural catastrophe. But much of the development of Israel's history with God takes place not through events of this kind, but through political and military history, and especially Israel's relation with the surrounding nations. In this era, in which God's guidance of his people is expressed primarily in social and political terms, the reference to natural events is less.

In the story of Jesus, however, the role of nature in God's judging and saving work is more emphasized, as we see in the darkening of the sun at the time of the crucifixion, and in the way in which, in the eschatological parts of the New Testament, nature is involved in the great changes of the consummation. These and similar statements expressed anew the conviction that God's history with man, as well as man's life itself, is embedded in the processes of nature, and that there is a continuous interrelation between both. God's salvation has wider dimensions than the existential one.

More important in the New Testament, however, is another line—the dominion of nature by the new man Jesus Christ. Usually we see Jesus' perfect manhood in his relation to God and to his fellow-men; but the authors of the Gospels were equally aware of a third dimension: Jesus' mastery over the forces of nature, as evidence of the messianic times. It is difficult, if not impossible, for us to distinguish in these pronouncements and stories between memories of real facts and expressions of the belief of the Early Church. No doubt this last element plays an important role; but it must have been based on and inspired by real facts which many had witnessed. We cannot draw a line between the two elements. For our subject this is less important, however. The main thing is that Jesus is seen and confessed as the New Man who has nature with its threatening powers under his control. "He was with the wild beasts" (Mark 1:13); he walks on the waters, signs of the chaos; he heals the sick and casts out the demons. All this is ascribed not to his Godhead, but to his true humanity; such a new relation to nature, therefore, cannot be completely alien to his followers either (Matt. 14:31; Mark 9:28 f.). At the same time this relation is the anticipation of the coming fulfilment of man's relation to nature, in which the roles of servant and of companion will be in full harmony (cf. Is. 11:6–9).

Here a word must be said about miracles. Does God's saving

relation disrupt the natural order by miraculous incidents? Or is this order a closed chain of causes and results? It was in this way that the contrast between orthodoxy and modernism was formulated in the nineteenth century. This contrast is now obsolete. Deeper study of the Bible, as well as modern science, has removed the problem in this form. Both consider the natural order as not a closed but an open reality. The Bible sometimes reports miracles which reflect either a primitive understanding of nature or a desire for the miraculous. In its central message, however, it is not interested in anomalous happenings as such, but only in "signs and wonders" (Heb. *otot umofetim*, Gk. *semeia kai terata*), events in which we see something of God's restoring and elevating work, pointing to the new creation. Where the eye of faith discerns how God uses the natural order as his instrument, signs and wonders are declared. Such words do not belong to an objective realm (the "sign" character of certain events can never be proved by scientific means), nor are they mere projections of subjective feelings; they express the discovery by faith of a higher reality which makes the lower realities instruments of, and windows for, its purposes.

The crucial miracle, on which the Christian's hope for the world and himself depends, is Christ's resurrection. This is indeed the "defining" miracle, on which the meaning of miracle as such has to be based. It is the powerful affirmation that in the life of Jesus of Nazareth the grace of the living God was present indeed; it is at the same time the dawn of God's new order, the first-fruits of the consummation. This new order includes our total existence, both body and soul. When we try to subsume this unique event under the laws of our ordinary life, we deny the meaning of the resurrection. What is possible and real with God is indicated by this sign disclosing the future order towards which we are under way. We now know that what we call "life," "history" and "nature" is part of a preliminary order surrounded and limited by the order of God's salvation and re-creation. The scientist may not deem himself qualified to affirm or to deny such extraordinary events. When as a Christian he believes their reality, he will welcome the new perspective they gave to the field of his research. He will beware of conceiving physical reality as a closed and ultimate reality, and he may find certain analogies and models which help him in a fruitful way, to confront his faith with his scientific pattern of thinking, though such never can furnish an explanation of the miracle.

IX. *Christian Faith and Technology*

During the last decade the conviction has often been voiced that modern technology is a fruit of the Gospel, a result of man's calling to dominate the earth in the name and as the image of God. There is a great deal of truth in this assertion, but a careful distinction has to be made. God's restoring and renewing work evokes in man abilities and attitudes which were previously underdeveloped, but it never creates them out of nothing. Man has always to some extent tried to control nature and to make tools which could help him in this struggle. Hampered, however, by his belief that nature was the external manifestation of the Godhead, and that a deep change of its course and function might evoke the wrath of the gods, his technical skill and outreach necessarily remained very limited. Graeco-Roman culture, however, already brought a certain turn in man's attitude towards nature. The greatest stumbling-block for a radical display of man's dominating force was removed when, as a result of Christian preaching in the Western world, nature was understood as the creation of a transcendent God, and was thus desacralized and de-demonized.

The relation between Christian faith and technology is nevertheless not a direct one, because centuries passed after the victory of Christianity before the technical age set in. The reason for this long delay was partly that under the deep influence of past traditions, European man stood in the same awe of nature as a divine revelation as did his pagan ancestors. Moreover, theological motives can never explain the whole of history any more than economic or social ones can. The great display of technical sciences after the eighteenth century had as its prerequisite specific scientific and economic conditions which were not previously ripe. It is nevertheless true that Christian faith prepared the soil and set man free for an ever more radical dominion over, and use of, nature. Christendom should not have hesitated, therefore, to welcome the immense progress in controlling and using nature which gave relief to innumerable men in their struggle for life, and disclosed innumerable riches for a deeper humanization of mankind. The ambiguous way in which many Christians regarded new inventions and new achievements, both criticizing and using them at the same time, has been a cause for shame. These achievements are signs of the kind of life which God has intended for his children at the consummation.

However, we still live this side of the consummation, in a sinful world. Technics are not sinful in themselves; on the contrary, they are a means towards fulfilling God's commandment. The means are in the hand of sinful man, and are therefore never free from the possibility of misuse for selfish ends. Here the Christian Church has to exercise a critical function. Not in an unfair way, as is often done when technical progress is labelled as Babylonian tower-building, yet at the same time is gladly used; nor by drawing a line where science and technics ought to stop (e.g. where research into and use of nuclear energy or of outer space begins), since it is against the nature of science and of technology to be given artificial limits. The Church has to exercise her critical function by putting three questions to this technical generation:

1. *What kind of dominion is being exercised?* Here the seven points in chapter VI should be recalled. Nature is both man's servant and his sister, and these two aspects have to be kept in balance. In this age, the desire for handling, changing, using and transforming nature is so one-sidedly developed, that man is in danger of forgetting what nature has to contribute in her sister-function. Man no longer gives names to the animals; they have mainly become objects. His housing areas devour the natural resources of open space. His industries defile the air and the streams. So he exercises a dominion which more and more makes the display of nature's sister-aspect impossible. Man will pay the price for this fault. This one-sidedness of his dominion will hollow out and undermine his humanity.

2. *What are the aims of man's technical dominion?* We all know that war and the preparation for war are the great promoters of technics. Whether technics are a blessing or not, depends entirely on man. His mastery of nature should be in harmony with

the fact that he is a child of God and a partner with his neighbour. Up to the present this harmony has been lacking. A joint effort of all industrialized nations could dispel hunger and poverty from the earth in not more than a few decades; yet man prefers to put his technical skill into the service of his narrow national aims, his anxiety, his pride and his competition. For outer space projects, there is far more money available than for anti-hunger campaigns. Nuclear fission has so far been applied more for constructing means to destroy mankind than for promoting welfare.

The question of aims has become far more crucial still in recent years, since not only nature but also man himself can now be manipulated and changed in many ways, not only through drugs but also through interference in the genetic code. Here questions of great import arise, all of which circle around the problem [of] what it means that man is a person and what the relation is between the core of man's personality and the objectifiable elements of his nature. We are no more than dimly aware as yet of these questions, which can be answered only through the co-operative effort of scientists and students of the behavioural sciences, of ethics and of theology.

3. *What is the result of man's actual technical dominion?* What are the results upon man as a human person? On the one hand, modern man is freed from bondage to nature to an extent of which his ancestors would never have dreamed. On the other hand, however, technics and industry have transformed man in such a way that he is now more than ever functionalized, and adapted to the laws of his own tools—and therefore, also, more in a hurry, more nervous, more a "mass man." He suffers from the relative hypertrophy of his mastery-relation to nature, the concomitant of which is too often the atrophy of his relationships with God and with his fellow-men. Modern man is deformed. He becomes a function and a product of his own achievements. First he was enslaved to nature, now he is enslaved to his mastery of nature. As a consequence of this situation, we even see the possible destruction of the human race, either by a nuclear war or by degeneration.

Nevertheless, we do not advocate a stop to technical development. Man has to do not less, but more. He has to subjugate his technical possibilities to the other relations of his life, instead of allowing technics to supersede these other relations. Otherwise he will lose as much as he gains, and in the long run he will lose far more than he gains. Already in many highly-developed countries complaints are heard of the menace of boredom, because man is satiated and has lost the notion that he is called to be more than a consumer. In less developed countries the joy of freedom, made possible by science and technology, is still rightly dominant. Everywhere, however, man has to be reminded of the fact that what seem to be the ambiguities of technics are in reality the ambiguities of man himself, and that in view of the immense power which he now possesses, it is high time for him to seek a fresh understanding of his nature and destiny.

X. God in Universal History

It has already been seen how Israel's concept of history, born out of her encounter with God in history, contrasted with the way in which history was conceived of before and around Israel. The self-revelation of the God of convenant and promise was directed towards one small particular nation, but it was never meant for that nation exclusively. On the contrary, in her meeting with the God of history Israel is treated as representative of the whole of mankind, and considered as suffering and acting on behalf of all mankind. In this very particular (and often seemingly particularistic) revelation, the unity of mankind is presupposed and aimed at. This is clear from the universal background which the writer of Gen. 2–11 gave to his account of Israel's history, from the universal outlook in the prophets (Isaiah, Deutero-Isaiah, Deutero-Zachariah, Jonah, etc.), and especially from the whole trend of the New Testament. Mankind is understood as a whole, with a common nature (created from one head), with common problems (sin, suffering, death), with a common future (the Kingdom of God for every nation, people and tongue, the uniting of all things in Christ), and with a common calling (to faith, love and hope). So God's history must sooner or later give birth to the conception of universal history, in the sense that all groups, tribes, nations, imperia, races, and classes are involved in one and the same history. This conviction was not without a certain preparation in former political events (Alexander the Great, Pax Romana) and philosophical thinking (Stoicism), but all this had no power to break through the feeling of separation, as it existed between Greeks and barbarians. So long as in the West Christianity was identified with a special "Christian culture," limited to Europe, no more could the germs of universality in the Christian message bear fruit either. The universalizing and unifying of history started in the ages of mission and colonialism, and is now in this generation penetrating human minds everywhere as never before. This last fact is not so much due to the impact of the Gospel as to the technological revolution, which in itself has a universal tendency. These different sources of universal history cannot, however, be separated, because, as has been seen, the advance of technological science and practice cannot be understood apart from the influence of the Gospel.

The present movement towards the unification of mankind and its history lays a heavy pressure on all the Christian Churches to seek, with greater earnestness and haste than ever before, the world-wide unity of the Christian Church. The prayer of our Lord "that they may all be one" (John 17:21) has always disquieted and inspired many Christians. However, now as never before, the Churches are challenged because the world needs the united witness and service of the Church. Only the one Church can be the adequate counterpart of the one world. We see it as the guidance of the Spirit that in our century, and exactly in face of the dividing forces of two world wars, the Churches everywhere have begun to seek a world-wide unity. The interdependence between this fact and the present search for world unity can help us to a deeper understanding of the meaning and the call of the Spirit, and stimulate us not to be disobedient to this call, lest the coming one world be deprived of the guidance of the partner who once sowed the seed of her unity.

The growing awareness of being involved in one universal history appeals to the Church, particularly because this fact has also an ethical thrust. It inspires men to react against all kinds of social, racial and economical discrimination and to strive with all their strength for world peace and world co-operation. In all this can be seen realizations of God's purposes for this world, signs of the coming Kingdom.

We dare not use a stronger word than "signs," however, because the present universalizing of history partakes of that ambiguity which is characteristic of this world in its preliminary and sinful phase. Christ evokes the powers of the Spirit—and at the same time those of the Anti-Christ. He brings new shadows as well as new light. Universal History, experienced apart from Christ, can become a threat as well as a blessing. What is the goal towards which Universal History is developing? For very many of our fellow-men there is no goal beyond the creation of a well-balanced, smoothly-organized, technically perfect universal welfare-state. Now already we see the indications that this will result in a society of boredom. A society which has no purposes beyond its own welfare must die. The alternative is that it devotes all its superfluous powers to new irrational and even anti-humane adventures. The unification of societies is not in itself a good thing. The value of universal history depends on the good it serves and the goal towards which it is directed. Here may be recalled Genesis 11, where the Tower of Babel is the expression of a strong universal will, but a will directed against God's purpose.

For this and other reasons, many are inclined to see little or no connexion between God's history in Israel and in Christ, on the one hand, and man's "profane" history, universal history included, on the other hand. But such a connexion does exist, and must be affirmed. History is one and indivisible. We partake today in that same history in which Abraham was called, Israel was judged and delivered, Jesus died and rose from the dead, and the Holy Spirit was poured out. What modern man sees around him are risks and detours, guilt and frustration. Things are ambiguous or inscrutable. The same is true, however, for God's history as it is told in the Bible, which, though it is a history of rebellion and failures, is nevertheless God's history. The difference is that God's work in Israel and in Christ is interpreted by the Word, that here we have to do with disclosure-situations in the highest sense of the phrase, that here and particularly in the appearance of Jesus Christ, God lays aside his anonymity. All this can be said only by faith. A double disclosure is needed: one in the events and one in men's hearts through the Spirit. The revelation which is given in this double disclosure is not exclusive, however, but inclusive. God's mind and purpose are here disclosed in their relevance for all times and nations. So we are summoned to understand all history, and especially our own history, with its good and evil, in the light of this History. The same God is present, there in a more disclosed way and here in a more hidden way; but it is one presence and therefore one history. He goes on with his judging and saving work on a world-wide scale. That is what we confess. And this confession, far from making us passive spectators, inspires us to share in the tensions and risks of human history. As God's fellow-workmen, we are called to make way for the healing forces of his love on a worldwide scale, through our mission and our service, knowing that in the Lord our labour is not in vain.

XI. God and Man in History

The God who historicizes human existence frees man from entangling bondage to the powers of nature, and calls him to come of age and to become the master of the powers whose slave he previously was. In this statement, which summarizes much of what has been said in the previous chapters, two confessions are inseparably connected: God's sovereignty over man and his history, and man's freedom in history. These two confessions, so often put over against one another, are in the Christian faith two sides of the same reality. And this not as a result of penetrating philosophical thinking, but of the reality which is discerned in the disclosure-situations. God frees man for responsibility. The terrifying mystery is that man is inclined to mobilize his freedom not to pursue his divine calling, but to act counter to God's will. Even so, God accepts him and grants him full room for his self-chosen role. The whole of Israel's history and particularly the life, death and resurrection of Jesus reflect the unity of man's autonomy and God's sovereignty. Man's freedom in history is unlimited: he can even expel God's presence. Nevertheless, God is not defeated, but victorious. He takes man's rebellious freedom into his service, bending man's aims and actions towards his purpose (cf. Gen. 50:20, Is. 10:5–21, Acts 4:27 f.). God's work through Christ and the Spirit everywhere in the world liberates man to autonomy; and man everywhere is tempted to use his new freedom against God. The history of Jesus' life, death and resurrection is displayed and repeated on an ever wider scale. For the world-wide scale on which it will be repeated in the final stages of history, the New Testament uses the images of Anti-Christ and the Millennium.

History is the work of the sovereign God. He is never a helpless spectator of man's autonomy. Nor does He use men as passive instruments. The divine character of his omnipotent grace is seen in the fact that it admits and even presupposes the highest measure of human liberty. God's freedom does not jeopardize nor even limit man's. The confession of God's Providence (a far too static and poor a word for his ways through history!) can never be an excuse for irresponsibility nor a shelter for passivity. It functions in the life of God's children, in the midst of so many baffling events, as a source of confidence, consolation and challenge.

These insights are particularly relevant since, through the knowledge of nuclear fission, the power fell to mankind to destroy itself and its world. From now on, we have to live with this terrifying possibility. This situation makes an appeal to our responsibility as never before. For Christians who know about the depth of sin in man, this implies a constant struggle to bring and to keep the powers of destruction under a strict control. We are challenged to pray and to work afresh for the renewal of the world through the powers of the Spirit. At the same time, we will do so in a deep confidence, knowing that our concern is far more God's own concern, and that his sovereign love for his sinful creatures will prove itself stronger than all our resistance.

XII. History and Nature in Consummation

In wide circles of Christendom the relation of history and consummation is mainly seen in a context of pessimism: this world will come to a drastic end, and on its ruins (if any are left) an entirely new world will be created. This presentation is in contradiction to even the most apocalyptical passages of the New Testament (cf. Matt. 24, Mark 13, Luke 21, I Cor. 15, II Thess. 2, Rev. 18–22), where the new world is found in the identical setting of the old, and where often even between this age and the age to come no sharp line can be drawn. This is quite different from the dualistic tendencies in the Jewish apocalyptic literature of that time. This applies even to the most "dualistic" passage in the N.T., II Pet. 3:5–10, where the fire is not so much destroying as purifying and where, according to the better manuscripts, the last words have to be read: "and the earth and the works that are upon it will be found" (instead of: "will be burned up").

The relation between history and consummation is one of both continuity and discontinuity. The new world will be this earth renewed. The eschaton will be the complete and glorified unfolding of what God has already begun in history in his Son and his Spirit. This work is in contrast with much in this world, which has to be removed. The world will be recreated according to the new humanity of the risen Christ. As he could become the new man only through suffering and death, so this whole creation has to undergo an analogous process: in this way "He will change our lowly existences to be like his glorious existence" (Phil. 3:21). That is what the dark features in New Testament eschatology want to express. The cross is the way to the resurrection; for this lower and sinful humanity there is no other way. But in all this are disclosed, not signs of frustration, but the travail of the coming glorious liberty of the sons of God (Rom. 8), which is the goal of human history.

Discontinuity serves continuity. It may be believed that our works in the Church of Christ (I Cor. 3:14) and our cultural achievements (Rev. 21:24, 26) will be used as building-stones for the Kingdom of God. All deeds and achievements which help the world to more freedom, humaneness and love, according to God's purposes, have such a function of continuity. But who knows which of his works will stand the great Test? (I Cor. 3:13).

Since there is some kind of continuity between history and consummation, the suggestion of a contrast between history and consummation is to be rejected. Of course the human mind is here at the limits of what can be thought or said. Nevertheless it should be boldly stated that the alternative, consummation as a timeless motionless eternity, is alien to the Christian faith. The historicizing of life has been experienced as God's own liberating work. The end of such a work never can mean its abolition, only its glorification, its preservation in a wider context of life. The expression in the New Testament that mankind in the consummation will reign with Christ (Rom. 5:17, II Tim. 2:12, Rev. 3:21, 5:10, cf. also Luke

19:17) seems to express this conviction. Consummation will mean a new and far more thorough-going display of man's freedom and dominion.

Nature in consummation has to be spoken of in an analogous way, because of the close unity between man and nature, and the continuity between this world and the consummation. The Revelation of John uses an illuminating imagery: the sea is no more, the waters are transparent like crystal, the trees yield their fruits each month. These images express the thought that nature will completely lose its uncertain, chaotic and threatening character to man, and will be entirely subservient to him. To modern man there is nothing strange in this message, except that what the Bible expresses in terms of substance, he prefers to express in terms of relation. Renewed nature is the product of a renewal of man in his relations to God and to his neighbour. Such renewal will affect our relation to nature in the widest sense, nature beyond our planet included. Man will participate more fully in the divine joy in creation, and be more fully aware of the meaning of this larger order. The renewal of nature in its relation to man will also and even primarily affect man's most intimate connection with nature—his body. The confession of the resurrection of the body means that man's corporality is not something accidental but essential, and that he lives with the promise that his complete rebirth will also imply that his bodily existence, now so often a burden and a hindrance, will become a perfect instrument of his personality in his communion with God and with man.

In the progress of technical and medical sciences may be seen the foreshadowing of this renewal of nature in the consummation. At the same time their limits, risks, darker sides and misuses are reminders of the fact that these sciences are still instruments in the hands of man as yet unrenewed. This ambivalent situation foreshadows the fact that the Kingdom will come only through the deep crisis of divine judgment.

XIII. Our Situation in History: Interpretation and Commitment

Can we interpret history? On this point we find two opposite opinions in Christian theology. The first is a clear "yes." Its defenders point to Matt. 16:3, where Jesus rebukes his adversaries with the words: "You know how to interpret the appearance of the sky, but you cannot interpret the signs of the times." They speak of the prophets as the great interpreters of their time, of the way in which Paul in Romans 11 and II Thess. 2 interprets the present and the near future, of the Book of Revelation and other apocalyptic passages, etc.

Over against this opinion the following objections can be made: man can never see more than very limited fragments of God's great history. He does not live in God's disclosed history, but in the midst of events in which He is present in a hidden way. We believe his presence; we cannot indicate it. Consider what is said in the Bible about those who wanted to explain contemporary events! (Cf. Job 42:7, Luke 13:1–5, which follows right after the Lucan version of "the signs of the times.") No survey, no blueprint of history, has been given. We are men, not God. We live on this side of the consummation. Prior to that, history remains still incomplete. And before the great divorce, good and evil are still inseparably mixed. In the Lucan version of "the signs of the times," Jesus asks: "Why do you not know how to interpret the present time?", i.e. the fullness of time, the meaning of his appearance. There is one great Sign of the time and of all times: Jesus Christ and none besides Him. Moreover, the history of all interpretations of "the signs of the times" is a strong warning. Hardly any of these interpretations has survived the interpreters. Think of the so-called "German Christians," who interpreted the Third Reich as a new outpouring of the Holy Spirit. All this should warn against interpreting special events and contemporary developments as signs of the work of Christ or of the work of the powers of evil. Christians are called not to interpretation, but to repentance and commitment.

It would thus seem that the "no" has far stronger arguments than the "yes." Yet this is not the case. The "no" separates between interpretation and commitment, which is impossible. Commitment always implies a decision in favour of something and against something else. Repentance is always repentence concerning concrete deeds, which now are rejected as being against God's will. Conscious human life is always interpreting. As responsible human beings we can never avoid it. Nor can we avoid it as Christians; for the same God who was revealed to us in Israel and in Christ, is He whose hidden presence we believe in the events of our time. We believe that the last secret of our world is the double secret of cross and resurrection. Christians are called to a life which in service, suffering and resistance will share in this ultimate reality of cross and resurrection. So they are obliged to take the risk of interpreting their historical situations to the extent that this is necessary for their commitment.

A parallel can here be drawn with what we do in our personal lives. The Christian believes that in everything God works for good and with those who love Him (Rom. 8:28). This faith is again and again a reason to try to discern God's guidance in daily life, in order to see what the next step should be. Our interpretation may, in the light of later events, be confirmed or be negated. In either case faith in God's guidance remains unshaken. The Christian's faith is independent of interpretations. At the same time, in its encounter with the ambiguities and decisions of life, it makes interpretations.

God calls us to make our decisions, in the light of his coming Kingdom, against hunger, suffering, poverty, discrimination and oppression, and for welfare, freedom, equality and brotherhood. The Christian has to know for himself where he sees the forces of the Spirit at work, in order that he may join them, and where he sees the forces of darkness at work, in order that he may resist them. It is often far from easy to make such interpretations. In this age good and evil are never present in pure forms. Always, or almost always, man has to do with a "more or less." This is a source of much difference among Christians in interpreting their historical situations. Interpretation is primarily a personal decision, but is never meant to remain a mere private opinion. It calls for confirmation, amendment or rejection by the common body of Christ. Christians need a fresh understanding of what, in the New Tes-

tament, is called "the gift of prophesy"; some members of the
Church receive more than others the ability to discern and to formulate the will of God in the problems of the present day.

There is no clear and absolute authority in interpreting history. The Church has no guarantee against great mistakes in this
realm. We think e.g. of the quite different views which we now
hold of the French Revolution, compared with that of contemporary Christians. This cannot make us passive, however, particularly not in our time when our commitment is required on a world-
wide scale.

Here the World Council of Churches has a major task. We
may hope that this body will sometimes speak the right prophetic
words on behalf of the Churches. On the whole, however, its main
task will be in preparing its member Churches for such a witness,
through bringing together their different interpretations, providing
fuller information, widening their horizons, and challenging them
to distinguish between pure and wrong motives in their initial interpretations. So the Churches in this community can wrestle to
find a common interpretation of the contemporary situation, as the
basis for their common endeavour.

All our interpretations have to be built on the foundation
which is laid, Jesus Christ (I Cor. 3:10–15). He, as the rejected
and victorious Lord, is the key to the understanding of our universal history. On this foundation, however, we can build in very different ways, with gold, silver and precious stones, or with wood,
hay and stubble. No authority can decide who is building well,
who is building badly. "The Day will disclose it, and fire will test
what sort of work each one has done." This is not said to make us
passive; on the contrary, it is an appeal to us to test ourselves,
"with all the saints," "that we may prove what is the will of God."

God is present in human history. He is present in a hidden
way. Even the forces which resist Him serve his purposes. At the
same time He is not present as an anonymous God. He has a
name. "Truly, thou art a God who hidest thyself, O God of Israel,
the Saviour" (Is. 45:15). This Saviour-name is the key to our understanding of nature and history. And in God's saving history man
is called to partake.

HISTORIANS AND
HISTORICAL STUDY

E. HARRIS HARBISON

What relevance does a Christian view of history have to the actual writing of history by historians? For Harbison (1907–64) the question was a crucial one which he discussed in several essays collected in his *Christianity and History* (1964). He strove to overcome any split which placed his Christian faith and his historical profession "in water-tight compartments." His special field as a historian at Princeton University was the sixteenth century. What intrinsic effect might his Christian view of the meaning of history and human nature have upon his teaching and his writing, such as his books *Rival Ambassadors at the Court of Queen Mary, 1553–1557* (1940), and *The Christian Scholar in the Age of the Reformation* (1956)?

A Christian historian, he thought, should by reason of his Christianity have an appreciation of the universality of history and the relativity of all human acts and institutions, overcoming thereby parochialism, nationalism, and similar tendencies. Because of his awareness of sin and redemption, there should be a sensitive realism in his view of human actions, and his historical judgments should be cautious, merciful, aware of the complexities of life. Some processes, like secularization, he might understand more profoundly than his secular colleagues, provided he did his homework like everyone else. Above all, says Harbison, the marks of a Christian historian are these: "It is *an attitude toward history* which is neither assurance nor doubt—*an understanding of history* which is something less than a philosophy but more than a mere frame of mind. . . ."

The Marks of
a Christian Historian

I

A theologian who had written an eloquent history of the Reformation is said to have met the historian Ranke in Berlin and embraced him effusively as one would a confrere. "Ah please," said the father of scientific history, drawing himself away, "there is a great difference between us: you are first of all a Christian, and I am first of all a historian."

It was with this anecdote that Lord Acton introduced the central argument of his inaugural lecture on "The Study of History." [1] The story dramatizes vividly the nineteenth century belief that history is a "science," and that science is knowledge of an utterly different order from religion. The "great difference" which Ranke saw between Christian and historian has undoubtedly narrowed in our own day as historians have grown more conscious of the subjectivity of their interpretation and more uneasy about calling history a "science." But a difference still exists in the academic mind between one who would call himself "first of all a Christian" and one who would call himself "first of all a historian."

Many years ago men would have looked at the same difference from the other side of the gulf. Imagine Acton's anecdote in reverse: Ranke (in a previous incarnation) enthusiastically embraces a great medieval saint, let us say Bernard, as a comrade; but the saint draws himself away saying, "You are a chronicler of

"Religious Perspectives of College Teaching: History," in E. Harris Harbison, *Christianity and History: Essays* (copyright © 1964 by Princeton University Press), pp. 3 through 34. Reprinted by permission of Princeton University Press. First published as a pamphlet by the Hazen Foundation in 1950.

the City of Man, I am a citizen of the City of God; between us
there is a great gulf fixed." The point is simply that in the Middle
Ages the tables would have been turned. Sainthood once had the
prestige which science (and "scientific" history) was to attain in
the nineteenth century. St. Bernard, in the position in which we
have imagined him, would have sensed the danger in Ranke's
desire to clothe his secular scholarship with the aura of Christian
sanctity. "You are first of all a historian," he might conclude, "I am
first of all a Christian."

In letting the imagination play upon the apparent difference
between professing Christian and professional historian, however,
it is easy to oversimplify. We know, for instance, that Ranke himself was a deeply religious person. "In all history," he wrote at one
time, "God dwells, lives, is to be seen. Every deed demonstrates
Him, every moment preaches His name." [2] I can find little information about the effusive theologian in the story, but I am sure
that if Ranke thought his history of the Reformation a bad job, it
was a bad job. Assuming that what Ranke objected to was the distortion of events "as they actually happened" to fit the demands of
sectarian prejudice, the cause of Christian truth certainly did not
suffer through his rebuke. The eager quest from Bayle to Voltaire
to cleanse the historical record of superstition and priestly distortion, the passion for accuracy, objectivity, and exhaustiveness in
the nineteenth century German school of "scientific" historiography—these things were certainly not anti-Christian in and
of themselves. It is far too simple to say that in our anecdote Ranke
represents something called "history" and the theologian something called "Christianity." Each in a different sense was a *Christian historian*. The question as Ranke stated it was which comes
"first of all," a man's vocation as Christian or his profession as historian.

II

There is a false sharpness in this apparent contradiction between
"Christian" and "historian" which results from the survival of a
naïve nineteenth century conception of "objectivity." Deep at the

heart of the American academic world is the belief that the word "scholar" cannot tolerate any qualifying adjective like "Christian." Has not the scholar had to battle the priest at every step of the way in his fight for freedom of inquiry? Did not the Church burn Bruno and humiliate Galileo? And in the search for historical truth, were not the real heroes those who (like Valla) exposed the arrogant forgeries of Popes or (like Bayle) laid bare the superstitions on which Christians had been nourished for centuries? Once a man allows himself to be *anything* before he is "scholar" or "scientist," so the argument runs, truth flies out the window and prejudice fills the classroom. The adjectives most feared today are of course not religious, but pseudo-religious—not "Christian" and "Jewish" but "Communist" and "Fascist." Fascist, Nazi, and Bolshevist regimes have attacked the disinterested pursuit of truth for its own sake as not only dangerous but fundamentally immoral, and it is no wonder that older convictions about the incompatibility of science and religion should be reinforced by the present-day evidence that disinterested scholarship cannot survive under the shadow of our great pseudo-religions. Such convictions are particularly strong among historians because they know what happens to the historical profession and the historical record in the hands of totalitarian governments. In any discussion of the hackneyed problem of "academic objectivity" it is important to remember that American academic communities are keenly aware of the overwhelming threat to the disinterested pursuit of truth which has driven a throng of scholarly exiles to our shores and onto our campuses. The jealous fear of coupling any adjective implying zealous faith with "scholar" is not altogether unjustified.

This was borne in upon me vividly at Bossey near Geneva during the summer of 1949, at a conference of professional historians and graduate students on "The Meaning of History." Years of totalitarian tyranny or war regimentation on the Continent have sapped any vitality which might have been left in the nineteenth century belief in "objectivity." Historians who lived under "thought control" learned to use "objectivity" as an escape from publicly committing themselves to the dominant political philosophy. Today their students have only contempt for the tendency they notice in the older academic generation to avoid commitment of any kind, on or off the lecture platform. On the other hand, they warm to teachers who believe something, even though it be a communism which most of them would reject. To most of them "objectivity" is either a hypocritical dodge designed to cover up unspoken assumptions or an immoral escape from the necessity of taking a stand on the vital issues of the day. Many European historians are so saturated in existential thinking as to deny the possibility of objectivity in any sense of the word. The only attainable objectivity, one member of the conference argued, is a frank and detailed confession of all subjective prejudices in the preface of a historical work. In other words, the dominant opinion in many European academic communities appears to be the opposite of the dominant American opinion. You must proclaim openly what sort of a historian you are—Communist, Bourgeois, or Christian. Words like "scholar" and "historian" must always and inevitably have qualifying adjectives attached to them or they have no meaning.

Contact with such thinking has a dual effect upon an American. On the one hand, it gives him a sense of pride and gratitude that belief in the possibility of disinterested inquiry is still alive and vigorous in American universities. On the other hand, it makes him sensitive to the naïveté and hypocrisy in much American talk about impartial objectivity. There is a sense in which "impartiality" has become a luxury which only those nations can afford which remained neutral or happened to avoid the worst physical and moral destruction during the late war. Swedish students at the conference mentioned were insistent that they and their friends were not a bit interested in the personal beliefs of their professors but solely in what they *knew*. Any teacher of history this side of the water will remember the same disposition in many students he has known. Faith in the possibility of "objective" knowledge is evidently still strong in these two parts of the world at least. But to most Europeans, and even to many Americans, teachers and students alike, impartiality is simply a pose adopted by fearful academicians with de-sensitized social consciences and dried-up emotions. Even in the United States all of us who face students in the college classrooms have at one time or another sensed the utter seriousness with which undergraduates ask, "But what is *your* relation to what you know? What is *your* concern with it? What do *you* think it's all about?" This is not the place to spell out what has happened to the concept of "objectivity" in recent epistemology—

and only a philosopher would do the job well. It is enough to point out that the contemporary teacher and writer of history is confronted in fact by an audience which includes an increasing number who think that Ranke was not necessarily any more "objective" than his theological friend. Europeans are simply a few steps ahead of Americans in popular awareness of the truth that the knower is intimately involved in the process of knowing.

III

The question which haunts any historian today who is at all sensitive to the deeper currents of the age in which he lives, the question his students constantly ask of him by implication even when they do not put it into words, is the question of the meaning of history. A great many of the veterans who flocked into courses in history and the social studies in such swollen numbers after the war made it clear to advisers and teachers that they were looking for answers they thought neither the arts and letters nor the natural sciences could give. Somewhere in history, many of them thought, the answer to how it all came about was to be found. This search is still on on many campuses, at least so far as history courses are concerned. Students who would hardly think of asking "What is the meaning of nuclear energy?" or "What is the meaning of the artistic impulse?" will ask in one way or another "What is the meaning of human history?" What they really mean to ask, of course, is "Where are we all headed?"

Questions like this are not fashionable among professional historians, but when a man reaches the top of the profession and no longer has reason to fear the sneers of his colleagues, it is a well-established custom to reflect upon such matters. Kenneth Scott Latourette, delivering the presidential address before the American Historical Association in 1948 on "The Christian Understanding of History," pointed out that "a survey of the presidential addresses made before this Association reveals the fact that no one single topic has so attracted those who have been chosen to head this honorable body as have the possible patterns and meanings of history." [3] In a recent discussion with a fellow historian Arnold J.

Toynbee remarked, "This job of making sense of history is one of the crying needs of our day—I beg of you believe me." [4] The philosophers and above all the theologians have been even more eager than the historians in recent years to make sense of history. Books on "The Meaning of History," "Meaning in History," "Faith and History," "Christianity and the Nature of History" have poured from the presses in fairly steady succession, particularly since the close of the war. The historian may perhaps be pardoned for thinking that this question of the whole meaning of his subject is pressed upon *him* more insistently these days by students and fellow scholars than it is upon any of his colleagues in other departments of higher learning.

There are two easy answers to this question of the meaning of history. One is to say that meaning is so woven into the texture of history that the pattern is self-evident to any interested and careful observer. All that is necessary is to study the historical record "objectively" and impartially, and a design of meaningful progress will become evident. The other is to say that there is no meaning in history and that the search for design is futile and stupid. The first is an attitude of assurance which is closely affiliated to the nineteenth century faith that if the facts are only heaped high enough they will amount to something. The second is an attitude of doubt which is generally born of disillusionment about the failure of exactly this kind of assurance.

It is not the purpose of this essay to present and preach a Christian "interpretation" of history. Rather it is to suggest that the question of meaning must be faced by every professional historian whether he likes it or not, both in his teaching and writing; that current secular answers generally end up either in a too-easy assurance or a too-abject doubt; and that there is a Christian way of looking at history which is something less than a philosophy of history but something more than a mere frame of mind, which constitutes the only really adequate alternative to either dogmatism or skepticism.

The men of assurance in the historical profession are perhaps not so numerous as they once were, but they are still an impressive group. They are generally the "social scientists" among historians, the heirs of a great hope, that science will save society. The study of history has always had its statistical side and the areas of it which are capable of semi-scientific treatment have received increasing attention during the past two centuries: geography, climate, demography, production and exchange, class struggle and social displacement. Historical study has profited immensely from this statistical emphasis, and the hard-boiled statisticians who keep reminding their colleagues of prices and wages, food production and population fluctuation, "forces" and "trends," are stimulating and indispensable members of any department of history. But the perception of trends and the drawing of graphs appear to exercise a fatal fascination on the academic mind. The trends become animated, and before we know it we are confronted with mechanisms and determinisms which "explain" history. Any practicing historian knows how deliciously seductive these magnificent simplicities can be to students who for the first time encounter the historical interpretation of Marx, for instance, or Spengler, or Sorokin.

If the men of assurance seize upon one of the emotional attitudes of modern science—its self-confidence and optimism—the men of doubt seize upon another—its tentative, skeptical, inquiring attitude, Descartes' *de omnibus dubitandum*. History to them is an unintelligible and meaningless process. Any meaning ascribed to the course of history is totally subjective; any determination of cause and effect is difficult and dubious; even the concept of cause itself, many of them maintain, is best dispensed with. There is an intellectual honesty about these people, a refusal to be taken in, an ascetic renunciation of wishful thinking, which are altogether admirable. But in the classroom this second attitude too often ends in a philosophy which proclaims that life is a mess, history a farce, and historical study a kind of intellectual game, interesting in a gruesome sort of way, but not enlightening and certainly not ennobling. All this is particularly appealing to a bewildered, disillusioned, and fearful post-war generation of students. In times of trouble pessimism is a surer balm than optimism. Men can enjoy misery if they know they have company in it. I have often seen students gain real emotional release through the discovery that a professor of history was more cynical and despairing about the state of the universe than they were themselves. But the anodyne is not permanent. And although doubt may be the beginning of wisdom, I know of no guarantee that it must end in wisdom. It is hard to nourish vigorous and creative historical thinking on the thin gruel of thoroughgoing skepticism.

IV

It should be the mark of a Christian attitude toward history that it resolves the antinomy of assurance and doubt about the meaning of the historical process on a higher plane. St. Augustine was the first Christian thinker to wrestle long and hard with the problem of how the Christian must look upon history, and it was Augustine who first saw clearly that to the Christian history is *neither* a deterministic system *nor* a meaningless chaos. The determinists of his day believed that history moved in cycles and that if only historians studied the process of recurrence carefully enough they could describe and predict the movements of history almost as they could predict the motions of the planets. Origen had seen that if this were true, then "Adam and Eve will do once more exactly what they have already done; the same deluge will be repeated; the same Moses will bring the same six hundred thousand people out of Egypt; Judas will again betray his Lord; and Paul a second time will hold the coats of those who stone Stephen."

"God forbid that we should believe this," Augustine wrote, "for Christ died once for our sins, and rising again, dies no more." [5] In other words, there is a decisiveness and unpredictability about history which is falsely annihilated in any view of history as mechanical recurrence, scientifically intelligible and predictable.

Augustine saw with equal clarity that history is not chaos. The rise and fall of states and civilizations is not meaningless process: "We do not attribute the power of giving kingdoms and empires to any save to the true God. . . . He who is the true God . . . gave a kingdom to the Romans when He would, and as great as He would, as He did also to the Assyrians and even the Persians. . . . And the same is true in respect of men as well as nations. . . . He who gave power to Augustus gave it also to Nero. . . . He who gave it to the Christian Constantine gave it also to the apostate Julian. . . . Manifestly these things are ruled and governed by the one God according as He pleases; *and if His motives are hid, are they therefore unjust?"* [6]

The very essence of a Christian understanding of history, despite the many sectarian forms it may take, is in this last sentence. The Hebrew prophets and the Christian fathers agreed in believing the strange paradox that God both *reveals* and *conceals* Himself in history. There is too much revelation for a Christian to think that there is no judgment or mercy in history, no moral meaning, no spiritual significance. On the other hand, the divine concealment is of such a character that no Christian may think that the judgment or meaning or significance is unambiguously clear to him as a human being. To Luther, who wrote eloquently about this "hiddenness of God" in history, there is mystery as well as majestic purpose in the historical pageant; and the one is meaningless without the other. God is Lord of history to Luther, but He does not work openly and visibly in the historical process. In typically extravagant imagery, he speaks of history as God's "play," God's "mummery," God's "joust and tourney." The actual course of secular history cannot be identified with God's will—nor can it be wholly divorced from His will. God wills to conceal as well as to reveal Himself in the fate of empires, and above all in the unplumbed depths of two central events, the Birth and Passion of Christ. In a famous comparison of God's grace to a passing shower of rain, Luther suggested in a single brief passage the simultaneous revelation and concealment of the divine will, the unity-within-diversity of human history, the uniqueness of events, and the decisiveness of the present moment in history for the individual: "For this shall you know, that God's word and grace are a passing shower of rain, which never comes again where it has once been. It was with the Jews, but what is gone is gone, they have nothing now. Paul brought it into Grecian land. What is gone is gone again, now they have the Turks. Rome and Latin land had it also. What is gone is gone, they now have the Pope. And you Germans must not think that you will always have it. So grasp on and hold to, whoever can grasp and hold." [7]

V

In developing the implications of these basic Christian insights into history, Christian thinkers and Christian sects have not escaped the danger of falling into one or the other of precisely the same attitudes which we have described in the case of secular historians. We might say that in the Christian case these are the "heresies" of over-assurance and over-diffidence about the meaning of history, the one closely parallel to the sin of pride, the other to that of sloth.

To Christian historians the Biblical record has always appeared to reveal a broad pattern of the divine activity in history. A Swiss scholar, Oscar Cullmann, has sketched this pattern with brilliant strokes as he believes it to appear in the New Testament.[8] As he sees it, the God who created the universe is the Lord of redemption and so of history. By the dual process of "calling" and "substitution," he directs the drama of salvation through its various stages to triumphant conclusion beyond the historical vision of mankind. He first calls or chooses mankind to stand for creation; then calls a nation, the Hebrews, to substitute for man in general; then summons a remnant to represent that nation when it falls away; and finally fixes upon one man, the Christ, to stand for all humanity and creation. The progressive reduction then gives way to progressive expansion and the process reverses itself. Through Christ the apostles are won, through the apostles the Church is founded, through the Church all mankind will be reconciled to God, and the new heaven and earth will complete the first creation. The fact that the Western world divides time into "A.D." and "B.C." is the most obvious evidence of the incalculable influence which this broad pattern of meaning envisioned by the early Christians has had upon historical understanding.

The point at which this pattern becomes controversial for Christian groups is naturally the concrete meaning given to the age in which we live, the age of the Church from the Resurrection to the present. Is the gradual unfolding of this age a significant part of the drama or not? Is God's hand still evident in every turn of events? If so, how and where and in what?

The answer has been clearest through the ages for the Roman Christian. For him, God's hand has been clearly evident in history since Pentecost in the Roman Catholic Church. There is a real progress in history: progressive unfolding of doctrines which were only implicit in New Testament times, progressive winning of the pagan, the infidel, and the schismatic in spite of all appearances of defeat. History has a central thread in Church history, in the growth of a visible divine institution—what Sir Thomas More called "the common, known church"—changeless in goal but constantly changing in its temporal position in relation to this goal. In different times and in different ways, such a conviction that God's hand in history is unmistakably revealed in a visible historical institution has been shared by Eastern Orthodox Christians as well as by Lutherans, Anglicans, and early Calvinists. Its remote source is undoubtedly the Old Testament Covenant of Jehovah with his chosen people.

Another form taken by Christian assurance about the meaning of history is the belief that God's hand is evident not so much in *institutions* as in *events*. In the Middle Ages, the most significant events were visions and miracles. To readers of the lives of the saints, God's love and power were constantly breaking in upon the ordinary course of human affairs in a direct and self-evident way. The successor to this belief in more sophisticated early modern times was the conviction, particularly evident in Oliver Cromwell and his Puritan contemporaries, that God's hand appears not so much in miracle as in the outcome of historical events like battles. This conviction that God guides men not by mystical vision or miraculous breaking of natural law but by his shaping of secular history, by what Cromwell called "dispensations," was rooted in the Hebrew prophets and widely prevalent among our seventeenth century American ancestors.

Among Protestants today assurance about the meaning of history is certainly not a besetting sin. Christians have never entirely recovered from the eighteenth century attack on the "theological interpretation" of history which had been dominant from Augustine to Bossuet. Nor should they, perhaps. Many of the things which Voltaire assailed in Christian historiography needed to be assailed: the narrow parochialism which funneled all ancient history into the story of "that miserable little people," the Jews; the neglect of non-Christian civilizations; the partisanship and axe-grinding so characteristic of monkish and priestly chronicle; the easy recourse to miracle as a short-circuit of causal explanation. Voltaire and his fellow-philosophers destroyed the older Christian pattern of meaning in history only to substitute another, that of secular progress. But the shattering experience of two world wars and the cold shadow of a third have effectually destroyed the naïve belief in inevitable progress, and most Protestant leaders today are concerned to extirpate the last traces of nineteenth century optimism about the course of secular history.

The result is a strong tendency on the part of Christian intellectuals today to adopt a kind of Christian skepticism about the meaning of history. Among Protestant theologians this group is clearly in the ascendancy today, in terms of prestige if not also of numbers. There is sound historical reason for this. Primitive Protestantism had at its center a passionate protest against identifying the will of God with any visible institution such as the Roman Church. Too often the result was simply to substitute the church of Wittenberg, Geneva, or England for that of Rome. But it is impossible in the long run for a Protestant to rest content with any theory of history in which a visible institution is the sole channel of God's grace. This is why Protestants turned so easily to something like Cromwell's doctrine of "dispensations." They soon abused this doctrine, to be sure, by seeing God's will in secular events or movements which pleased them, all the way from parliamentary government and democracy to liberalism and socialism. Led by Karl Barth, Protestant theologians today are moving in strong reaction to such tendencies. In spite of the widespread current interest in history among theologians, the deepest currents in Protestant theology, particularly in Europe, can only be described as *anti-historical*. These currents find their source in Kierkegaard, in Barth, in Berdyaev, and in secular philosophers of the existentialist school. Diverse as they are in their sources and present courses, they have some things in common: a deep distrust of everything associated with "progress"; a sense that God is the "wholly Other" and hence not to be identified with any historical institution or movement, whether it stem from Rome or Geneva or Moscow; a radical Christian relativism in viewing all historical achievements.

This Christian skepticism about the possibility of discerning any pattern of meaning in secular history bulks large in recent theological works. "There never has been and never will be," a recent writer concludes, "an immanent solution of the problem of history, for man's historical experience in one of steady failure. . . . History is, through all the ages, a story of action and suffering, of power and pride, of sin and death. . . . The importance of secular history decreases *in direct proportion to* the intensity of man's concern with God and himself. . . . A 'Christian history' is non-sense." [9] I have heard a similar view eloquently expressed by a deeply spiritual Danish professor of church history who was arguing "the impossibility of a Christian conception of history." Since real knowledge presupposes simultaneity, he maintained, we can never actually know the past and the past can never have real significance for us. The mere unrolling of history has no visible meaning for a converted Christian. "Christian belief," he concluded, "is to trust God in the uncertainty of life. It is the most abominable arrogance to make false certainties by interpreting history in a Christian way." [10] The trend toward a Christian agnosticism with respect to any self-evident meaning in the course of history is very strong indeed, particularly in Europe. Evidently the Christian historian does not avoid the twin dangers of dogmatism and doubt simply by being a Christian.

VI

The historian who happens also to be a Christian is thus besieged, as it were, by four attacking armies of colleagues, students, and friends who come at him from the four points of the compass. His secular colleagues who have all the answers tell him to put aside childish things like religion now that he has become a man and to open his eyes to the great material mechanisms which determine history. A few of his Christian friends are perhaps equally dogmatic on the other side of the matter, exposing the naïve assumptions of the materialists and pointing out with equal assurance just where the hand of God is to be discerned in history. The agnostics among his colleagues both in history and in theology come at him from two different and opposite quarters—each with *Nescio* inscribed on their banners, but for quite different reasons. Each group maintains that history has nothing much to do with Christianity, the first because Christianity is nothing, the second because history is nothing. In this plight I think the Christian historian may well stand up and make a brief speech which might run something like this:

"I am neither a philosopher nor a theologian. I am interested as any educated man is in philosophy and theology, but as a professional historian you must not expect of me a fully-rounded philosophy or theology of history. Thanks to my training, I am suspicious of big words and big ideas. I believe that Marx was wrong in his interpretation of history for the same reason that the authors of saints' legends were wrong—that human history cannot be reduced to magnificent simplicities, either material or spiritual. I have a feeling that agnosticism, not assurance, is the first step toward wisdom, provided that it does not sink away into cynicism and despair. But I cannot agree that history has nothing to do with the religious insights of Christianity, or that Christianity has nothing to do with secular history. I could not long remain either a believing Christian or a practicing historian with my convictions about Christianity and history in water-tight compartments. I believe, in spite of secular skeptics, that Christianity offers a profound insight into the general nature of the historical process, even though both as historian and Christian I am too diffident to think that I can discern a clear-cut pattern. I believe, in spite of the theological skeptics, that secular history is important to the Christian and that Christianity always suffers when its historical character is minimized, because the immediate result is always a loss of ethical vigor among Christians. I think I see a fine traditional ambiguity in the word 'vocation' as the call of God both to religious commitment and to service in a job. I see no reason why I cannot find a reconciliation between my two 'vocations' on the practical working level of teaching and writing history, if not on the loftier levels of philosophy and theology."

VII

To the professional historian, much of what has been discussed thus far may seem highly theoretical and only very tenuously related to the practical work-a-day problems of the classroom. It is my conviction, however, that in any discussion of religious perspectives in teaching history—whatever may be true of other subjects—it is impossible to separate the theoretical and the practical, just as it is impossible to split apart the historian's dual function as teacher and writer. The real problem is to find a practical working form of Augustine's or Luther's understanding of history which takes account of the immense recent progress of historical knowledge and technique, which conforms to the idiom of twentieth century thought in general, but which remains true to the basic insights of Christianity into the nature of man, of God, and of time.

On this level the first illusion to be got rid of is the idea which I have heard expressed by enthusiastic theologians that being a Christian will make a man a better professional historian—nay, that it is the very condition of being a true historian at all, since it was Christianity which nurtured the modern historical sense of unique events happening in irreversible sequence in straight-line time. Christian belief is obviously no substitute for competent scholarship at the technical level, and it would be intolerable pride in a Christian to suggest that on this level his religion gives him an advantage over the non-religious historians. I cannot see how Christian belief contributes anything significant to the careful study of matters like the laws of Solon, medieval land-tenure, or the impact of gunpowder on the history of military tactics. Furthermore, sectarian prejudice has long been a notorious obstacle in the path of historical understanding.

There is an important truth, however, at the basis of this illusion, a truth most eloquently developed in Herbert Butterfield's penetrating and exciting lectures on *Christianity and History*. It is that the Christian understanding of the nature and destiny of man—created yet free, fallen yet redeemable, bounded by history yet able to transcend it by his imagination and creativity—cannot fail to deepen and enrich any historian's understanding of his subject. It cannot be said too often that historical understanding is never merely a matter of reading documents. A child cannot comprehend Luther's experience in the monastery until his own human experience and powers of imagination are mature enough to provide at least some common ground of understanding. A student cannot understand the complexities of the movement Luther started, its contradictions and confusions, the mixture in it of lofty ideals and base motives, until he has absorbed something at least of how the politics and mass movements of his own day operate. In the same way, the truly great historian cannot afford to ignore the thinking about human nature and the problem of evil which has been done by the most sensitive and intelligent observers. To the Christian, the profoundest view is the Hebraic-Christian as it has been developed from the prophets and Christ through the apostles and later teachers of the Church.

There is an opposite illusion which may also be dismissed briefly. This is that a man will be a better Christian for being a historian. Stated in this form, the proposition is of course absurd. Learning of any sort has never been a condition of Christian perfection. But again there is a truth at the basis of the illusion. The Christian faith was born among a people which had developed a relatively strong historical sense, and the New Testament is saturated with temporal terminology used naïvely: "then," "straightway," "when the time was fulfilled," "in the fullness of time." At the Last Judgment men are judged by what they have done in history, even though their righteousness or unrighteousness is not evident to them during their historical existence. The Apostles' Creed is a statement of belief about events which happened in time, not a statement of truths which are eternally true apart from time. To Augustine, as to the Hebrew prophets before him, there was significant development in time of God's purpose; and to Dante, the destiny of Rome was linked firmly and surely to the destiny of the Church.[11] In other words, the Hebraic-Christian tradition, unlike others which arose in India and China, is a history-valuing tradition; and it is no accident that when it became partially secularized, the result was the modern idea of progress. Except when Greek or Oriental influences have become dominant, Christians have never looked upon time as something to be fled or annihilated. There is a sense in which a man must be historically minded in an elementary way in order to be a Christian.

Let us grant that Christian belief will not improve a historian's standing with his fellow scholars, nor professional historical knowledge a Christian's standing among the saints. On the practical level the gulf between Christian and historian is nevertheless by no means so wide as Ranke implied it was. There are some qualities and attitudes which are equally admired by Christians and by professional historians, and which may serve as guide-posts for the man who wishes he were both a better Christian and a better historian.

One of these is *universality* or catholicity of outlook. The best historians are not satisfied until by a rigorous intellectual asceticism they have risen as far as humanly possible above all parochialism of both time and place which narrows or distorts their historical vision. It was part of Ranke's greatness that he strove so hard and so self-consciously to rise above sectarian and national prejudice and to judge past ages by their own standards rather than by those of a later day. The most obvious source of this rationalistic universalism was the Stoic conception of the natural equality of all men and the eighteenth century cosmopolitanism so akin to it. This outlook blended easily with the catholicity preached by a religion which insisted from the beginning upon the fatherhood of God and the brotherhood of all men. The monotheism of the Hebrew prophets and the belief in the universal fatherhood of the Christian God formed the basis upon which the first clear conception of the unity of history was built in the West. Christian historiography, with all its failings, constituted a notable step beyond the parochialism and nationalism of Greek and Roman historical writing; and even if it developed a new parochialism of its own, it never entirely lost the belief that all local histories are really one history. The Christian believed that though one nation may be "chosen," the mission of a chosen people is world-wide, more is demanded of it than of others, and if it falters, its mission may pass to the Gentiles. Amid all the welter of histories written in the interests of class, nation, race, or sect, this ideal of universality of perspective still stands as that of professional historian and Christian alike.

Closely related to universality is the difficult matter of *judgment*. The secular historian would dislike any theological terminology here, but a reading of the ablest contemporary historians I think would suggest that they believe in something very close to the Christian belief in a justice completed, though never annihilated, by mercy. Most historians are aware that they cannot avoid judgment of men and movements, either in their writing or their teaching. Monographs and textbooks which simply "give the facts" betray underlying judgments in the very choice and arrangement of such facts—especially when they are read after the lapse of a generation or so. Students are quick to sense the judgment implicit not only in the conscious choice of material for presentation but even more in the unplanned and half-conscious tone of voice or facial expression which betrays the teacher. Granted the necessity of making judgments, the real question is on what basis they are to be made, and here the historian and the Christian are in general agreement. Justice requires that all the relevant data be used and fairly weighed before judgment is given. The usual result of a long and honest attempt to get at all the historical evidence about any disputed event or personality is an overwhelming sense of the complexity and relativity of the issues, a sense of *tout comprendre, c'est tout pardonner*. The desire to be fair ends often enough in the desire to extend mercy, even on the level of purely secular historical labor. In the Gospels "Woe unto you, Scribes and Pharisees . . ." is balanced by "Judge not that ye be not judged." The historian knows—or should know—that the limits of judgment lie for him too between these same two extremes, between a sense of righteousness which refuses to blink the fact of evil, and a sense of mercy which follows from the complexity of human affairs and the frailty of human judgment.

To take a concrete case, any historian who writes, lectures, or talks with students about Luther is sooner or later forced to take up an attitude toward him. A Roman Catholic teacher may vent his righteous indignation upon the reformer; a pious Lutheran may make a spotless prophet of him; a Marxian may point out that Luther was a mere puppet in the grip of irresistible economic forces. It may be suggested, without any intent to blaspheme, that the best professional historian's ideal here is theoretically the same as the Christian's: to see Luther as nearly as possible as his own Lord saw him, in all his weakness and strength, his compromises and triumphs, his freedom and his compulsion, so that in the resulting judgment justice is perfectly tempered with mercy. As a matter of fact, close and persistent study of Luther and his whole age by professional historians has brought us closer at least to the possibility of such a judgment than was conceivable a century ago, simply because we knew too little then. Mere knowledge is no guarantee of sound judgment of men and movements, either in

THE MARKS OF A CHRISTIAN HISTORIAN

historical study or in ordinary Christian living, but it is often the beginning of true understanding. The kind of judgment the best historians strive for is not so far as some may think from the kind of judgment the truest followers of Christ have striven for.

A third quality or attitude which is characteristic of both historians and Christians on different levels is best described as *realism*. Generally it is the "humanists" among historians, not the traditional Christians, who are shocked by the realities of human nature as they are encountered in history. The historian and the social scientist habitually deal with human nature at its lowest level, the level at which "moral man" is absorbed in "immoral society." Much of the time they are concerned with the competition of groups for wealth and power, the game of power politics, the awful destruction of revolution and war. My guess is that the ratio of cynicism among historians is higher than that among, say, professors of literature or of physics. At any rate the historian is not apt to be a Pollyanna at the present moment of world history. Nor is the Christian. Both succumbed for a time to the eighteenth century belief in the goodness of human nature and the inevitability of progress, but a good many non-Christian historians today would be impelled to agree with Herbert Butterfield when he writes, "We have gambled very highly on what was an over-optimistic view of the character of man. . . . It is essential not to have faith in human nature. Such faith is a comparatively recent heresy and a very disastrous one." [12] The tough-mindedness about which many professional historians pride themselves is not so far from a Christian attitude toward human nature as a soft and idealistic optimism.

Tough-mindedness must be balanced, however, both with the historian and the Christian, by *open-mindedness*. By this I mean openness to unforeseen possibilities in human nature and history. The historian who is merely cynical is obviously going to be blind to the unexpected and unexplainable good in human nature, the movements which turn out better than their sordid origins would lead one to expect. "Good" events in history have a disconcerting way of producing unlovely results. But many of the results which we later call "good" have been the by-product of selfish conflicts—civil liberties in English history, for instance, were partly the product of self-interested squabbles over privilege by social or religious groups. The great historians have invariably had a certain open-mindedness to the infinite possibilities in human nature which is certainly akin to, though it is not identical with, the Christian's sensitivity to the redemptive possibilities in any human situation. In the mental make-up of a historian, realism must be balanced by a certain naïveté and wonder, a sense of the kindliness in human beings that is the ultimate foundation of societies and of the resilience which human beings keep demonstrating in the face of disaster and evil. On a different level the Christian would call this kindliness and resilience evidence of the workings of grace. Luther's warning that to talk of the Law and forget the Gospel is "to wound and not to bind up, to smite and not to heal, to lead down into Hell and not to bring back again," has its clear implications for the historian as well as for the Christian.

Finally there is a sense in which both historians and Christians are *relativists*. One of the major counts brought against teachers of history by moralists in our day is that they instill into the minds of our youth a corrosive relativism, a feeling that there are no universal and unchanging standards and that moral codes are always relative to time and place. In this view, for instance, there is no justification for saying that Democracy is any better than Naziism, or "civilization" any better than "barbarism." Undoubtedly there are radical skeptics among historians (as we have already pointed out) who appear to enjoy fostering the amoral relativism they find ready-made among their students. But the Protestant Christian at least will find some common ground more readily with one of these relativists than he will with an absolutist who deifies some historical institution or movement or individual. The Christian is too deeply rooted in history to be unconcerned about the strivings and achievements of his own class, nation, or civilization in history. But his nature and destiny can never be understood from the historical perspective alone since man transcends history in addition to being immersed in it. In other words, the prospect of the collapse of our civilization is important (as it is not to a Buddhist), but not all-important (as it is to a humanistic believer in progress). If God is really Lord of history, then no man or group or idea is lord of it. The Christian can never compromise with men who see the meaning of history exhausted, for instance, in the rise of the Aryan race to world empire under the leadership of a

Fuehrer; but he can find a beginning of mutual understanding with men who refuse to deify any hero or cause in history.

In all this there is meant to be no implication that the attitudes of professional historians and of Christians are *necessarily* the same, or even that when parallel attitudes emerge they spring from the same underlying motives. It is simply to say that from the perspective of the mid-twentieth century, Ranke was wrong. There is no inherent and necessary contradiction between being a Christian believer and being a professional historian.

VIII

We are left with a final question. Is there anything *distinctive* about a historian who is also a Christian? What are his marks and how will he be known? How will he understand history as how will he attempt to teach others to understand it?

To many—students, colleagues, and friends—the chief test will be quantitative: the amount of time and attention a historian devotes in his writing and teaching to the place of religion in history. Important as this test undoubtedly is, I believe it is generally over-emphasized. A good historian, whether he is a person of religious belief or not, should give religion its due just as he gives every other factor—economic, political, intellectual—its due in his study of the historical process. The current tendency is to ignore or minimize the role of religion in history as the story gets closer to the present. It is no particular surprise to most historians to learn that while the average college text in European history devotes about 30 percent of its space to religious developments in the Middle Ages, only 2 percent or less of its space is taken up with specifically religious movements after about 1800.[13] There is no question that a glib unexamined assumption that "religion is through" is often behind this progressive neglect of religious factors as the textbook writers skim over the modern centuries. In any truly impartial search (if such were possible) for what made the nineteenth century tick, religion would bulk much larger than it does in most of our texts. But this is a matter for historians in general to settle with their scholarly consciences. Naturally a his-

torian of Christian leanings will be interested in the religious factors in history and he will probably give them due space. But being
human, he will be in constant danger of giving them *too much*
space, of "dragging religion in," like the Marxian who distorts the
historical picture by overweighting the economic factors. The plain
fact is that specifically religious ideas, religious images, religious
institutions, and religious influences in general were nowhere near
so dominant in the Europe of 1800 as they were in the Europe of
1300, and any historian who blurs this fundamental fact is not
being honest. There is no simple quantitative test of a Christian
historian. His mark is not the quantity of time he devotes to religious matters, but the quality of his whole treatment of his subject.

To follow out the example chosen, how will a Protestant
Christian historian view the "secularization" of European society
since the Middle Ages? How will his view differ, if at all, from the
average textbook and classroom treatment? In terms of time and
space devoted to religious movements it may differ very little, and
yet I fancy there should be a profundity to it which is generally
lacking in the ordinary treatment. "Secularization" is an extremely
complex and subtle sort of historical process. In many ways people
in the Middle Ages were as worldly and immoral as people in our
own day, and considerably more brutal and insensitive in some respects. True, the Church dominated their daily existence, their
whole culture became infused with Christian ideals, and there was
no real alternative to Christianity as a system of ultimate truth. But
when we ask whether the hold of Christianity upon their lives was
more or less "totalitarian" than the hold of Naziism upon Germans
under Hitler or of Marxism upon Russians under Stalin, the answer is that the hold was probably less total. Naziism and Communism are not religions, but they appeal to the religious emotions of
men, they organize themselves along lines strikingly similar to the
Medieval Church, and they make demands upon their followers
that are best described as religious. If we grant that they are
pseudo-religions, it could even be argued that we live in a more
"religious" age than the Middle Ages. Christianity itself is more
widely spread over the earth's surface than ever before, and even
the economic and political philosophies of our day have to be given
a "religious" dynamic in order to move great masses of men. This

suggests that "religion," often in a bewildering variety of perverted and idolatrous forms, is still one of the major forces in the twentieth century world, as it was in the thirteenth. This is an exaggeration, of course, but it may serve to suggest dimensions of the problem of "secularization" which generally remain unseen by "secular" historians and which should be evident to those of Christian belief. The latter should be aware that the concept of secularization is only one of many—and a crude and clumsy one at that—which historians need to describe the historical change which has taken place since 1300. The Western world has become more "worldly" since Dante's day, but to anyone who knows the history of the "Dark Ages," the present battle of the Christian churches with "worldliness" is surely nothing new. The "secularization of society" is a far more subtle affair than it appears to be in most textbooks.

The Christian who is also a historian, then, will be known neither by any fully-rounded "philosophy of history" which is the necessary outcome of his Christian belief, nor by the amount of time he spends talking or writing about Christianity. He will be known by *his attitude toward history*, the quality of his concern about it, the sense of reverence and responsibility with which he approaches his subject. This attitude will of course be determined by the quality of his Christian faith and life. The intensity and character of Christian belief varies enormously. An indifferent Roman Catholic will differ a great deal in his attitude toward history from a recent convert, and a Calvinist will see things differently from a Quaker. But I believe it possible to sketch the characteristics of a sort of composite Christian historian, provided the reader remembers that the author of the sketch is a Protestant, and provided both remember that although it is given to all men to follow Christ in any profession, it is given to none to become like his Master.

The attitude of the Christian historian toward the past will be like that of the Christian toward his contemporary fellow beings. He may seldom mention the name of God, of Christ, or of the Church, but in every remark he makes in the classroom and in every paragraph he writes in his study there will be a certain reverence and respect for his material, a certain feeling for human tragedy and human triumph in history which is closely parallel to the

Christian's respect for human personality in general. He will try to understand before he condemns, and he will condemn with a sense that he too, being human, is involved in any judgment he may make. He will not bleach the moral color out of history by steeping it in corrosive skepticism. Nor on the other hand will he use history as a storehouse from which deceptively simple moral lessons may be drawn at random. He will admire Lord Acton's unquenchable moral fervor in urging historians "to suffer no man and no cause to escape the undying penalty which history has the power to inflict on wrong," but he will not be impressed either by Acton's historical wisdom or by his Christian humility in this famous passage. He will have too lively a sense of his responsibility to his students, his community, and his society, too deep a sense of the urgency and crisis of his time, to dismiss the whole story of the past as a tale told by an idiot, signifying nothing. He will know that to see any meaning at all in history is an act of faith, not a result of studying documents, but he will not dodge the question for that reason. He will be aware that every man in his beliefs belongs to *some* school or party or church, and he will not be afraid to admit that his own beliefs have their source in a church. He will say that he thinks them to be far better beliefs than those which stem, for instance, from the school of skepticism or the Communist party.

At the same time he will remember that he is a teacher, not a preacher or a pastor; a layman rather than a clergyman. He will remember that as a layman and a historian he has no more right to pontificate about the ultimate meaning of history than his students or his friends. If he is a Protestant, he will not grant this right to any human being, whether priest or lay. Where materialists may see mere blind process, where rationalists may see evident progress, he will see providence—a divine *providing* in both the conscious decisions and the unintended results of history, a purpose partly revealed and partly concealed, a destiny which is religious in the deepest meaning of the word, in which human freedom and divine guidance complete each other in some mysterious way.

He will not blink the fact of evil in history. He will not be so naïve as to relegate it to a past which is progressively being left behind, or to an "environment" which can be changed merely by a little human goodwill, or to some convenient historical scapegoat such as a "bad" nation, an "inferior" race, or a "degenerate" class.

But he will not leave his hearers or readers to wallow in masochistic enjoyment of history's folly and brutality. He will be sensitive to the unpredictable and sometimes unbelievable redemptive forces in history. He will not "know it all." He will neither sell his fellow human being short, nor will he over-rate them. Behind both the personal decisions and the vast impersonal forces of history he will see an inscrutable purpose. He will look for the working of God both in the whirlwinds and in the still small voices of history. He will give a sense of pondering and wondering more than of either dogmatizing or doubting. ". . . And if God's motives are hid, are they therefore unjust?"

There is a sense in which the Christian historian is justified by faith. No man can *know* the meaning of history, but his faith that there is meaning in history may perhaps be counted to him as knowledge in the same sense that faith is counted to the Protestant believer as righteousness. The Christian historian's faith may nourish, enrich, and deepen the faith of those about him for the very reason that it is *not* knowledge. Let us insist upon it again that it is *an attitude toward history* which is neither assurance nor doubt—*an understanding of history* which is something less than a philosophy but more than a mere frame of mind—it is these that are the marks of a Christian historian. In the last analysis, the attitude a Christian takes toward the history of which he himself is a living part will determine his attitude toward the history which is past.

This will not be enough to some—to an Orthodox Jew, for instance, to a Roman Catholic, or to a fundamentalist Protestant. To many others it will be too much. A professing Christian member of the historical profession will be constantly aware that he is fighting a two-front war, against non-Christians who think he believes too much and super-Christians who think he believes not enough. From the subjective point of view this consciousness that there is no wall for him to put his back to may be the ultimate mark of his calling. Deep within him will be the faith, counted to him perhaps as righteousness, that in spite of the conviction of Ranke with which we began, a man may be "first of all a Christian *and* a historian."

NOTES

1. Lord Acton, *A Lecture on the Study of History* (London and New York, 1895), p. 50 and note p. 115. Acton quotes an article of Victor Cherbuliez in *Revue des Deux Mondes,* XCVII (1872), 537, in which the historian is not identified.

2. James Westfall Thompson, *A History of Historical Writing* [New York, 1942], II, 171.

3. *American Historical Review,* LIV (1949), 261 [see p. 46].

4. *Can We Know the Pattern of the Past?* Discussion between P. Geyl . . . and A. J. Toynbee . . . (Bussum, Holland, 1948), 30.

5. Augustine, *De Civ. Dei,* Book XII, chap. 13. The passage from Origen (*Peri Archon, II,* chap. 3) is quoted by Lynn White, Jr., "Christian Myth and Christian History," *Journal of the History of Ideas, III* (1942), 147.

6. *De Civ. Dei,* [Book] V, chap. 21.

7. Luther, *Werke* (Weimar ed.), XV, 32.

8. See Oscar Cullmann, *Christus und die Zeit* (Zürich, 1946) (English trans., *Christ and Time,* Philadelphia, 1950), particularly Part 1, chap. VIII.

9. Karl Löwith, *Meaning in History* (Univ. of Chicago Press, 1949), pp. 190–197. Italics mine.

10. P. G. Lindhardt, of the University of Aarhus, Denmark, at the conference at Bossey mentioned above.

11. The most significant passages for study of the general problem seem to me the following: Acts II, III, X, XI; Romans VI; Galatians IV; I Corinthians XV. Augustine, *De Civ. Dei,* Book V, chap. 21; Book XII, chap. 13; Book XVIII, chap. 46. Dante, *De Monarchia,* and *Purgatorio,* cantos 16, 20.

12. Herbert Butterfield, *Christianity and History* (London, 1949), pp. 34, 47.

13. *College Reading and Religion: A Survey of College Reading Materials sponsored by The Edward H. Hazen Foundation* . . . (Yale Univ. Press, 1948), pp. 209–211.

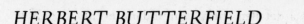

HERBERT BUTTERFIELD

A historian's Christianity can suggest two ways of entry into historical study, says Butterfield in his famous book *Christianity and History* (1949). First, it can provide an orienting interpretation of history which is "the key to his conception of the whole human drama," and which fills the details of history with significance. To achieve this view of the whole, we need the poet, the prophet, the philosopher, and the theologian.

Second, Christian faith can suggest a method of approach to historical study which deflates the role of science in life and which acknowledges the limited task of the historian. Academic history, according to Butterfield, legitimately fulfills its responsibility when, following the tradition of Ranke, it is restricted to the critical investigation of documents, working thereby to yield very concrete and particular information about the past. This technical history can "provide us with a reasonable assurance that certain things did happen, that they happened in a certain order, and that certain connections exist between them." He believes that information such as the date of his grandfather's birth can be established independently of a philosophy or creed, and can act as a bridge between the versions constructed by "the liberal, the Jesuit, the Fascist, the Communist." To be sure, as Butterfield stressed later, only a small portion of what the historian deals with—and not even the most important—can be "historically established" by this method.

Butterfield comments in *History and Human Relations* (1951) that such a restricted and technical method may be "a specifically Christian one." In any case, he believed that Christians, starting with their view of the whole and of Providence, "can safely embark on [such] a detailed study of mundane events, if only to learn through their interconnections the ways of Providence."

Historical Scholarship and Its Relation to Life

It was often noted in the earlier decades of the present century how greatly it had become the habit of Protestants to hold some German scholar up their sleeves—a different one every few years but always preferably the latest one—and at appropriate moments strike the unwary Philistine on the head with this secret weapon, the German scholar having decided in a final manner whatever point might have been at issue in a controversy. From all of which the charge arose that for the Protestants the unanswerable pope was always some professor—a system more inconvenient than that of Rome, partly because the seat of authority might change overnight and be transferred to a new teacher who had never been heard of before, and partly because if one has to have a pope it is at least better that he should be subject to certain rules and traditions, and appointed by a properly constituted authority. The tendency was not confined to Protestants, however, for almost a century ago the young Acton was warned not to play this game of waving German professors at his fellow Catholics; though he not only failed to take the advice, but added the weight of his influence to a tendency that was making historical scholarship perhaps over-arrogant and certainly too pontifical. When, therefore, the other week I happened to hear two theologians congratulating one another that the very advanced German professors who had been thrown at our heads in the days of my youth had long been exploded, I had the feeling that we who study the past must be all alike; the new school of thought in the 1940's is evidently as sure of itself as the old one of the 1920's used to be.

The perfect parable for those who are interested in the relations between religion and any form of science is provided by the conflict between Galileo and the Church on the subject of the rotation of the earth. On the one hand Galileo's conduct in the particular circumstances of the case required—if he was to be justified—that he should make good his claim that he had actually demonstrated the earth's motion; but, as he imagined that the action of the tides was the clinching argument which proved his thesis, he was wrong at a critical point—mistaken in his science and premature in his dogmatism. On the other hand it is clear from Galileo's case as well as many others, that much unnecessary anguish has been produced for Christians throughout the ages because the Church has so often imagined the gospel to be tied to the science of a particular epoch (Aristotelian physics, and Ptolemaic astronomy for example), with the result that men have felt that the one must stand or fall with the other. On both sides of the Galileo controversy, therefore, we see the effect of the mind's presumption—we see a little of that intellectual arrogance, or mental rigidity, or stiff-necked self-assurance which manages to interpolate itself into all forms of scholarship and science. If anybody were to doubt the existence of this, it is always sufficiently evident when we turn back to examine the dogmatisms of scholarship in any generation previous to our own.

In the case of history, for reasons that are understandable, such presumption insinuates itself into the study more regularly, more powerfully and with more dangerous guile than in all other forms of scholarship and science put together. And if it infiltrates into the upper regions of the study it comes with much mightier force into all popularisations of knowledge, all forms of sub-scholarship. As regards historical learning we may begin by noting, therefore, that when attached to other things—when geared into some specific outlook on life for example—it results in a product colossal in its comprehensiveness and almost frightening in the power that it has over men. When it is envisaged in itself, however, its scientific authority is limited by the character of its apparatus and the nature of the evidence which it can employ. Taken by itself historical scholarship as such must be regarded as fulfill-

ing a more limited and humble rôle than many people take for
granted.

We can do many things with the past apart from scientifically
studying it—we can sing songs about it, like Browning in his *Cav-
alier Songs,* or we can let our fancy play around the Roman wall,
as Kipling did, and simply use the past as a thing to tell tales
about. Thinking vaguely about the founders of our ancient colleges
we may be moved almost by a sense of piety towards them; and it
is clear that some men have found a part of themselves reaching
strangely out to the past as they have gazed for a moment on the
ruins of Rome. Sometimes there has existed a nostalgia for the
past that is almost a form of disease, as in the case of that roman-
ticising which in the eighteenth and nineteenth centuries many
European nations began to do over their primitive history—their
fairy-tales and folk-lore and heroic poetry—a phenomenon which
helped to bring about the evils of romantic nationalism. But a different set of factors is involved if we note the peculiar interest—
beyond that of the academic historian—which the twentieth-century Protestant must have in the Reformation; while the claim has
been made that every man must have an attitude to the French
Revolution—must make a decision about it somehow—as part of
the stand that he generally takes in life. Another aspect of our relations with our predecessors is illustrated in the whole question of
the power of tradition which, whether by its unconscious operation
or as a result of certain doctrines and institutions, may go so far as
to imply an exaggerated subservience to the past. It is even true
that the recovery of the past has never been solely or even prin-
cipally the work of what we usually call the historian—as can be
seen in classical education, Biblical scholarship, and much of our
study of architecture, painting and literature. The Renaissance
had the design of salvaging and actually reinstating the arts and
sciences, the wisdom and the learning, and indeed the whole civilisation of antiquity—a plan of resurrection much more radical and
far-fetched than anything which the mere historian pretends to
undertake. The past in fact must never be regarded as a fossil or as
having existed merely to be the object of the historian's scientific
curiosity.

But however much I may have loved my grandfather I may be
convinced that he was always mistaken, or always tried to cheat

me, about his age; and, without diminishing my affection for him, but holding it in suspense so to speak, and freezing out any wishful thinking, I may set myself to discover by a scientific procedure the precise date of his birth. In the nineteenth century such a critical attitude to historical data—such an enquiry for those facts which could be established in a watertight manner—received its great development and recognition, though the fundamental features of the method had been practised on and off, or applied in certain fields, for many centuries. The nineteenth century, on the one hand, illustrated the truth that owing to the laxity of the human mind and our tendency to float at ease on what we too readily regard as established facts, there are certain lessons of critical awareness that easily drop out of our traditions and have to be discovered over again in successive generations. The same century, on the other hand, vastly intensified the technical discipline and extended its application, carrying the sceptical or critical attitude into further realms of what had hitherto been too easily accepted as established facts.

For students of modern history it was an important moment when the young German historian Ranke, looking at the age of the Renaissance, took various authors of that period, who had written the chronicles of their own times, and by various forms of detective-work undermined their credibility. The novelty of his technique was perhaps exaggerated in the nineteenth century, but it established the fact that you were foolish to depend on the contemporary chroniclers and narrative-writers of the sixteenth century if you wished to know what really happened in that period—you must go to official documents. For some time Ranke himself as an historian made great use of the despatches sent by Venetian ambassadors resident in foreign countries to their government at home; but there was a period when he laid himself open to the charge that he who had torn the contemporary chroniclers to pieces with his criticism did not think to exercise a parallel criticism upon the despatches of Venetian ambassadors in turn. He relied on their descriptions for many kinds of information, whereas we to-day would feel dissatisfied if for a knowledge of the sixteenth-century economic life of England we had to depend upon the reports of a foreign ambassador resident in London. Ranke himself was to learn later that a considerable degree of human frailty is liable to insert itself into any species of mere reporting that is done by a man in circumstances in which there is likely to be no immediate check on him.

In the nineteenth century, then, and even in the work of Ranke himself, the scientific method went on developing. The intensity of criticism, and the awareness of the possible pitfalls, increased in a remarkable manner as time went on. You were in a position to learn a great deal more than before about the diplomacy of Europe when the archives of the British Foreign Office became available to scholars for a particular period; but it soon transpired that if you worked up the story from that body of documents alone you were simply locking yourself up in the British Foreign Office view of what was happening in that period; and this needed to be squared with evidence coming from other quarters. The total result was that the labours of the historian were multiplied a hundredfold. A Napoleonic battle reconstructed from the vast collection of orders issued during its course, and supplemented by the constant flow of reports from officers to their superiors while the action was developing, is a colossal piece of labour for the student, but it stands in a different class from an account of a battle compiled merely from eye-witnesses' reports, or the later recollection of participants, both of which are forms of evidence gravely discredited if we look at the history of historical science as a whole.

Once we pass beyond the establishment of what I have called specific facts, however, and particularly when we come to the reconstruction of a complicated episode or the attempt to put a whole story together in its proper bearings, then a certain feature of historical science makes its appearance which it is important above all other things that people should realise, and which is more generally overlooked than anything else. The only appropriate analogy to the authentic work of historical reconstruction is the case of the detective working out the solution of a crime-problem in a conventional work of fiction. At the first stage you have the stupid inspector from Scotland Yard who sees all the obvious clues, falls into all the traps, makes all the common-sense inferences, and lo! the criminal is self-evident. The whole story of the crime in fact is immediately made clear to us; there is a plausible rôle in that story for each of the characters concerned; the solution satisfied the mind, or at any rate the mind at a given level; and

indeed for this poor Scotland Yard inspector one would say that
the study of history ought to be the easiest occupation in the
world. Detective stories may not in other ways be true to life, but it
is the case in human affairs that the same set of clues, envisaged
at a higher level of thought, with or without additional evidence—
the same set of clues reshaped into a new synthesis by a Sherlock
Holmes—may produce a new map of the whole affair, an utterly
unexpected story to narrate, and possibly even a criminal where in
the first place we had never thought to look for one. And the same
thing is liable to happen when an historical episode is reconsidered
and reconstructed after, say, a century of learned controversy.

In other words, the development of the scientific method in
nineteenth-century historiography did not merely mean that this
or that fact could be corrected, or the story told in greater detail, or
the narrative amended at marginal points. It meant that total re-
constructions proved to be necessary, as in the detective stories,
where a single new fact might turn out to be a pivotal one; and
what had been thought to be an accident might transform itself
into an entirely different story of murder. In these circumstances,
evidence which had seemed to mean one thing might prove to be
capable of an entirely different construction.

In the *British Documents on the Origins of the War* the crucial volume for July, 1914, contains some interesting scraps of
documents—only a few lines of them in particularly small print—
belonging to a class of evidence which the editors had some difficulty in getting published, and which will not be published in the
parallel series of documents now appearing for the Second World
War. A person who looks hard at those half a dozen lines, and
broods over them till their implications simply stare him in the
face, will find them so important that he must go back to the
beginning again—he must re-read hundreds of pages of documents before and after the critical point, to find what they now
mean in the light of those few significant sentences. Here, as on so
many occasions, it is something small which proves to be a clue or
turns out to serve as a hinge—a few sentences that would not have
been missed if (as so nearly happened) they had not been printed
with the rest of the collection at all.

There exists in most historical writing, therefore, an appearance of definitiveness and finality which is an optical illusion—and

this is particularly the case as the period under study becomes more recent, and the history becomes more nearly contemporary. If historical education gets into the hands of heavy pedagogues, who teach a hard story in a rigid framework and expect it to be memorised, then new depths of unimaginativeness will have been reached, not possible of attainment without an education in history. If men at twenty learn to see the events of history in a certain framework, and learn that framework so thoroughly that it remains on their minds in after-years—if they learn it without acquiring imagination and elasticity of mind—then we can say (and the words let fall by some of our leaders and by the framers of public opinion would tempt one to say it already), that by the study of history a merely probable national disaster can be converted into a one hundred per cent. certainty.

Now if history is a science of this peculiar structure there are certain comments to be made on this whole form of scholarship which may be relevant to a study of the relations between Christianity and History. First of all it transpired in the nineteenth century that the critical method, as applied in this field, could be pursued with a scepticism that overstepped the bounds of common sense. Over a century ago this possible extravagance had become the subject of satire in a work intitled *Historic Doubts concerning Napoleon,* where, by rejecting things alleged to be too improbable for belief, the author purported to demonstrate that the great Napoleon himself must have been a mythical personage. Of course if Ranke showed the untrustworthiness of old narrators, when compared with official documents, his destructive criticism has a striking application to the narrative in the Bible and to ancient history generally. Indeed Ranke only transferred to modern history a critical method which had already been applied long before in the various fields of ancient history. I must confess that, as a modern historian, when I consider the terrible effects of criticism even on the most respectable of contemporary memoirs—those of Sir Edward Grey, for example—or remember the suppressions of which both good Protestants and good Catholics have been so often guilty, with the most pious of intentions, in their writing of history; when I think that the future student of the 1930's and the 1940's is going to have to pick his way even amongst faked diaries and narratives of pretended eye-witnesses; and when I recall how much more easy it is for a camel to go through the eye of a needle than for the most excellent trained historian to repeat a piece of gossip or an anecdote at the dinner-table without adding a little varnish—putting all these things together I have wondered sometimes how such a thing as ancient history, whether secular or sacred, could be taken seriously at all. It was not surprising that sooner or later somebody should raise the question whether Jesus Christ Himself were not perhaps a myth, possibly even a syndicate.

I have an impression, however, that the purely sceptical method almost gave us the measure of itself in the nineteenth century; for it produced some prime specimens of ludicrousness in the way of conjectural interpretation, and the centre of gravity in these ancient studies seems to me to have shifted in the other direction. A remarkable factor affecting both classical and Biblical history has been the archaeological discoveries which confirmed the literary documents sometimes in unexpected points of detail. The general fact emerges that in a great deal of historical work mere scepticism carries one nowhere and everything depends in the last resort on the very delicate balancing of the mind as it makes what we call an "act of judgment." From what has been already noted concerning the nature of history it will be apparent that in reality there are reasons why we ought to have a great respect for ancient studies. The weight of scholarship is imposing in realms where year in and year out, for generation after generation, century after century, minds have been traversing and re-traversing the same field, one hypothesis after another being put forward and tested, every permutation and combination tried, a tremendous amount of detective work carried out over every square inch of the area, all the jealousies and rivalries of scholars adding to the intensity of the debates. It always seems to me that such long centuries of study result in history of an entirely different order—not to be compared with those hurried superficial compilations of recent happenings which have their currency with us to-day for a moment because they happen to be the first in the field.

Secondly, history is a peculiar science in that it depends so much on things which can only be discovered and verified by insight, sympathy and imagination. The historian does not have direct acess to the insides of the people he deals with; he imagines that they must have profundities of mind and motive, tremendous corridors and recesses within, just as he has himself; but he has to piece these out from scraps of external evidence and he must use his imaginative sympathy, must give something of himself, to the reconstruction of an historical character. Thomas Carlyle is supposed to have provided the world with the clue it had long been needing for the production of anything like a plausible personality for Oliver Cromwell; and it is held that he achieved his effect by the process of reading something of himself into that historical character. That method may give easy results when the historian is dealing with a temperament that has some special degree of affinity with his own; but the resources of history are bound to be very limited if a given historian can only achieve understanding in the case of men who are somewhat like-minded with himself. Carlyle showed his weaknesses when he began to read too much of his own personality into other historical characters for whom the procedure was bound to be less happy than it had been in the case of Oliver Cromwell.

Because it is so difficult to attain an internal knowledge of historical personages it is extremely hazardous for the historian to venture on certain interesting questions—for example to pretend that he can show that one generation was really more happy than another. Because the historian cannot reach the seat of the personality it is not he who, when confronted by a pleasing character on the one hand and an unpleasant character one the other hand, can decide quite what was due to merit in the one case and what to misfortune in the other. If I claimed to be the reincarnation of Beethoven, any man would have as much right as any other to put me down as a lunatic, but it is not by the apparatus of the historian that I could be proved to be actually wrong. If any man were to say that history had scientifically established or scientifically disproved the Divinity of Christ, he would for the same reason be guilty of that intellectual arrogance which works in all the sciences as each of them transgresses its bounds in order to gain an usurped authority.

Thirdly, if I demonstrate that my grandfather was born, shall we say, on January 1st, 1850, then that thesis must be equally valid whether I present it to Christian or atheist, whig or tory, Swede or Dane. In respect of points which are established by the evidence, or accepted by the judgment of common sense, history has a certain validity of its own, a certain minimum significance that is independent of philosophy, race or creed. It is recorded somewhere that the group of men who founded the Royal Society in seventeenth-century England resented the waste of time that was liable to occur in their discussions. when—as in the case of some societies in our present-day universities—every topic would be carried back to the region of first principles and fundamental beliefs, so that the debate was for ever returning to the same issues and they could not discuss the ordinary operations of nature without perpetually coming back to their basic theological or philosophical differences. Only when these men learned to keep their conversation fixed on the mere mechanical operations of nature— the observable effects of heat on a certain substance for example (where what was true for one was true for all of them)—could they short-circuit that tantalisingly unprogressive form of general debate.

In historical science, and particularly in the upper regions of the study, a similar policy of abstraction has become customary. Historians, limited by the kind of apparatus they use and the concrete evidence on which they must rely, restrict their realm to what we might almost call the mechanism of historical processes: the tangible factors involved in an episode, the displacements produced in human affairs by an observed event or a specific influence, even the kind of movements that can be recorded in statistics. All this tends to give historical narrative and historical scholarship a mundane and matter-of-fact appearance. I must confess that if in the ordinary course of teaching I were to ask for what I should carefully call the "historical explanation" of the victory of Christianity in the ancient Roman Empire, I should assume that there could be no doubt concerning the realm in which the problem was to be considered, no doubt that I had in mind the question "how" Christianity succeeded and not the more fundamental question "why." As a technical historian, that is to say, I should not be satisfied with the answer that Christianity triumphed merely because it was true and right, or merely because God decreed its victory. I remember taking part in a *viva voce* examination in Oxford over ten years ago when we were left completely and permanently baffled by a candidate who ascribed everything to the direct interposition of the Almighty and therefore felt himself excused from the discussion of any intermediate agencies.

Yet it seems true to say that nothing in the work of the technical historian causes so much dissatisfaction at the present time as this mater-of-fact policy—this way of setting out the concrete story, the observed phenomena, and leaving it for people of all beliefs to make their varied commentaries. And so it is that the liberal and the Jesuit, the Marxist and the Fascist, the Protestant and the Catholic, the rebel and the patriot—all cry out against our modern forms of exposition, saying what a bloodless pedestrian thing academic history is. Above all, the young student who does not know where he stands amongst all these partisans but goes round with a hungry look seeking for something like an interpretation of life—even the student who comes to history itself for his education, on the assumption that life will somehow explain itself if you study a greater length of it—he tells us that whereas he asked for bread, he is in reality only being given a stone. More serious still, it happens that the historian has to try to see Christian and Mohammedan, black man and white man, conservative and socialist all somewhat from their own point of view—he must include all men and parties in a comprehensive effort of understanding. And some people have complained that by such a policy they have found themselves doomed to a perpetual relativism, as though between Christianity and Islam it were a matter of indifference—they have been trapped into a habit of mind which sees no values as absolute in themselves. This last point is particularly important and it equally affects the students of the natural sciences; because it is true that we fall into certain habits of mind and easily become the slaves of them, when in reality we only adopted them for the purpose of a particular technique. It is as though people could be so long occupied in tearing flowers to pieces and studying their mechanism that they forget ever to stand back again and see the buttercup whole. It is possible that in the transition to the modern oulook the world was guided much less by any deliberated philosophy than is often assumed, and I think that few people could be said to have come to that modern outlook by an authentic process of thinking things out. Men are often the semi-conscious victims of habits of mind and processes of abstraction like those involved in technical historical study or in physical science. They decide that for purposes of analysis they will only take notice of things that can be weighed and measured, and then they forget the number they first started from and come to think that these are the only things that exist.

If men have found no philosophy or religion in their actual experience of life, it can hardly be claimed that the academic study of history—the mere concrete study of the workings of events—will itself provide the remedy, or that the attempt to learn more scientifically when things happened or how they happened can solve the whole problem of human destiny or achieve anything more than a better statement, a better laying-out, of the essential riddle. Certainly academic history is not meant for all people and is often a somewhat technical affair; and those are gravely wrong who regard it as the queen of the sciences, or think of it as a substitute for religion, a complete education in itself. Those who promoted its study in former times seemed to value it rather as an additional equipment for people who were presumed to have had their real education elsewhere, their real training in values (and in the meaning of life) in other fields. Those who complain that technical history does not provide people with the meaning of life are asking from an academic science more than it can give and are tempting the academic historian himself to a dangerous form of self-aggrandisement. They have caught heresy from the secular liberals who, having deposed religion, set up scholarship in its place and unduly exalted it, assuming that the academic historian was fitted above all others to provide out of his technique an interpretation of life on the earth. Academic history would be subject to fewer attacks if our educational system as a whole had not gone adrift, and we had not allowed the administrative mind to throw overboard the very things which (precisely because they had elements of the imponderable) provided a training in values.

If it is the assured Christian who is reading academic history these problems—these objections to a technical form of study—can hardly be said to exist; for, having in his religion the key to his conception of the whole human drama, he can safely embark on a detailed study of mundane events, if only to learn through their inter-connections the ways of Providence. When we have reconstructed the whole of mundane history it does not form a self-explanatory system, and our attitude to it, our whole relationship to the human drama, is a large affair altogether—it is a matter not of scholarship but of religion. It depends on the way in which we decide to set our personalities for the purpose of meeting the whole stream of events—depends ultimately on our attitude to life as we actually live it. If academic history cannot provide a man with the ultimate valuations and interpetations of life under the sun, neither is it generally competent to take them away from the person who actually possesses them; and if there is internal friction and tension when the religious man puts on the technical historian's thinking-cap, the strain is just as constant between religion and one's actual experience in the world—in both cases we might say that, for the Christian, the friction which is produced is of a generative kind.

It is true that technical history and historical research only comprise a specialised part of our attitude to the past, and their realm is restricted by the character of the apparatus which they use and the kind of evidence which is available. They provide us with a reasonable assurance that certain things did happen, that they happened in a certain order, and that certain connections exist between them, independent of any philosophy or creed of ours. But for the fulness of our commentary on the drama of human life in time, we have to break through this technique—have to stand back and see the landscape as a whole—and for the sum of our ideas and beliefs about the march of ages we need the poet and the prophet, the philosopher and the theologian. Indeed we decide our total attitude to the whole of human history when we make our decision about our religion—and it is the combination of the history with a religion, or with something equivalent to a religion, which generates power and fills the story with significances. We may find this in a Christian interpretation of history, or in the Marxian system or even perhaps in H. G. Wells's *History of the World*. Nothing can exceed the feeling of satisfaction that many people have when they meet some such system which helps them through the jungle of historical happenings and gives them an interpretation of the story seen as a whole. In such cases our interpretation is a thing which we bring to our history and superimpose upon it, however. We cannot say that we obtained it as tech-

nical historians by inescapable inferences from the purely
historical evidence.

Therefore, the liberal, the Jesuit, the Fascist, the Communist,
and all the rest may sail away with their militant versions of history, howling at one another across the interstellar spaces, all
claiming that theirs is the absolute version, and admitting no place
even for an academic history that shall be a bridge between them.
In a cut-throat conflict between these and other systems for the
control of schools and universities (in other words for predominance in society) it is not clear that a specifically Christian or
Biblical interpretation would in fact prevail at the present day, or
would be acceptable to the world at large, unless it were seriously
corrupted. But while we have Marxists and Wellsians, Protestants
and Catholics with their mutually exclusive systems (historical assertion confronted by counter-assertion), many people, confounded
by the contradictions, will run thankfully in the last resort to the
humbler academic historian—to the man who will just try to show
what can be established by the concrete external evidence, and
will respect the intricacy and the complexity of events, bringing
out the things which must be valid whether one is a Jesuit or a
Marxist.

Technical historical study has its place, therefore, and we
shall find further reasons later why perhaps the Christian should
be the last person in the world to object to historical reflection,
even if it only serves to deepen our understanding of human relations, and to provide a limited knowledge of the demonstrable connections between events. The cry for an interpretation of the
human drama is a cry not for technical history but for something
more like "prophecy." Those Christians who wish to have their history rich in values, judgments and affirmations about life, can find
the clue and the pattern to its interpretation very easily; for they, of
all people, ought to be the most inveterate readers and students of
the Bible. Those who complain of the aridity of technical history
which strands itself in petty discussions about the date of a de-
spatch or the mechanical operation of a constitutional device,
while evading the majestic issues that relate to man's larger destiny, are crying out for precisely the thing which the Biblical
writers were doing with the human drama, and to the dignity of

which the academic historian could not pretend to reach. Even within the range of what I might call mundane comment on human affairs and on the moral problems involved—even in the things that would still be valid if there were not a word of truth in supernatural religion itself—there is a profundity of long-term historical comment in some of those ancient writers which it is surprising that our civilisation should have allowed itself so tragically to forget.

On the decisive question of the posture one should adopt towards life or the interpretation one would give to the whole human story, it would be unwise to surrender one's judgment to a scholar, any more than one would expect a scholar by reason of his technical accomplishments to be more skilled than other people in making love or choosing a wife. Neither should one be guided in the great decision by the spirit of an age—for, concerning the spirit of any age, even technical history can find many disillusioning things to say. Our final interpretation of history is the most sovereign decision we can take, and it is clear that every one of us, as standing alone in the universe, has to take it for himself. It is our decision about religion, about our total attitude to things, and about the way we will appropriate life. And it is inseparable from our decision about the rôle we are going to play ourselves in that very drama of history.

ARTHUR S. LINK

Professor Link (b. 1920), of Princeton University, probably knows American political history during the presidency of Woodrow Wilson better than anyone else. His many books include *Wilson* (5 volumes, 1947–65), *Woodrow Wilson and the Progressive Era* (1954), and *Papers of Woodrow Wilson* (16 volumes, 1966–73). But when he, in this essay, reviews what he knows he is impressed that he has "seen only the small tip of the historical iceberg." His is merely "fragmentary knowledge of [a] single brief isolated episode or period."

Like Butterfield's, Link's Christianity leads him to stress the limits of the historian's methodology. The Christian historian, Link affirms, is free "from the tyranny of the ego's insatiable demands for its own understanding and control of history." Furthermore, because God is the creator and reality is his creation, the historian may rely upon "the faith and knowledge that every single fact of history has its own objective existence and integrity." The study of history is, for Link, a sacred vocation wherein he examines historical reality as a given truth which is independent of our constructs about it and which he endeavors to understand faithfully for the good of all people.

For Link what matters is not sweeping generalizations about history, but "the myriad seemingly small and unimportant details" of history. Consequently he finds the attempts to build a Christian interpretation of the whole course of history fruitless. Instead, Christian historians should be content with using the insights of a biblical view of such matters as human nature and the lordship of Christ over history as guides in uncovering the truth of historical reality in all its particularity.

The Historian's Vocation

It is probably accurate to say that man's first conscious intellectual endeavor was his effort to know and remember his past. Long before he had a written language or began to evolve a primitive understanding and control of his natural environment, he and his fellow-clansmen and tribesmen recorded and preserved in song and saga the origins of tribes and peoples and the memory of migrations to green pastures, of wars and heroic deeds, and of natural occurrences and catastrophes. It would seem, indeed, that man has always known instinctively that knowledge of his past is one of the basic items of his equipment for survival. He learned this fact presumably at the dawn of human history.

It seems equally safe to say that one of the ego's basic drives is toward understanding of the self in time. This is more than a conscious act of survival. It stems from the self's innate curiosity about the self. To be sure, the sophistication with which the individual conducts his search depends upon his own equipment of mind and even more upon the intellectual resources of his culture. But all peoples, whether they be herdsmen in Ur or scholars in twentieth-century universities, have had an innate curiosity about the past. It is not enough to say, as one of my distinguished colleagues once said, that men study history because they enjoy it. It is more important to say that men study history, whether around the council fire or in universities, because their egos demand such activity for their own fulfillment, because they tell them that they must know their past if they will vindicate their superiority over the rest of the natural world.

Reprinted by permission of *Theology Today* and Arthur S. Link from *Theology Today*, XIX (1962–63), 75–89.

I

Man is not content merely to study history. The ego will not be satisfied with this, because the ego in its unredeemed or natural state is not able to see history apart from itself. It is the center of creation; history, therefore, has no meaning outside its understanding. Thinking that it is the creator, the ego drives toward the reduction of history in order to assimilate and master history. What occurs when this takes place is that the ego compels its finite mind to reduce the infinite to finiteness, in order that the mind may understand, control, and use the infinite of history.

If you are thinking that all this sounds theoretical, permit me to say that there is nothing theoretical about it at all. It is a plain statement of simple fact, which I am inclined to believe goes a long way toward describing techniques that men most often use to delude themselves. But I must resist the temptation to talk about cases, like that of primitive men in a so-called natural state or even of the rank and file of people today, which obviously illustrate my generalizations. My space is limited, and I must get directly to the practicing historian, the man upon whom I want to concentrate my attention. I want to say a specific word about his condition.

Journeymen of the historical craft live as much in bondage to the ego as do their less sophisticated or learned fellowmen. This fact is all the more significant because in the western Christian world, at least, they have been trained to live according to the law. That law is what the profession calls methodology, that is, the way in which one should go about studying history and doing research and writing. This methodology was based in its inception either upon Biblical affirmations about the reality of truth or upon Newtonian-Darwinian concepts of scientific certainty. A fact is a fact, for all that; two plus two equals four, and so on. Now, the historian, along with most other intellectuals in the modern world, long ago concluded that Biblical faith was irrelevant, that it did not validate his methodology; he has long since ceased to see its meaning for his methodology. No sooner had he repudiated the Biblical foundations, however, than scientists themselves began to undermine reasons for believing in scientific certainty. These two great erosions have by our own day gone a long way toward destroying the intellectual and faithful foundations of historical methodology.

Some members of our profession have been frank enough to admit that this is true and honest enough with themselves to try to find a new *modus operandi*. The more extreme among them have embraced and practiced a pure subjectivism, an out-and-out egocentric understanding of history. There is, they say, no such thing as absolute historical truth; facts mean altogether different things to different people, depending upon culture, environment, and so on. History, consequently, has no meaning outside the mind of the historian; indeed, in an existential sense the historian creates history. The historian should approach his subject by constructing hypotheses based upon what he knows to be true. He should then write his history after marshaling evidence to support his hypotheses.

This is too strong doctrine for most historians to profess openly, or even to accept consciously. It may be that they have been trained in seminars too rigorously in the rules of evidence and in respect for the formalities to be willing to abandon the old methodology for the new subjective anarchy. Perhaps they have also done enough work in historical sources to have come to feel the strange power that evidence itself can exert over the mind of the researcher. In either event, most historians go about their daily work on the common sense assumption that historical truth must have its own existence because otherwise their work would be meaningless and their careers a fraud. They live not in total darkness but, it might be said, in the dim light of natural revelation. And in many instances they live scrupulously, morally, righteously by the law of historical method. For them it is no longer a divine law, handed down on some Sinai; they know the law's formalities, not its life. But it is a seemingly viable way of professional life. Carefully observed, it enables one to write acceptable monographs and to teach seminars of his own.

I have, I suspect, just been describing the situation of the vast majority of historians whom I happen to know. I mean no derogation of them when I say that living by the law as historian amounts to precisely the same thing and has precisely the same inevitable results as living by the law in all of life. We are not able to fulfill our true vocation, that is, to be good and faithful historians, because we simply do not have it in us to fulfill the law's demands. That, I can hear you say, is a big statement and easy enough to make, but what about the proof? All that I can say in reply is that we are moving now on a level where theories and speculations have no relevance. We are dealing with experience, not theory. In trying to explain to the Christian community at Rome the futility of striving after righteousness, even under divine law, Paul appealed to the facts of Israel's history and, most importantly, to the truth that he had been given the grace to see in his own experience. And so it is when we talk about what happens when the historian tries scrupulously to live by the law.

To begin with, as I can testify from my own experience, the law of historical methodology, most especially the law as most historians understand it, leaves us in vast darkness. It tells us that there are facts but does not tell us what they mean. It says that there is such a thing as history, but it does not tell us what it is. In other words, it does not answer our first questions about the meaning of history, even the meaning of our own lives in history. The law fails, more importantly, because it makes onerous demands without giving the power to fulfill its high and worthy standards. It tells me that as historian I must be scrupulous, honest, and fair, that I must honor truth by respecting its integrity, that I must marshal my evidence and relate the facts as I see them. Well and good; the rules are clear enough. But what happens when I try to put the facts together for a lecture or a book? I find that the harder I try the more I fail to satisfy the law's demands. I am not just parroting Paul at this point. Over and over I have found from my own experience that my ego drives inexorably toward its own control, that is to say, it seeks to impose its own pattern upon events, selects its own evidence and discards evidence when it is not useful, in short, writes its own history. And so I find that the so-called subjectivists were right, at least in their diagnosis of our situation. Scientific objectivity, as present-day historical methodology understands it, is a snare and delusion for me.

II

The most pretentious thrust of the historian's mind takes form in the construction of theories and philosophies of history. This occurs in the first place because the mind is overwhelmed, baffled, and disorganized by the immensity and complexities of history. The human mind, if for no other reason than its sheer physical inadequacy, can never assimilate more than a minute segment of the historical record. Long and laborious research according to the best canons of historical method and invoking the assistance of all the tools of modern technology, can yield only fragmentary knowledge of any single brief isolated episode or period. If, for example, we study the history of a single presidential administration in the United States, we do well if we attain a degree of mastery over the most obvious facts about a few leaders of the government in Washington and the larger forces and movements in the country that were operating to shape important policies during this brief period in one country. At best we will have seen only the small tip of the historical iceberg. We can never know all the thoughts and actions and decisions of the millions of Americans in their daily lives and work, to say nothing of the vast stream of events in the rest of the world, even those parts of the world with close ties to the United States. This is true only secondarily because the historical record is fragmentary; it is true more importantly because our finite minds are not capable of comprehending the infinitude of history.

It is altogether understandable why both philosophers and historians (and ordinary folk, too, for that matter) through the ages have sought release from the bonds of finiteness by devising theories or philosophies of history. As I said a moment ago, the ego drives powerfully and inexorably toward its own control of history. In its finiteness it cannot truly, fully know history; none the less, it will be satisfied with nothing less than its own understanding of history. Hence it must reduce history's complexities, dilemmas, and baffling uncertainties to some comprehensible, manageable system. The results, obviously, are theories and philosophies of history.

There have, of course, been many different kinds. This is not the time and place for description and analysis of their varied assumptions and understandings, but it is, I think, important to note that all theories and philosophies of history have at least four characteristics in common. First, all of them, at least all that have been fully developed, pretend to nothing less than a world view, a cosmology, a complete and total understanding. As Richard Hofstadter said of Herbert Spencer's social Darwinism, "It offered a comprehensive world view, uniting under one generalization everything in nature from protozoa to politics." Second, ironically, in view of their aspirations, all theories and philosophies of history have been the product of their peculiar culture and their culture's understanding of human affairs. That is to say, they cannot be understood outside the total context of the culture that spawned them. Third, all these well-developed systems attain comprehension and symmetry by rigorously imposing their own order on history, and they do this by quite ruthlessly ignoring, excluding, or discarding evidence that is not susceptible of assimilation. This is, I think, as true of Greek idealism as it is of dialectical materialism. Fourth, most if not all great philosophies of history have not been content merely to describe but have ranged beyond and have attempted to discover the dynamics of history, to discern and isolate the forces that move men and nations.

I hope it is obvious that I would not want to be understood as passing moral judgment on theories and philosophies of history. The interesting and significant fact is that most ordinary workaday historians have never derived much help or understanding from them. To be sure, monolithic interpretations and theories have had their vogue from time to time, and individual historians have sought refuge from their bafflements in them. But it would seem that some automatic device always sets to work to prevent such commitment by the rank and file. Indeed, it is not too much to say that the average working historian is almost inherently suspicious of too much theory. His methodology has trained him to be this way. Perhaps by natural revelation he has come to see if not to understand the infinitude of history and to know that commitment to theory or philosophy can never open doors that now seem locked to him. If philosophy and theory do not provide the way out, then what? The historian, it would seem, has no recourse but to live by a law that pronounces the sentence of death upon him because it fails to give power for fulfillment of its impossible demands.

III

The historian is set free, that is to say, enters into new life in which he can know and live with the truth of history and be the kind of historian that God means him to be, when he is justified, when he is set in a right relationship to God. I do not mean to imply that he is justified merely as professional teacher and scholar. When it occurs, justification is a radical transformation of the entire person—body, mind, and spirit. It is a new state of being, not an attitude of mind or a new way of looking at things. It is a complete turning around of personality, from inward looking toward self to outward looking toward God. It is the experience that all men have felt when they have known the redeeming power of God. We do not need to say at this point precisely how this occurs. Let it suffice to say that justification occurs when the Holy Spirit, whether in response to human submission or by God's own loving grace alone, comes to the individual in his helplessness and despair, restores his health by smashing the fortress walls of selfishness and pride, and gives him the ability to love God and hence to love creation.

The point that concerns us most as teachers and students is what all this means to us in our particular vocations. I realize clearly enough the difficulties of undertaking any explanation. And yet I cannot escape the conviction that we cannot begin to know what it means to be Christians in our vocations until we have abandoned the absurd practice of compartmentalizing our lives and come to see that living by faith means living by faith as historians, economists, scientists, and so on, in every detail of daily work.

I think that we can best approach this subject by trying to see what happens to the historian when he is given the gift of the Holy Spirit. It is hard to know where to begin, because he is made a new creature. He is given, for one thing, the ability to see all things a new way—to know himself as creature, finite being, whose creative powers have been dulled or destroyed by pride, selfishness, ambition, lust for power. He is given the ability to live with himself because God has accepted and forgiven him. He is given not perfection or sanctification, for the old man has not yet been entirely destroyed, but a mighty helper, guide, corrector, and friend in the Holy Spirit, who never leaves him even in his darkest perplexities. He is given, among other things, the grace to be grateful, even joyful, in response to God's goodness in giving him family and friends, a university with colleagues and students to serve and love, and the sustaining fellowship of the Church. He is given, finally, the sight to see his vocation for what God intended it to be.

For the historian in his daily work of trying to learn, teach, and write, all this has very specific meaning. To begin with, it means the liberation of the self from the tyranny of the ego's insatiable demands for its own understanding and control of history. I do not mean to imply that this happens all at once, or that we are ever completely liberated from our bondage. But the Holy Spirit works and prays for us even in our persistent, stubborn rebellion. And he does break through to reclamation. He gives us the ability first of all to know that truth without which there can be no understanding of history—that God exists, and that because he exists truth lives in resplendent power and glory. The historian will no longer say with Descartes, "Cogito, ergo sum." He will now say "Deus est, ergo sum," *ergo* creation, being, truth, history. Think what this means to the historian in so vital a matter as his methodology. It means that historical truth exists not in his imagination or because of his whim, but because God himself, the Creator of the universe, has brought human history into being and has himself lived in human history. Man, a finite creature, can know and understand truth only partially, imperfectly, corruptly, it may be. But by God's grace he can at least honor, respect, and treasure it. That is to say, the historian, while readily acknowledging that only God knows all historical truth, can now affirm, profess, and confess that he stands in the presence of something far greater than himself, something that gives meaning to his life and work—the faith and knowledge that every single fact of history has its own objective existence and integrity. We may ignore, warp, or deny those facts, but in the very act of doing violence to them we stand already condemned.

I suspect that these generalizations have much to say to the present sometimes very warm discussion in the historical profession about whether it is possible to write so-called objective history, by which is meant history purged of the ego's distortions and

perversions. As we usually do, we begin this discussion by asking
the question the wrong way. We should ask, instead, whether historical truth has its own existence, in short, whether there is such
a thing as objective history. If we answer this question in the affirmative, we will not ask the essentially foolish question of whether
we can in fact write objective history. We will know only that we
must try even if we are bound to fail, and that we must trust in the
power of God to give us the ability partially to succeed. For when
God justifies and calls us, that is, gives us the ability to accept historical truth in humility, he also gives us the ability to be good and
faithful historians. This is a fact of experience, not a theory, and it
is difficult to explain because its precise meaning will vary according to the individual experience. But let me try for a moment to
elaborate upon it.

The first result of justification is to free the historian from the
tyranny of the law. This is rather inaccurately put, as in fact justification gives the historian ability for the first time to know and
understand the majesty and righteousness of the law. It would, I
think, be more accurate to say that the first great result of justification is to lift the law's sentence of death upon us as historians.
It does this by giving us the ability to observe the law. There is no
great mystery about how this happens. In his natural state, the
historian is such a slave of ego that he cannot observe the law's
demands no matter how hard he tries. In justification, God in the
Holy Spirit not only restores health to the ego, the mind, the whole
person, as I have already tried to say; he also gives the historian,
the whole person, power to live in new freedom from day to day, in
the classroom and the study.

For example, there is the freedom that comes from new understanding of daily tasks. The historian set right knows that he is
God's chosen man. God has called him to study history for a specific vital purpose—to preserve the historical record in truth and
integrity, not merely because history is a record of God's work in
time, but because mankind cannot be truly free unless and until it
knows the truth about itself. The truth is revealed most fully in the
record of the past. In the classroom or in the study writing articles
and books, the historian is God's man. He is not the servant of
students who might want to be entertained or of governments and
cultures which demand glorification and deification. He is God's

servant. And just as God calls the historian to this service, so also does he give the historian courage and power in time of need to perform it.

There is liberation, too, in the historian's new understanding of how he should proceed to the service to which God has called him. Freed, at least in part, from the ego's drive toward its own understanding and use of history, he can now see his reasonable service to be the discovery and relation of events of the past. In short, he can see that he is called to be a mere chronicler of the past. To be sure, he will be eager to know and understand theories and philosophies of history, because they constitute an important part of the record of human intelligence at work. But he does not have to be concerned about imposing his own system to control events. He accepts his own finiteness. He knows that he can never know all of history's complexities. He knows that imperfection and mortality stamp his work with ephemeral character. This apprehension, however, brings not tension and anxiety but release from the compulsion to be original, masterful, cosmic. It frees the historian to live creatively.

I have said that the historian justified will have the grace to see his proper role as being that of mere chronicler. The adjective is adequate but somewhat misleading. Seen in the light of faithful service, being a mere chronicler is an awesome task indeed. It means not only taking history seriously, but also taking one's discipline seriously. It means never being satisfied, and working relentlessly because there is so little that is known and so much to do. It means knowing that the good chronicler is not one who merely records events, even events in their vastness, but one who tries to understand *why* things turned out as they did—one who attempts to analyze and interpret as well as to relate. It means rigorous regard for a methodology that is grounded in truth, and being a good scholar and a good citizen of the academic community, because this only is service acceptable to God. It means knowing that alleged piety is no substitute for hard and excellent work, and that one can truly love God as historian only if he is willing to go far beyond the law's demands.

I come back to the most wonderful and amazing fact about this justification of which I have been speaking. It is simply that God gives us power to fulfill our vocation's demands. I am reminded at this point of Georg Neumark's great seventeenth-century hymn of trust, "If Thou but Suffer God to Guide Thee," and particularly of the last two verses which follow:

> Only be still, and wait his leisure
> In cheerful hope, with heart content
> To take what e'er thy Father's pleasure
> And all-discerning love hath sent;
> Nor doubt our inmost wants are known
> To him who chose us for his own.

> Sing, pray, and swerve not from his ways,
> But do thine own part faithfully;
> Trust his rich promises of grace,
> So shall they be fulfilled in thee;
> God never yet forsook at need
> The soul that trusted him indeed.

God stands with us in the classroom as we seek to relate the facts of the coming of the French Revolution or the American Civil War. His Spirit works with us in the library as we search through newspapers and magazines, and in the study as we struggle to reconstruct the evidence of past events. Do we go off on our own tangents? Do we seek to fit the evidence into our own molds? Then the Spirit can, if he will, correct and guide us back to faithful chronicling. Perhaps he will not so use us; perhaps he will use our willfullness for our larger training as historians. Even so, he gives us the ability to live with our mistakes and to learn from them, and to go on in daily work in trust that he will turn all our imperfect work to good purposes.

There is great and rich significance for the historian in the experience of the compilers of the historical books of the Bible. Judged by modern standards, they were unlettered men with only a primitive methodology. And yet they laid the foundation for historiography; indeed, in their understanding of history and scrupulous regard for the truth of historical events they set standards to which all historians might well aspire. But we miss the point of their achievement if we regard their work as being some special act of grace, never to be repeated. The point is that God inspires all history that is well and faithfully written. If the writers of the

Biblical record were "inspired," that is, given grace to be true historians, then we, too, can be "inspired" even as we are justified.

Permit me to add one final word about the justification of the historian, or of any scholar or person, for that matter. I said at the very beginning that we too often ask the question about the meaning of faith to our vocations in the wrong way, as if the matter involved our own superior goodness or our skill as scholars. I have tried to show what being justified by faith means to the historian, but I have completely failed if I have imputed any righteousness to the individual whom God has been pleased to justify. I have failed in an even worse way if I have implied that we are competent to say whom the Holy Spirit claims and helps. Thank God, it is no concern of ours whom God loves and helps. We can only be thankful for the gift of the Holy Spirit, who is the author of all good work and who enables us to love all our colleagues and live with ourselves even while we know our own unworthiness.

IV

In the brief space remaining I want to shift my attention from what it means to be a Christian as historian to what it means to understand history as a Christian. I must apologize for the sketchiness of what I am about to say, because this subject deserves a great deal more careful attention than I can give at this point. My only excuse for making the effort at all is that there are several important things that ought to be said to point up the larger meaning of justification.

God does not leave the historian to grope in darkness, not knowing what history is. In justification he gives the historian power to see all things anew through the eyes of faith. I do not mean a private faith, such as might come from the self communing with the self. I mean that faith not built by human minds but what is called Biblical faith, which is to say the record of God speaking by the prophets, the law, Jesus Christ, and the Holy Spirit in the Church. Biblical faith speaks clearly and forcefully to us, if we will but listen.

It tells us, first of all, I suspect, that history is not the product of the human mind. It does not consist of the kind of abstracted reality that theory and philosophy would have it be. These are part of the stream of history, to be sure, but they are not history in the sense that they pretend to be. Biblical faith knows nothing about philosophy of history, except to say that it is the foolishness of the Greeks and another evidence of the corrupted ego's effort to deify itself. Biblical faith tells us that history is the sum total of all actions and events, the record of every movement of mind or matter since creation. This record exists because God has called it into existence in space and time. He who brought matter into existence has given a matter-of-fact reality to matter. He who swung the planets into their courses also created man a part of matter with a consciousness of time.

I think that it is important to add that Biblical faith tells us most emphatically that there is no such thing as a so-called Christian interpretation of history. At least this is the conclusion to which I have come, or to which the Holy Spirit has brought me, after trying for years to work out a Christian interpretation. History is simply history, the same for Christians, Jews, Moslems, people of no faith. We do not shape, change, or control it by trying to force it into a so-called Christian mold according to our understanding. A Christian interpretation would not be much better than another rival to other interpretations.

Biblical faith, I think also, tells us something very special about the historical record. It tells us that it is stored in its incredible totality in the mind and memory of God. He has numbered the hairs of our heads as well as the days of princes and kings. Not a sparrow falls to the ground without his knowing it. He knows our going in and our coming out. It is to him a precious thing because it is his truth. Think what this says to us as historians. It says, does it not, that because history belongs to God we violate the divine sovereignty when we tamper with it. It says that history is a whole, and that no one part is more important than the other. It says, finally, that all history is local, personal history, that the truth of history lies not in sweeping and obscuring generalizations, but in the myriad seemingly small and unimportant details of the vast unknowable record. Is this not something of what we see when we see history through the eyes of faith?

Biblical faith gives additional vital insight to the historian in its view of man. Faith tells me that it is the only true and authentic view of man, and that it is authentic precisely because it is the only view that sees man beyond the limits of human understanding. The historian can, I suggest, derive enormous help in understanding even when he cannot affirm that the Biblical view reflects God's knowledge of man.

This is true because the Biblical view is the only view that takes man seriously in history. It takes him seriously as a part of nature. It does not reduce him to idea by ignoring or relegating to unimportance his material nature. On the other hand, it affirms his personality and possibility for free creative existence beyond the slavery of ego or great forces. It does not reduce him to an economic cipher or a cog in a machine of progress. In other words, the Biblical view accepts man for what he is—a creature, fallen, corrupted, confused, rebellious, yet worthy of respect, love, and honor because he remains God's creature even in his fallen-ness.

Because the Biblical view takes man for what he is, it is an honest view with no purpose to serve other than to reveal man to himself. We have no better proof of the sturdy reliability of its honesty than the Biblical record itself. As Woodrow Wilson once put it, "The Bible has revealed the people to themselves." It strips bare all pretension to human righteousness. Its pages are filled with the record of human sin—of idolatry by people freed from slavery, adultery by kings, betrayal and denial by disciples. It says that the economic interpretation, Freudian psychology, and all other insights of all other views of man are partially right, insofar as they go. But in its honesty, the Biblical record tells us more. It tells us that human kind bear the stamp of divinity on their brow, and that we cannot take an honest view of human history unless we acknowledge God's work through human kind in history.

To the historian, I suspect that Biblical faith would say that he cannot be a true and faithful chronicler of events outside its understanding. For outside the context of faith there are only partial, imperfect, earth-bound understandings of man. Bound to these corrupted understandings, the historian can never escape the bondage of human kind. Only in Biblical understanding can he know the truth that sets him free.

Biblical faith tells us, finally, that the great authenticator of history is also the living Lord of history, the same then, now, and ever more. Faith impels us to acknowledge the sovereignty of the Lord of history. Faith gives us the capacity to know that history, even the record of human affairs, is the record of God's work in time in all the places of the earth. He is the Lord of the Soviet Union and the United States, just as he is the Lord of the pharaohs, of Cyrus, and of Nero and Titus. Nothing has happened or will happen except by his will or permission; he uses men and nations to achieve his inscrutable purpose. History is also the special record of this same God's redeeming activity—what the Germans call *Heilsgeschichte* and we rather imprecisely call "sacred history"—which culminated in God's direct, personal participation in human affairs in the Incarnation and the coming and living of the Holy Spirit in the Church.

For the historian who sees through the eyes of faith, God's lordship is the central, supreme, and essential fact of history. He knows that all of history must be understood in terms of God's eternal, unending work in redemption. He knows, for example, the meaning of God's life on earth and how the Cross and Resurrection condemn all human pretension and pride and vindicate forever God's lordship. Standing under the shadow of the Cross, the historian finally sees the truth, the reality of history. He knows that this is the great watershed, that human affairs can never be the same again because of God's sacrificial act of love.

All this is to say, of course, what God's lordship and activity in history mean to all men who live in faith. But what does God's lordship say to the historian in his daily vocation, in his work as historian? It will mean different things, I am sure, to different men, but to me it says something very specific and practical. It tells me that I can be a true and faithful historian only as I remember that God, the Lord of history, is also the sole judge of history. I serve and glorify him only as I remember that my precious, single task is to preserve the historical record in purity and integrity. I am a chronicler, not a prophet. It is not my task to prove God's existence or even his lordship over history. I am not competent to render judgment on righteousness and evil. I cannot know how and where and when God works, except as he has revealed himself to the Church. It is not given to me to say, "Thus saith the Lord." This is the prophet's word, the word of the Church. It is given to me to preserve the record, even in its fragmentary and imperfect form, without which the prophet cannot know how to speak.

What I am trying to say is that we historians have enough to do without trying to play God. "Do not pronounce judgment before the time, before the Lord comes, who will bring light to the things now hidden in darkness and will disclose the purposes of the heart." We are surely tempted to do this, and we often succumb. We feel, for example, that we must defend the Church by revealing its righteousness in the historical record, or that we must vindicate God's lordship by showing how he has acted at precise moments in human affairs. We are not competent to do this anyway, but when we try, we deny God's lordship by our refusal to believe that the historical record, like the Gospel, which is the vital part of that record, has its own integrity and power, gives its own testimony, and pronounces its own answers. Let us remember that for the historian, as for other men, the fear of the Lord, that is, the knowledge of his lordship, is the beginning of wisdom.

HENRI-IRÉNÉE MARROU

Marrou (b. 1904), a specialist in the era of Augustine, and professor in the University of Paris, agrees with Butterfield and Link about the danger of hubris in historical study. He readily supports Link's point about the objectivity of historical reality. But he is more impressed than either with the decisive role of the historian in gaining access to the truth of that reality even in detail. Marrou is aware of the pitfalls of positivism as well as its antithesis, idealism, and is very conscious of defining his own Christian viewpoint in distinction from both philosophies. His inquiry into a Christian philosophy and theology of history is published in two works, *The Meaning of History* (1966), from which this selection is taken, and *Time and Timeliness* (1969).

He concurs with a statement by V. H. Galbraith: "History, I suppose, is the Past—so far as we know it." Historical study is, in other words, a humble relationship. On the one hand, there is the "baffling reality" of the past which is so complex and so elusive. On the other, there is the searching of the historian who ferrets out knowledge of that past. To understand how this relationship functions one must start not with the objective past, nor with the documents as intermediaries, but with "the inquiring mind of the historian." Writes Marrou, "Any knowledge the historian may acquire will obviously depend on the question or questions he chooses to investigate. And this choice will in turn be directly attributable to his personality, the orientation of his mind, the level of his learning, and finally the general philosophy which underlies his mental categories and his principles of judgement."

History and the Historian Are Inseparable

When it is stripped of polemical excesses and paradoxical formulations, the critical philosophy of history consists essentially in revealing the decisive role which the active participation of the historian (including both his mind and personality) must necessarily assume in the elaboration of historical knowledge. We shall no longer say, "history, alas, is inseparable from the historian." [1]

Gide's remark comes to mind: "So much the worse!" said Ménalque. "I prefer believing that if something does not exist, it is because it could not exist." However, neither *alas* nor *So much the worse!* can be called philosophical categories.

We can only acknowledge the simple fact—without surprise or feelings of anger—as inscribed in the very structure of reality. We must frankly recognize the actual situation imposed on the historian by the conditions of knowledge, including the structure of the mind and the nature of the object. It is in terms of these necessities that we shall try to show on what conditions, and within what limits, an authentic (that is, *true*) knowledge of the human past is really accessible.

It is at this point that I part company with Raymond Aron whose point of view, in my opinion, still seems to be excessively polemical. The sub-title of his thesis is very revealing: "An essay on the limits of historical objectivity." (Is a universally valid historical science possible at all? To what extent would this be so?) [2] The real problem is the "Kantian" question: On what conditions is historical knowledge possible? In other words, this is the problem of

Reprinted by permission of Helicon Press, Inc., from *The Meaning of History* (1966). The original French edition was published in 1954 with the title *De la Connaissance Historique*.

the truth of history, if objectivity is not to be the supreme criterion.

It has become classic—and may still be pedagogically useful—
to contrast this attitude (which sufficiently defines what is proudly
called the new approach to history and is a fundamental principle)
with the illusions of our positivist predecessors. I do not believe it
would be slanderous to say that they dreamed of bringing history
into alignment with the "exact" sciences—a very revealing expression, incidentally, by which they meant physics, chemistry and biology. But their conception of these sciences was very naïve, and
in fact so elementary as to be utterly false. We shall have occasion
to return to this matter when we explain the distinction—no doubt
essential but requiring careful precision—between the sciences of
nature and sciences of the mind. Dazzled and somewhat intimi-
dated by the undeniable triumphs of the natural sciences, the positivist theorists tried to determine the conditions with which history
would have to comply in order to attain, in its turn, the honorable
status of a positive science offering objective knowledge "valid for
everyone." Their avowed objective was to foster "an exact science
of things of the mind." That was Renan's term for it. We would
have to cite his book, *The Future of Science,* to reveal fully the
degree of tragic assurance with which men of 1848 committed
themselves and all European scholarship generally to a course
which has since proved to be merely a dead-end. If there still
remains a little bitterness in our voices when we mention these
men who were our teachers, I would ask my younger readers to
consider the great amount of rectification which we were obliged
to undertake.

If we now attempt to set forth their position in terms of a
formula, using the same symbols as before we would say:

$$h = P + p$$

In their opinion, history is the Past, objectively recorded,
plus, *alas!* an inevitable intervention of the present of the historian. It is something like the personal equation of the observer in
astronomy or the astigmatism of the ophthalmologist: a symbiotic
datum or quantity which must be rendered as small as possible—
or even made quite negligible, tending toward zero.

In this conception there seems to be a belief that both the historian and the witness before him whose report is utilized could

only damage or diminish the objective integrity of truth by their personal contribution. But whether positive or negative—omissions, misunderstandings or errors in the second case; trivial considerations, and literary embroidery in the first—this contribution is always regrettable and ought to be eliminated. They would have liked to make the historian and his informers of the past purely passive instruments: a kind of recording apparatus which would simply reproduce the object, the past, with mechanical fidelity—or would photograph it precisely, as they probably said in the year 1900.

But the image would have been quite deceptive. We have since learned to recognize all that is personal and everything that is constructed and profoundly informed by the active intervention of the operator in all those images which are obtained with such objective means as a camera lens or an emulsion of silver bromide, from Nadar's *Baudelaire* to the *Images à la sauvette* of Cartier-Bresson.

Let us glance through an exemplary manual of the positivist scholar, our old companion, the work of Langlois and Seignebos. In their opinion, history is the sum total of "facts" derived from documents. History exists in the documents in a latent but real manner prior to the intervention of the historian's research. But let us follow the latter's technical procedures attentively. The historian finds the documents and then proceeds to sift and cull them. This is the task of external criticism, a "technique of purging and piecing," which separates the good grain from the straw. The critique of interpretation concentrates on the testimony of the witnesses, whose value is determined by a severe "internal, negative criticism of sincereity and exactness." (Could the witness have been mistaken? Did he perhaps want to deceive us?) Little by little, the pure wheat of the "facts" accumulates in our notebooks and memos. The historian need only report them with precision and fidelity, wholly concealing himself behind the testimony and evidence regarded as valid. In short, he does not construct history but simply discovers it. Collingwood, who does not hide his contempt for such a conception of "pre-fabricated historical knowledge, needing only to be gulped down and then disgorged," calls it "history compiled with scissors and paste." [3] The irony of his remark is fully deserved, for nothing could be less accurate than an analysis or enquiry that completely overlooks the actual proceedings of the historian's mind.

Such a methodology simply resulted in debasing history to mere erudition, and in fact it had exactly that consequence in the case of one of its theorists who took it all seriously in practice: Charles V. Langlois no longer dared to write history toward the end of his career, but was content to offer his readers merely a selection of texts. But what ingenuousness! As if the choice of selected evidence was not already a very considerable intervention of the author's personality, with his particular orientations, prejudices and limitations! (See for instance, *La connaissance de la nature et du monde d'après les écrits français à l'usage des laïcs*, 1911, and republished in 1927 as volume 3 of *La vie en France au moyen âge du XIIe au milieu du XIVe siècle*.)

In any case, "there is no *historical reality*, ready-made prior to knowledge, which need only be reproduced with fidelity." [4] History is the result of the creative effort by which the historian, as the conscious subject, establishes a relationship between the past which he evokes and the present which is his own. It is tempting at this point to make another comparison with idealism because of its insistence that knowledge receives its form, if not its entire reality, from the activity of the mind. But this time I hesitate to do it, for I am fully aware of the dangers which the misuse of such references may entail. Excessive emphasis upon the creative contribution of the historian would lead to the description of the elaboration of history as a kind of gratuitous game. In this view it is the free exercise of a story-weaving imagination lightly dallying with an anomalous collection of texts, dates, deeds and sayings, with all the freedom of a poet juggling verses to write a sonnet. [5] This kind of conception simply destroys the serious import of our discipline and the validity of its truth. It could hardly serve as an adequate description of the real activity of the historian, according to our own experience of such activity in the course of our daily task. Consequently, it is better to avoid making any comparison that is excessively far-fetched. We should try instead to express ourselves without metaphorical subterfuges. In my own opinion, and without pretense or paradox, I would not hesitate to accept the formula proposed by one of our British colleagues, Professor V. H. Galbraith of Cambridge, who said, *"History, I suppose, is the Past–so far as we know it."* [6]

Indeed, this is far better than the pride of the idealist philosopher who is convinced that he can construct reality (as he says) with the resources of his mind alone, and certainly much better than the conscientious short-sightedness of the positivist scholar, satisfied with the accumulation of "facts" in his little notebooks. It seems to me that the moderation and logical preciseness of Professor Galbraith's formula more truly sums up the essential aspect of our real experience as historians. It cannot be described in terms of the quiet labor of the one or the triumphant expansion of the other. It is something much more hazardous, in the tragic sense. We emerge from it gasping and humbled, always more than half-defeated, rather like the struggle of Jacob with the Angel of Yahweh at the Jabbok ford.

We are not really alone in our work, for in the shadows we meet with a mysterious *other* (which I mentioned before as the noumenal reality of the past). It is a reality that is felt to be both dreadfully present and yet apparently resistant to our efforts. We try to lay hold of it and compel its submission, but invariably it ultimately eludes us at least in part. History is a struggle of the mind, an adventure. Like all human quests it knows only partial successes, wholly relative and never proportionate with the original ambition. As in any encounter with the baffling depths of reality, man ends up with an acute awareness of his limitations, his weakness and his humble status.

We are quite aware of the task we must be able to undertake. By dint of grappling with this baffling reality, we finally fix its position well enough to know what we would need and what we are lacking in order to know the historic past in an authentic and total way. We realize at last what kind of mind the historian must possess to become capable of such knowledge (in the sense in which an arc in geometry is capable of a given angle). He would, in fact, have to know everything—including all that was ever felt, thought and accomplished by men of the past. He would have to perceive the complexity clearly without overlooking, shattering or changing the internal relations—so delicate, multiple and interwoven—which bind together all the manifestations of human activity in the real world. It is the knowledge of these relations that makes everything understandable. However limited our experience may be, it is sufficient to reveal to us the existence of this close network of relations. It is a web in which the causes prolong the effects and the consequences cross-check each other, becoming entwined or opposed; and the most trivial "fact" (on which the whole course of a man's lifetime may hinge) is the culminating result of a complete, convergent series of reactions. Every problem in history, no matter how small, gradually and eventually demands a knowledge of universal history in its entirety.

I could cite the example, already quite classic, which was proposed by C. Morazé: the general situation when Jules Ferry became head of the French government.[7] A historian would doubtless have to know the exact conditions of his rise to power, the circumstances that brought it about, and consequently the French parliamentary situation in 1880. But instead of this let us refer more generally and more fundamentally to the political, and therefore the social and economic situation of France. The international ramifications cannot be neglected either. The whole enquiry must be carried out at new levels. But with regard to Jules Ferry, who was this man? We may describe him in terms of a particular character and personality, as the culmination in 1880 of a personal history that was already a long one. Our colleague, the psychoanalyst, might even insist on extending it back to the pre-natal stage! But was Ferry, the man, merely the product of a process of development that began at the moment of his conception? Jules Ferry was also Saint-Dié, where he was born; and he was the Alsatian emigration, the cotton-mill workers of Mulhouse, French Protestantism, etc. We could go back to the very beginnings of Christianity. But there is still another trail to explore: the industrial middle class, the collapse of agricultural prices, and a whole new chain of events and circumstances that will lead us as far back as the prehistoric clearing of the land as we study the arrangement and allocation of the French countryside. In all of this we are mentioning only the enquiries that our mind conceives as possible. But we certainly know what mere chance or accident may underlie the fact that we are aware of the possibility of each of them. It is clearly quite legitimate to postulate the existence of other causal series than those we have just suggested.

Accordingly, in extension as in comprehensiveness, the problem posed by the human past reveals a structure that is doubly and infinitely complex. Pascal's idea of the double infinite could be transposed to the object of history, but I shall not pursue the matter any further. We have already felt a sudden spell of dizziness!

If our conception of history raises a problem of such magnitude, what mind would ever be able to encompass it? We can reply immediately that such a mind exists. It is the mind of the Lord our God, יהוה, whose uncreated Wisdom "is really in itself a discerning, intelligent mind, subtle, perceptive, clear, trenchant, incoercible, firm and unerring, wholly adequate for everything, governing all things and penetrating all things. . . ." [8]

It is surely right and fitting that the philosopher pause to pronounce the ineffable Name with adoration, for such a moment of meditation will help to deliver him from the most dangerous temptation, always a threat to every philosophy of history, a really fatal error, the sin of immoderation: ὕβρις. The historian must always remember that he is merely a man and that it is best for mortals to think as mortal men should: θνητὰ φρονεῖν.

I have been speaking as a Christian, but the formula of Euripides shows that this *truth* possesses an absolute value. Reference to Christian thought is imperative for everyone in our Western civilization. We see this, for instance, in Raymond Aron who felt constrained to say, "Only God could weigh the value of every deed, put in their place the contradictory episodes, and unify character and behavior. The whole idea of this absolute truth will disappear with theology." [9] As a matter of fact, however, it is not disappearing, for it is still conceivable as a possibility. But the theologian, whether Christian or pagan—or rather the philosopher—insists that it is not within man's reach.

With our young students in mind, the first principle of practical conduct which we must formulate will be an admonition: *You are not God. Never forget that you are only a man.* This reminder should not be considered as an admission of powerlessness or a call to renunciation and despair. St. Thomas, who extolled the virtue of *magnanimitas*, puts us on guard against this sinful deceit: it is merely a form of pride. The philosopher should rejoice to have given clear expression to the truth regarding our being and nature, no matter what it implies—in this instance it is the truth about the

nature and capacity of the historian. Indeed, young man, you are
only human. But that is no reason to give up your life-work, your
own calling as a man and a historian. It may be humble and difficult, but within its limits it is most certainly fruitful and worthwhile.

Our philosophy also is only human, and can go forward only
one step at a time. This fruitfulness—genuine but limited—will be
demonstrated at the proper time. For the present, however, the
first point had to be clearly established: the fundamental dispro-
portion between the object with which history is concerned (the
noumenal, historic reality which only God can encompass and perceive) and the limited means available to historical research (the
pathetic little efforts of the human mind with its methods and instruments). I remember standing on a high crag overlooking a
mountain lake, watching the exertions of a fisherman. I could see
the beautiful trout that he was excitedly sighting from the shore as
they playfully sported and frolicked far from his much too short
line. The historian often faces the same situation. His limited
means do not allow him to sweep the whole extent of the lake of
the past into his nets. History can only be *the Past so far as . . .* it
can be encompassed by his nets. Even this is something, of
course, but it is not everything. And what is still more important, it
is not the same thing. History is whatever the historian succeeds
in reaching in the past. But while passing through his instruments
of knowledge this very past has been so re-elaborated and so
worked-over that it has been made into something quite new and
has become ontologically quite different. But we must now devote
our serious attention to this process of transmutation.

In order to discover what history will become, we shall have to
stop concentrating on its object—that indeterminate something,
ἄπειρον, transcending experience—and begin instead with the
historian himself, following his endeavors in the procedure that
will lead him to knowledge. History will be whatever he finally
succeeds in elaborating.

Let us now consult our Langlois-Seignobos manual: Book I,
Chapter 1, first line. We learn that "history is constructed with
documents." This is a formula we find again in the conclusion,
which assures us that "history is merely the applied utilization of
documents." [10] This is quite understandable, but logically it is not

the document that is the point of departure. After all, the historian is not a factory-worker intent upon the transformation of raw material; nor is the historical method a funnel-shaped piece of machinery into which documents in the rough state can simply be poured, with a fine and continuous fabric of knowledge emerging from the other end. Our work presupposes original activity resulting from personal initiative. History is the response (obviously elaborated by means of documents, as we shall see later) to a question which the curiosity, concern, and existential anxiety—as some would say—but in any case the inquiring mind of the historian asks of the mysterious Past. At first the past appears to him rather indistinctly, like a phantom, without shape or solidity. To lay hold of it the historian must encompass it tightly within a network of questions that leave no room for evasion, compelling it to reveal itself frankly. As long as we fail to set upon it in this way, it remains veiled and silent. Logically, the process of the elaboration of history is set in motion not by the existence of documents but by an initial step, the "posed question" inscribed in the choice, delimitation and conception of the subject.

In practice, of course, it sometimes happens that a historical study is undertaken as the result of the casual reading of some document. The goat grazes wherever it happens to be tied. How often I have heard this reason given by my colleagues when asked about their work! The proximity of some collection of records and documents, the resources of a particular library, the accidental discovery of some new monument by archeologists (a frequent occurrence in the study of Ancient History, in which documents are rare and any new material is given a welcome)—any of these may appear to be the starting-point of historical studies. But this changes nothing with regard to the logical priority of the "question" which the historian poses in the presence of the documents.

The apparently superficial analysis of Langlois and Seignobos can be explained (let us be fair!) in terms of the rather limited conception of history that was prevalent for such a long while. Whatever its value may have been, it held them captive. It was limited in practice to what was called general history. This is the study of the "great" historic events: primarily the wars and the diplomatic negotiations that prepared the way for them or somehow ended them. It also included the vicissitudes of internal politics, studied with reference to men at the top: the king, his ministers, the royal court; or else the leaders of political movements, the assemblies and their parliamentary life. If a few natural calamities were added to all this, such an epidemic of the plague, we would possess practically all that Thucydides considered useful to report about Greece in his day; and for centuries historians were content with that kind of outline. At the very most, since Voltaire they have added to their account a portrayal of the state of the sciences, letters and arts as an appendix or a kind of digression. In these circumstances the outline was completely delineated, the questions were all posed in advance, and the subject's conception simply amounted to the choice of some particular period.

But in our day a wholly different conception of history has triumphed which is both "greater in scope and more extended in depth." This was Marc Bloch's comment.[11] It is only fair to emphasize the part taken in France by the team of Lucien Febvre and Marc Bloch in the victorious struggle against the old idol of political, episodal history, which was a kind of "historicizing history."

In any case, the reaction was very widespread and was never restricted to any particular school of thought. Lord Acton had already given his students the following suggestion: "Study problems rather than periods." All during the nineteenth century we can see the progress of the history of civilization, *Kulturgeschichte,* in opposition to its old rival, the "history of battles."

Political history is nearly stifled by the proliferation of studies concerning "special" history. This would include for instance economic and social history, the history of ideas, points of view, *Weltanschauungen,* the history of the sciences, philosophy, religion and art. This specialization has been carried so far that perhaps it is now necessary to react against it, at least at the pedagogical level. In its excessive quest for comprehensiveness and depth, the study of history runs the risk of forsaking concrete reality and simply dissolving in abstract pipe-dreams. We must constantly remind younger historians that the history of civilization (and each special history) must be based upon a close web of names, dates and actual happenings; and that political facts—ordinarily the best documented—provide the solid background for such a sketch.

Accordingly, whenever the historian undertakes the study of a certain time or place there is no method of inquiry established *a priori* and serving somehow as a master-key, which is either obligatory for him or even available. The method or outline is something which the historian must personally decide upon. Consequently the entire later development of the study—and the knowledge itself in its final culmination—will be oriented and predetermined by the questions that were posed. I say "questions" for the sake of brevity. But when the mind elaborates a question it immediately formulates one or several possible answers. A precise question (and only a question that is precisely formulated can serve any purpose in history) presents itself in the form of a hypothesis to be verified. "Could it be true that . . . ?" No doubt in the process of verification the hypothesis will often be restated, corrected and changed until it becomes unrecognizable. But the fact remains that there was a creative effort by the historian at the start, beginning with the elaboration of a provisional description of the past.

Once again, we must be careful to rid ourselves of the dangerous phantom of idealism. Let us limit the part of autonomous "construction" which such an elaboration of the questions and their related hypotheses may entail. Apart from the fact that the validity of the hypothesis is dependent on the process of verifying its suitability in relation to the documentary data, it must certainly be obvious that historical knowledge does not begin with an absolute zero. It is by analogy with a human situation already known that we formulate a hypothetical description of the past to become known. The part or role of transposition is of little importance in this. Except in the case of a newly discovered civilization that is wholly exceptional (and what could ever be really known about it?), the historian ordinarily knows in general which questions can possibly be asked. He knows what are the sentiments, ideas, reactions and technical achievements that can be attributed to the men of a particular time and place. His initial hypotheses will be all the more fruitful if they contain the least possible extrapolation.

We must now consider the idea of progress within the homogeneous development of the study. Whenever historians approach some new field of study, it is almost impossible for them to avoid committing the frightful sin of anachronism. They do not yet know what questions to pose and the mind does not have access to analytical instruments of sufficient precision to construct a satisfactory set of questions.

That is why I would not, for instance, throw stones at Michelet for having made of Abelard a free-thinker, an apostle of rationalism challenging the "Scholastic obscurantists." The categories inherited from the *Aufklärung* did not provide this romantic liberal with the mental equipment necessary for an understanding of Christian thought of the twelfth century. If we are more successful in this respect today it is because of the progress achieved and the efforts continuously put forth from Michelet himself to Etienne Gilson.

It must be kept in mind that knowledge of an historical object may be dangerously distorted or diminished by the crude or narrow point of view by which it was approached at the start. An example of a badly formulated question is evident in the controversy that lasted for a whole generation concerning St. Augustine. It was asked whether he was converted to Neoplatonism or Christianity in the year 386 at Milan. But P. Courcelle has since proved that Neoplatonism was the official philosophy of the Christian intellectual milieu of Milan in that era, beginning with its bishop, St. Ambrose himself.[12]

Insufficient, diminished knowledge is especially exemplified in two historical works on the little town of Gap.[13] They cover hardly more than the medieval era. Even this period is reduced to a series of monographs on the successive bishops, pertaining almost exclusively to their political quarrels with the municipality, the lord paramount, Count de Forcalquier, or with the Dauphin. We are told nothing about the history of the people of this little human cell; nothing of their economic activity, their social structure, or the development of either. Nevertheless, I did seem to catch a glimpse of a prosperous middle class transforming itself into a landed gentry, such as J. Schneider investigated so thoroughly in his book on the city of Metz.[14] Nor is there anything concerning their spiritual life, although the crisis of the Reformation was extremely serious in the region of Gap—as indeed everywhere in Dauphiné. Farel, one of the leading French Reformers, came from Gap. But we learn nothing about the place except the political events and religious wars. There are only banal comments concerning the origins of the town, although like A. Déléage's book on Burgundy [15] there could have been a systematic utilization of the toponymy represented by particular "place-names." These are attested as fully in our own day as in the medieval records. They would enable a historian, by etymological analysis, to reconstitute the successive stages of settlement of the area (and consequently of the population itself) going all the way back to the pre-Celtic clearing of the land. Moreover, by studying the hagiographic legends and investigating the distribution of titular saints of the various churches of the region, it would have been possible to reconstitute the stages of the implanting of Christianity in that part of France at the end of the era of Antiquity and the beginning of the Middle Ages. [16]

I must, however, interrupt this analysis of possibilities, which are unlimited. It must be emphasized that every period, every human environment, every historical object always presents a great number of problems and, logically speaking, is likely to raise innumerable questions. Any knowledge the historian may acquire will obviously depend on the question or questions which he chooses to investigate. And this choice will in turn be directly attributable to his personality, the orientation of his mind, the level of his learning, and finally the general philosophy which underlies his mental categories and his principles of judgment.

Let us consider a specific historical phenomenon: Christian monasticism, for example, in its beginnings in fourth century Egypt. This can be studied from the perspective of the history of Christianity, in so far as it represents a particular episode of that time and place. Or it can be considered as an aspect of the development of the Christian religion. We can study it from the comparative point of view of the history of religions, as one of the manifestations of the ideal of solitude, asceticism and contemplation which has found expression in so many other ways among men (Brahmanism, Jainism, Buddhism, Taoism, and perhaps even in the pre-Columbian civilizations). There is a social aspect in this phenomenon which could be stressed: the flight to the desert. Devotion to an "anchoretic" life (which means literally to "take refuge in the wilderness"), was a very common phenomenon in Greco-Roman

Egypt. The desert was a favorite haunt of criminals, debtors, and especially insolvent tax-payers, together with non-social individuals of every kind who were not exclusively religious men. There could also be a study of their economic function. The cenobites of St. Pachomius left their monasteries by the thousands to harvest the crops in the Nile Valley and thus earn their meager subsistence for the whole year in a few days' time. They were a kind of reserve labor force resembling the migratory farm workers of California who were described in Steinbeck's *Grapes of Wrath*.

Each of these perspectives is intrinsically legitimate, and perhaps fruitful also. Each apprehends the reality of the past in part, or under some particular aspect. But we shall delay our examination of the umbilical cord that binds each of them to the historian's individuality, and the resulting consequences for the validity of the knowledge obtained. In our attempt to outline the virtues of the historian gradually, we shall for the moment simply lay stress on the fact that the copiousness of historical knowledge will depend directly on the skilfulness and ingenuity with which the initial questions are posed. It is this which conditions the general orientation of all subsequent research. The great historian will be one who, within his own system of thought, is able to pose the historical problem or question in the richest and most fruitful manner. No matter how extensive his learning may be, or his broadmindedness either, he will recognize the limitations that form necessarily imposes, and will readily see what question would be worth asking of the past. The value of history (and by this I mean its human interest as well as its validity) is therefore strictly dependent on the ability of the historian. As Pascal said, "In proportion as we possess greater ingenuity, we find that there are more original men," or in other words, greater treasures to be retrived in man's past.

Consider, for example, the singularly enriched vision of Hellenic civilization which the genius (as well as the vast erudition) of the great Rostovtseff opened up to us.[17] We now see it as the admirable maturity of ancient civilization—"that long summer under the perpetual sunlight of the south." No longer is it depicted as decadent. This was the evaluation of a certain narrow kind of humanism utterly obsessed with the idea of a Golden Age, and the desire of romatic history, which was almost uniquely concerned about evidences of originality, creativity and initial spontaneity. All this led the romantic historians to become primarily interested in the "archaic" aspects of "youth" of an art, an idea or a whole civilization.

NOTES

1. L. I. Halkin, *Initiation à la critique historique* [2] (1953), p. 86, quoting P. Valéry.

2. R. Aron [*Introduction to the philosophy of history: an essay on the limits of historical objectivity* (Boston, 1961)], p. 10.

3. [R. G. Collingwood], *The Idea of History* [Oxford, 1946], p. 257; cf. p. 246.

4. R. Aron, p. 120.

5. Cf. my discussion with Denis de Rougemont concerning his book, *L'amour et l'Occident*, in *Esprit*, September, 1939, pp. 760–768.

6. *Why We Study History* (Historical Association Publications, no. 131, 1944). I have separated the formula from the context, which is sometimes rather sceptical.

7. *Trois essais sur Histoire et Culture* ([Paris], 1948), pp. 1–10.

8. [*Book of Wisdom* 7:22–23.]

9. R. Aron, p. 71.

10. [Ch. V. Langlois and Ch. Seignobos], *Introduction aux études historiques* [Paris, 1898], pp. 1, 275.

11. *Apologie pour l'histoire, ou Métier d'historien* [Paris, 1949], p. 17.

12. See especially his *Recherches sur les Confessions de saint Augustin* ([Paris], 1950).

13. Th. Gautier, *Histoire de la ville de Gap et du Gapençais* (1842, published by P. P. Guillaume, Gap, 1909); J. Roman, *Histoire de la ville de Gap* (1892).

14. *La ville de Metz aux XIIIe et XIVe siècles* (Nancy, 1950).

15. *La vie rurale en Bourgogne jusqu'au début du XIe siècle* (Mâcon, 1941).

16. G. de Manteyer tried to do this, but his method was not rigorous enough. Cf. *Les origines chrétiennes de la IIe Narbonnaise* (Gap, 1924).

17. *The Social and Economic History of the Hellenistic World* (3 vol., Oxford, 1942).

GEORGES FLOROVSKY

Georges Florovsky (b. 1893) is also interested in the relationship between the objective givens of historical reality, the documents, and the historian. Like Marrou, he emphasizes the role of the historian, and in contrast with Butterfield, he gives priority, not to technical history, but to the larger problems of achieving historical understanding. His Christianity leads him to stress that history is a study of other *people*. He writes, "The ultimate purpose of a historical inquiry is not in the establishment of certain objective facts, such as dates, places, numbers, names, and the like, as much as all this is an indispensable preliminary, but in *the encounter with living beings*." Historical study is a committed engagement by the historian whose own concerns enable him to understand the lives and concerns of others. Because the Christian historian has made the ultimate commitment to Christ, he is prepared to appreciate the most profound and most urgent questions faced by the people he studies.

The end of Florovsky's essay takes us back to the questions of the meaning and nature of history. In contrast with Butterfield, he believes that this is the major predicament of the historian: "No historian can, even in his limited and particular field, within his own competence, avoid raising ultimate problems of human nature and destiny, unless he reduces himself to the role of a registrar of empirical happenings and forfeits his proper task of 'understanding'."

Florovsky's career began in Russia, moved to Prague, then Paris, and finally the United States, where he was professor at Harvard and Princeton. His special fields are Russian history and Eastern Orthodoxy.

The Predicament of the Christian Historian

Veritas non erubescit nisi abscondi.—Leo XIII

I

"Christianity is a religion of historians." [1] It is a strong phrase, but the statement is correct. Christianity is basically a vigorous appeal to history, a witness of faith to certain particular events in the past, to certain particular data of history. These events are acknowledged by faith as truly eventful. These historic moments, or instants, are recognized as utterly momentous. In brief, they are identified by faith as "mighty deeds" of God, *Magnalia Dei*. The "scandal of particularity," to use the phrase of Gerhard Kittel,[2] belongs to the very essence of the Christian message. The Christian Creed itself is intrinsically historic. It comprises the whole of existence in a single historical scheme as one "History of Salvation," from Creation to Consummation, to the Last Judgment and the End of history. Emphasis is put on the ultimate cruciality of certain historic events, namely, of the Incarnation, of the Coming of the Messiah, and of his Cross and Resurrection. Accordingly, it may be justly contended that "the Christian religion is a daily invitation to the study of history." [3]

Now, it is at this point that the major difficulties arise. An average believer, of any denomination or tradition, is scarcely aware of his intrinsic duty to study history. The historical pattern

"The Predicament of the Christian Historian" by Georges Florovsky from *Religion and Culture: Essays in Honor of Paul Tillich,* edited by Walter Leibrecht. Copyright © 1959 by Walter Leibrecht. Reprinted by permission of Harper & Row, Publishers, Inc.

of the Christian message is obvious. But people are interested rather in the "eternal truth" of this message, than in what they are inclined to regard as "accidents" of history, even when they are discussing the facts of the Biblical history or of the history of the Church. Does not the message itself point out beyond history, to the "life of the Age to come"? There is a persistent tendency to interpret the *facts* of history as images or *symbols*, as typical cases or examples, and to transform the "*history* of salvation" into a kind of edifying *parable*. We can trace this tendency back to the early centuries of Christian history. In our own days we find outselves in the midst of an intense controversy precisely about this very matter.

On the one hand, the essential *historicity of Christian religion* has been rediscovered and re-emphasized, precisely during the past few decades, and a fresh impact of this reawakened historical insight is strongly felt now in all fields of contemporary theological research—in Biblical exegesis, in the study of Church history and liturgics, in certain modern attempts at the "reconstruction of belief," and even in the modern ecumenical dialogue. On the other hand, the recent plea for a radical *demythologizing* of the Christian message is an ominous sign of a continuing antihistorical attitude in certain quarters. For to demythologize Christianity means in practice precisely to de-historicize it, despite the real difference between myth and history. In fact, the modern plea is but a new form of that theological liberalism, which, at least from the Age of the Enlightenment, persistently attempted to disentangle Christianity from its historical context and involvement, to detect its perennial "essence" ("*das Wesen des Christentums*"), and to discard the historical shells. Paradoxically, the Rationalist of the Enlightenment and the devout Pietists of various description, and also the dreamy mystics, were actually working toward the same purpose. The impact of German Idealism, in spite of its historical appearance, was ultimately to the same effect. The emphasis was shifted from the "outward" facts of history to the "inward" experience of the believers. Christianity, in this interpretation, became a "religion of experience," mystical, ethical, or even intellectual. History was felt to be simply irrelevant. The historicity of Christianity was reduced to the acknowledgment of a permanent "historical significance" of certain ideas and principles, which originated under particular conditions of time and space, but were in no sense intrinsically linked with them. The person of Christ Jesus lost its cruciality in this interpretation, even if his message has been, to a certain extent, kept and maintained.

Now, it is obvious that this anti-historical attitude was itself but a particular form of an acute historicism, that is, of a particular interpretation of history, in which the historical has been ruled out as something accidental and indifferent. Most of the liberal arguments were, as they still are, historical and critical, although behind them one could easily detect definite ideological prejudices, or preconceptions. The study of history was vigorously cultivated by the Liberal school, if only in order to discredit history, as a realm of relativity, or as a story of sin and failure, and, finally, to ban history from the theological field. This "abuse of history" by the liberals made even the "lawful" use of history in theology suspect in the conservative circles. Was it safe to make the eternal truth of Christianity dependent in any way upon the data of history, which is, by its very nature, inextricably contingent and human? For that reason Cardinal Manning denounced every appeal to history, or to "antiquity," as both "a treason and a heresy." He was quite formal at this point: for him the Church had no history. She was ever abiding in a continuous present.[4]

After all—it has been persistently asked—can one really "know" history, that is, the past? How can one discern, with any decent measure of security, what actually did happen in the past? Our pictures of the past are so varied, and change from one generation to another, and even differ from one historian to the next. Are they anything but subjective opinions, impressions, or interpretations? The very possibility of any historical knowledge seemed to be compromised by the skeptical exploits of the learned. It seemed that even the Bible could no longer be retained as a book of history, although it could be kept as a glorious *paradeigma* of the eternal Glory and Mercy of God. Moreover, even if one admits that Christians are, by vocation, historians, it can be contended that they are bound to be bad historians, or unreliable historians, since they are intrinsically "committed" in advance. It is commonly agreed that the main virtue of a historian is his impartiality, his freedom from all preconceptions, his radical *Voraussetzungslosigkeit*. Now, obviously, Christians, if they be believing and practicing Christians, cannot conscientiously dispense with their formidable "bias," even if they succeed in preserving their intellectual honesty and integrity. Christians, by the very fact of their faith and allegiance, are committed to a very particular interpretation of certain events of history, and also to a definite interpretation of the historic process itself, taken as a whole. In this sense, they are inevitably prejudiced. They cannot be radically critical. They would not agree, for instance, to handle their sacred books as "pure literature," and would not read the Bible simply as the "epic" of the Jews. They would not surrender their belief in the crucial uniqueness of Christ. They would not consent to rule out the "supernatural" element from history. Under these conditons, is any impartial and critical study of history possible at all? Can Christians continue as Christians in the exercise of their profession? How can they vindicate their endeavor? Can they simply divorce their professional work, as historians, from their religious convictions, and write history as anyone else may do it, as if they were in no way informed by the faith?

The easiest answer to this charge is to declare that all historians have a bias. An unbiased history is simply impossible, and actually does not exist.[5] In fact, "evolutionary" historians are obviously no less committed than those who believe in the Biblical revelation, only they are committed to another bias. Ernest Renan and Julius Wellhausen were no less committed than Ricciotti or Père Lagrange, and Harnack and Bauer no less than Bardy or Lebreton, and Reitzenstein and Frazer much more than Dom Odo Casel and Dom Gregory Dix. They were only committed to different things. One knows only too well that historical evidence can be twisted and distorted in compliance with all sorts of "critical" preconceptions, even more than it has been done sometimes in obedience to "tradition."

This kind of argument, however, is very ambiguous and inconclusive. It would lead, ultimately, to a radical skepticism and would discredit the study of history of any kind. It actually amounts to a total surrender of all claims and hopes for any reliable historical knowledge. It seems, however, that, in the whole discussion, one operates usually with a very questionable conception of the historical study, with a conception derived from another area of inquiry, namely, from the natural sciences. It is assumed in advance that there is a universal "scientific method" which can be applied in any field of inquiry, regardless of the specific character of the subject of study. But this is a gratuitous assumption, a bias, which does not stand critical test and which, in fact, has been vigorously contested, in recent decades, both by historians and by philosophers. In any case, one has, first of all, to define what is the nature and specific character of "the historical" and in what way and manner this specific subject can be reached and apprehended. One has to define the aim and purpose of historical study and then to design methods by which this aim, or these aims, can be properly achieved. Only in this perspective can the very question of "impartiality" and "bias" be intelligently asked and answered.

II

The study of history is an ambiguous endeavor. Its very objective is ambiguous. History is the study of the past. Strictly speaking, we have at once to narrow the scope of the inquiry. History is indeed the study of the *human* past. An equation of human history and natural history would be an unwarranted presupposition or option. Much harm has been done to the study of history by such naturalistic presuppositions, which amount, in the last resort, to the denial of any specific character of human existence. Anyhow, "the past" as such cannot be "observed" directly. It has actually passed away and therefore is never given directly in any "possible experience" (to use the phrase of John Stuart Mill). The knowledge of the past is necessarily indirect and inferential. It is always *an interpretation.* The past can only be "reconstructed." Is it a possible task? And how is it possible? Actually, no historian begins with the past. His starting point is always in the present, to which he belongs himself. He looks back. His starting point is his "sources," the primary sources. Out of them, and on their authority, he proceeds to the "recovery" of the past. His procedure depends upon the nature and character of his information, of his sources.

What are these sources? What makes a certain thing a source for the historian? In a certain sense, almost everything, *omnis res scibilis,* can serve as a historical source, provided the historian knows how to use it, how *to read the evidence.* But, on the other hand, no thing at all is a historical source by itself, even a chronicle, or a narrative, or even an autobiography. Historical sources exist, in their capacity as sources, only in the context of a historical inquiry. Things are mute by themselves, even the texts and speeches: they speak only when they are understood; they render answers only when they are examined, as witnesses are examined, when proper questions are asked. And the first rule of the historical craft is precisely to cross-examine the witnesses, to ask proper questions, and to force the relics and the documents to answer them. In his admirable little book, *Apologie pour l'Histoire, ou Metier d'Historien,* Marc Bloch illustrates this rule with convincing examples.

> Before Boucher de Perthes, as in our own days, there were plenty of flint artifacts in the alluvium of Somme. However, there was no one to ask questions, and there was therefore no prehistory. As an old medievalist, I know nothing which is better reading than a cartulary. That is because I know just about what to ask it. A collection of Roman inscriptions, on the other hand, would tell me little. I know more or less how to read them, but not how to cross-examine them. In other words, every historic research presupposes that the inquiry has a direction at the very first step. In the beginning there must be the guiding spirit. Mere passive observation, even supposing such a thing were possible, has never contributed anything productive to any science.[6]

This remark of a conscientious and critical scholar is revealing. What he actually suggests is that all historical inquiry is, by definition, as a true inquiry, "prejudiced" from the very start—prejudiced because directed. Otherwise there would have been no inquiry, and the things would have remained silent. Only in the context of a guided inquiry do the sources speak, or rather only in this context do "things" become "sources," only when they are, as it were, exorcised by the inquisitive mind of the historian. Even in the experimental sciences, facts never speak by themselves, but only in the process, and in the context, of a directed research, and no scientific experiment can ever be staged, unless an "experiment in mind" has been previously performed by the explorer.[7]

Observation itself is impossible without some interpretation, that is, understanding.

The study of history has been sorely handicapped by an uncritical and "naturalistic" conception of historical sources. They have been often mistaken for independent entities, existing before and outside of the process of the historical study. A false task was consequently imposed on the historian: he was supposed to find history *in* the sources, while handling them precisely as "things." Nothing could come out of any such endeavor but a pseudo history, a history made "with scissors and paste," [8] a "history without the historical problem," as Benedetto Croce aptly has styled it. [9] Certain historians have deliberately sought to reduce themselves to the role of reporters, but even reporters must be interpretative and selective, if they want to be intelligible. In fact, historical sources cannot be handled simply as "relics," "traces," or "imprints" of the past. Their function in the historical research is quite different. They are *testimonies* rather than traces. And no testimony can be assessed except in the process of interpretation. No collection of factual statements, no compilation of news and dates, is history, even if all facts have been critically established and all dates verified. The best catalogue of an art museum is not a history of art. A catalogue of manuscripts is not a history of literature, not even a history of handwriting. No chronicle is history. In the sharp phrase of Benedetto Croce, a chronicle is but a "corpse of history," *il cadavere*. A chronicle is but "a thing" (*una cosa*), a complex of sounds and other signs. But history is "an act of the spirit," *un atto spirituale*. [10] "Things" become "sources" only in the process of cognition, in relation to the inquiring intellect of the student. Outside of this process historical sources simply do not exist.

The question a historian asks is the question about *meaning* and *significance*. And things are then treated as *signs and witnesses* of the past reality, not simply as relics or imprints. Indeed, only signs can be interpreted, and not "pure facts," since the question about meaning points beyond pure giveness. There are things insignificant and meaningless, and they cannot be understood or interpreted at all, precisely because they are meaningless, just as in a conversation we may fail to understand certain casual remarks, which were not intended to convey any message. Indeed, historical cognition is a kind of conversation, a dialogue with those in the past whose life, thoughts, feelings, and decisions the historian endeavors to rediscover, *through the documents* by which they are witnessed to or signified. Accordingly, one can infer from certain facts, words or things, *as from a sign to the meaning,* only if and when these objective things can be lawfully treated as signs, that is, as bearers of meaning, only when and if we can reasonably assume that these things have a dimension of depth, a dimension of meaning. We do not assign meaning to them: we should detect meaning. Now, there is meaning in certain things, in our documents and sources, only in so far as behind them we are entitled to assume the existence of other intelligent beings.

History is accordingly *a study of the human past,* not of any past as such. Only man has history, in the strict sense of this word. R. G. Collingwood elaborates this point with great clarity. Close similarity between the work of an archaeologist and that of a paleontologist is obvious: both are diggers. Yet, their aims are quite different. "The archaeologist's use of his stratified relics depends upon his conceiving them as artifacts serving human purposes and thus expressing a particular way in which men have thought about their own life." In the study of nature, on the other hand, there is no such distinction between the "outside" and the "inside" of the data. "To the scientist, nature is always and merely a 'phenomenon,' not in the sense of being defective in reality, but in the sense of being a spectacle presented to his intellectual observation; whereas the events of history are never mere phenomena, never mere spectacles for contemplation, but things which the historian looks, not at, but through, to discern the thought within them." [11] Historical documents can be interpreted as signs because they are charged with meaning, as expressions or reflections, deliberate or spontaneous, of human life and endeavor.

Now, this meaning is available for others only in so far as a sufficient identification can be achieved between the interpreter and those whose thoughts, actions, or habits he is interpreting. If this contact, for any reason, has not been established, or cannot be established at all, no understanding is possible and no meaning can be elicited, even if the documents or relics are charged with meaning, as it is, for instance, in the case of an undecipherable script. Again, "testimonies" can be misunderstood and misinterpreted, just as we often misunderstand each other in an actual conversation or fail to find a "common language"—then no communication is possible; just as we may misinterpret a foreign text, not only because we simply make mistakes in translation, but also when we fail to enter congenially into the inner world of those persons whose testimonies we are deciphering. An *Einfühlung* into the witnesses is an obvious prerequisite of understanding. We are actually deciphering each other's words even in an ordinary conversation, and sometimes we fail sorely to achieve any satisfactory result. The problem of semantics, that is, of intelligent communication—a communication between intelligent beings—is inherent in the whole process of historical interpretation. In the phrase of Ranke, "history only begins when monuments become intelligible." [12] One should add that only "intelligible documents" are, in a full sense, *historical* documents, historical *sources*—as H. I. Marrou puts it, *"dans la mesure où l'historien peut et sait y comprendre quelque chose."* [13] Consequently, the person of the interpreter belongs to the actual process of interpretation no less than the data to be interpreted, just as both partners in a conversation are essential for a successful dialogue. No understanding is possible without some measure of "congeniality," of intellectual or spiritual sympathy, without a real meeting of minds. Collingwood is right in pointing out that

> historical inquiry reveals to the historian the power of his own mind.
> . . . Whenever he finds certain historical matters unintelligible, he
> has discovered a limitation of his own mind, he has discovered that
> there are certain ways in which he is not, or no longer, or not yet,
> able to think. Certain historians, sometimes whole generations of his-
> torians, find in certain periods of history nothing intelligible, and call
> them dark ages; but such phrases tell us nothing about those ages
> themselves, though they tell us a great deal about the persons who
> use them, namely that they are unable to re-think the thoughts
> which were fundamental to their life.[14]

It is the first rule of the true *exegesis:* we have to grasp *the mind of the writer,* we must discover exactly what he intended to say. The phrase, or the whole narrative, or the whole document, can be misunderstood when we fail to do so, or when we *read* our own thought *into* the text. No sentence, and no text, should be dismissed as "meaningless" simply because we fail to detect meaning. We misread the text when we take literally that which has been said metaphorically, and also when we interpret that which was meant to be an actual story just as a parable.

> You cannot find out what a man means by simply studying his spoken or written statements, even though he has spoken or written with perfect command of language and perfectly truthful intention. In order to find out his meaning you must also know what the question was (a question in his own mind, and presumed by him to be in yours) to which the thing he has said or written was meant as an answer.[15]

It is true of our actual conversations, in the intercourse of the current life. It is true of our study of the historical sources. Historical documents are *documents of life.*

Every historian begins with certain data. Then, by an effort of his searching and inquisitive mind, he apprehends them as "witnesses," or, as it were, "communications" from the past, that is, as meaningful signs. By the power of his intellectual intuition, he grasps the meaning of these signs, and thus recovers, in an act of "inductive imagination," that comprehensive setting in which all his data converge and are integrated into a coherent, that is, intelligible, whole. There is an inevitable element of guess, or rather of "divination," in this process of understanding, as there is, unavoidably, a certain element of guess in every attempt to understand another person. A lack of congenial guess, or imaginative sympathy, may make any conversation impossible, since no real *contact of minds* has been established, as if the participants spoke different languages, so that utterances of one person did not become messages for the other. In a sense, any act of understanding is a "mental experiment," and divination is always an indispensable element therein. Divination is a kind of mental vision, an indivisible act of insight, an act of imagination, inspired and controlled by the whole of one's acquired experience. One may suggest it is an act of "fantasy," but it is fantasy of a very special kind. It is a *cognitive fantasy* and, as Benedetto Croce eloquently explains, without it historical knowledge is simply impossible: *senza questa ricostruzione o integrazione fantastica non e dato ne scrivere storia, ne leggerla e intenderla.* It is, as he says, a "fantasy in the thought" (*la fantasia nel pensiero e per pensiero*), a "concreteness of the thought" which implies judgment and is therefore logically disciplined and controlled, and thereby clearly distinguished from any poetical license.[16] *"Understanding is Interpretation,* whether of a spoken word, or of the meaningful events themselves," as it was stated by F. A. Trendelenburg: *Alles Verständniss ist Interpretation, sei es des gesprochenen Wortes oder der sinnvollen Erscheinungen selbst.*[17] The art of hermeneutics is the core of the historical craft. And, as it has been aptly put by a Russian scholar, "one must observe as one reads, and not read as one observes." [18] "To read," whether texts or events themselves, means precisely "to understand," to grasp the inherent meaning, and the understanding intellect cannot be ruled out of the process of understanding, as the reader cannot be eliminated out of the process of reading.

Historians must be critical of themselves, probably even more critical of themselves than of their sources as such, since the sources are what they are, that is, "sources," precisely in proportion to the questions which the historian addresses to them. As H. I. Marrou says, "a document is understood precisely in the measure in which it finds a historian capable of appreciating most deeply its nature and its scope," *dans la mesure où il se rencontrera un historien capable d'apprecier avec plus de profondeur sa nature et sa portée.*[19] Now, the kind of questions a particular historian is actually asking depends ultimately upon his stature, upon his total personality, upon his dispositions and concerns, upon the amplitude of his vision, even upon his likes and dislikes. One should not forget that all acts of understanding are, strictly speaking, personal, and only in this capacity of *personal acts* can they have any existential relevance and value. One has to check, severely and strictly, one's prejudices and presuppositions, but one should never try to empty one's mind of *all* presuppositions. Such an attempt would be a suicide of mind and can only issue in total mental sterility. A barren mind is indeed inevitably sterile. Indifference, or neutrality and indecision, are not virtues, but vices, in a historian as well as in a literary critic, as much as one should claim "objectivity." Historical understanding is ultimately an intelligent response to the challenge of the sources, a deciphering of signs. A certain measure of relativity is inherent in all acts of human understanding, as it is inevitable in personal relations. Relativity is simply a concomitant of relations.

The ultimate purpose of a historical inquiry is not in the establishment of certain objective facts, such as dates, places, numbers, names, and the like, as much as all this is an indispensable preliminary, but in *the encounter with living beings*. No doubt, objective facts must be first carefully established, verified and confirmed, but this is not the final aim of the historian. History is precisely, to quote H. I. Marrou once more, "an encounter with the other"—*l'histoire est rencontre d'autrui*.[20] A narrow mind and an empty mind are real obstacles to this encounter, as they obviously are in all human relations. History, as a subject of study, is *history of human beings*, in their mutual relationship, in their conflicts and contacts, in their social intercourse, and in their solitude and estrangement, in their high aspirations and in their depravity. Only men live in history—live, and move, and strive, and create, and destroy. Men alone are *historic beings*, in a full sense of the word. In the historical understanding we establish contact with men, with their thoughts and endeavors, with their inner world and with their outward action. In this sense, Collingwood was undoubtedly right in insisting that "there are no mere 'events' in history."

> What is miscalled an "event" is really an action, and expresses some thought (intention, purpose) of its agent; the historian's business is therefore to identify this thought.[21]

In this sense, Collingwood insisted, "history proper is the history of thought." It would be unfair to dismiss this contention as a sheer intellectualism, as an unwelcome ghost of obsolete Hegelianism. Collingwood's emphasis is not so much on the thought as such, but on *the intelligent and purposeful character of human life and action*. In history, there are not only happenings and occurrences, but actions and endeavors, achievements and frustrations. This only gives meaning to human existence.

In the last resort, history is history of man, in the ambiguity and multiplicity of his existence. This constitutes the specific character of historical cognition and of historical knowledge. Accordingly, methods must be proportionate to the aim. This has been often ignored in the age of militant and doctrinaire positivism, and is still often forgotten in our time. Objective knowledge, *more geometrico*, is impossible in history. This is not a loss, however, since historical knowledge is not a knowledge of *objects,* but precisely a knowledge of *subjects*—of "co-persons," of "co-partners" in the quest of life. In this sense, historical knowledge is, and must be, *an existential knowledge.* This constitutes a radical cleavage between the *"study of Spirit"* and the *"study of Nature,"* between *die Geisteswissenschaften* and *die Naturwissenschaft.* [22]

III

It has been often contended, especially by the historians of the old school, that historians are led, in the last resort, in their study, by the desire "to know the past as an eyewitness may know it," that is, to become, in some way, just a "witness" of the past events. [23] In fact, this is precisely what the historian cannot do, and never does, and never should attempt to do, if he really wants to be a historian. Moreover, it is by no means certain that an eyewitness of an event does really "know" it, that is, does understand its meaning and significance. An ambition to perform an impossible and contradictory task only obscures the understanding of that which a historian actually does do, if only he does a "historical" work.

The famous phrase of Leopold von Ranke, suggesting that historians "wish to know the actual past"—*wie es eigentlich gewesen*—has been much abused. [24] First of all, it is not fair to make of a casual remark by the great master of history a statement of principle. In any case, in his own work, Ranke never followed this alleged prescription of his, and was always much more than a chronicler. He always was aiming at an interpretation. [25] Obviously, historians want to know what actually has happened, but they want *to know it in a perspective.* And, of course, it is the only thing they can actually achieve. We can never remember even our own immediate past, exactly as we have lived it, because, if we are really *remembering,* and not just dreaming, we do remember the past occurrences in a perspective, against a changed background of our enriched experience. Collingwood described history as "re-enactment of past experience," [26] and there is some truth in this description, in so far as this "re-enactment" is an integral moment of "understanding identification," which is indispensable in any conversation. But one should not mistake one's own thoughts for the thoughts of others. Collingwood himself says that the objects of historical thought are "events which *have finished* happening, and conditions *no longer in existence,*" that is, those events which are "no longer perceptible." [27] Historians look at the past in a perspective, as it were, at a distance. They do not intend *to reproduce* the past event. Historians want to know the past precisely *as the past,* and consequently *in the context of later happenings. "Un temps retrouvé,"* that is, recaptured in an act of intellectual imagination, is precisely *"un temps perdu,"* that is, something that really *did pass away,* something that has been really lost, and only for that reason, and in this capacity of a "lost moment," can it be searched for and rediscovered.

Historical vision is always *a retrospective vision.* What was a future for the people of the past, is now for historians a past. In this sense, historians know more about the past than people of the past themselves were ever able to know. Historians are aware of the impact of the past, of certain past events, on the present. As historians, we cannot visualize the glorious *Pentekontaetia* of Pericles, except in the perspective of the subsequent doom and collapse of Athenian democracy. Or, in any case, such an attempt, even if it were possible (which it is not), would in no sense be a historical endeavor. A perspective and a context are constitutive factors of all true historical understanding and presentation. We cannot understand Socrates properly and historically if we ignore the impact of his challenge and thought, as it has been actually manifested in the later development of Greek philosophy. Indeed, we would know much less about the "true," that is, historical, Socrates if we endeavored to see him, as it were, *in vacuo,* and not against the total historical background, which for us includes also that which for Socrates himself was still an unrealized and unpredictable future.

After all, history is neither spectacle nor panorama, but a *process.* The perspective of time, of concrete time, filled with events, gives us the *sense of direction* which was probably lacking in the events themselves, as they actually happened. Of course, one can make an effort to forget, or to ignore, what one does actually know, that is, the perspective. Whether one can really succeed in doing so is rather doubtful. But even if this were possible, would this be really a historical endeavor? As has been recently said, "to attempt to make oneself a contemporary of the events and people whose history one is writing, means, ultimately, to put oneself in the position which excludes history." *No history without a retrospect,* that is, without perspective.[28]

No doubt, retrospection has its dangers. It may expose us to "optical illusions." In retrospect, we may discover in the past, as it were, "too much," not only if we happen to read anything into the past events, but also because from a certain point of view certain aspects of the past may be seen in a distorted or exaggerated shape. We may be tempted to exaggerate unduly and out of proportion the role and impact of certain historic personalities or institutions, because their images have been disproportionately magnified in our apprehension by the particular perspective in which we are looking at them. And very often the perspective is simply imposed upon us: we cannot change our position. We may be tempted to establish wrong ancestries of trends and ideas, mistaking similarities for actual causal links, as has been done more than once in the history of Early Christianity, and indeed in many other fields. In brief, we may look at the past in a *wrong* perspective, without knowing it and without any means of correcting our vision. In any case, our perspective is always limited. We can never have a total perspective. Yet, on the other hand, we can never see the past in no perspective at all. The ultimate aim of the historian is indeed to comprehend the whole context, at least in a particular "intelligible, that is self-explanatory field" of research (the phrase is Toynbee's). Obviously, this aim is never achieved, and for that reason all historical interpretations are intrinsically provisional.

The historian is never content with a fragmentary vision. He tends to discover, or to presuppose, more order in the flux of events than probably there ever was. He tends to exaggerate the cohesion of various aspects of the past. As H. I. Marrou describes the historian's procedure, he endeavors, *for the sake of intelligibility,* to substitute "an orderly vision," *une vision ordonnée,* for that "dust of small facts" of which the actual happening seems to consist.[29] No historian can resist doing so, and no historian can avoid doing so. It is at this point, however, that utter caution must be exercised. Historians are always in danger of overrationalizing the flux of history. So often instead of living men, unstable and never fully "made up," historians describe fixed characters, as it were, some typical individuals in characteristic poses. It is, more or less, what the painters of portraits sometimes do, and by that device they may achieve impressiveness and convey a vision. This was the method of ancient historians, from Thucydides to Polybius and Tacitus. This is what Collingwood described as the "substantialism" of ancient historiography, and it was what made that historiography, in his opinion, "unhistorical." [30] But the same method has been persistently used by many modern historians. It suffices to mention Mommsen (in his *Roman History*), George Grote, Taine, Ferrero. To the same category belong the numerous stories of Christ in modern historiography from Keim and Ernest Renan to Albert Schweitzer. In a sense, it is a legitimate device. A historian tends to overcome, in a synthetic image, the empirical complexity and often confusion of individual bits, and occurrences, to organize them into a coherent whole, and to relate the multiplicity of occurrences to the unity of a character. This is seldom done in a logical way, by a rational reconstruction. Historians act rather as *inductive artists,* go by intuition. Historians have their own visions. But these are *transforming visions.* It is by this method that all major generalizations of our historiography have been created: the Hellenic mind; the medieval man; the bourgeois; and the like. It would be unfair to contest the relevance of these *categorical* generalizations, which must be clearly distinguished from the *generic* generalizations. And yet, it would be precarious to claim that these generalized "types" do really exist, that is, exist in time and space. They are, as it were, *valid visions,* like artistic portraits, and, as such, they are indispensable tools of understanding. But "typical men" are different from real men of flesh and blood. Of similar character are also our sociological generalizations: the city-state of Ancient Greece; the feudal society; capitalism; democracy; and so on. The main danger of all these generalizations is that they overstress the inner "necessity" of a particular course of behavior. A man, as a "type" or a "character," seems to be predestined to behave in his "typical" manner. There seems to be a typical pattern of development for each kind of human society. It is but natural that in our time the mirage of "historical inevitability" had to be exposed and disavowed, as a distorting factor of our historical interpretation.[31] There is indeed an inherent determinism in all these *typical* and *categorical* images. But they are no more than a useful shorthand for the "dust of facts." The actual history is fluid and flexible and ultimately unpredictable.

The tendency toward determinism is somehow implied in the method of retrospection itself. In retrospect we seem to perceive the *logic* of the events, which unfold themselves in a regular order, according to a recognizable pattern, with an alleged inner necessity, so that we get the impression that it really could not have happened otherwise. The ultimate *contingency* of the process is concealed in the rational schemes, and sometimes it is deliberately eliminated. Thus, *events are losing their eventuality*, and appear to be rather inevitable *stages of development or decay*, of rise and fall, according to a fixed ideal pattern. In fact, there is less consistency in actual history than appears in our interpretative schemes. *History is not an evolution*, and the actual course of events does not follow evolutionary schemes and patterns. Historical events are more than happenings; they are actions, or complexes of actions. History is a field of action, and behind the events stand agents, even when there agents forfeit their freedom and follow a pattern or routine, or are overtaken by blind passions. Man remains a free agent even in bonds. If we may use another biological term, we may describe history rather as *epigenesis* than as "evolution," since evolution always implies a certain kind of "pre-formation," and "development" is no more than a disclosure of "structure." [32] There is always some danger that we may mistake our conceptual visions for empirical realities and speak of them as if they were themselves factors and agents, whereas, in fact, they are but rational abbreviations for a multiplicity of real personal agents. Thus we venture to describe the evolution of "feudalism" or of "capitalistic society," forgetting that these terms only summarize a complex of diverse phenomena, visualized as a whole for the sake of intelligibility. "Societies," "categories," and "types" are *not organisms*, which only can "evolve" or "develop," but are *complexes* of co-ordinated individuals, and this co-ordination is always dynamic, flexible, and unstable.

All historical interpretations are provisional and hypothetical. No definitive interpretation can ever be achieved, even in a limited and particular field of research. Our data are never complete, and new discoveries often compel historians to revise radically their schemes and to surrender sometimes their most cherished convictions, which may have seemed firmly established. It is easy to quote numerous examples of such revision from various areas of historical study, including church history. Moreover, historians must, from time to time, readjust themselves to the changes in the surrounding world. Their vision is always determined by a certain point of view, and thereby limited. But the perspective itself unfolds in the course of actual history. No contemporary historian can commit himself to the identification of the Mediterranean world with the *Oicoumene,* which was quite legitimate in the ancient time. These limitations do not discredit the endeavor of historians. It may even be suggested that a "definitive" interpretation of events would eliminate the "historicity" of history, its contingency and eventuality, and substitute instead a rational "map of history," which may be lucid and readable, but will be existentially unreal. Again, our interpretations are also facts of history, and in them the depicted events continue their historical existence and participate in the shaping of historical life. One may argue whether the "Socrates of Plato" is a "real" Socrates, but there is little doubt that this Socrates of Plato had its own historical existence, as a powerful factor in the shaping of our modern conception of "philosopher." It seems that our interpretations disclose, in some enigmatic way, the hidden potentialities of the actual past. It is in this way that traditions are formed and grow, and the greatest of all human traditions is "culture," in which all partial and particular contributions of successive ages are melted together, synthetically transformed in this process of melting, and are finally integrated into a whole. This process of formation of human culture is not yet completed, and probably will never be completed within the limits of history. This is an additional reason why all historical interpretations should be provisional and approximative: a new light may be shed on the past by that future which has not yet arrived.

IV

It has been recently suggested that "if history has meaning, this meaning is not historical, but theological; what is called *Philoso-*

phy of history is nothing else than a *Theology of history,* more or less disguised." In fact, the term "meaning" is used in different senses when we speak of the meaning of particular events or of the sets of actions and events, and when we speak of the Meaning of History, taken as an all-inclusive whole, that is, in its entirety and universality. In the latter case, indeed, we are speaking actually of the ultimate meaning of human existence, of its ultimate destiny. And this, obviously, is not a historical question. In this case we are speaking not of that which has happened—and this is the only field in which historians are competent—but rather of that which is to happen, and is to happen precisely because it "must" happen. Now, it can be rightly contended that neither "the ultimate" nor "the future" belongs to the realm of historical study, which is, by definition, limited to the understanding of the human past. Historical predictions, of necessity, are conjectural and precarious. They are, in fact, unwarranted "extrapolations." Histories of men and societies are history, but the History of Man, a truly universal and providential History, is no longer just history.

In fact, all modern "philosophies of history" have been crypto-theological, or probably pseudo-theological: Hegel, Comte, Marx, even Nietzsche. In any case, all of them were based on beliefs. The same is true of the modern substitute for the Philosophy of history, which is commonly known as Sociology, and which is, in fact, a *Morphology of history,* dealing with the permanent and recurrent patterns or structures of human life. Now, is Man, in the totality of his manifold and personal existence, a possible subject of a purely historical study and understanding? To claim that he is, by itself is a kind of theology, even if it turns out to be no more than an *"apotheosis* of man." On the other hand—and *here lies the major predicament of all historical study*—no historian can, even in his limited and particular field, within his own competence, avoid raising ultimate problems of human nature and destiny, unless he reduces himself to the role of a registrar of empirical happenings and forfeits his proper task of "understanding." In order to understand, just historically, for instance, "the Greek mind," the historian must, of necessity, have his own vision, if not necessarily original, of the whole range of those problems with which the "noble spirits" of Antiquity were wrestling, in conflict with each other and in succession. A historian of philosophy must be, to a certain extent, a philosopher himself. Otherwise he will miss the problems around which the quest of philosophers has been centered. A historian of art must be, at least, an *amateur*— otherwise he will miss the artistic values and problems. In brief, the problem of *Man* transpires in all problems of *men*, and accordingly cannot be skipped over in any historical interpretation. Moreover, in a certain sense, historical endeavor, as such, aims in the last resort at something which, of necessity, transcends its boundaries.

The process of historical interpretation is the process in which the Human Mind is built and matures. It is a process of integration, in which particular insights and decisions of various ages are accumulated, confronted, dialectically reconciled, vindicated or discriminated, or even discarded and condemned. If history, as the process of human life through ages, has any meaning, any "sense," then obviously the study of history, if it is more than a matter of curiosity, must also have a meaning, a certain "sense." And if historical understanding is the historian's "response" to the "challenge" of that human life which he is exploring, it is of utter importance that historians should be prepared, and inwardly equipped, to meet this challenge of human existence in its fullness and in its ultimate depth.

Thus, contrary to the current prejudice, in order to be competent within his proper field of interpretation, a historian must be responsive to the whole amplitude of human concerns. If he has no concerns of his own, concerns of the others will seem nonsensical to him, and he will hardly be able to "understand" them and hardly competent to appraise them. A historian indifferent to the urgency of the philosophical quest may find, with full conviction, that the whole history of philosophy has been just a story of intellectual vagaries or "vain speculations." In the same way, an areligious historian of religion may find, again with naïve conviction and with an air of superiority, that the whole history of religions has been but a history of "frauds" and "superstitions," of various aberrations of the human mind. Such "histories of religion" have been manufactured more than once. For similar reasons, certain sections and periods of history have been denounced, and consequently dismissed and ignored, as "barbarian," "dead" or "sterile," as "dark ages," and the like. The point is that even a pretended neutrality, an alleged freedom from bias, is itself a bias, an option, a decision. In fact, again contrary to the current prejudice, commitment is a token of freedom, a prerequisite of responsiveness. Concern and interest imply commitment. Now, obviously, one cannot be committed in general, *in abstracto*. Commitment is necessarily discriminative and concrete. And consequently, not all commitments would operate in the same manner and not to the same effect. In any case, the openness of mind is not its emptiness, but rather its comprehensiveness, its broad responsiveness, or, one is tempted to say, its "catholicity." Now, there is here more than just a gradation, as it were, in volume or capacity. "The whole" (*to kath'olou*) is not just a sum total of various "particularisms" (*ta kata merous*), even if these particularisms are dialectically arrayed (as they were, for instance, in the Hegelian map of intellect) or discriminated as "stages of the progress" (as was done, for instance, by Auguste Comte). Particularisms must be done away, and catholicity of mind can be achieved only by a new, integrating reorientation, which would necessarily imply a certain radical discrimination. For in the last resort one cannot evade the ultimate discrimination between "yes" and "no"—and the compromise of "more or less" is just "no" in polite disguise.

In any case, historical interpretation involves judgment. The narrative itself will be twisted and distorted if the historian persists in evading judgment. There is little difference, in this case, between discussing the Greco-Persian War and World War II. No true historian would escape taking sides: for "freedom" or against it. And his judgment will tell in his narrative. No historian can be indifferent to the cleavage between "Good" and "Evil," much as the tension between them may be obscured by various speculative sophistications. No historian can be indifferent, or neutral, to the challenge and claim of Truth. These tensions are, in any case, historical facts and existential situations. Even a denial is a kind of assertion, and often a resolute one, charged with obstinate resistance. Agnosticism itself is intrinsically dogmatic. Moral indifference can but distort our understanding of human actions, which are always controlled by certain ethical options. An intellectual indifferentism would have the same effect. Precisely because human actions are existential decisions, their historical interpretation cannot avoid decisions.

Accordingly, a historian, precisely as historian, that is, as interpreter of human life as it has been actually lived in time and space, cannot evade the major and crucial challenge of this actual history: *"Who do men say that I am?"* (Mark 8:28). For a historian, precisely in his capacity of an interpreter of human existence, it is a crucial question. A refusal to face a challenge is already a commitment. A refusal to answer a certain question is also an answer. Abstention from judgment is also judgment. An attempt to write history, evading the challenge of Christ, is in no sense a "neutral" endeavor. Not only in writing a "Universal History" (*die Weltgeschichte*), that is, in interpreting the total destiny of mankind, but also in interpreting any particular sections or "slices" of this history, is the historian confronted with this ultimate challenge— because the whole of human existence is confronted with this challenge and claim. A historian's response prejudges the course of his interpretation, his choice of measures and values, his understanding of human nature itself. His response determines his "universe of discourse," that setting and perspective in which he endeavors to comprehend human life, and exhibits the amplitude of his responsiveness. No historian should ever pretend that he has achieved a "definitive interpretation" of that great mystery which is human life, in all its variety and diversity, in all its misery and grandeur, in its ambiguity and contradictions, in its basic "freedom." No Christian historian should lay such claims either. But he is entitled to claim that his approach to that mystery is a comprehensive and "catholic" approach, that his vision of that mystery is proportionate to its actual dimension. Indeed, he has to vindicate his claim in the practice of his craft and vocation.

V

The rise of Christianity marks a turning point in the interpretation of history. Robert Flint, in his renowned book, *History of the Philosophy of History,* says:

The rise of ecclesiastical history was more to historiography than was the discovery of America to geography. It added immensely to the contents of history, and radically changed men's conceptions of its nature. It at once caused political history to be seen to be only a part of history, and carried even into the popular mind the conviction—of which hardly a trace is to be found in the classical historians—that all history must move towards some general human end, some divine goal.[33]

Contemporary writers are even more emphatic at this point. For, indeed, the rise of Christianity meant a radical reversal of man's attitude toward the fact of history. It meant actually the discovery of the *"historic dimension,"* of the *historic time.* Strictly speaking, it was a recovery and extension of the Biblical vision. Of course, no elaborate "philosophy of history" can be found in the books of the Old Testament. Yet, there is in the Bible a comprehensive *vision of history,* a perspective of an *unfolding time,* running from a "beginning" to an "end," and guided by the will of God, leading His people to His own goal and purpose. In this perspective of dynamic history early Christians have assessed and interpreted their new experience, the Revelation of God in Christ Jesus.

Classical historians held a very different view of human history. The Greeks and the Romans were indeed a history-writing people. But their vision of history was basically unhistorical. They were, of course, desperately interested in the facts of history, in the facts of the past. It might be expected that they would accordingly be well qualified for the historian's task. In fact, by their basic conviction they were rather disqualified for that task. The Greek mind was "in the grip of the past." It was, as it were, charmed by the past. But it was quite indifferent and uncertain with regard to the future. Now, the past itself acquires its historic character and significance only in the perspective of the future. "Time's arrow" was totally missing in the classical vision of human destiny. Great historians of Greece and Rome were not, in any sense, philosophers. At their best, they were fine observers, but rather moralists or artists, orators and politicians, preachers or rhetoricians, than thinkers. Ancient philosophers, again, were not interested in history, as such, as a contingent and accidental flux of events. They endeavored, on the contrary, to eliminate history, to rule it out, as a disturbing phenomenon. Philosophers of ancient Greece were looking for the permanent and changeless, for the timeless and immortal. Ancient historiography was emphatically pessimistic. History was a story of unavoidable doom and decay. Men were confronted with a dilemma. On the one hand, they could simply "resign" and reconcile themselves to the inevitability of "destiny," and even find joy and satisfaction in the contemplation of harmony and splendor of the cosmic whole, however indifferent and inimical it might be to the aims and concerns of individuals and societies. This was the *catharsis* of tragedy, as tragedy was understood in the classical world. Or, on the other hand, men could attempt an escape, a "flight" out of history, out of this dimension of flux and change—the hopeless *wheel of genesis and decay*—into the dimension of the changeless.

The ancient pattern of historical interpretation was "cosmic," or "naturalistic." On the one hand, there was a biological pattern of growth and decay, the common fate of everything living. On the other hand, there was an astronomical pattern of periodical recurrence, of circular motion of heavens and stars, a pattern of "revolutions" and cycles. Indeed, both patterns belonged together, since the cycles of the earth were predetermined and controlled by the circles of the heavens. Ultimately, the course of history was but an aspect of the inclusive cosmic course, controlled by certain inviolable laws. These laws were implied in the structure of the universe. Hence the whole vision was essentially fatalistic. The ultimate principle was *tyche* or *heimarmene*, the cosmic "destiny" or *fatum*. Man's destiny was implied and comprehended in that astronomical "necessity." The Cosmos itself was conceived as an "eternal" and "immortal," but periodical and recurrent, being. There was an infinite and continuous reiteration of the same permanent pattern, a periodical renewal of situations and sequences. Consequently, there was no room for any pro-gress, but only for "re-volutions," re-circulation, *cyclophoria* and *anacyclosis*. Nothing "new" could be added to the closed perfection of this periodical system. Accordingly, there was no reason, and no motive, to look forward, into the future, as the future could but disclose that which was already preformed in the past, or rather in the very nature of things (*physis*). The permanent pattern could be better discerned in the past, which has been "completed" or "perfected" (*perfectum*), than in the uncertainty of the present and future. It was in the past that historians and politicians were looking for "patterns" and "examples."

It was especially in the later philosophical systems of the Hellenistic age that these features of "permanence" and "recurrence" were rigidly emphasized—by the Stoics, the Neopythagoreans, the Platonics, the Epicureans alike. *Eadem sunt omnia semper nec magis est neque erit mox quam fuit ante.*[34] But the same conviction was already dominant in the classical age. Professor Werner Jaeger admirably summarizes the main convictions of Aristotle:

> The coming-to-be and passing-away of earthly things is just as much a stationary revolution as the motion of the stars. *In spite of its uninterrupted change nature has no history* according to Aristotle, *for organic becoming is held fast by the constancy of its forms in a rhythm that remains eternally the same. Similarly the human world of state and society and mind appears to him not as caught in the incalculable mobility of irrecapturable historical destiny, whether we consider personal life or that of nations and cultures, but as founded fast in the unalterable permanence of forms that while they change within certain limits remain identical in essence and purpose.* This feeling about life is symbolized by the Great Year, at the close of which all the stars have returned to their original position and begin their course anew. In the same way cultures of the earth wax and wane, according to Aristotle, as determined by great natural catastrophes, which in turn are causally connected with the regular changes of the heavens. That which Aristotle at this instant newly discovers has been discerned a thousand times before, will be lost again, and one day discerned afresh.[35]

In this setting of thought there was no room for any conception of "history," whether of the world or of man and human societies. There was a *rhythm* in the cosmic process, and consequently in the destiny of man, but *no direction.* History was not going or moving anywhere. It was only rotating. It had no end, as it had no goal. It had only structure. The whole of ancient philosophy was, in fact, a system of "general morphology" of being. And it was also essentially political or social. Man was conceived as an essentially "social being," *zoon politicon,* and his personal uniqueness was hardly acknowledged at all. Only "typical" situations were regarded as relevant. Nor was the uniqueness of any event acknowledged. Only "patterns" were relevant. There was a great variety of views and shades of opinion within this general and common pattern of the Greek and Hellenistic thought; there were inner tensions and conflicts therein, which must be carefully discerned and acknowledged. But the basic vision was the same in all these variations on the same theme: an "eternal Cosmos," the "endless returns," the ominous "wheel of genesis and decay." [36]

Against this kind of background, and in this perspective, Christianity meant an intellectual revolution, a radical reversal of standards, a new vision and orientation. Christianity is an *eschatological religion* and, for that very reason, is *essentially historical*. Recent theological controversy has sorely obscured the meaning of these terms, and some explanation is required to prevent confusion and misunderstanding.

The starting point of the Christian faith is the acknowledgment of certain actual events, in which God has acted, sovereignly and decisively, for man's salvation, precisely "in these last days." *In this sense these facts*—Christ's coming into the world, his Incarnation, his Cross and Resurrection, and the Descent of the Holy Spirit—*are eschatological events:* unique and "ultimate," that is, decisive, "critical" and crucial, wrought once forever, *ephhapax.* In a certain sense, they are also *final events,* the accomplishment and fulfillment of the Messianic prophecy and promise. In this sense, they assume their significance in the perspective of a past history which they "conclude" and "fulfill." *They are eschatological because they are historical,* that is, because they are situated in a sequence of the antecedent events, and thereby validate retrospectively the whole series. *In this sense, Christ is "the end of history,"* that is, of a particular "section" of history, though not of history as such. History, as such, is far from being terminated or abrogated by Christ's coming, but is actually going on, and *another eschatological event* is anticipated and expected to terminate history, *the Second Coming.* This entire pattern of interpretation is definitely *linear,* running from the beginning to the end, from Creation to Consummation, *but the line is broken, or rather "bent,"* at a particular "crucial" or "turning" point. *This point is the center of history,* of the "history of salvation," *die Heilsgeschichte.* Yet, paradoxically, "beginning," "center," and "end" coincide, not as "events," but in the person of the Redeemer. Christ is both *alpha* and *omega,* "the First" and "the Last," as well as the center. *In another sense, Christ is precisely the Beginning.* The *new aion* has been inaugurated in his coming. "The Old" has been completed, but "the New" just began.

Time was in no sense "devaluated" by Christ's coming. On the contrary, time was validated by his coming, by him and through him. It was "consecrated" and given meaning, the new meaning. In the light of Christ's coming, history now appears as a "progress," inwardly toward "the end," to which it unfailingly precipitates. The hopeless "cycles" have been exploded, as St. Augustine used to say. It was revealed that there was no rotation in history, but, on the contrary, an unfolding of a singular and universal purpose. In this perspective of a unique and universal history, all particular events are situated in an irreversible order. "Singularity" of the events is acknowledged and secured.

Now, it can be contended that the Biblical vision of history was not, in fact, a "history of man," but rather "the history of God," the story of God's rule in history. Indeed, the main emphasis of the Bible is precisely on God's lordship, both in the world at large and in history in particular. But *precisely because history was apprehended as "God's history," the "history of man" was made possible.* Man's history was then apprehended as *a meaningful story* and no longer as a reiteration of the cosmic pattern, nor as a chaotic flux of happenings. The history of men was understood in the perspective of their salvation, that is, of the accomplishment of their destiny and justification of their existence. Man's action has been thereby justified and stimulated, since he was given a task, and a purpose. God has acted, and His ultimate action in Christ Jesus was a consummation of His continuous actions in the past, "at sundry times and in diverse manners." Yet, His manifold actions were *not simply particular cases* or instances of a certain general law, *but* were *singular events.* One can never suppress personal names in the Bible. The Bible can never be, as it were, "algebraized." Names can never be replaced by symbols. There was a dealing of the Personal God with human persons. And this dealing culminated in the Person of Jesus Christ, who came "in the fullness of time," to "complete" the Old and to "inaugurate" the New. Accordingly, there are two basic themes in the Christian understanding of history.

First, there is *a retrospective theme:* the story of the Messianic preparation. Secondly, there is *a prospective theme*, opening the vistas of the "end of history." *The Christian approach to history, so radically different from that of the ancient world, is by no means just a subjective reorientation of man in time.* An existential revaluation of time itself is implied. Not only was the human attitude changed when a new and unique term of reference was inserted into the flux of events, but the character of historical time itself has been changed. What was of decisive importance was that God's revelation in Jesus Christ was of an *ultimate* character, disclosing *a new dimension of human existence.* The decisive contribution of the Christian faith to the understanding of history was not in the detection of the radical "historicity" of man's existence, that is, of his finite relativity, but precisely in *the discovery of perspective in history,* in which man's historical existence acquires relevance and meaning. Therefore, the modern existentialist emphasis on "man's historicity" is, in fact, neither historical nor distinctively Christian. It is, in many instances, rather *a relapse into Hellenism.* "Man's historicity" means, in certain existentialist interpretations, nothing more than man's essential temporality, his inextricable involvement in the comprehensive context of passing occurrences, which brings him, finally, to extinction, to death. This diagnosis reminds one, however, more of the tragic insight of the Ancients than of the jubilant News of the Gospel. The original Christian *kerygma* not only intended to expose the misery and "nothingness" of sinful man, and to announce the Divine judgment, but above all it proclaimed the value and dignity of man—God's creature and adoptive child—and offered empirical man, miserable and spiritually destitute, God's "enemy," and yet beloved of God, the way of salvation. It was not only a condemnation of the Old, but an inauguration of the New, of "the acceptable year of the Lord."

Now, it is precisely at this point that a radical disagreement among Christian interpreters arises. Is there anything else to happen "in history" which may have any ultimate existential relevance for man, after Christ's coming? Or has everything that could be accomplished *in history* already been achieved? History, as a natural process, is, of course, still continuing—a *human history.* But does the *Divine history* continue as well? Has history any constructive value now, after Christ? or any "meaning" at all? It is sometimes contended that, since the ultimate Meaning has been already manifested and the *Eschaton* has already entered history, history has been, as it were, "closed" and "completed," as a meaningful process, and eschatology has been "realized." This implies a specific interpretation of the "turning-point" of history which was the coming of Christ. It is sometimes assumed that there was, indeed, a *sacred history* in the past, just up to the coming of Christ Jesus, in which it was "consummated," but that after him there is in history only an empty flux of happenings, in which the nothingness and vanity of man is constantly being exposed and manifested, but nothing truly "eventful" can ever take place, since *there is nothing else to be accomplished within history.* This assumption has been variously phrased and elaborated in contemporary theological thought. It may take a shape of the "realized Eschatology," and then meaning is shifted from the realm of history to the realm of sacramental experience, in which the *Eschaton* is present and reenacted.[37] It may take the shape of a "consequent Eschatology," and then history appears to be just a great *Interim* between the great events in the past and in the future, between the "first" and "second" comings of the Lord, devoid of any constructive value, just a period of hope and expectation. Or else history may be "interiorized," and the realm of meaning would be confined to the experience of individual believers, making "decisions." [38] In all these cases, history as an actual course of events in time and space is denied any "sacred" character, any positive significance. Its course is apprehended as a continuous unfolding of human vanity and impotence.

It has been, in fact, recently suggested that "a Christian history" is simply nonsense. It has been contended that "the message of the New Testament was not an appeal to historical action, but to repentance," and that this message "dismantled, as it were, the hopeless history of the world." [39] This radical eschatologism, which simply "dismantles" all human history, is open to serious theological doubt. Indeed, it is a theological, and not a historical, assumption. It is rooted in a one-sided theological vision in which God alone is seen active, and man is just an object of Divine action, in wrath or mercy, and never an agent himself. But it is this "inhuman" conception of man, and not "the message of the New Testament," which makes nonsense of human history. The message of the New Testament, on the contrary, makes sense of history. In Christ, and by him, Time was itself, for the first time, radically and existentially validated. History has become *sacred* in its full dimension since "the Word was made flesh," and the Comforter descended into the world for its cleansing and sanctification. Christ is ever abiding in his Body, which is the Church, and in her the *Heilsgeschichte* is effectively continued. The *Heilsgeschichte* is still going on. It is obviously true that in practice it is utterly difficult to discern the pattern of this ongoing "history of salvation" in the perplexity of historical events, and historians, including Christian historians, must be cautious and modest in their endeavor to decipher the hidden meaning of the particular events. Nevertheless, the historian must be aware of that new "situation" which has been created in history by the Coming of Christ: there is "now" nothing "neutral" in the human sphere itself, since the Cross and Resurrection, since the Pentecost. Accordingly, the whole of history, even "the hopeless history of the world," appears now *in the perspective of an ultimate, eschatological conflict*. It was in this perspective that St. Augustine undertook his survey of historical events in his story of the "Two Cities." It may be difficult to relate the *Heilsgeschichte* to the general history of the world. On the other hand, the Church is *in the world*. Its actual history may be often distorted by worldly accretions. Yet "salvation" has also a historical dimension. The Church is the leaven of history. As Cyril C. Richardson has aptly observed recently, the history of the Church bears a *prophetic* character, no less than the sacred history of the Bible. "It is a part of revelation—the story of the Holy Ghost." [40]

One may suggest that in the modern "hyper-eschatologism," with its implicit radical devaluation of history, we are facing in fact a revival of the Hellenic anti-historicism, with its failure to ascertain any constructive value in temporal action. Of course, eschatologists of various descriptions protest their allegiance to the Bible and abhor and abjure all Hellenism. They would indignantly repudiate any charge of philosophism. However, the close dependence of Rudolf Bultmann upon Martin Heidegger is obvious. In fact, they advocate the same position as the Greek philosophy, so far as the understanding of history is concerned. Obviously there is a profound difference between a subjection to the *fatum*, whether it is conceived as a blind *heimarmene* or as a "fiery Logos," and the proclamation of an impending and imminent judgment of the eternal God. Yet in both cases *human action* is radically depreciated, if for different reasons, and is denied any constructive task. This makes the understanding of history an impossible and even a nonsensical endeavor, except in the form of a general exposure of man's vanity and pride, of his utter impotence even in his ambition and pride. Under the guise of prophecy, history of this kind is in danger of degenerating into homiletic exercise. It is true that, in a certain sense, the modern radical eschatologism may be regarded as a logical consequence of the reduced conception of the Church, which was so characteristic of certain trends of the Reformation. The Church was still recognized as the area of an "invisible" action and operation of God, but she was denied precisely her historical significance. The modern recovery of the integral doctrine of the Church, which cuts across the existing denominational borders, may lead to the recovery of a deeper historical insight and may restate history in its true existential dimension.[41]

Strangely enough, for those who reduce the Church to the role of *an eschatological token* and refuse to regard her as a kind of *proleptic eschatology,* history inevitably becomes again essentially a "political history," as it was in classical times. It is again conceived as a story of states and nations, and as such it is denounced and condemned. Paradoxically, it ceases to be, in this interpretation, the history of man. It is assumed that man has nothing to do, that is, to create or to achieve. He simply expects judgment, or, in any case, stands under it. But in fact, man is becoming—or, indeed, is failing to become—himself precisely in his historical struggle and endeavor. Eschatologism, on the contrary, condemns man to a dreamy mysticism, that very trap and danger which eschatologists pretend and attempt to evade. He is doomed to detect and contemplate, unredeemably, the abyss of his nothingness, is exposed to dreams and nightmares of his own vanity and spiritual sickness. And a new mythology emerges out of these unhealthy dreams. Whatever kind of "man's historicity" may be claimed as a discovery of such an impoverished Christianity, the actual historicity of man is thereby, implicitly or often quite explicitly, denied and prohibited. Then history, in such an interpretation, actually becomes "hopeless," without a task, without a theme, without any meaning. Now, the true history of man is not a political history, with its utopian claims and illusions, but *a history of the spirit,* the story of man's growth to the full stature of perfection, under the Lordship of the historical God-man, even of our Lord, Christ Jesus. It is a tragic story, indeed. And yet the seed matures, not only for judgment, but also for eternity.

The Christian historian does not proceed actually "on Christian principles," as is sometimes suggested. Christianity is not a set of principles. The Christian historian pursues his professional task of interpreting human life in the light of his Christian vision of that life, sorely distorted by sin, yet redeemed by Divine mercy, and healed by Divine grace, and called to the inheritance of an everlasting Kingdom. The Christian historian will, first of all, vindicate "the dignity of man," even of fallen man. He will, then, protest against any radical scission of man into "empirical" and "intelligible" fractions (whether in a Kantian fashion or in any other) of which the former is doomed and only the latter is promised salvation. It is precisely the "empirical man" who needs salvation, and salvation does not consist merely in a kind of disentanglement of the "intelligible character" out of the empirical mess and bondage. Next, the Christian historian will attempt to reveal the actual course of events in the light of his Christian knowledge of man, but will be slow and cautious in detecting the "providential" structure of actual history, in any detail. Even in the history of the Church "the hand of Providence" is emphatically hidden, though it would be blasphemous to deny that this Hand does exist or that God is truly the Lord of History. Actually, the purpose of a historical understanding is not so much to detect the Divine action in history as to understand the human action, that is, human activities, in the bewildering variety and confusion in which they appear to a human observer. Above all, *the Christian historian will regard history at once as a mystery and as a tragedy—a mystery of salvation and a tragedy of sin.* He will insist on the comprehensiveness of our conception of man, as a prerequisite of our understanding of his existence, of his exploits, of his destiny, which is actually wrought in his history.[42]

The task of a Christian historian is by no means an easy task. But it is surely a noble task.

NOTES

1. Marc Bloch, *Apologie pour l'Histoire, ou Metier d'Historien,* "Cahiers des Annales," 3 (Paris, 1949); English translation, *The Historian's Craft* (New York, 1953), p. 4.

2. Gerhard Kittel, "The Jesus of History," in *Mysterium Christi,* ed. by G. K. A. Bell and Adolf Deissman (Longmans, 1930), pp. 31 ff.

3. F. M. Powicke, *Modern Historians and the Study of History* (London, 1955), pp. 227–228.

4. H. E. Manning, *The Temporal Mission of the Holy Ghost: or Reason and Revelation* (New York, 1866), pp. 227 ff.

5. An interesting discussion of this issue took place at the Anglo-American Conference of Historians, July, 1926; three addresses given at the conference by C. H. McIlwain, A. Meyendorff, and J. L. Morison are published under the general title, "Bias in historical writing," in *History,* XI (October, 1926), 193–203.

6. M. Bloch, pp. 64–65.

7. See the penetrating analysis of experimental method by Claude Bernard, in his classical essay, *Introduction à l'étude de la médecine experimentale* (Paris, 1865). Bergson compares this book with the *Discours sur la methode* of Descartes: "The Philosophy of Claude Bernard," in *The Creative Mind* (New York, 1946), pp. 238 ff.

8. See the caustic remarks of R. G. Collingwood, *The Idea of History* (New York, 1946), pp. 257 ff.

9. Benedetto Croce, *La Storia come Pensiero e come Azione,* 4th ed. (Bari, 1943); English translation, *History as the Story of Liberty* (London, 1949), pp. 85 ff.

10. Benedetto Croce, *Teoria e Storia della Storiografia,* 6th ed. (Bari, 1948), p. 11.

11. Collingwood, p. 214.

12. Leopold von Ranke, *Weltgeschichte,* Theil I, 3 Aufl. (Leipzig, 1883), "Vorrede," s. VI.

13. Henri-Irenée Marrou, *De la connaissance historique* (Paris, 1954), p. 83.

14. Collingwood, *op. cit.,* pp. 218–219.

15. Collingwood, *An Autobiography* (New York, 1949), p. 31.

16. Croce, *Teoria e Storia,* pp. 29 ff.; cf. Collingwood, *The Idea,* pp. 214 ff.

17. Fr. Ad. Trendelenburg, *Logische Untersuchungen,* Bd. II. 2, s. 408.

18. G. Spet, "Istorija kak predmet logiki" ("History as the Matter of Logic"), in *Nauchnyja Izvestija,* coll. 2 (Moscow, 1922), pp. 15–16.

19. Marrou, *op. cit.,* p. 120.

20. Marrou, *op. cit.,* p. 101.

21. Collingwood, *Autobiography,* pp. 127–128.

22. For the whole section 2 of this article see my essay, "O tipakh istoricheskago is-tolkovanija" ("The types of historical interpretation"), in *Sbornik v chest' na Vasil N. Zlatarski* (Sofia, 1925), pp. 523–541 (in Russian). It is gratifying for the author

to discover that this conception is now widely shared by many historians and philosophers, although his Russian article was hardly likely to have been read by many. In addition to the studies by Croce, Collingwood, and Marrou, already quoted, one should mention: Raymon Aron, *Introduction à la Philosophie de l'Histoire, Essai sur les limites de l'objectivité historique* (Paris, 1948); *La Philosophie critique de l'Histoire, Essai sur une théorie allemande de l'histoire* (Paris, 1950). Of earlier writers one should mention Wilhelm Dilthey; on him see H. A. Hodges, *Wilhelm Dilthey, An Introduction* (London, 1944); *The Philosophy of Wilhelm Dilthey* (London, 1952). On Benedetto Croce see A. Robert Caponigri, *History and Liberty: The Historical Writings of Benedetto Croce* (London, 1955). For other points of view see, e.g., Patrick Gardiner, *The Nature of Historical Explanation* (New York, 1952); S. G. F. Brandon, *Time and Mankind* (London, 1951); G. N. Renier, *History, Its Purpose and Method* (Boston, 1950).

23. V. V. Bolotov, *Lekzii po istorii drevnej cerkvi* ("Lectures on the History of the Early Church") (St. Petersburg, 1907), I, 6–7.

24. Ranke, "Geschichte der Romanischen und Germanischen Völker von 1494 bis 1514," in *Vorrede zur ersten Ausgabe* (October, 1824), *Samtliche Werke*, 3 Aufl., Bd. 33 (Leipzig, 1885), s. VII.

25. See von Laue, *Leopold Ranke, The Formative Years* (Princeton, 1950), and especially H. Liebeschutz, *Ranke* (Historical Association, G 26, 1954); cf. Eberhard Kessel, "Rankes Idee der Universalhistorie," in *Historische Zeitschrift*, Bd. 178.2, ss. 269–308 (with new texts of Ranke).

26. Collingwood, *The Idea*, pp. 282 ff.

27. *Ibid.*, p. 233.

28. Cf. H. Gouhier, "Vision retrospective et intention historique," in *La Philosophie de l'Histoire de la Philosophie* (Rome–Paris, 1956), pp. 133–141.

29. Marrou, *op. cit.*, p. 47.

30. Collingwood, *The Idea*, pp. 42 ff.

31. See Isaiah Berlin, *Historical Inevitability* (New York, 1954), and Pieter Geyl's remarks in *Debates with Historians* (London, 1955), pp. 236–241.

32. See my earlier articles: "Evolution und Epigenesis, Zur Problematik der Geschichte," in *Der Russische Gedanke*, Jh. I, Nr. 3 (Bonn, 1930), ss. 240–252; "Die Krise des deutschen Idealismus," in *Orient und Occident*, Hf. 11 & 12, 1932.

33. Robert Flint, *History of the Philosophy of History* (Edinburgh and London, 1893), p. 62.

34. Lucretius, *De rerum natura*, III, 945.

35. Werner Jaeger, *Aristoteles. Grundlegung einer Geschichte seiner Entwicklung* (Berlin, 1923); English translation: *Aristotle, Fundamentals of the History of His Development*, translated with the author's corrections and additions by Richard Robinson (2nd ed.; Oxford, 1948), p. 389 (italics mine). Cf. O. Hamelin, *Le Système d'Aristote* (2nd ed.; Paris, 1931), pp. 336 ss.; J. Chevalier, *La Notion du Nécessaire chez Aristote et chez ses prédécesseurs, particulièrement chez Platon* (Paris, 1915), pp. 160 ss.; R. Mugnier, *La Théorie du Premier Moteur et l'Evolution de la Pensée Aristotelienne* (Paris, 1930), pp. 24 ss.; J. Baudry, *Le Problème de l'origine et de l'éternité du Monde dans la philosophie grecque de Platon à l'ère*

chrétienne (Paris, 1931), especially chapters on Aristotle (pp. 99–206) and conclusion (pp. 299 ss.).

36. B. A. van Groningen, "In the Grip of the Past, Essay on an Aspect of Greek Thought," in *Philosophia Antiqua*, ed. by W. J. Verdenius and J. H. Waszink (Leiden, 1953), vol. VI; Pierre Duhème, *Le Système du Monde, Histoire des Doctrines Cosmologiques de Platon à Copernic* (Paris, 1913), t. I; (Paris, 1914), t. II; Hans Meyer, "Zur Lehre von der Ewigen Wiederkunft aller Dinge," in *Festgabe A. Ehrhard* (Bonn, 1922), ss. 359 ff.; Jean Guitton, *Le Temps et l'Eternité chez Plotin et St. Augustin* (Paris, 1933); John F. Callahan, *Four Views of Time in Ancient Philosophy* (Cambridge, Mass., 1948); Victor Goldschmidt, *Le système stoicien et l'Idée de temps* (Paris, 1953); Mircea Eliade, *Der Mythos der Ewigen Wiederkehr* (Duesseldorf, 1953); Henri-Charles Puech, "Temps, Histoire et Mythe dans le Christianisme des premiers siècles," in the *Proceedings of the 7th Congress for the History of Religions, Amsterdan, 4th–9th September 1950* (Amsterdam, 1951), pp. 33 ff.; "La Gnose et le Temps," in *Eranos*, Bd. XX, *Mensch und Zeit* (Zurich, 1952), pp. 57 ss. An attempt of Wilhelm Nestle to prove that there existed a certain "philosophy of history" in ancient Greece was unsuccessful; see his "Griechische Geschichtsphilosophie," in *Archiv fur die Geschichte der Philosophie*, Bd. XLI (1932), ss. 80–114. Nor are the remarks of Paul Schubert convincing; see his chapter, "The Twentieth-Century West and the Ancient Near East," in *The Idea of History in the Ancient Near East*, ed. by Robert C. Dentan, American Oriental Series (New Haven, 1955), vol. 38, pp. 332 ff.

37. See, *e. g.*, C. H. Dodd, *History and the Gospel* (London, 1938); cf. "Eschatology and History," an Appendix in *The Apostolic Preaching and Its Developments* (New York, 1936 [new ed. in 1944]).

38. Rudolf Bultmann, *History and Eschatology*, The Gifford Lectures, 1955 (Edinburgh, 1955).

39. Karl Loewith, *Meaning in History: The Theological Implications of the Philosophy of History* (Chicago, 1949), pp. 196–197; cf. also his articles: "Skepsis und Glaube in der Geschichte," in *Die Welt als Geschichte*, Jh. X. 3 (1950); "Christentum und Geschichte," in *Christentum und Geschichte, Vortraege der Tragung in Bochum vom 5. bis 8. October 1954* (Duesseldorf, 1955).

40. Cyril C. Richardson, "Church History Past and Present," in *Union Seminary Quarterly Review* (November, 1949), p. 9.

41. For a further elaboration of this topic see my Dudleian Lecture, *The Christian Dilemma*, delivered at Harvard University on April 30, 1958.

42. The problem of "Christian history" (in the double meaning of the word: "actual history" and "historiography") has been extensively discussed in recent years, and literature is enormous. There are several competent surveys: G. Thils, "Bibliographie sur la theologie de l'histoire," in *Ephemerides Theologicae Lovanienses*, 26 (1950), pp. 87–95; F. Olgiati, "Rapporti fra storia, metafisica e religione," in *Rivista di filosofia neoscholastica* (1950), pp. 49–84; P. Henry, "The Christian Philosophy of History," in *Theological Studies*, XIII (1952), 419–433; see also R. L. Shinn, *Christianity and the Problem of History* (New York, 1953); M. C. Smit, *De Veroudingvan Christendom en Historie in der huidige Roms-Katholicke geschicolbeschouwing* (Kampen, 1950) [with a French résumé]).

The following publications also should be especially mentioned in the context of the present article: Oscar Cullmann, *Christus und die Zeit* (Zurich, 1945); English translation, *Christ and Time* (London, 1951); Karl Barth, *Kirchliche Dogmatik*, Bd. III. 2 (Zollikon-Zurich, 1948), ss. 524–780; John Marsh, *The Fulness of Time* (London, 1952); Jean Danielou, *Essai sur le Mystère de l'Histoire* (Paris, 1953); *Le Mystère de l'Avent* (Paris, 1948); *Papers of the Ecumenical Institute*, 5: "On the Meaning of History," in *Oikoumene* (Geneva, 1950); Erich Frank, *Philosophical Understanding and Religious Truth* (New York, 1945); "The Role of History in Christian Thought," in *The Duke Divinity School Bulletin*, XIV, No. 3 (November, 1949), pp. 66–77; H. Butterfield, *Christianity and History* (New York, 1950); E. C. Rust, *The Christian Understanding of History* (London, 1947); Reinhold Niebuhr, *Faith and History* (New York, 1949); Pietro Chichetta, *Teolgia della storia* (Rome, 1953); John McIntyre, *The Christian Doctrine of History* (Edinburgh, 1957); Christopher Dawson, *Dynamics of World History*, ed. by John J. Mulloy (New York, 1957); Jacques Maritain, *On the Philosophy of History*, ed. by Joseph W. Evans (New York, 1957).

ERIC COCHRANE

Roman Catholicism has produced one of the strongest traditions of Christian historiography. As Eric Cochrane (b. 1928) notes, it is visible institutionally in the history departments of Catholic universities in all parts of the world and in professional societies like the American Catholic Historical Association. Cochrane, a professor at the University of Chicago, and a specialist in Renaissance and post-Renaissance Italy, presented this paper as president of that society in December 1974.

According to Cochrane, the Catholic tradition of historiography has not been altogether worthwhile. He would not for that reason, however, want to give up on it as some have done, but he would like to see it taken in fresh directions. "The task," he concludes, "consists not simply in sweeping away the remnants of an older, and no longer useful, form of Catholic historiography. It consists rather in creating a new Catholic historiography to take its place—a historiography constantly in dialogue with the latest currents of non-Catholic historiography, yet one still faithful to the lasting values of its own 2,000-year-old tradition."

Cochrane believes that Catholic historians—and this could be said of other Christian historians—possess certain insights helpful to historical study: they understand the significance and place of theology and religion in history, they hold to a view of personality that resists any deterministic approaches to history, they recognize their work as a sacred vocation for the blessing of others, they understand the limited competence of historical study, and they work with a genuine universality of viewpoint. Catholic historians today, he believes, have the special duty to help resurrect a sense of history which respects the constancies of history and truth as well as the relativity and changeableness of history.

What Is Catholic Historiography?

The question, "What is Catholic historiography?" could have been answered much more easily a few decades ago then it can be today. To be sure, there were even then some critics who questioned the propriety of its identification as historiography at all and who classified it instead as "theology of history." [1] There were others who identified it solely by the objects toward which it was directed and by the judgments it passed on those objects rather than by any special methods or particular insights it might have.[2] Moreover, many Catholics had long practiced history in the same way that other Catholics practiced dentistry or pipe fitting. That is, they performed, and even excelled in, tasks whose standards and aims were defined without regard to a confessional commitment. And they produced works like the *Cambridge Modern History,* which can no more be called "Catholic," notwithstanding the profound Catholicism of its founder, than the *English Historical Review* can be called Anglican or the *Annales* Jewish.

Nonetheless, no one would have denied the existence of a special Catholic historiography, at least in its institutional form. It had long been represented by the Görresgesellschaft in Europe and, in the United States, by the numerous state and regional associations that prepared the way for the establishment of the American Catholic Historical Association in 1919. It was represented by history departments in Catholic universities all over the world. It was represented by such prestigious periodical publications as the *Analecta Gregoriana,* the *Revue d'historie ecclésiastique,* and, after 1945, the *Rivista di storia della Chiesa in Italia.*

Reprinted by permission of the Catholic University of America Press from *The Catholic Historical Review,* LXI (1975), 169–90.

Nor would anyone have denied that Catholic historians were animated by a certain spirit of solidarity. They organized historical
conferences of their own, and they generally shunned conferences
organized by non-Catholics—as they did, for example, in occasion
of the 1947 conference on the history of the Council of Trent.
"They whispered," said one of the organizers, "about getting into
trouble with the hierarchy," which, they feared, would look with
disfavor "upon their bringing up ticklish or embarrassing subjects
or their collaborating with persons of different persuasions, some
Protestants, some *laïcs*." [3] Apparently, commented another, "the
history of the Church is meant to be a monopoly of certain people
specially chosen for reasons that have nothing to do with as-
siduousness in research and historiographical preparation." [4] More
important still, Catholic historiography was inspired by certain explicitly stated objectives. According to the founders of the *Illinois
Catholic Historical Review* in 1918, it aimed at filling up the la-
cunae left by Protestant historians of the state. "The glorious history of Catholic Illinois," they noted, "has but few worshipers,
because for the most part it has been a hidden shrine." [5] According
to Bishop Thomas Shahan in his presentation of the *Catholic Historical Review* three years earlier, it sought both to "add to the intellectual reputation and stature of American Catholicism" and to
promote the principle "that God rules over the affairs of mankind
and disposes of all things according to His own purposes." [6] According to no less an authority than Jean Daniélou, it was supposed to be concerned with one alone of the two traditional kinds
of history—not with the history which "men make because of pride
in the flesh, imperialism, and domination," but rather with "the
history which God makes" and which can be apprehended fully
only with the help of the Holy Spirit. [7] "Whoever writes history in
which there is no trace of the transformation of humanity brought
about by the coming of Christ into the world," according to another authority, "is not a Christian." [8]

It is therefore not surprising that Catholic historiography
should have acquired certain characteristics that distinguished it
from what was considered correct historiography *extra ecclesiam*.
Catholic book reviewers were expected to make use of theological
as well as critical principles in their judgments. For example, they
could reprimand an author for not having found the modern for-

mulae of papal supremacy in the writings of the Church Fathers.[9]
They could applaud others for being "correct in regard to faith and
morals" and even advise them occasionally to "withhold the facts"
out of "reverence for those in authority."[10] Catholic historians
were permitted to denounce as heretical those Catholic movements of the past that failed to anticipate subsequent doctrinal pronouncements. The opposition of Gallicans to papal infallibility in
the eighteenth century could be defined as heterodox even then.[11]
The theory of double justification presented at Trent could be labelled "seductive."[12] And sixteenth-century requests for communion in both kinds could be seen "as nothing but dirty political ma-
neuvers."[13] Moreover, Catholic historians were often permitted, as
their secular counterparts have not been since the advent of humanism, to admit metahistorical constants as causes for single historical phenomena. "Providence," they could say, was responsible
for the preservation of Augustine's library during the Vandal invasion.[14] "Someone, somehow" could be credited with having scat-
tered gold coins and piled up wood by the door in response to the
prayers of the poor, cold Theatines at Cremona.[15] A thesis about
the relationship between soul and body and form and matter could
be used to explain the conflicts between the bishop and the gover-
nor of Piacenza.[16] And the solicitude of "The Church"—at all times
and in all places—"for the proper moral and intellectual training of
the clergy" could be made into a chief cause of the seminary legislation at Trent.[17] Needless to say, the term "Church" in such occasions usually referred exclusively to the special meaning given it
by one particular man at one particular time, namely, by Pope Pius
IX in the mid-nineteenth century—as at least one diligent observer
has noted.[18]

Thanks to these special prerogatives, Catholic historians were
able to produce a fairly original scheme of historical development.
First of all, they exempted certain institutions completely from the
normal effects of human fallibility and temporal change—namely,
the Papacy and several of the religious orders. Pope Alexander VI
was praised by one of them for having provided "a stable organization for the Church" and for having launched "the whole en-
terprise of the Americas, from Christopher Columbus on down."[19]
Pope Pius VII—and not the political economists of the eighteenth
century—was credited by another for having invented free trade

laws.[20] All the generals of the Society of Jesus were found to have been equally without blemish, and the Jesuits' best-known antagonists, Galileo and Pascal, were pronounced worthy of contempt.[21] Even though he admitted the loss of all the relevant documents, another historian affirmed that "we can be sure that our fathers [of the Tuscan Capuchins] were all spotless mirrors . . . of the Holy Rule, vivid rays of the saving wisdom that shines forth from our inspired constitutions." [22] If any of these fathers turned out in fact to have been not quite so spotless, the historian could quietly erase them from his roster—which is what the seventeenth-century historian of the Servites did to Paolo Sarpi.[23] And if their critics turned out to have been somewhat less than diabolical, he could anathematize them with loaded adjectives: hence such phrases as the "radical preaching" of Zwingli, the "gloomy apostolate" of Calvin, the "pitiful rhetorical superficiality" of Savonarola, the "unctuous form" of Quesnel, the "burning, fanatical" anticurialism of Antonio Genovesi.[24]

Similarly, according to this scheme, some historical phenomena were wholly good—the Scholasticism of the thirteenth century and the neo-Thomism of the nineteenth century, for instance. Some phenomena, on the other hand, were wholly bad. Nominalism could have appealed only to "the corrupt tastes of a time of decadence." [25] The Spiritual Franciscans were "an heretical and divisive force" in the Church.[26] Renaissance humanism was in general "disrespectful of the Catholic priesthood," even though, strangely enough, many of the humanists were priests.[27] Jansenism was "nothing but an adulterous union of politics and theology." [28] And, needless to say, "the Protestant flood" left a "silt of moral corruption" "enshrined in a crabbed and forbidding German [language]." [29] Some historical periods too were wholly good—no longer, perhaps, the Age of the Apostles and the Age of the Fathers that had inspired the Tridentine Reformers, but at least the Age of Thomas Aquinas [30] and Francis of Assisi. Other ages were wholly bad. The Renaissance, for example, "separated itself progressively from the Incarnation" and "encouraged the worst of human inclinations." [31] The first decades of the sixteenth century were given over to "licentious morals" and "the triumph of the flesh," from which the Catholic clergy was providentially saved by the reforms of the Council of Trent.[32] The eighteenth century was an age of rationalism and anticlericalism.[33] And the French Revolution marked the greatest calamity in European history before the advent of Marxism. Along with good and bad ages, finally, went a distinction between good and bad men. Paul IV, Pius V, Robert Bellarmine, and, once he was found to have been antirationalist, Giambattista Vico [34] were assigned to the gallery of heroes. Into the inferno of villains, on the other hand, were thrown William of Ockham, Lorenzo Valla (who tried to destroy the Papal State), Machiavelli,[35] "wily old Michael Baius," [36] and, at least before he was found to have been a scholastic at heart, the destroyer of the scholastic synthesis, René Descartes.[37]

In its day, this vision of history provided a frame of reference almost as satisfying for ordinary Catholics as the metaphysical and moral frame of reference provided by neo-Thomism. It gave credible answers to the embarrassing questions raised by non-Catholic and anti-Catholic polemicists—questions about "Bloody Mary," about Jesuit subversives, and about Spanish inquisitors. Better yet, it put the blame for whatever was amiss in the present not on the present, but on the past;[38] and it then covered the past with a "patina of antiquarianism" to prevent its causing any trouble in the present. No one need make nasty speeches about scribes and pharisees today, in other words, because, *Deo gratias,* Titus took care of them once and for all at the fall of Jerusalem.[39]

But unfortunately, Catholic historiography turned out in the long run to have several troublesome defects. First, its aims and methods were generally unacceptable to those of other current schools of historiography—be they Marxist, neo-positivist, *Annales,* or just plain American social sciences-oriented history.[40] True, some efforts were made to bridge the gap. The Fliche-Martin *Histoire de l'Église* was modeled upon the Halphen-Saignac *Peuples et Civilisations* series, and Amintore Fanfani's journal *Economia e Storia* was originally intended to stimulate interest among Catholic historians in a field in which their participation previously had been minimal. But none of these efforts fully met the standards prescribed by their non-Catholic models, and they thus failed to open up the kind of interconfessional dialogue called for by Vatican Council II.[41]

Secondly, this vision was found not really to be the direct descendant of late Roman and medieval Catholicism, but rather the product of the special circumstances of relatively recent times. It was born amid the religious controversies of the late sixteenth and early seventeenth centuries. It thus inherited Baronius's unconscious break with the then current schools of humanist historiography, particularly after Baronius's *Annales Ecclesiastici* was raised to the rank of a definitive authority in church history.[42] It inherited the hostility of Roman liturgical authorities of the age toward historical rectifications in the Breviary, even by such impeccably orthodox critics as the Bollandists.[43] It also inherited the closed-archives policy adopted by the post-Tridentine Papacy in order to safeguard the privileges of the Congregation of the Council—a policy still observed until recently even by some diocesan archivists.[44] This vision of history was nourished in the eighteenth century first by the efforts of the Papacy to tone down theological controversy by imposing silence and then by the success of Alfonso de' Liguori's campaign against the biblical-patristic piety of the Muratorians in Italy.[45] In the nineteenth century, it was further molded by the fear of historicism among the theologians and by the antihistorical bias of the Aristotelian philosophy to which they sought to wed theology.[46] And it was carefully circumscribed by the fear of ecclesiastical censors that calling Pierluigi Farnese the son (rather than the "nephew") of Pope Paul III might tarnish the reputation of Pope Leo XIII.[47] The vision finally reached maturity as a result of the anti-Modernist decrees, which made explicit what even Lorenzo Valla had once timorously admitted—that historical investigation poses a threat to the a-temporal, eternal validity of doctrinal pronouncements.

Third, Catholic historiography was found to contain a number of internal contradictions that even its most devoted protagonists could not comfortably overlook. Upgrading Pope Paul IV, they discovered, could be accomplished only at the cost of downgrading Pope Pius IV—and by writing off Paul's Roman opponents as a bunch of "Jews, Trasteverines, and escaped convicts."[48] Exalting the Jesuits could be accomplished only by denigrating, one by one, the Dominicans, the Oratorians, the French Capuchins, and even a pope, Clement XIV. Downgrading Erasmus ("anticipato modernista del suo tempo"),[49] Pascal, and the Benedictines of Saint-Maur could be accomplished only by upgrading such now distasteful personages as Alberto Pio da Carpi and Melchior Cano. Looking for signs of the immutable—including natural law—in historical time could sometimes be accomplished only at the risk of lending support to retrogressive political policies, as that versatile master of many fields of historical research, Walter Ong, has pointed out.[50] And separating heroes from villains could often be accomplished only by introducing distinctions—distinctions of doubtful theological validity and of clear McCarthy-era overtones—between what was "totally Catholic" and what was "not always completely orthodox"—*non sempre del tutto ortodossa*.[51] Similarly, Catholic historiography frequently resorted to somewhat unsatisfactory explanations of historical phenomena. It maintained that the conversion of a third of Europe to Lutheranism derived from "the unheard-of deformation in the conscience" of one man.[52] It credited one of its heroes both with consistently sacrificing offers of even the most modest benefice to his personal commitment to poverty, and then with endowing, out of his own pocket, an orphanage and dowries for some 200 girls.[53] It made good periods of history arise almost miraculously from bad periods—as the Tridentine reformation did from the Renaissance—and it put the sole blame on a few villains, or on a single metaphysical principle (like "secularism"), for the subsequent collapse of good periods into bad. The darker the niche, in other words, the brighter the statue—and vice versa.[54] Finally, Catholic historiography often ended up destroying one of the most peculiar characteristics of the Christian religion: the recognition of the irreducibility of individual human beings to categories. Following the example of traditional hagiography, it turned people into abstractions; and even such highly individualistic people as the fifteenth-century Italian mystics often became little more than reshufflings of the same bundle of virtues.[55]

As Catholic historiography thus became discredited among Catholic historians themselves, it also became increasingly unacceptable to theologians. Far from "liberating" Catholics, in the Pauline sense of the term, it was found actually to be "enslaving them to particular temporal solutions and to particularly worldly structures."[56] Far from bringing them back to the Bible and to the "essentially social and historical way of life" reflected in the Bible, it was reinforcing the individualistic, a-historical, and a-social tendencies of eighteenth- and nineteenth-century piety—what Italians call *devozioncine*.[57] Even those theologians who most needed the support of tradition, rather than logical deductions or authoritative pronouncements, for their theses frequently turned away from history entirely; and they jumped insouciantly over the nineteen hundred years that separated the Apostolic Age from the relevant problems of their own times.[58]

Most historians, however, were unwilling to make such a radical break. Some of them sought to use traditional methods to new ends. That is, they attempted to show not how Catholics were different, but how well they fitted into a pluralistic society—how many of them had fought with distinction in the Civil War and how many had been elected to public office. Others tried to close the gaps in traditional Catholic periodization schemes. They discovered a "Christian" Renaissance parallel to Burckhardt's "pagan" Renaissance.[59] They made Paul III and Charles Borromeo, rather than Zwingli and Calvin, the chief agents of what was the "real" Reformation.[60] And they pushed the current alliance between Catholics and political conservatives in Italy back into a "real" Risorgimento of the nineteenth century.[61] Still others tried to turn traditional historical judgments upside down. Luther and Melanchthon were the real Catholics of the sixteenth century, they proposed, and the Counter-Reformation papal nuncios were intolerant oppressors. The Tridentine reformation was indeed imposed by autocratic masters on unwilling subjects, and the "Catholic reform" that supposedly preceded it was a figment of Hubert Jedin's wishful imagination. But many historians just gave up. Either they joined one of the current non-Catholic schools of historiography, or else they limited themselves merely to accumulating facts, without thesis and without the slightest trace of a personal religious commitment.[62] Consequently, history in Catholic high schools was swallowed up by "Social Studies." History in Catholic seminaries was reduced to chronologies of particular religious orders. History in Catholic colleges was eliminated from the list of required courses. And subscriptions to the *Catholic Historical Review* declined abruptly—as the editor noted with dismay ten years ago.[63]

It may be that those who give up are correct. After all, no one has ever pretended to write "Catholic mathematics"—not even the pious monks of the eighteenth century who imported the latest theories of probability from schismatic England and applied them to such delicate questions as population growth and pensions in the Most Catholic Duchy of Milan.[64] If history is history, if the same standards, methods, and objectives are valid for all historians alike,[65] then the only admissible kinds of hyphenated histories are those defined by subject matter—medieval history, church history, economic history. If historians should be "suspicious of loyalty oaths, religious creeds, or affiliations with political parties," as Edmund Morgan says they should be, then the very existence of a separate, Catholic historiography is incompatible to the pursuit of truth.[66] Consequently, the American Catholic Historical Association should be reduced to a kind of historians' Holy Name Society, with the president as organizer of communion breakfasts (or, in San Francisco, of wine-and-cheese parties) and the secretary as spiritual director.

In my opinion, however, such a course would constitute an impardonable shirking of responsibility. For one thing, some non-Catholic historians have recently begun to take note of—and to declare themselves stimulated by—the "ferment, the intellectual restlessness, and the novelty of themes" they observe among Catholic historians, at least in Europe, where historical research is still animated by ideological discussions.[67] And while traditionally *laici* journals like the *Rivista storica italiana* have opened their pages to such committed Catholics as Romeo De Maio, Catholics have responded by inviting even Marxists to their conferences. For another thing, several Catholic historians—like Giuseppe De Luca, Ernst Walter Zeeden, and Gabriel Le Bras, who have usually worked outside the mainstream of Catholic historiography—have founded a new field of historical research, one that has aroused considerable interest among their secular colleagues—namely, the history of piety and religious practices.[68] More important still, Catholic historians have at last opened a campaign against the remnants of the various Whig myths, Weber-Tawney theses, and black legends that still populate school textbooks—and, alas, some learned articles as well. Unless they take the trouble to point out the historical error involved in identifying all Catholicism in the early sixteenth century with the theological pronouncements of the Sorbonne,[69] unless they point out that Caravaggio's realism cannot possibly be attributed to the influence of Protestantism,[70] unless they show that Francisco de Vitoria was not obliged either as a Catholic or as a Dominican to approve of every papal claim to temporal jurisdiction,[71] unless they expose the myth of an international Catholic plot to pull off the Massacre of St. Bartholomew,[72] unless they show that Sarpi, for all his merits, is no authority on the resistance to the Tridentine decrees (particularly when he is made to speak in Jacobean English),[73] unless they rescue the Counter-Reformation from the responsibility for every frown in every late mannerist painting, they cannot complain about the persistence of such historical misrepresentations.[74] The spirit of Foxe, Flacius Illyricus, and Voltaire will live on in those age-old, but unwitting allies of "Catholic" historiography—Calvinist, Lutheran, and Liberal historiography. And the discipline as a whole will suffer as a consequence.

To be sure, none of these are tasks that need necessarily be accomplished by Catholics alone. After all, the Marxist historian Delio Cantimori was as fully aware as any Christian of the primacy of religious conviction as the cause of much of what took place in sixteenth-century Italy. One of his disciples who is also a Marxist, Antonio Rotondò, has consistently explained the activities of the Italian heretics as a result of their free acceptance of theological doctrines. Another of his disciples who is neither a Marxist nor a Catholic, John Tedeschi, can claim credit, as no Catholic can, for finally sweeping away a four-century accumulation of legends about the Roman Inquisition.

Nevertheless, a historian who is also a Catholic has several notable advantages over his secular colleagues. First, he is obliged to know something about theology, as Henri Bremond pointed out long ago, and thus to appreciate the historical importance of theological questions.[75] Second, he is obliged to recognize just the opposite of the rule prescribed by David Potter in 1961.[76] That is, he must recognize the value of the individual man as an object of historical investigation and to admit the possibility that individual wills, passions, and perceptions of the divine, no matter how hemmed in they may be by economic curves and social structures, can be active agents in the historical process. As Ernesto Balducci once said:

> There exists a spiritual causality which penetrates material causes and which always preserves the power not, perhaps, to destroy those causes, but to turn them to purposes that it itself freely choses.

[Hence] while for idealists, history is the history of ideas, and while for Marxists history is the history of structures, for us it is the history of ideas and structures together in all the infinite variety of their relationships.[77]

More important still, Catholic historians have an obligation to apply in their professional work a theological doctrine first proposed by Paul, then revived by Erasmus and Ignatius of Loyola, and finally fully elaborated by Pierre Teilhard de Chardin— namely, the doctrine of the sanctity of vocations. They must regard the work of historical inquiry not as a way of gaining social prestige, of building academic empires, or of making payments on suburban swimming pools. Rather, they must regard it as a way of sanctifying themselves, others, and eventually the whole universe. While realizing that talent rains on the just and unjust alike, and while admitting that success is no measure of the quality of the intention, Catholic historians have an added incentive to be diligent, hard-working, and honest—even when honesty, i.e., fidelity to the documents, forces them "to speak contrary to the usual ideas on the subject." [78] For although their discipline has for centuries been defined with only minimal regard for the specifically religious aspects of Catholicism, it is one to which they have been called not by men, but by God. As Giuseppe Alberigo puts it: "All historical research conducted with scientific rigor is a spiritual adventure; and research into the history of the Church is also a religious experience." [79]

If history, then, is a holy occupation, the Catholic historian will have no reluctance to consider seriously—and critically—all the methodological and substantive innovations of whatever provenance proposed by any of his colleagues of all ideological or religious persuasions. At the same time, he will inevitably recognize that the history he writes is not necessarily the same as the history written by his non-Catholic colleagues. First, he will insist that history not be just the pastime of an elite, but an essential category of human thought and action of great importance to mankind as a whole. He will, therefore, avoid isolating himself in wall-to-wall think-tanks, surrounded only by specialists and Ph.D. candidates. He will be solicitous for the teaching of history at all levels, from elementary to graduate schools, and for the diffusion of historical information and attitudes to the general public. And he will put science and rhetoric back together, in accordance with the humanist dictum: "What's not well written won't be read." Second, he will take on a special commitment to the history of religion in general and of Catholic Christianity in particular, since that is a field which his predecessors often neglected or mistreated. He will not permit religious motives to be suffocated—or explained away—by social, psychological, or economic determinants. And he will admonish his colleagues not to exclude Puritanism from histories of Puritan England [80] or moral preoccupations from histories of Florentine merchant-bankers. Third, while insisting upon the autonomy of history as a discipline, he will remember that history is not identical with the whole of reality. "We Christians know," said Hubert Jedin, "that beyond the tragedy and apparent irrationality of history there is a supreme Wisdom that gives meaning to human events. . . ." [81] Rather than dismissing as irrelevant such related disciplines as metahistory, theory of history, philosophy of history, as some historians did during the debates over Toynbee,[82] he will look to them for suggestions with the same respect that most historians today look to the social sciences. And he will remember that the end of history is to occur at the end of time, not in some Prussian, Communist, or American terrestial paradise.

Fourth, the Catholic historian will take care to remain uncontaminated by the most insidious heresy of modern non-Catholic historiography: nationalism. As a member of a universal, multinational church, he will never let himself be trapped within the confines of an "American" or a "German" school of historiography. He will be able at least to read all the languages of current historical scholarship. And he will feel as much at home in the Kirchengeschichtliches Institut at Bonn or the Instituto per le Scienze Religiose at Bologna as he is in the Center for Reformation Research at St. Louis.

Finally, the Catholic historian will seek to rediscover, revivify, and look for inspiration to what, as a matter of fact, was a vital and distinctive tradition of historiography within Catholicism centuries before the appearance of what until recently has been known as "Catholic historiography." While never admitting that any particular moment in that tradition can be considered normative, and while insisting that the tradition never has been, and never will be, complete, he will realize that he can still learn something from it.

As the Renaissance humanists admired Livy for his style, and as
early twentieth-century historians admired Ranke for his impartiality, so Catholic historians today can still admire Eusebius' respect
for documents, Orosius' search for a world-historical pattern, Otto
of Freising's attention to detail, Platina's interest in individual personalities, Baronius' zeal for thorough research, Muratori's understanding of the relevance of the past to the present, Pastor's care to
avoid confessional polemics, the Maurists' ability to engage in *tra-
vaux d'équipe*. And he will take comfort in the principle that a
recent representative of that tradition, Pope John XXIII, borrowed
from the Maurists: that "the best apology for the Church is the impartial history of its life." [83]

Yet Catholic historians today have yet another, and perhaps
even more important obligation: that of reintroducing a sense of
history among their fellow-Catholics. More than any other of the
great world religions, Christianity is basically historical in outlook:
and it is to the Christian historians of late antiquity that Western
civilization today owes its notion of progress in history through
successive historical epochs. "Christianity is a historical religion,"
says M. C. D'Arcy. "It began at a certain date. It continued in a visible society." And, he might have added, it seeks to direct the
course of history toward a definite goal.[84] Catholicism, which insists upon the theological value of a post-Apostolic tradition, is the
most historical of all the forms of Christianity. As Michael Novak
puts it:

> What do I mean by Catholicism? Not merely an institution, a set of
> practices, a liturgy and a creed, but more than that: a history, a his-
> torical people in continuity.[85]

Unfortunately, this historical orientation began to wane
among Catholics within a century after Trent had raised it to the
level of doctrine. As Novak says elsewhere:

> The theology which has been entrenched for the last four hundred
> years . . . might fairly be described as "non-historical" or even "anti-
> historical." It favors speculation which is not called to the bar of his-
> torical fact, past or present; [indeed], it often seems to fear principles
> which would make it face such a bar.[86]

As a consequence, Catholicism has lost much of what Teilhard de Chardin insisted is one of its most essential characteristics. The omnipresence of God in the universe, he warned, is comprehensible only when it can be seen as radiating:

> from an historical centre and . . . [being] transmitted along a traditional and solidly defined axis. . . . If you suppress the historical reality of Christ, the divine omnipresence which intoxicates us becomes, like all other dreams of metaphysics, uncertain, vague, conventional. . . . The mystical Christ, the universal Christ of St. Paul, has neither meaning nor value in our eyes except as an expansion of the Christ who was born of Mary and who died on the Cross.[87]

At the same time, Catholic theology has often lost its ability to understand fully certain pressing problems of the modern world. "The question 'what is a free man,' " warned Gabriel Marcel,

> cannot usefully be discussed in the abstract, that is, without regard to concrete historical situations. . . . We should ask not what is a free man in himself, as an essence . . . , but rather how freedom can be conceived of and witnessed in the particular historical situation that we, *hic et nunc,* have to face.[88]

Catholic theology has also at times lost its ability to explain the relevance today of doctrinal statements put forth in response to very different circumstances in the past. For example, it has permitted one theologian to define "obedience" in terms utterly incomprehensible either in the United States, where he published his article, or in South Korea, where he wrote it. Obedience, he says, consists in

> our [positive] response to the explicit statements of our Holy Father, Paul VI, concerning moral questions of marriage and procreation, our acceptance of directives of bishops' conferences regarding ecumenical actions, and the submission of the active parishioner to the will of the parish priest.[89]

Indeed, obedience so defined would have been just as incomprehensible to Ignatius and Peter Canisius, whom the author, a Jesuit, would probably regard as authorities on the question.

This a-historicism has also permitted Catholics in general to attribute infallibility to doctrinal pronouncements which, however logically impeccable, are utterly devoid of specific references to concrete historical situations; and it has enabled them to ignore, or bury in platitudes and abstract formulae, such pressing problems of their own times as racism, imperialism, political corruption, and over-population. It has encouraged American Catholics in particular to ignore their own specific experience and simply to import acritically the answers to their theological questions from the very different environment of Western Europe.[90] It has impeded the progress of ecumenical dialogue, as Hubert Jedin pointed out.[91] And it has left any number of so-called "Progressive" Catholics—from Pentecostals and commune members to liturgical reformers and social activists—bereft of the experience accumulated over two millennia by such of their forerunners as Teresa of Avila, Benedict of Nursia, Philip Neri, and Joseph of Calasanz.

Fortunately, the work of rehistorization has already begun—thanks, it must be admitted, more to the theologians than to the historians. Emile Mersch demonstrated as early as the 1930's that the doctrine of Christ's Mystical Body could be understood only in so far as it is investigated historically—and only in so far as that investigation is inspired by "the conviction that the message, just as God has given it [in various times and places], is worth infinitely more than anything which mere human reason might substitute in its place."[92] As early as the 1940's Yves Congar reminded all Catholics, laymen as well as ecclesiastics, of their duty to work toward the "plentification" of Christ in this world in preparation for the eventual historical parousia.[93] In the early 1960's Gaetano Chiavacci pointed out that time and eternity were incomparable only in the minds of men, and that the study of the single manifestations of eternal truth was the best way for men to approach what in itself was beyond their comprehension.[94] More recently, Hans Küng has led the way toward a deeper understanding of the doctrine of infallibility in accordance with Cardinal Bea's admonition—namely, by studying it as it has been expressed "according to the mentality and the language of men" in all past ages.[95]

Recently, however, some historians too have taken up the cause. After all, the Second Vatican Council's decree on "The Legitimate Autonomy of Terrestial Affairs" (De iusta rerum terrenarum autonomia) is based in part on Pio Paschini's researches into the life and works of Galileo.[96] The decree on the authority of bishops is based in good measure on Giuseppe Alberigo's study of the historical episcopacy. And a past president of the American Catholic Historical Association, Brian Tierney, has added still more evidence to the inquiry begun by Küng.[97] The reunification of systematic and positive theology proposed by Bernard McGinn some four years ago may be still far in the future.[98] So also may be the substitution of courses in the Christian tradition for the currently required courses in philosophy and systematic theology in the curricula of Catholic colleges and seminaries. But the increasing possibility that such hopes may one day be realized should be sufficient to remind historians of the true nature of the task before them. This task consists not simply in sweeping away the remnants of an older, and no longer useful, form of Catholic historiography. It consists rather in creating a new Catholic historiography to take its place—a historiography constantly in dialogue with the latest currents of non-Catholic historiographies, yet one still faithful to the lasting values of its own 2,000-year-old tradition.

NOTES

1. Sandro Fontana, "Cultura cattolica," *Il ponte* (November, 1962), pp. 1510 ff.

2. Cf. Arnaldo Momigliano in *Rivista storica italiana*, LXXIII (1961), 118.

3. "Avvertenza" to *Contributi alla storia del Concilio di Trento e della Controriforma* ("Quaderni di Belfagor," 1 [Florence, 1948]). It continues: "Ancora una volta ci siamo amaramente convinti che la Chiesa cattolica non può fare e non ama fare la storia." And it then adds: "Ma il *cattolico profondamente cristiano . . .* affronta la responsabilità del suo giudizio critico e la sua collaborazione impegnativa con i malfamati e pretesi 'castaldi del demonio'; mentre il *cattolico conformista* è, al solito, pieno di dubbi e di cautele" [italics added].

4. Delio Cantimori in preface to Giuseppe Alberigo, *I vescovi italiani al Concilio di Trento* (Florence, 1959).

5. Frederic Siedenburg, S.J., in preface to Vol I (1918).

6. *Catholic Historical Review*, I (April, 1915), 5. Cf. Carl Wittke, "The *Catholic Historical Review*—Forty Years," *ibid.*, XLII (April, 1956), 1–14. See further: Peter Guilday, "The American Catholic Historical Association," *ibid.*, VI (April, 1920), 1–14.

7. "Marxist History and Sacred History," *Review of Politics*, XII (October, 1951), 505.

8. Giuseppe Prezzolini, *Machiavelli anticristo* (Rome, 1954), p. 31.

9. See review of Jaroslav Pelikan, *The Christian Tradition* (Chicago, 1971) in *Catholic Historical Review*, LVIII (January, 1973), 578–580.

10. W. H. Kent, "Catholic Truth and Historical Truth," *ibid.*, VI (October, 1920), 275–293.

11. Enrico Dammig in *Il movimento giansenista a Roma nella seconda metà del Settecento* (Vatican City, 1945), p. 17. "Tuttavia oltre al primato anche l'infallibilità era riconosciuta dalla Chiesa universale fin dall'antichità. . . . Se quindi a quei tempi mancando una solenne definizione, la negazione dell'infallibilità . . . tuttavia non era . . . conforme alla dottrina cattolica."

12. James Brodrick, S.J., *The Origin of the Jesuits* (Westport, Connecticut, 1971), p. 191.

13. Brodrick, *Saint Peter Canisius* (New York, 1935), p. 473.

14. F. Van der Meer, *Augustine the Bishop* (New York, 1965—Harper Torchbook edition), p. 16. Similarly, Adeodatus' death is seen by the author "as a punishment for Augustine; . . . but we can believe that he [Adeodatus] was found fit to see God" (p. 3), although no evidence is given as a foundation for this belief.

15. Paul H. Hallet, *Catholic Reformer: A Life of St. Cajetan of Thiene* (Westminster, Maryland, 1959), pp. 191–192.

16. Franco Molinari, *Il Card. Teatino Beato Paolo Burali e la riforma tridentina a Piacenza (1568–1576)* ("Analecta Gregoriana," Vol 87 [Rome, 1957]), p. 361.

17. James A. O'Donohoe, *Tridentine Seminary Legislation* (Louvain, 1957), p. 171.

18. E.g., Walter Binni's comments in *Rassegna di letteratura italiana,* LXX (1966), 466, on a review of Adam Wandruszka's biography of Emperor Leopold II published in *Civiltà cattolica,* Anno 117, Vol. II (1966), 154–155: "la persistenza in certi ambienti cattolici di concezioni che identificano il risveglio religioso e la 'libertà' con i criteri di Pio IX."

19. That was too much even for G. B. Picotti, who reviewed the Accademia di Oropa's edition of *Alessandro VI e Savonarola: Brevi e lettere* (Turin, 1950) in *Rivista di storia della Chiesa in Italia,* V (1951), 110–111. "Truly," he commented, "I would like to suggest that the honorable founders and financers of the Accademia di Oropa consider directing their activities toward a better end."

20. Armando Lodolini in *Economia e storia,* VI (1959), 402.

21. Note review by Kurt Dietrich Schmidt in *Historische Zeitschrift,* CLXXIV (1952), 720–721, of Hubert Becher's *Die Jesuiten* (Munich, 1951).

22. Sisto da Pisa, *Storia dei Cappuccini toscani* (Florence, 1906), I, 37: "limpidissimi specchi a tramandarne il puro splendore della santa regola, i vividi raggi di quella saluberrima sapienza che rifulge nelle nostre ispirate costituzioni. . . ." Hence Alberigo's comments in *I vescovi italiani . . .* , pp. 111–112: "Quasi ogni ordine ha dedicato più di una pubblicazione ai propri confratelli intervenuti al Concilio, fenomeno che però raramente si è risolto in un vantaggio per la ricerca storica. . . . Frequentemente si è infiltrato l'amore per la grandezza dell'ordine . . . , allontanando da una ricerca seria ed oggettiva."

23. See my *Florence in the Forgotten Centuries* (Chicago, 1973), pp. 209–10.

24. These expressions come from Robert E. McNally, S.J., "The Council of Trent and the German Protestants," *Theological Studies*, XXV (March, 1964), 1–22, and from Giuseppe Cacciatore, *Sant'Alfonso de' Liguori e il giansenismo* (Florence, 1944).

25. Carlo Giacon, *La seconda scolastica* (Milan, 1944), p. 167. This judgment is discredited by Heiko Oberman in "The Shape of Late Medieval Thought," in Oberman and Charles Trinkaus (eds.), *The Pursuit of Holiness in Late Medieval and Renaissance Religion* (Leiden, 1974), pp. 3–25.

26. Colman J. Barry (ed.), *Readings in Church History* (Westminster, Maryland, 1959), I, 401.

27. Giles-Gérard Meersseman, "Il tipo ideale di parroco secondo la riforma tridentina nelle sue fonti letterarie," in *Il Concilio di Trento e la riforma tridentina* (Rome, 1965), I, 42.

28. Metodio da Nembo in *L'Italia francescana*, XXXII (1957), 33. Note criticisms by Jean Mesnard in *Pascal, l'homme et l'oeuvre* (Paris, 1951) with reference to E. Baudin, *La philosophie de Pascal* (Neuchâtel, 1946–1947), which "définit la casuistique et le probabilisme d'une manière idéale, peu conforme à la réalité que Pascal avait sous les yeux." The same reduction of concrete historical phenomena to abstractions is evident in Giuseppe Maria de Giovanni, S.I., "Il giansenismo a Napoli nel secolo XVIII," published in *Nuove ricerche storiche sul giansenismo* ("Analecta Gregoriana," Vol. LXXI [Rome, 1954]), pp. 195–210, which makes Jansenism the ally of "il regalismo, il giurisdizionalismo [e] il febronianesimo" and the parent of "illuminismo" and "incredulità," not by any documentable historical process, but "per logica connessione d'idee."

29. Brodrick, *The Origin of the Jesuits*, pp. 182 and 188.

30. E.g., Jacques Maritain in *Integral Humanism* (1936), tr. Joseph W. Evans (Notre Dame, 1968), p. 13.

31. *Ibid.*, p. 15.

32. M. Grosso and M. F. Mellano in *La Controriforma nella arcidiocesi di Torino* (Vatican City, 1957), I, 56, on which see Pio Paschini's chastizing comments in *Rivista di storia della Chiesa in Italia*, XIII (1959), 301–302. An authoritative statement of this periodical scheme was given by Cardinal Alfonso Capecelatro in his presentation of *Il terzo centenario di San Filippo Neri* (Padua, 1895), p. 13. It was repeated by Renato Canestrari in *Sisto V* (Turin, 1954), p. 3: "Il vecchio mondo in cui trionfava la carne. . . . Solo nel XVI secolo si tolse la maschera, assunse una personalità, un volto, un nome, e si chiamò Martino Lutero. Gli Dei falsi e bugiardi tornarono a gioire. . . ." More examples in my "New Light on Post-Tridentine Italy," *Catholic Historical Review*, LVI (July, 1970), 291–319.

33. "The barbarian may be the eighteenth-century philosopher, who neither anticipated nor desired the brutalities of the Revolution . . . , but who prepared the way for the Revolution by creating a vacuum which he was not able to fill": John Courtney Murray, "America's Four Conspiracies," in John Cogley (ed.), *Religion in America* (New York, 1938), p. 23.

34. Cf. L. Belfiore, *La dottrina della provvidenza in G. B. Vico* (Padua, 1962), reviewed enthusiastically in *Osservatore Romano*, April 27, 1963, p. 6. Vico, accord-

ing to the reviewer, was a "buon conoscitore e ammiratore del Tomismo. . . . La provvidenza vichiana è unicamente nel solco del Cristianesimo" and a "risposta . . . profonda all'invadenza del razionalismo moderno."

35. Pietro Conte, *L'errore logico di Machiavelli e i fondamenti metafisici della politica* (Rome, 1955)—one among many examples.

36. Marvin R. O'Connell, *Thomas Stapleton and the Counter Reformation* (New Haven, 1964), p. 42.

37. Francesco Olgiati, *Cartesio* ("Pubblicazioni dell'Università Cattolica del Sacro Cuore," Vol. XX [Milan, 1934], esp. pp. 94 ff.: "L'opposizione cattolica a Descartes."

38. Cf. Herbert Weisinger, "The Attack on the Renaissance in Theology Today," *Studies in the Renaissance*, II (1955), 176–189, especially p. 189: "If the world is as bad today as the theologians tell us it is, the blame rests not with Michelangelo or Shakespeare or Bacon but with us, and the remedies lie not in their hands but ours."

39. Ernesto Balducci, *Stagioni di Dio* (Brescia, 1960), p. 157.

40. Cf. Richard Trexler's discussion of C. C. Calzolai, *Frate Antonino Pierozzi* (Florence, 1960), in *Studies in the Renaissance*, XIX (1972), 7. He politely uses the term "clerical" rather than "Catholic" to designate this kind of history writing.

41. Note Ellis Waterhouse's comments on Enrico Castelli's *Simboli e immagini* (Rome, 1966), in *Renaissance Quarterly*, XX (1967), 364: "No dialogue between the two is possible." Note also Mario Rosa's comments on "i criteri e i modi della storiografia ecclesiastica tradizionale" and "una generica visione ottimistica che si sovrappone . . . a date ed elementi che parlano spesso altro linguaggio": *Rivista di storia della Chiesa in Italia*, XVI (1967), 552 ff.

42. See Cyriac Pullapilly's forthcoming "Caesar Baronius, Counter-Reformation Historian" (Notre Dame, 1975). The roots, however, are already apparent in certain antiphilological tendencies present at the Council of Trent, e.g., the attempt of one party to fix up the words of St. Cyprian to make them conform to the Vulgate, an attempt which evoked a violent reaction on the part of the still humanist majority of the fathers. See Paolo Prodi, *Il cardinale Gabriele Paleotti (1522–1597)* (Rome, 1959, 1967), I, 110.

43. E.g., the case of "St. Dionysius the Areopagite": Pierre Batiffol, *Histoire du Bréviaire romain* (3d ed.; Paris, 1911), pp. 354 ff. According to George H. Dunne in *Catholic Historical Review*, XLVIII (July, 1962), 255, Benedict XIV's ban on further discussion of the rites issue was still on the books in 1961. That is the reason why Georgius Mensaert, O.F.M., left the relative documents out of his edition of *Sinica Franciscana*.

44. Fully described by Luigi Firpo in *Rinascimento*, IX (1954), 97–98.

45. Cf. Sergio Bertelli, *Erudizione e storia in Ludovico Antonio Muratori* (Naples, 1960), p. 415, on the antihistorical bias of certain persons in the Roman Curia.

46. Giuseppe Martini, *Cattolicesimo e storicismo: Momenti d'una crisi del pensiero religioso moderno* (Naples, 1951). On the incompatibility of philosophy and history, see Henri-Irénée Marrou, *De la connaissance historique* (Paris, 1966): "L'histoire de la philosophie, telle que la pratiquent en général les philosophes, est une cause de perpétuel agacement pour l'historien tout-court: il voit entre leurs mains le passé perdre sa réalité concrète, la pensée devenir comme impersonnelle et même intem-

porelle. . . ." For a non-Catholic historian's view of the violent philosophical-theological reaction against historicism, see Heinz Lubasz in *History and Theory,* II (1962), à propos of Karl Löwith's *Gesammelte Abhandlungen: Zur Kritik der geschichtlichen Existenz* (Stuttgart, 1960). Says Löwith, the whole trouble with modern man is that he has abandoned Aristotle and cosmological order and reduced everything, himself included, to the one dimension of time. The effects of imposing philosophical concepts on history are evident in Raffaele Cioni's *Niccolò Stenone* (Florence, 1953), which constantly argues from what Steno should have done (as a saint) to what he in fact did—even when the latter is wholly undocumentable.

47. G. P. Gooch, *History and Historians in the Nineteenth Century* (2nd ed.; London, 1952), p. 355.

48. See Romeo De Maio, *Alfonso Carafa Cardinale di Napoli* (Vatican City, 1961).

49. Pietro Tacchi Venturi, *Storia della Compagnia di Gesù in Italia,* Vol. II (Rome, 1950), p. 168.

50. Walter J. Ong, *Frontiers of American Catholicism* (New York, 1957), pp. 118–119.

51. Giuseppe Vincenzo Vella, *Il Passionei e la politica di Clemente XI* (Rome, 1953), p. 10 (à propos of the Maurists). The same distinction is made by Tacchi Venturi (*op. cit.,* I[1], 290) between the proponents and the opponents of frequent communion in the sixteenth century.

52. Ferdinand Cavallera in *Bulletin de littérature ecclésiastique,* XLVI (1954), 59.

53. E. Vaccaro in *A Cesare Baronio: Scritti vari* (Sora, 1963), p. 25.

54. E.g., Arturo da Carmignano, *San Lorenzo da Brindisi* (published by the Venetian Capuchins) (Venice, 1960), I, 152, of which the most important source is, not surprisingly, Tacchi Venturi. However, Paul Broutin says almost the same thing in *La réforme pastorale en France* (Tournai, 1956), I, 1: "Dans le désarroi provoqué par la Renaissance païenne, l'Eglise se ressaisit dans ses chefs et dans ses membres. . . ."

55. Numerous examples in the still-standard *Figure della riforma pretridentina* by Antonio Cistellini (Brescia, 1948).

56. Fontana, in the article cited in fn. 1, *supra.*

57. Michael Novak in *Commonweal,* March 24, 1961, p. 652.

58. E.g., Gregory Baum in "Catholic Homosexuals," *Commonweal,* February 15, 1974, p. 480, where, after reflecting upon the position of the Apostolic Church in Greek society, he states: "This has been the voice of tradition." The next paragraph begins: "In recent years, however, ..." Not a word concerning what preachers and confessors had been saying over and over since the early Middle Ages about what went on in monasteries and seminaries.

59. Thus Louis Bouyer threw Machiavelli, Guicciardini, and Giovio out of the Renaissance in *Erasmus and His Times* (Westminster, Maryland, 1959) and reproached Pope Clement VII for associating with them.

60. Cantimori makes fun of this attempt in his *Prospettive di storia ereticale italiana* (Bari, 1960), p. 24.

61. Augusto Del Noce, "Per una interpretazione del Risorgimento," *Humanitas*, XVI (January, 1961), 16–40.

62. And, at least in one case, without any real reason for writing in the first place. Note E. E. Reynolds's review of a recent book by "a well-known Catholic biographer" in *American Historical Review*, LXXII (January, 1967), 566–567.

63. *Catholic Historical Review*, L (April, 1964), 64–65.

64. I copy this charming title from Giovanni Levi's article in *Rivista storica italiana*, LXXXVI (1974), 210: *La dottrina degli azzardi applicata ai problemi della probabilità di vita, delle pensioni vitalizie, reversioni, tontine, . . . trasportata dall'idioma inglese, . . . e presa per argomento di pubblica esercitazione matematica tenuta nell'aula della Regia Università di Pavia dal padre don Roberto Gaeta, monaco cistercense, sotto l'assistenza del padre don Gregorio Fontana delle Scuole Pie . . .* (Milan, 1776).

65. This is the well-reasoned position of Wittke in the article cited in fn. 6, *supra*.

66. "Curiosity and Communication," *Yale Alumni Magazine* (November, 1959), pp. 10–13.

67. Lucio Villari, "Recenti studi cattolici sulla storia dell'Italia contemporanea," *Studi storici*, IV (1963), 123–141.

68. See Carlo Russo, "Studi recenti di storia sociale e religiosa in Francia: Problemi e metodi," *Rivista storica italiana*, LXXXIV (1972), 625–682.

69. As in Aurèle La Rocque's introduction to his translation of Bernard Palissy's *Admirables discours* (Urbana, 1957).

70. "Il Caravaggio è dunque l'artista che porta a Roma dal Settentrione, dove più frequenti erano le infiltrazioni della Riforma, il fermento di una religiosità nuova . . .": Giulio Carlo Argan in "Il 'realismo' nella poetica del Caravaggio," *Scritti di storia in onore di Lionello Venturi* (Rome, 1956), II, 39–40.

71. Gesina H. J. van der Molen, *Alberigo Gentili and the Development of International Law* (2nd ed.; Leiden, 1968), p. 8.

72. As in Nicola Mary Sutherland, *The Massacre of St. Bartholomew* (London, 1973).

73. Donald R. Kelley, *François Hotman* (Princeton, 1973) (which also credits Peter Canisius with promoting "ultramontanism"), p. 170.

74. As in Federico Zeri, *Pittura e Controriforma* (Turin, 1957). Note similarly John Jay Hughes' battering down of the preconceptions about the omniscient Jesuits in Anthony Rhodes' *The Vatican in the Age of the Dictators* in *Journal of Modern History*, XLVI (1974), 726.

75. In *Prière et poésie* (Paris, 1926), repeated by Augustin Renaudet in his comments in *Bibliothèque d'humanisme et renaissance*, VI (1952), 26.

76. ". . . The historian is concerned with human beings . . . , but not primarily as individuals. Instead he deals with them in groups—in religious groups, in cultural groups, in ideological groups, in interest groups. . .": "The Historian's Use of Nationalism and Vice Versa," *American Historical Review*, LXVII (July, 1962), 924.

77. *Testimonianza*, No. 46 (July–August, 1962), 403–404.

78. Lucien Ceyssens, O.F.M., in *Revue d'histoire ecclésiastique*, LI (1956), 168–169.

79. *I vescovi italiani al Concilio di Trento*, p. 1.

80. As Max Beloff did in "La storiografia inglese contemporanea," *Rivista storica italiana*, LXXII (1960), 304–316.

81. "Esame di coscienza di uno storico," *Quaderni di Roma*, I (1947), 206–217.

82. M. C. D'Arcy, *The Sense of History, Secular and Sacred* (London, 1959), p. 72; (American edition) *The Meaning and Matter of History: A Christian View* (New York, 1959), p. 73.

83. *Il Cardinale Cesare Baronio* (3d ed.; Rome, 1961), p. 41. A similar statement by Ludovico Antonio Muratori in his *Epistolario,* ed. Matteo Campori (Modena, 1901–1915), IX, 4074.

84. D'Arcy, *op. cit.,* p. 158.

85. *National Catholic Reporter*, March 2, 1973, p. 7.

86. *Loc. cit.* (v. fn. 57, *supra*).

87. *Le milieu divin* (London, 1960), pp. 104–105.

88. *Les hommes contre l'humain* (Paris, 1951), p. 17.

89. *American Benedictine Review*, XIX (September, 1968), 358–369.

90. So says Daniel J. Callahan in *Commonweal*, April 8, 1960, pp. 31 ff.

91. In "Mutamenti dell'interpretazione cattolica della figure di Lutero," *Rivista di storia della Chiesa in Italia*, XXIII (1969), 361.

92. Quoted from the introduction of *The Whole Christ* (Milwaukee, 1938), p. 17.

93. Cf. *Jalons pour une théologie du laïcat* (2nd ed.; Paris, 1954), pp. 101 and 309.

94. "Quid est Veritas?" *Giornale critico della filosofia italiana*, XL (1961), 219–289.

95. In "La liberté des consciences," *Informations catholiques internationales*, No. 185, February 1, 1963, p. 2. Cf. Charles Curran in *Christian Morality Today* (Notre Dame, 1966), p. xx: "Moral theology in general has been very slow in investigating the historical backgrounds of the teaching of the Church on particular matters. . . . The work of historical scholarship is slow and tedious [but it is] absolutely necessary for a true understanding of the traditional teaching of the Church."

96. *Conciliorum Oecumenicorum Decreta* (3d ed.; Bologna, 1973), p. 1090.

97. *Origins of Papal Infallibility, 1150–1350* (Leiden, 1972).

98. "An Approach Toward the Problem of Historical Theology," *Criterion* (Winter, 1970).

BIBLIOGRAPHY
for Further Reading

The primary intentions of this anthology are to demonstrate that there is a renewal of Christian views of history in our time, especially since 1939, that many important thinkers in various fields have devoted themselves to it, and that the range of issues which a Christian perspective thereby illuminates is much wider than we are accustomed to think.

In a limited way this anthology can also serve as an entrée to the systematic questions which a careful theoretical and philosophical inquiry into history should raise. Some of the ideas suggested here show what a Christian perspective does have to offer for theology of history, philosophy of history, and historiography, for the theologian, the philosopher, as well as the historian at work. Because of the disagreements and diversity among the authors, each one of us will have to criticize the essays for ourselves and sort out what indeed we find insightful.

A few of the authors have attempted, in their complete writings, to treat a range of themes nearly as wide as that in this anthology. The names of Maritain, Butterfield, Dooyeweerd, Marrou, Dawson, and Toynbee stand out, all of them historians or philosophers. Others probe more extensively into one or two areas, like Niebuhr, Tillich, and Pannenberg.

A good way to pursue further reading is to pick up the entire book from which a selection in the anthology is taken. For example, the whole of Niebuhr's *Faith and History* and Maritain's *On the Philosophy of History* are important reading. Then it is easy to move on, in some cases, to other works by the same author, or to read books and articles by authors not represented in the anthology.

It is obvious that most writing on a Christian view of history relates to Part I. The themes of Part II and Part III nonetheless have already attracted considerable attention, and we can expect more people to work on them in the future, perhaps especially historians themselves. Cochrane's article is suggestive of this.

While all three parts of the bibliography are very selective, the works listed under Part I represent a smaller proportion of the appropriate literature than those given under the other parts. Also, many of the books listed cover themes which fall into more than one area. In general, a book has been placed under the category to which it seems to make the best contribution, even though much or even the bulk of the book might pertain to other parts. An attempt has been made to include titles which represent a diversity of viewpoints and approaches, and a wide range of themes.

IN GENERAL

"Bibliography of works in theology and history." Compiled by Robert North. *History and Theory*, XII (1973), 55–140.

Bibliography of Works in the Philosophy of History (History and Theory. Middletown, Conn.: Wesleyan University): John C. Rule, *1945–1957* (Beiheft 1, 1961, with Supplement, Beiheft 3, 1964); M. Nowicki, *1958–1961* (Beiheft 3, 1964); Lewis D. Wurgaft, *1962–1965* (Beiheft 7, 1967, with addenda, Beiheft 10, 1970); Lewis D. Wurgaft and others, *1966–1968* (Beiheft 10, 1970, with addenda, Beiheft 13, 1974); Sylvia Pruitt and Astrid Witschi-Bernz, 1969–1972 (Beiheft 13, 1974).

Rienstra, M. Howard. "Christianity and history: a bibliographic essay." *A Christian View of History?* Eds., George M. Marsden and Frank Roberts. Grand Rapids: Eerdmans, 1975.

Journals which sometimes publish articles on a Christian view of history include: *The Catholic Historical Review, Church History, Fides et Historia, History and Theory, Journal of Religion, Religion in Life, Theology Today, Cross Currents*.

PART I   THE MEANING OF HISTORY

a. General

Balthasar, Hans Urs von. *A Theology of History*. New York: Sheed & Ward, 1963.

Berdyaev, Nicholas. *The Meaning of History*. New York: Scribners 1936.

Berkhof, Hendrikus. *Christ the Meaning of History*. Richmond, Va.: John Knox, 1966.

Connolly, James M. *Human History and the Word of God: the Christian Meaning of History in Contemporary Thought*. New York: Macmillan, 1965.

Daniélou, Jean. *The Lord of History*. Chicago: Regnery, 1958.

Guilday, Peter, ed. *The Catholic Philosophy of History.* New York: Kenedy, 1936.

Löwith, Karl. *Meaning in History: the Theological Implications of the Philosophy of History.* Chicago: University of Chicago Press, 1950.

Markus, R. A. *Saeculum: History and Society in the Theology of St. Augustine.* New York: Cambridge University Press, 1970.

Niebuhr, Reinhold. *Beyond Tragedy: Essays on the Christian Interpretation of History.* New York: Scribner's, 1937.

* ———. *Faith and History: a Comparison of Christian and Modern Views of History.* New York: Scribner's, 1949.

———. *The Nature and Destiny of Man.* 2 vols. New York: Scribner's, 1941, 1943.

Patrides, C. A. *The Grand Design of God: The Literary Form of the Christian View of History.* Toronto: University of Toronto Press, 1972.

Rust, Eric, E. *Towards a Theological Understanding of History.* New York: Oxford University Press, 1963.

Shinn, Roger L. *Christianity and the Problem of History.* New York: Scribner's, 1953.

Tillich, Paul. "History as *the* Problem of our Period." *Review of Religion,* III (1939), 255–64.

———. *The Interpretation of History.* New York: Scribner's, 1936.

b. Kingdom of God, Liberation, and History

Dussel, Enrique. *History and the Theology of Liberation: A Latin American Perspective.* Maryknoll, N.Y.: Orbis, 1976.

Ellul, Jacques. *False Presence of the Kingdom.* New York: Seabury, 1972.

* Gutiérrez, Gustavo. *A Theology of Liberation: History, Politics, and Salvation.* Maryknoll, N.Y.: Orbis, 1973.

Laurentin, Rene. *Liberation, Development, and Salvation.* Maryknoll, N.Y.: Orbis, 1972.

Marrou, Henri-Irénée. *Time and Timeliness.* New York: Sheed & Ward, 1969.

Moltmann, Jürgen. *Religion, Revolution, and the Future.* New York: Scribner's, 1969.

———. *The Theology of Hope.* New York: Harper & Row, 1967.

Pannenberg, Wolfhart. *Theology and the Kingdom of God.* Philadelphia: Westminster, 1969.

* An asterisk indicates a volume from which a selection in the anthology is taken.

Ridderbos, Herman N. *The Coming of the Kingdom*. Philadelphia: Presbyterian & Reformed, 1962.

Segundo, Juan Luis. *A Theology for Artisans of a New Humanity*, 5 vols. Maryknoll, N.Y.: Orbis, 1973–74.

* Tillich, Paul. *Systematic Theology*, III. Chicago: University of Chicago Press, 1963.

Wood, H. G., *et al. The Kingdom of God and History*. New York: Willett, Clark, 1938.

c. *The Bible, Jesus, and History*

Braaten, Carl E. *History and Hermeneutics*. New Directions in Theology, II. Philadelphia: Westminister, 1966.

* Bultmann, Rudolf. *The Presence of Eternity: History and Eschatology*. New York: Harper & Row, 1957.

Cullmann, Oscar. *Christ and Time*. Philadelphia: Westminster, 1950; rev. ed., 1964.

Guthrie, Harvey H. *God and History in the Old Testament*. Greenwich, Conn.: Seabury, 1970.

Henry, Carl F., ed. *Jesus of Nazareth: Savior and Lord*. Grand Rapids: Eerdmans, 1966.

MacKenzie, Roderick. *Faith and History in the Old Testament*. Minneapolis: University of Minnesota Press, 1963.

Marshall, I. H. *Luke: Historian and Theologian*. Grand Rapids: Zondervan, 1971.

Pannenberg, Wolfhart. *Basic Questions in Theology*, I. Philadelphia: Fortress, 1971.

*————, ed. *Revelation As History*. New York: Macmillan, 1968.

Robinson, James M. *A New Quest of the Historical Jesus*. Naperville, Ill.: Allenson, 1959.

Stevenson, W. Taylor. *History as Myth: The Import for Contemporary Theology*. New York: Seabury, 1969.

PART II   THE NATURE OF HISTORY AND CULTURE

a. *Providence and Laws in History*

* Barth, Karl. *Church Dogmatics*, III, part 3. Edinburgh: T. & T. Clark, 1960.

Case, Shirley J. *The Christian Philosophy of History.* Chicago: University of Chicago Press, 1943.

Casserley, V. Langmead. *Toward a Theology of History.* New York: Holt, Rinehart & Winston, 1965.

D'Arcy, Martin C. *The Meaning and Matter of History: A Christian View.* New York: Farrar, Straus & Giroux, 1959.

Dawson, Christopher. *Progress and Religion: An Historical Enquiry.* New York: Sheed & Ward, 1929.

*———. *The Dynamics of World History.* Ed., John J. Mulloy. New York: Sheed & Ward, 1956.

Dooyeweerd, Herman. *A New Critique of Theoretical Thought,* II. Philadelphia: Presbyterian & Reformed, 1955.

*———.*In the Twilight of Western Thought.* Philadelphia: Presbyterian & Reformed, 1960.

Halecki, Oscar. *The Limits and Divisions of European History.* New York: Sheed & Ward, 1950.

———. "The moral laws of history." *Catholic Historical Review,* XLII (1956–57), 409–40.

Kasper, Walter, *et al. The Crisis of Change: Are Church and Theology Subject to Historical Laws?* Chicago: Argus, 1969.

* Maritain, Jacques. *On the Philosophy of History.* Ed., J. Evans. New York: Scribner's, 1957.

Niebuhr, Reinhold. *The structure of nations and empires: a study of the recurring patterns and problems of the political order in relation to the unique problems of the nuclear age.* New York: Scribner's, 1959.

Pittenger, Norman. *Christian Faith and the Question of History.* Philadelphia: Fortress, 1973.

Richardson, Alan. *History Sacred and Profane.* Philadelphia: Westminster, 1964.

Smit, M. C. *The Divine Mystery in History.* Kampen: J. H. Kok, 1955.

Sullivan, John Edward. *Prophets of the West: An Introduction to the Philosophy of History.* New York: Holt, Rinehart & Winston, 1970.

Teilhard de Chardin, Pierre. *The Phenomenon of Man.* New York: Harper and Row, 1965.

Toynbee, Arnold. *A Study of History.* 12 vols. New York: Oxford University Press, 1934–61.

Voegelin, Eric. *Order and History.* 4 vols. Baton Rouge: Louisiana State University Press, 1956–74.

Wood, H. G. *Freedom and Necessity in History.* London: Oxford University Press, 1957.

b. *History and Culture*

* Brunner, Emil. *Christianity and Civilization.* 2 vols. New York: Scribner's, 1948–49.
Dawson, Christopher. *The Formation of Christendom.* New York: Sheed & Ward, 1967.
————. *The Historical Reality of Christian Culture.* New York: Harper & Row, 1960.
Eliot, T. S. *Notes Toward the Definition of Culture.* London: Faber & Faber, 1948; New York: Harcourt, Brace, 1949.
Niebuhr, H. Richard, *Christ and Culture.* New York: Harper & Row, 1951.
van Leeuwen, A. T. *Christianity in World History.* London: Edinburgh House, 1964.

PART III HISTORIANS AND HISTORICAL STUDY

Albright, William F. *History, Archaeology and Christian Humanism.* New York: McGraw-Hill, 1964.
* Butterfield, Herbert. *Christianity and History.* London: Bell, 1949; New York: Scribner's, 1950.
————. *History and Human Relations.* London: Collins, 1951.
————. *Man on his Past: The Study of the History of Historical Scholarship.* Cambridge: Cambridge University Press, 1955.
————. "The Christian and history." *The Christian Newsletter* (1949), no. 333, 88–96; no. 336, 136–44; no. 341, 215–23, 224–32.
Cairns, Earle E. "Christian faith and history." *Christianity and the World of Thought.* Ed., Hudson T. Armerding. Chicago: Moody, 1968.
Clouse, Robert G. "History." *Christ and the Modern Mind.* Ed., Robert W. Smith. Downers Grove, Ill.: Intervarsity, 1972.
Dyson, A. O. *The Immortality of the Past.* London: SCM, 1974.
Ellis, John Tracy. "The ecclesiastical historian in the service of Clio." *Church History,* XXXVIII (1969), 106–20.

* Harbison, E. Harris. *Christianity and History*. Princeton: Princeton University Press, 1964.

Harvey, Van A. *The Historian and the Believer: The Morality of Historical Knowledge and Christian Belief*. New York: Macmillan, 1966.

Kearney, H. F. "Christianity and the study of history." *Downside Review*, LXVII (1949), 62–75.

Marrou, Henri-Irénée. "From the logic of history to an ethic for historians." *Cross Currents*, XI (1961), 61–77.

*———. *The Meaning of History*. Baltimore: Helicon, 1966.

Marsden, George M., and Roberts, Frank, eds. *A Christian View of History?* Grand Rapids: Eerdmans, 1975.

McIntire, C. T. "Historical study: a Christian approach." *Perspective*, X (1976), supplement.

———. *The Ongoing Task of Christian Historiography*. Toronto: Institute for Christian Studies, 1974.

Montgomery, John Warwick. *Where Is History Going?* Grand Rapids: Zondervan, 1969.

Outler, Albert C. "Theodosius' horse: reflections on the predicament of the church historian." *Church History*, XXXIV (1965), 251–61.

Reid, W. Stanford. "Absolute truth and the relativism of history." *Christian Perspectives*, II (1961), 89–129.

Smith, Page. *The Historian and History*. New York: Knopf, 1964.

Stevenson, W. Taylor. "Christian faith and historical studies." *Faith and Learning Studies*, II. New York: Faculty Christian Fellowship, 1964.

Toynbee, Arnold. *An Historian's Approach to Religion*. New York: Oxford University Press, 1956.

Ward, Paul. "The Christian and history teaching." *Religion in Life*, XXVI (1956–57), 490–500.

INDEX

1. Important Names, Movements, Philosophies

2. Main themes